SUBJECTS OF THE SULTAN
Culture and Daily Life in the Ottoman Empire

SURAIYA FAROQHI

I.B. TAURIS
LONDON · NEW YORK

Reprinted in 2011 by I.B. Tauris & Co Ltd
6 Salem Road, London W2 4BU
175 Fifth Avenue, New York NY 10010
www.ibtauris.com

In the United States of America and in Canada distributed by Palgrave Macmillan, a
division of St Martin's Press, 175 Fifth Avenue, New York, NY 10010

First published in 1995 as *Kultur und Alltag im osmanischen Reich* by
C. H. Beck'sche Verlagsbuchhandlung, Munich

C. H. Beck'sche Verlagsbuchhandlung, München, 1995
This translation first published in 2000 by I.B. Tauris & Co Ltd
Paperback edition first published in 2005, Reprinted in 2007, 2010
Translation by Martin Bott © I.B. Tauris & Co Ltd, 2000, 2005

The translation of this work has been supported by Inter Nationes, Bonn

A full CIP record for this book is available from the British Library
A full CIP record for this book is available from the Library of Congress
Library of Congress catalog card number: available

ISBN 978 1 85043 760 4

Set in Monotype Ehrhardt by Ewan Smith, London
Printed and bound in India by Replika Press Pvt. Ltd.

Subjects of the Sultan

IN MEMORY OF ZDENKA VESELÀ

FOR RUDOLF VESELY

Contents

Maps and Illustrations

Maps

Illustrations

A Note on Transliteration

The modern Turkish Roman typeface has been employed throughout. In order not to trouble the reader with two differing transliteration conventions, the few Arabic and Persian words that occur in the text are also written in Turkish Roman characters.

The following letters differ from English pronunciation:

c – dsh;
ç – tsh;
ğ – aspirate, often hardly audible;
ı – as in unaccented syllables in English;
j – as in French '*jaune*';
ş – sh;
^ – long vowel.

The orthography adheres to the recommendations of *Redhouse Yeni Türkçe – İngilizce Sözlük* (Istanbul: Redhouse Press, 1968), of which there are several editions.

Preface

During the years in which I wrote this book I enjoyed a great deal of sympathetic support. Above all, I must thank those of my colleagues who read and commented upon certain chapters or even the whole manuscript. Halil Inalcık gave me many ideas, for which I am very grateful. I am indebted to Fikret Adanır (Bochum), Doris Behrens-Abouseif (London), Barbara Flemming (Leiden), Cemal Kafadar (Cambridge MA), Machiel Kiel (Utrecht), Klaus Roth (Munich), Andreas Tietze (Vienna) and, in particular, Christoph Neumann (Istanbul) for all their advice. They helped draw my attention to unfortunate phrases, factual errors and problematic assertions. No doubt much remains to be criticized, for which I, of course, accept sole responsibility.

Tülay Artan (Istanbul), Halil Berktay (Istanbul), Cemal Kafadar (Cambridge MA), Gülru Necipoğlu (Cambridge MA), Christoph Neumann (Istanbul) and Isenbike Togan (Ankara) have contributed more than they themselves are aware to the writing of this book, thanks to their published and unpublished work and our useful conversations. Without their previous studies I doubt that I should have come to the conclusion that a book such as this one, in which unofficial and informal matters play so important a part, might be feasible. I thank them all most sincerely and hope that the result is not too disappointing.

In addition, I must thank all the persons who helped me obtain the literature I required, above all Wilfried Riesterer (Staatsbibliothek, Munich). Cem Behar (Istanbul), Wolfgang Birus (Munich), Hadumod Bußmann (Munich), Cristina Feneşan (Bucharest), Wolf Dieter Hütteroth (Erlangen-Nuremberg), Andreas Schachner (Munich), Laszlo Vajda (Munich) and Nicolas Vatin (Paris) were also very helpful. I received further assistance from booksellers Ibrahim Yılmaz (Istanbul) and Ahmet Yüksel (Ankara). Ayda Arel (Istanbul) was good enough to put photographs at my disposal. I am also extremely grateful to Filiz Çağman, then Curator and now Director of the Topkapı Sarayı Museum (Istanbul) for making illustrations available to me. Hans-Georg Majer (Munich) let me use two engravings which added greatly to the value of the illustrative material. The helpfulness and patience of Özgür Savaşçı, Elfriede Eberl and Christl Catanzaro helped save me from being overwhelmed by the tricks of the computer.

The most difficult part of this book is probably its Introduction, as complexity cannot be avoided when account is taken of the work of many fellow researchers. Anyone wishing to plunge in without preamble might prefer to begin with the second chapter and return later to the Introduction – or even ignore it completely.

1

Introduction

This book deals mainly with the practice and reception of certain arts in the Ottoman Empire, and in particular with architecture and the related decorative arts. Its focus, however, is not so much on the works of the great masters – although it will occasionally touch upon these – but rather on a question. Namely, to what extent and how did those Ottoman townspeople who were literate, or who at least enjoyed indirect access to written culture, have a stake in the buildings, books and festivals which were created in their midst? This means that we are concerned with the relationships between patrons, artists and audiences, as well as with the relationships between the various arts which interacted in, for example, a festival. As well as the architecture and the decorative arts, we must look at the dramatic performances which accompanied Ottoman festivals, at everyday writing such as diaries and letters, and last but not least at the culinary arts. Cooking was and is an everyday activity, but it is an outlet for artistic inspiration, however modest in scope.

In addition, we shall examine the human networks through which the knowledge relevant to artistic production was transmitted. Thus, if we wish to understand an Ottoman building, we must know something of how architects were educated. It is equally important to locate information about any writers in the court environment who wrote, for example, about the symbolic content of certain architectural forms and festivals, or who discussed the qualities a building needed to possess if it were to be considered beautiful. This is because, if we are fortunate, their writings may have been read by members of the sultan's inner circle, and the thoughts expressed in them may have been incorporated into official building policy. Indirectly at least, such texts tell us of the political aims which a particular sultan hoped to pursue via the construction of a building or the instigation of a public festival. It is true that in a book of limited scope it is possible to discuss only a part of the networks which were of cultural importance. Moreover, those which are treated here have been chosen because they are relatively well documented, and some of them may in fact have been less significant to artistic production than others which are not discussed here due to a lack of sources. Nevertheless, in this way it is possible to make clear the connection between everyday communication of knowledge and artistic production.

A Belated Synthesis

Such an overview of the Ottoman domain has rarely been attempted before, although there are of course numerous examinations of its architecture, painting and theatre. The main preoccupation in architectural history, apart from documenting buildings (which dominated for a substantial period), has been the historical elucidation of ground plans and elevations.[1] In the history of painting, attention has been paid to those forms of representation which did not contravene the religious prohibition against depicting people and animals: for example, calligraphy and abstract ornamentation, as well as illustrations of plants and flowers. However, equally or even more important to historians are those cases – mostly in the context of the sultans' courts – in which this ban was qualified or even evaded.[2] Researchers concerned with the theatre have taken an interest both in improvised theatre, which has a long tradition in the Ottoman domain, and the repertory theatre inspired by European practice, which gradually gained in popularity in Istanbul in the second half of the nineteenth century. However, there have been virtually no attempts to treat these various arts together and in their social context. This can be explained at least partly by the conservatism which is apparent in the methodology of many specialists in Near Eastern and Turkey studies. A debate about the relative merits of political and cultural history began as early as the late nineteenth century, but the cultural historians were able to assert themselves only to a limited extent and the debate did not influence Ottoman history, which at that time had hardly emerged as a distinct area of study.[3]

A greater degree of familiarity with the material, making it possible to examine the relationship between various cultural phenomena, arrived only in the 1930s, when more works by modern Turkish historians began to appear. However, the help afforded by these secondary sources was limited. Until five or ten years ago, most Turkish historians had shown little interest in the relationship between culture and society, at least after Fuat Köprülü had abandoned the field in the late 1940s. In the absence of such research, the question of the connections between literature, art and everyday culture cannot be resolved.[4] Later, only a few individuals worked on the relationship between culture and society, above all Sabri Ülgener and Abdülbaki Gölpınarlı. The latter wrote several works on the dervish order of the Mevlevîs and the literary activity of its members. Since the 1960s, Şerif Mardin has been concerned with the religion, political ideology and literature of the nineteenth and early twentieth centuries.[5]

Most historians turned their attention to political, economic and social structures, or they edited texts. This avoidance of cultural history can doubtless be partly explained by the fact that this branch of history cannot possibly avoid dealing with religion, a subject which was foreign to the often vehemently secular historians of the 1930s and 1940s. Yet at the same time, it was and still is frowned upon in Turkey to articulate clearly any disaffection with religion *per se*, as opposed to its external manifestations. As a result, it was rare for the role of religion as a totality to be treated at all, even in a historical context. Moreover, a considerable effort was required to process the Ottoman archives, the riches of which are still only partly known. Even if it was not always put into words, there was a definite feeling that the 'hard data' which would justify history as a science could be obtained only by analysing archive material.[6] In addition, collaboration with urban and regional planners had a lasting impact on Turkish socio-economic history. In consequence, analyses of trade, crafts and political institutions, along with their impact upon humanly inhabited space, were more in demand than studies of political ideology, cultural symbolism or even the expression of personal feelings.

The Discovery of Everyday Culture

Today, however, the situation is beginning to change: religious movements are far more visible in Turkey than they were just twenty years ago, and, as a result, the social role of cultural factors appears in a rather different light. Moreover, particularly among the cultural élite, there is a growing scepticism towards the state itself, which was previously so revered, and the social dynamic beyond the state can be examined only by taking cultural factors into account.[7] However, the debate among Europeanist historians has also made its mark: the definition of cultural history has changed very considerably in the last twenty-five years.[8] Today the term covers not just art, science and literature, but also everyday culture. 'Everyday culture' refers to a wide range of phenomena, from the etiquette of visiting a neighbour to the ways in which food is prepared or children are brought up. The symbolism of colour has a place in everyday culture, as do the stories told by men in the café and women at the spinning-wheel. Most of the areas dealt with under the heading of everyday culture are also of interest to folklorists and ethnologists.[9]

This interest in everyday culture can be partly explained by the fact that today's democratic impulses play an important role in the thinking of many historians.[10] It is for this reason that apart from the 'high culture' which touched relatively few, the cultural attitudes of 'ordinary' people have come to be examined. At first craftsmen, farmers and servants were considered of particular interest, because of their involvement in the economic sphere, and, not rarely, in the market. However, since the 1970s there has been an increasing awarenesss of the fact that, actually, members of these very groups often behaved in a manner contrary to the norms of the market, obeying instead their own social value systems. Obviously behaviour which, even in the nineteenth century, the heyday of the 'free market', systematically contravened the laws of that market, could be explained only by using social and cultural models; and this situation certainly has helped bring everyday culture to the attention of economic and social historians.[11]

So far as the Ottoman realm is concerned, the results of research into everyday culture have begun to accumulate without the term itself necessarily being applied. There are, for instance, several works dealing with lifestyle and with festivals instituted by the sultan and celebrated on the streets of Istanbul, and sometimes also on the Bosphorus and at the Golden Horn. Ottoman observers such as the seventeenth-century traveller Evliya Çelebi, as well as many Europeans, extensively described the festivities celebrating victories in battle, the births of princes and princesses, or the safe return of pilgrims from Mecca.[12] More recently, studies have appeared dealing with first-person narratives and memoirs.[13] These works came as something of a surprise as, for a long time, memoirs and literature in the first person in general had been widely regarded as virtually absent from the Ottoman domain. This gap was often explained by the supposed lack of an individual consciousness until the middle of the nineteenth century. However, recent discoveries have shown that this assertion must at least be heavily qualified.[14] Last but not least, estate inventories have provided a fairly accurate idea of the furnishings of wealthy households of the late sixteenth to early nineteenth centuries. However, as is the case in virtually every other part of the world, our knowledge of the poorer people is altogether less satisfactory.

High Culture, Folk Culture and Popular Culture

The class of those men and women who had a stake in Ottoman culture as creators or simply as consumers is also important. In earlier times the terms 'high culture' and 'folk culture' were common currency. However, a closer examination soon reveals that it is hard to do justice to the complexity of reality in an analysis founded on these two terms.[15] So far as high culture is concerned, the issue at first seems clear-cut: to be recognized as a member of the Ottoman upper class, cultural conformity was a prerequisite. In other words, it was necessary to be a Muslim (the exceptions, which certainly existed, merely prove the rule), to be fluent in both the spoken and written forms of the Ottoman language, and to be familiar with upper-class etiquette.[16] The culture of this group, or at least the culture of its most cultured members, is what would be described as Ottoman high culture.

Yet even within this culture, in which only a very limited circle of people participated and which at first glance appears entirely uniform, there were clearly discernible subcultures. A man who dedicated himself to religious law and Islamic theology was recognized as a member of the learned class (*ulema*) teaching these subjects and eventually becoming a judge (*kadı*). Such a person would concern himself mainly with the relevant Arabic texts. He would therefore develop an outlook very different from that of a court dignitary with an interest in Persian and Ottoman *belles- lettres*. This was because in the circles of the Ottoman central bureaucracy – few of whose members had, in the second half of the sixteenth century, been educated in a school of theology (*medrese*) – a relatively secular culture predominated.[17] Most Ottoman bureaucrats seem to have taken their religion for granted to the extent that they hardly referred to it in routine correspondence. In addition, there were the dervishes, who came from both the upper class and the lower orders of society. Here too there existed several cultural traditions. Thus, the Mevlevîs, who included many members of the upper classes, practised the ceremonial dance as the central mystical experience – this was anathema to many theologians.[18] Despite consensus on basic principles, the Ottoman upper class was divided into smaller groupings with rather widely diverging subcultures. Many beliefs developed initially within one specific group, later becoming accepted across a wider spectrum. This was the case, for example, with the relatively secular culture of the bureaucrats (*kâtip*) who had not been educated as jurists or theologians. These officials developed a variant of Ottoman culture which was to have a considerable impact upon the 'modern-style' cultural practice of the nineteenth and early twentieth centuries.[19]

Of course, there were also people, many of the most creative among them, who tried to form a personal synthesis from the various subcultures accessible to them. In the middle of the nineteenth century Ahmed Cevdet, who later became a historian, arrived in Istanbul to complete his *ulema* education and was not satisfied with what he found himself learning in the *medrese*.[20] He therefore sought out private tutors and attended the meetings of a group of Nakşbendî dervishes, with whom he studied Persian and literature. In the sixteenth century the historian and bureaucrat Mustafa Âlî, a most learned individual, prided himself on having conjoined the *medrese* subculture with that of the *kâtips* and the particular practices of the dervishes.[21] It goes without saying that figures who attempted this kind of cross-fertilization sometimes felt the pressure of the conflicting demands made upon them by the various circles to which they belonged. All his life Mustafa Âlî suffered from the resulting frustrations.

The term 'folk culture' is even more problematic. In the debate among Europeanist historians of early modern times, it used to denote the culture of those people who did not participate in the culture of the upper class, which was based on a classical education.[22] Yet the European town- and country-dwellers who were excluded from scholarly and court culture cannot be said to have constituted a homogenous group. Among them were craftsmen, country squires, and women of all levels of society who were literate only in their native languages. These were the readers of almanacs, prayer books and broadsheets. Yet their culture can hardly be described as 'folk culture' in that these people had access to the world of books, and as a result their attitudes and ways of thinking were only in part determined by oral tradition. Today, many cultural historians therefore consider that the dichotomy of high and folk culture is too crude. However, this dual model has proven to be as hardy as a weed, suddenly reappearing just when it was thought to have been eradicated.[23]

There are two possible alternatives. One is to create a third category, which denotes the culture of those people literate in their native languages but excluded from the privileged 'high' culture associated with the language of their time and place.[24] Such a culture has come to be known as 'popular culture', predominant among the Christian peoples of the Balkans until the late nineteenth or early twentieth century. Except for a small élite educated in the academy of the Greek patriarchs or in foreign universities, only very few Ottoman Christians of this period had access to any form of high culture. Moreover, the 'popular culture' of the Ottoman-Turkish domain has hardly been investigated. Both historians and philologists have tended to concentrate instead on court and scholarly culture, while the folklorists have busied themselves with the difficult subject of the partly oral, partly written tradition of the so-called 'folk poets' (halk şairleri).[25] We still know very little of the writing, printing and distribution of popular literature in Ottoman-Turkish. There is nothing, at any rate, to compare with the equivalent research concerning Bulgaria or Greece.

In face of an unsatisfactory dichotomy between 'high' and 'folk' culture, the other option would be to avoid such categories altogether. French historians writing about domestic, court and street culture in eighteenth-century Paris, for example, do not generally attempt to arrange the newspapers, broadsheets, testimonies and other materials with which they are concerned into a dual or triple scheme.[26] Rather, they will merely state that some item of true or false information was slipped to the gazette writer by, say, a royal official. In fact it would be difficult satisfactorily to categorize such an event, by no means uncommon in eighteenth-century France: the king and his official function here as the creators of popular literature! Any attempt at classification is made even harder by the fact that both people and works of literature can easily pertain to more than one culture. Even among the male members of the European nobility in the seventeenth century there were individuals who understood so little Latin that they could not follow mass. Such people were sometimes prominent members of the court, and doubtless they participated in court culture. However, as non-readers of Latin, who might perhaps tell their beads during mass, they can also be considered to belong to the realm of popular culture.[27]

I have decided to avoid expressions such as high culture, popular culture and folk culture as far as possible. This decision is based on pragmatic considerations, or to put it differently, on the lacunae in our information. Thus, for example, the relative lack of earlier research into book production in Ottoman Turkey has already-been mentioned. The scarcity of printing presses is not at issue here, as even handwritten material can be produced in considerable quantities for sale to a wider public.[28] However, because so little is known about what might be termed popular culture, it is hard to determine whether we may assume the existence of a unitary popular culture common to all those townspeople who were Muslim and who could write in Turkish. It is also conceivable that the regional, and perhaps also the social, differences were so great that it would be necessary to assume a plurality of such cultures. When more research has been completed, it will be possible to operate at this abstract level. For the time being, however, it seems more practicable to concentrate on the culture of the Muslim townspeople, with occasional reference to the non-Muslims. When these people participated in festivals organized by the sultan's court, or wrote down the religious legends recounted by peasants and nomads, they emerged from the narrow confines of their own sectional culture, and we shall attempt to follow them.[29]

Cultural Diversity

The Ottoman Empire was much more culturally heterogeneous than European states of the early modern era. In most European countries only small religious minorities remained after the expulsion of the Jews in the late middle ages and the various reformations and counter-reformations.[30] In the Ottoman Balkans there existed more or less compact Greek Orthodox and – to a lesser degree – Catholic communities, and in the vassal state of Transylvania, there were some Protestants. Compact Jewish communities of varying sizes existed in many Ottoman towns, particularly in Istanbul and Salonica. In Anatolia, there lived both Greek Orthodox and Armenian Christians, even if there seem to have been fewer Greeks in western Anatolia during the sixteenth century than there were to be later, after immigration from the Aegean islands in the nineteenth century. Each of these groups had its own liturgical language, separate from the spoken one. Thus, for example, in normal conversation the Sephardic Jews used a dialect of Spanish, which Evliya Çelebi, the seventeenth-century Ottoman traveller, a man proficient in languages, regarded as 'Jewish'.[31] Among the Greek Orthodox inhabitants of central Anatolia there was a Turkish-speaking community, whose members bestowed Turkish names upon their children; the Greek language was used only by the clergymen in the liturgy. On the other hand, among the Anatolian Muslims there was also a very large heterodox group. Unlike the non-Muslims, these people were subjected to persecution, but survived nevertheless. Known as Alevî, they are still a significant religious minority in modern Turkey. Fervent Kızılbaş ('red heads', as they were called on account of their headgear) avoided the mosques and shunned state institutions as far as was possible. Many of them believed in the occasional appearance of God incarnate in the world; Ali, the son-in-law of the prophet Muhammad, and Ismail, the first Safavid Shah (1487–1524), were seen as such. A substantial part of Kızılbaş culture was handed down orally and therefore only fragments are known. There was also, however, a written tradition in poetry, which is regarded as the most important contribution made by this group to the culture of modern Turkey.[32]

Beside the culture of the palace and the *ulema*, we also find written cultures in several subject communities, and today these are seen as more important than was true just ten or twenty years ago. From the seventeenth century onwards, when the medieval conflict between the followers of the Greek Orthodox Church and the Catholics had lost some of its virulence, a significant number of Greeks studied in Padua or other Italian universities.[33] Scholarly activity was supported by the Phanariots, wealthy Greek merchant families from Istanbul, who were also active patrons of the arts. The necessary resources stemmed partly from lucrative appointments as Ottoman governors in Moldavia and Wallachia, today's Romania.[34] Certain provinces also developed their own building styles; thus in Egypt during the eighteenth century the commanders of the various Cairene militias sponsored the construction of numerous buildings. These mosques, schools and public fountains united elements of the Ottoman 'imperial style', as favoured by the sultans since the fifteenth century and introduced into every province, with impulses arising from medieval (Mamluk) Egyptian architecture.[35] When dealing with provincial scholarly production or sophisticated architecture in the Ottoman context, it makes even less sense to insist on a simple dichotomy between high culture and folk culture than in the case of early modern France, where historians have long since demolished this two-tiered model. Yet some traces of this easy simplification seem all but ineradicable, and may be detected even in the present account.

Muslim Townspeople in the Core Regions of the Ottoman Empire

A multi-volume work rather than a single book would be necessary to deal with all these aspects of Ottoman culture, and such a work would probably require more than one author. A process of selection is therefore unavoidable. If, despite the attempt to shun it, the term 'high culture' occasionally creeps in here, it refers to the culture of the *ulema* on the one hand, and the culture of those state officials not educated in religious law on the other. Both these subcultures developed mainly in Istanbul and, to a lesser degree, in major regional centres such as Edirne. Court culture should not be forgotten, as it was an important source of inspiration for townspeople, particularly with regard to non-religious matters in the widest sense. For our purposes, however, it is significant only in so far as people who were not themselves members of the court involved themselves in it.

Of the men and women who had only limited access to this high culture we shall be concerned mainly, but not exclusively, with the Muslim townspeople of Anatolia, Istanbul and the Balkan peninsula. Balkan Muslims often wrote in Turkish, even if their mother-tongue might be Bosnian or Albanian. Those individuals with some knowledge of court culture and theological education tended to use more Arabic and Persian loan-words than other people did; but in the case of less well-educated writers, loan-words from local languages were common currency. Orthodox and Catholic Christians in the territory occupied until recently by the Yugoslavian federation often referred, and continue to refer, to their Bosnian Muslim neighbours as Turks. This tendency is probably linked to the formerly widespread use of the Turkish language among Balkan Muslims.[36]

The inhabitants of Istanbul have a particular role to play in our study. In this city the number of people who could read and write Ottoman-Turkish was greater than anywhere else in the Ottoman Empire. Moreover, the large number of libraries in mosques and dervish convents meant that the inhabitants of the city enjoyed easier access to written culture than was possible elsewhere. Libraries also functioned as relatively secure storage places for manuscripts; as a result, more manuscripts produced by 'common' people are preserved in Istanbul than elsewhere. These libraries tended to be stone buildings, and therefore offered greater protection against the fires which destroyed so many papers stored in private homes.

Anatolian townspeople are relatively obscure by comparison. This reflects the fact that Anatolia is one of the least-researched of the great regions of the Ottoman Empire. Because many Anatolian towns were not very large, there were correspondingly fewer places of learning where literate townspeople could congregate. Such centres were to be found mainly in the former capital, Bursa, where there were many pious foundations, and in Konya, where the principal convent of the Mevlevî order had built up a great library which still exists.[37]

In geographical terms, then, we shall be dealing with the area which historians have long identified as the core of the Ottoman Empire, that is with south-eastern Europe on the one hand and western and central Anatolia on the other.[38] By south-eastern Europe we mean the area which today includes Greece, Bulgaria, Albania, Macedonia, Serbia and Bosnia-Herzegovina. The Dalmatian coast, which is largely Croatian territory today, at least partly belongs to the core of the Ottoman area as well. Moldavia and Wallachia, today in Romania, are excluded; although the governors of these two provinces were appointed and dismissed by the Sublime Porte, there was no indigenous, Islamicized upper class there and there were relatively few Muslim Turks. Hungary is also excluded, principally because the Ottoman period there was relatively short (1540–1683), and it was a much disputed territory. Eastern Anatolia is omitted for similar reasons. In that area there were few urban centres, and those that did exist lost many of their libraries and archives in the wars of the nineteenth and twentieth centuries. Diyarbakır, Gaziantep, Bitlis and Van might, admittedly, have merited more attention than they have been given here. However, the number of surviving primary sources from this area is limited, and so is the number of secondary studies analysing them. The most unfortunate exclusion is without doubt that of the Arabian provinces, today's Syria, Egypt and Iraq, as well as Libya, Tunisia and Algeria. On the other hand, a considerable amount has already been published on many of these territories, particularly on Syria, Egypt and Tunisia, and much of it is available in European languages.[39] Readers will be able to fill some of the gaps unfortunately found in this book.

As was the case in nearly all pre-industrial societies, townspeople represented but a small minority of the total population. The vast majority of the inhabitants of the Ottoman Empire were peasants. In some areas, above all in central Anatolia, nomads and semi-nomads were also significantly represented. On the cultural history of these people, our information is as yet minimal. Outside the towns there were few mosques and other religious institutions and, doubtless, again as in other pre-industrial, rural societies, few people were literate. Moreover, the few available sources have often not been published or commented upon. Reluctantly, therefore, we must content ourselves with just occasional glances at the culture of the rural population, the vast majority of the sultans' subjects.

The History of Attitudes in the Ottoman Realm

The so-called history of attitudes has been an important element in the reinvigoration of European cultural history in the last thirty years.[40] It involves searching for traces of those people who seldom wrote. By looking at the changing formulae with which people began their testaments, at the inscriptions with which they commemorated their dead, at clumsy letters home from soldiers, and at memorials in cemeteries and parks, historians attempt to find answers to questions upon which traditional sources shed little light. Which social groups distanced themselves from organized religion and which ones, by contrast, embraced it, how were new political systems regarded, or in what way were emotions such as love and friendship expressed? The process involves assembling sequences of evidence with the aim of achieving as great a degree of continuity as possible, and then arranging the material in tables, graphs and diagrams. From these it is possible to detect changes in people's behaviour. There are, of course, many cases in which even this procedure is limited in its effectiveness by the sheer lack of sources. Surprisingly often, though, it seems that once the questions have been asked it is possible to locate the necessary primary sources.

In the Ottoman area this procedure is particularly helpful for the period beginning in the late seventeenth century. From this period relatively plentiful source material deriving from private persons is available; examples include tombstones, or notebooks in which selections from texts were occasionally copied to create private anthologies. The inscriptions from drinking-water outlets and other inexpensive pious foundations, as well as the corresponding deeds of foundation, might also be taken into account. Records of accidents, not infrequently found in the *kadi* registers of larger towns, were meant to determine whether anyone was responsible for deaths and injuries and could be forced to make reparations; these protocols also constitute a possible source for the historian. Evaluating this material is difficult, however, because the necessary preliminary research has been undertaken only in a few cases, such as in that of the tombstones of Istanbul. Intensive research into local history is often necessary, and these studies frequently have to be undertaken with virtually no institutional support.[41] Only with the help of such research, however, can we hope to elucidate how Ottoman non-élite townspeople viewed their religion. This book is intended as a possible framework for such studies.

Cultural Conflicts and Social Tensions

As Ottoman society contained social groups which were openly or covertly at odds with one another, and because many of these groups possessed their

own cultures, social conflicts often had cultural repercussions. The refusal of
sixteenth-century Anatolian nomads to hand over a theologian regarded by
the central government as a heretic, instead offering shelter to both the fugitive
and his books, was of course a political act.[42] At the same time, however, the
leaders of this group of nomads made it clear that their outlook on certain
matters, which we label 'cultural', differed from that of the central government. They took a different view of the duties of hospitality, possibly also of
their obligations towards fellow tribesmen (if indeed the accused theologian
was a member of the tribe) and maybe of the distinction between orthodoxy
and heresy. These cultural conflicts were far more profound than a mere
confrontation with a provincial governor and his mercenaries. Similarly, when
craftsmen tried to denigrate unwanted competitors as insufficiently qualified
(*hamdest*), they were appealing to more than just the economic interests of
potential customers.[43] Until their organizations dissolved in the nineteenth or
early twentieth century, Ottoman guildsmen often made reference to the
fütüvvet, a system of ceremonies and rules of moral behaviour designed to
ensure the integration of craftsmen in urban society. A craftsman who did
not adhere to the rules of the guild was thus marginalized not just in economic
terms, but socially as well. In the course of this book we shall encounter
many such instances of cultural conflicts with social foundations.

This is something which needs to be emphasized for the Ottoman context
most particularly. For many years the view predominated that, until the middle
of the nineteenth century, social conflicts in the widest sense of the term
were confined to disputes between various factions within the Ottoman ruling
class. In addition to these, the traditional view of social history mainly
recognized occasional quarrels between the members of particular religious
and ethnic groups (*millets*). Outside the political class, Ottoman society saw
itself as arranged not in upper and lower social strata but rather in vertical,
parallel 'columns'. Because of this conception, society was thought to be
'classless', that is, free of most social conflicts. The same difference of
opinions, incidentally, persisted in European social history for many years,
particularly in the case of pre-industrial France. Following that debate, many
French social historians today take the view that the numerous revolts of the
seventeenth century, directed against ever-increasing royal taxes, were carried
out by coalitions of provincial noblemen and peasants. They should therefore
not be compared to the class conflicts of the nineteenth and twentieth centuries.[44] On the other hand pre-industrial France saw quite a few bloody
conflicts between rich and poor at local level.

I see Ottoman society in terms of a similar basic structure. In everyday
political life, conflicts between nomads and sedentary farmers or between de-
mobilized soldiers and villagers were more conspicuous than those between

rich and poor. However, in analysing many such conflicts, we should not neglect the opposition between affluent merchants and poor craftsmen, or between privileged soldiery belonging to the class of untaxed sultan's servants (*askerî*) and mercenaries without any secure position. In many cases it can be hard to determine which was the decisive antagonism underlying a given conflict; thus we have not been able to locate ideological disputes clearly linked to the antagonism between 'established' servitors of the sultan and the 'out-group' of aggressive mercenaries. Yet careful research into well-documented conflicts is likely to throw up a few surprises. Cultural history, though, is inconceivable without cultural conflict. Neither is it possible to imagine social history, which is so closely tied to cultural history, without social conflicts, as soon as differences in power and wealth have been institutionalized – a process in which the state itself plays a key role.

Insisting on a close link between cultural conflicts and social tensions does not in itself imply a statement on the priority of the 'social' or the 'cultural' realm. However, I would suggest that social tensions are generally the primary phenomena, even though, in many cases, it will be hard to prove or disprove this assumption. If we wish to consider the social background to a cultural conflict, we need to adhere closely to the extant documentary evidence. Unprovable assertions that a certain social conflict underlies some literary controversy, or some quarrel between rival dervish sheikhs, are entirely unhelpful. In the worst cases such assertions can discredit a model which I believe to be a reasonable one. Of course, statements about arcane religious or literary questions, which may appear to be divorced from everyday life, have to be seen initially within the specific dynamic of their subject area, that is religious or literary history as the case may be. Yet the social position of the person making the statement is of relevance. If, for example, a member of the Ottoman upper class such as the historian Mustafa Âlî (1541–1600) insists upon the significance of a theological and legal training for future Ottoman public servants, this demand must be seen in the light of the writer's own career interests.[45] However, the social interpretation of intellectual statements can lead to satisfactory results only if sufficient sources are available and if all the relevant material is taken into account.

Mediators

Until now we have regarded culture as a medium for the expression of social conflict and as a means of social demarcation; in the sixteenth century an accomplished literary man such as Mustafa Âlî regarded many inhabitants of Anatolia as 'uncouth' and 'deprived of culture'.[46] Certain cultural traits were paraded in front of Ottoman subjects by the upper class, in order to draw attention to the distinction between rulers and ruled. As an example, we may cite the sumptuary laws affecting dress enacted repeatedly through the centuries (but not necessarily obeyed). After all, in the view of an educated Ottoman such as Mustafa Âlî, the barrier between the upper class and the humble taxpayer was a fundamental element in the smooth functioning of the whole political system.[47] Accordingly, until the middle of the nineteenth century there were few attempts to spread upper-class culture among the generality of Ottoman subjects. Exceptions proving the rule were the repression of the Kızılbaş, who were regarded as heretics and were supposed to become 'normal' Sunni Muslims, or else the sporadic forced settlement of nomads from the late seventeenth century onwards. This latter project had cultural as well as social, political and economic dimensions; after all former nomads needed to adapt to village culture. However, culture was spread even without the active efforts of the ruling classes. Proof of this includes the writing skills which were brought even to remote little market towns in Anatolia and the Balkans by dervishes, itinerant *medrese* students and mosque preachers. It is to such people that we are indebted for the biographies of local figures regarded as saints, often composed long after the death of the person in question.[48]

The greatest insights of modern historical research into the activities of the dervishes have concerned their role as cultural mediators. This activity began in the period from the eleventh century onwards (modern calendar) when Turkish tribes were migrating to Anatolia, but it clearly persisted in later eras. Thus the great Bektashi convent of Hacı Bektaş was located on the central Anatolian plain, far from all urban settlement. Yet despite its isolation, this place was sought out by members of the Ottoman upper class who wished to pay their respects to the saint.[49] In the nineteenth century the dervishes possessed an impressive library. Members of the order would take advantage of visits to a large city to copy texts for their own use, which they might in turn pass on to the library of their favourite convent. Libraries continued to be used in this way right up to the end of the nineteenth century.

One question, long studied and yet by no means resolved, concerns the transmission of the cultural innovations which came to Ottoman society from Europe from the eighteenth century onwards. The traditional explanation, still to be found in many studies, assumes that the Ottoman upper class was prepared to accept European reforms only under the pressure of repeated military defeats. Moreover, only indispensable technical innovations would be taken on, leaving the substance of Ottoman culture untouched. There is certainly a great deal of truth in this explanation; even today this is the kind of policy espoused in conservative circles. On the other hand, those historians who accept such a model concede that young men who had learnt French to further their careers could not be prevented from reading books beyond their school texts, and above all *belles-lettres*. Moreover, it is difficult to determine in individual cases just what constituted an indispensable part of a technical education. Physics and mathematics, for instance, were the basis for the study of ballistics, while many mathematicians regarded philosophy as a vital foundation for their own work. Certainly some novel branches of learning found Ottoman followers in this fashion, but many questions still remain unanswered. It would be interesting to know, for example, why certain books were particularly popular among those young men who ventured beyond the standard textbooks for their field of study.[50] More research into the role of teachers in the Ottoman military – and, later, civilian – academies is needed. On the basis of both French and Ottoman sources, much work also remains to be done on the studies and subsequent activities of those young people who, from the mid-nineteenth century onwards, were sent by the Ottoman government to study in Europe. These individuals must have played a particularly important part in transmitting cultural changes.[51]

Moreover, today there is less certainty about the absolute priority of military matters which is implicit in the traditional model. There is now more scepticism about the previously uncontested assumption that the Ottoman Empire was 'a (near) perfect military society', and that all cultural change thus stemmed from military expediency. After all, in early modern Europe war was also the central activity. In 1789 the *ancien régime* in France finally toppled under the weight of so many wars, while Prussia's contemporary army was of course positively hypertrophic.[52] The Ottoman Empire can hardly be considered more or less warlike than its European neighbours, and there is thus no basis for the assumption that members of its upper class were motivated by exclusively military concerns.

This new perspective grants a central role to direct and indirect contacts between Ottoman Muslims and contemporary Europe. Today we know that it was wrong to imagine that Ottoman Muslim merchants of the sixteenth and seventeenth centuries piously avoided all contact with 'unbelievers'.[53] They visited Venice in such large numbers that even in the early seventeenth century the Serenissima considered it necessary to create the Fondacco dei Turchi specifically to accommodate them. There were also opportunities for contacts within the Ottoman Empire itself with the many foreigners who had arrived either as prisoners or of their own volition and had settled there. Moreover, there was a substantial population of Turkish-speaking Christians in Anatolia in particular. Although the books these people wrote (and later printed) were probably not read by more than a very few Muslims, some oral communication of their contents, in the countryside of Konya or Kayseri, is not impossible.[54]

Spanish, French and Italian fishermen, soldiers and craftsmen found their way into the Ottoman Empire and sometimes made contacts with local people, of which the more highly educated of both cultures knew nothing; this state of affairs has recently been highlighted in a most valuable study.[55] Similarly, Ottoman merchants, fishermen and soldiers experienced life in the lands bordering the Mediterranean. As real human contact, frequently reported in European sources, can take place only if both sides desire it, I would argue that many Ottoman Muslims of the lower orders in particular knew a great deal more about Europe than is apparent in the books of the period.

A Caveat: 'Traditional Culture'

There is one term which appears frequently in publications on our subject dating from the 1950s and 1960s and which is deliberately avoided in this book. This is the so-called 'traditional culture' which many researchers perceive among the lower orders of all pre-industrial societies. Social scientists who operate with this term regard those aspects of modern culture which became widespread only in the late nineteenth or even in the twentieth century as defining characteristics of non-traditional societies. Reading newspapers is one example, but listening to radio broadcasts or taking part in elections have also been used. All societies in which such activities were absent are described as traditional, and of course by this definition rural peoples remain traditional much longer than members of the political upper class. The term 'traditional culture' implies in addition that such a society is characterized not by anonymity, but rather by the cooperation of people who know each other either at first hand or at least by repute.[56]

For our purposes the concept of 'traditional culture' is useless, not least because we shall be concerned with only very few human relationships which can be described as 'modern' in the sense of such a terminology. Labels are useful only in so far as they define situations and concepts in contradistinction to one another. However, there is another, more serious objection. 'Traditional culture' tends to mean a system relatively free of internal contradictions, or at least one in which those contradictions which do exist are not perceived as such by those living within it. This book is in fact concerned precisely with the discontinuities and contradictions inherent in Ottoman culture, meaning that it can hardly treat Ottoman culture as a traditional one in that sense.

Regarding Periodization

At first glance, dividing history into periods appears merely to be a means of making a vast amount of material manageable. From this point of view, any discussion of the specific dates marking off particular eras must appear entirely academic, not to say whimsical. Closer inspection will, however, show that such dates are never chosen at random, but rather show how particular historians perceive social changes. To select a battle or the rise of a dynasty as the limit of an era even when dealing with cultural history is to imply that political events take priority over cultural changes, at least in this particular case. Ottoman history, and Ottoman cultural history in particular, is a discipline which has tended to cling obstinately to certain long-established assumptions, and unfortunately this makes it necessary to reconsider the issue of eras.

In European cultural history it has long been customary to broaden the scope of labels deriving from the history of art to refer to a whole era. Thus we speak of baroque lyric, classical prose and so forth. Ottoman cultural history is still at such an early stage that no specific system of periodization has yet been developed. Architectural and literary historians, on the other hand, have made better progress in their particular fields. In each instance an early period has been identified in which the so-called classical synthesis of Ottoman court culture which predominated in the late fifteenth and the sixteenth centuries had not as yet emerged. This era, which ended as early as the second half of the fourteenth century so far as architectural historians are concerned, continued in literary history until the middle of the fifteenth century.[57] During the fourteenth and fifteenth centuries, Turkish emerged as a literary language. In the course of this process many words and also many grammatical structures were assimilated from Arabic and above all from Persian. By the second half of the sixteenth century, Mustafa Âlî was able to claim that in the Ottoman Empire Arab and Persian scholars and writers had finally found a home for the only culture he recognized, that is the culture of the court and *medrese*. Âlî did not, however, take that state of affairs for granted, but rather regarded court and *medrese* culture as a delicate plant which depended for its survival on constant care and support from the sultan.[58]

The middle of the fifteenth century was a turning-point in both literature and architectural history. Following the conquest of Istanbul, Mehmed the Conqueror (reign: 1451–81) instigated a great building programme in Edirne and, above all, in his new capital where, in the Topkapı Palace, 'exotic' motifs, meaning in particular Iranian ones, were incorporated.[59] The caesura was somewhat later in mosque architecture, where the so-called T-shaped mosque design, which consisted of two main domes and annexes on each side, was finally set aside around 1500.[60] In its place there emerged a design involving a central dome supported by semi-domes, and with a square or rectangular ground-plan. Albeit with many modifications, this design was ultimately adopted throughout the Ottoman Empire. Its emergence therefore represents a significant turning-point in architectural history, the beginning of the so-called classical style, dominated by the work of Mimar Sinan (the Chief Architect from 1538 to 1589). The style developed by 'Sinan the Architect' remained the obligatory model for Ottoman monumental architecture until the early eighteenth century.[61]

Another turning-point can be identified in the 1570s. At that time, at least from today's perspective, classical architecture achieved a culmination with the completion of Selim II's great mosque in Edirne (1574–75).[62] However, many contemporary figures sensed the beginning of a political decline, presaged by deteriorating coinage, organizational problems in the military and lengthy wars in which great conquests featured less and less frequently.[63] Today, some historians are inclined to relativize such suggestions: the topos of the decline of the times can be traced back as far as the beginning of the sixteenth century, as it is found in the writings of Prince Korkud, when the Ottoman sultans still had their greatest conquests before them.[64] It is nevertheless interesting that educated people of the 1570s and 1580s should perceive themselves to be living in a different age from that of the revered and only recently deceased Sultan Süleyman (reign: 1520–66).

This book will deal rather briefly with developments up to the second half of the sixteenth century and more fully with those of the late sixteenth, the seventeenth and the early eighteenth centuries. There is a practical reason for this: documentary evidence suddenly increases for the period from around 1560–70 onwards, no doubt as a result of the growth of the state bureaucracy. As we today know only too well, a greater number of bureaucrats invariably produces a greater quantity of written material. However, since we are here concerned not just with 'official' matters, but also with the culture of intimate and private spheres, literacy must be sufficiently widespread for a respectable amount of source material to accumulate. Moreover, my own field of research is the early modern period, and a certain degree of familiarity with the period is required to surmount the considerable difficulties often encountered in the search for sources.

The period which is here discussed in detail, and which is divided thematic-ally, ends around the middle of the eighteenth century. Practical constraints made it impossible to extend the study in such detail to the year 1789, for example (1789 has often been taken to mark the end of one era and the beginning of the next, being the year in which Sultan Selim III, a man of artistic interests and a military reformer, ascended the throne). The eighteenth century throws up particular difficulties, as very little research has been undertaken even though documentation is quite abundant. However, only a small part of the rich archive material for the period has been catalogued and thus opened up to researchers. The period from 1730 therefore receives short shrift, something which is all the more unfortunate in view of its potential interest. Recent studies have shown that there is much still to discover; by and large, however, we can still only speculate.

On the other hand, the period dealt with here does include the so-called 'Tulip Age' from 1718 to 1730, a time of particular interest in terms of cultural history. Impulses from the European baroque and rococo arrived in the Ottoman area at this time, albeit finding greater acceptance in the decorative arts than in structural architecture.[65] This style has long been disparaged by art historians. Nationalist researchers of the republican period were able to focus on the intense opposition of a part of the population of Istanbul to the style and the courtly pomp with which it was associated. They therefore interpreted it as a foreign import, brought in by a court negligent of its national traditions.[66] European historians, on the other hand, were far too strongly influenced by romantic conceptions of national singularity to find much merit in such a 'cosmopolitan' style. Only in recent years, when at least some writers have begun to look beyond the traditional way of thinking associated with national history, have the elegance and occasional exuberance of these buildings begun to attract greater attention. This new interest is part of the general rehabilitation of the eighteenth century not just among historians dealing with the Ottoman realm, but also among those concerned with India.[67] Where previously the eighteenth century was dismissed as a time of Ottoman cultural decline in the face of increasing European influence, now the vivacity and elegance characterizing the arts in this epoch are coming to be appreciated.

It is hard to pinpoint the exact end of this 'long eighteenth century' (1718-c. 1840). However, it does appear that a new attitude towards foreign influences set in from about 1840. No longer was it a question of incorporating the odd more or less exotic cultural element into a system which functioned adequately without such imports; rather, there was a reorganization of the whole culture of the Ottoman upper class. This process resulted in the introduction and popularization of new artistic forms such as the novel, oil-painting, the theatre and later the cinema. Everyday culture was also affected. Confectioners' shops, where food could be consumed on the premises, found in only a few parts of Istanbul at the end of the nineteenth century, began to spread throughout the city. In the republican period they gained a particular significance as places for social contact between women or mixed groups of people, while the café remained the preserve of the men.

Two final chapters deal with the period between 1770 and the first Tanzimat decree of 1839 on the one hand and, on the other, with the period from 1839 to 1908, which has been dubbed 'The Empire's Longest Century'.[68]

Here 1770 has been used to mark approximately the end of one era and the beginning of the next. This is because between 1760 and 1770 the economic cycle had moved from prosperity to depression, and the ensuing scarcity of money left its mark on the building trade. On the other hand, 1839 was a watershed in the cultural sphere as well. The heavy lines of the monument marking the tomb of Sultan Mahmud II, which can still be seen at Istanbul's Divanyolu, proclaim the end of Ottoman rococo.[69]

This book concludes in the year 1908, with the revolution of the so-called Young Turks. This was the end of the absolute rule of Sultan Abdülhamid II, who was toppled from his throne a year later, possibly after a failed attempt to regain power. Only four years remained until the outbreak of the Balkan War in 1912. The ensuing period of hostilities, which continued through the Balkan wars, the First World War and the war of Turkish independence until the peace treaty of Lausanne in 1923, was marked by severe confusion and destruction. It brought to a halt all cultural activities requiring any significant expenditure. Since, for our purposes, this period offers only literature and everyday culture, it has been omitted altogether.

This is a book largely based on the selection and reinterpretation of particular trends which have already been discussed elsewhere. Such a work is inevitably more strongly coloured by the author's fundamental outlook than an ordinary monograph would be. One aspect of that outlook therefore needs to be spelt out at this point, namely the belief that any culture, not least the Ottoman one, is an inextricable part of the lives lived by its creators. This does not mean that these people have no option but to behave according to predetermined cultural stereotypes. Rather, I work on the basis that even quite ordinary people, in their various circumstances, built on existing elements of their culture to develop new solutions. This book will investigate the men and women who availed themselves of such opportunities and the circumstances under which they did so.[70]

2

The Emergence of an Empire

In the late eleventh century Turkish immigrants, arriving from central Asia and sometimes travelling through Iran, began to settle in Anatolia and, in smaller numbers, the Balkans. The battle of Malazgird (Manzikert, 1071), in which the Byzantine Emperor Romanos Diogenes was defeated and taken prisoner by the Seljuk Sultan, Alp Arslan, represents a landmark in this process.[1] After the battle at Myriokephalon (1176), the Turks also began to settle in western Anatolia. By the end of the thirteenth century the Byzantines had lost virtually the whole of Anatolia: they were left with only Philadelphia (Alaşehir), Trabzon and a few small enclaves.[2] Even Nicaea (Iznik), which until 1258 had been the residence of Palaeologues driven from Constantinople by the so-called Latin conquest (1204), fell into Ottoman hands in 1331.

Anatolian Nomads: Religion and Rebellion

The vast majority of the Turkish immigrants were probably nomads. They bred sheep and used camels to transport their belongings; the more affluent among them rode horses. Nevertheless, most of the immigrants quickly settled down. This process was made easier by the fact that even in the driest areas of inner Anatolia it was (and still is) possible to farm without the need for irrigation.[3] By the second half of the fifteenth century, when Ottoman tax registers gave a first overview of land use, Anatolia was once again largely populated by sedentary farmers. The preponderance of the sedentary lifestyle grew markedly in the sixteenth century, although summer migrations to nearby high pastures were practised even by many twentieth-century villagers.

These immigrants were generally Muslims, albeit in many cases rather superficially so. Some groups settled in Byzantine territory and became Christians, among the most significant of which were the Gagauz, who today still inhabit Romania. Some researchers believe that the Karamanlı, who until their evacuation to Greece (1923) spoke Turkish and used Greek only in the liturgy, are descended from a Turkish ethnic group converted to Christianity in the middle ages.[4] But even in this early period, Turkish Christians were a tiny minority.

Most of the Muslim nomads, however, had practically no contact with the theologically-based piety of educated townspeople. Dervishes, often known as *abdal*, played a central role in the religion of the nomads, and so did the *babas*, spiritual leaders incorporating various elements from nature cults and in some cases also from shamanism in their religious practices.[5] Gradually dervishes and *babas* created a new religious synthesis with its own dynamic. From a Sunni Islam point of view this was heterodox religiosity, but over the centuries it came to play an important role in Ottoman and in particular in Anatolian cultural history. Most *babas* had little contact with written culture and are not therefore named in books and treatises. There were, however, exceptions such as Barak Baba, who was active in Anatolia, Syria and western Iran in the late thirteenth century, and whose unorthodox manner and heterodox attitudes scandalized theologians. In 1307–8 he was finally executed in Gilan, south of the Caspian Sea.[6]

About a generation before Barak Baba, in the thirteenth century, there were rebellious *babas* whose supporters have become known to posterity as Babaîs. Before 1240, Baba Ilyas and Baba Ishak led a great rebellion against the Seljuk sultans then ruling in Konya.[7] A refined courtly and urban culture flourished in the large towns of the state which these sultans had founded in central Anatolia in 1079. Meanwhile, in the remoter provinces, the leaders of nomad confederacies were at most indirectly and loosely controlled by the central government.

The Babaîs' rebellion was particularly violent in south-eastern Anatolia, as well as in the area of Amasya, not far from the Black Sea, where rebellions were frequent events in the Ottoman era as well. In 1240 the rebel Babaîs were massively defeated in the battle of Malya, near the central Anatolian town of Kırşehir. So-called 'Frankish' soldiers, from southern or western Europe, fought on the Seljuk side in this battle. It marked the beginning of the end for the Anatolian Seljuk state, which fell to the Mongols just three years later, at the time when the Mongols also reached central Europe. Hacı Bektaş and Sheikh Edebalı may have been among the *babas* who in the general confusion were able to escape the bloody reprisals Seljuk officers meted out to the rebels. In Ottoman historical writing, Hacı Bektaş and Sheikh Edebalı are seen as dervishes, that is, as men of God, who sought to draw nearer the Godhead by mystical practices. It was thus that at least some *babas*, whose rebellion initially probably had nothing to do with religion, were accepted into the increasingly Islamic society of Anatolia. Dervishes sought the way towards God in groups which resembled religious orders, at times paying scant regard to conventional religion. It was among the dervishes that the *baba*s, scantily clad in animal pelts, with their shaven heads and fondness for loud music, were welcomed with the fewest reservations.

Possibly after escaping from the battle of Malya, Hacı Bektaş retreated to the village of Suluca Karahöyük (today known as Hacıbektaş) and founded a hermitage destined to become the centre of the Bektashi. This was a dervish order which played a significant role throughout Ottoman history, although its organizational structure emerged only in the fifteenth and sixteenth centuries.[8] Sheikh Edebalı seems to have joined the Ottoman sultans, who at that time controlled only a small principality in north-western Anatolia around Iznik and Bilecik. The sheikh probably became spiritual adviser to Sultan Osman I (died 1326), who took his teacher's daughter as his wife. A chronicle dating from the fifteenth century suggests that Sheikh Edebalı interpreted one of Sultan Osman's dreams, in which a tree growing from the ruler's navel overshadowed the whole world, as an indication of future world domination.[9]

Nomads and semi-nomads clung on to their heterodox form of Islam despite the defeat at Malya. A sheikh from the Babaî tradition probably played a key part in the foundation of the Karaman principality which, in the fourteenth century, took over from the Seljuks in central Anatolia and later became an ally of Hungary against the Ottomans.[10] There was, however, no noteworthy nomad rebellion against the authority of the Ottoman state until about 1500, when the nomads and semi-nomads, for whom Ottoman rule had become a distant and alien entity, finally found a focus for their political discontent. This happened at the accession of Sheikh Isma'il, of the Safavid order of dervishes, to the Persian throne as Shah Isma'il I (1501), in whose state nomad groups were allowed a considerable political role. The Safavids, descended from Sheikh Safî al-Dîn Ishakî (1252–1334), initially resided in the town of Ardabil in western Iran. But in the fifteenth century the ancestor of Shah Isma'il, Sheikh Cunayd, emigrated to Anatolia. There, among a group of nomads, already heterodox from a conventional Sunni Islam point of view, he began to preach an extreme version of the Shia.[11] In the sermons of Sheikh Cunayd and later in those of Isma'il himself, Ali, the son-in-law and nephew of the Prophet Muhammad, was accorded a cosmic significance which far exceeded his historical role. As the religious leaders of extreme Shiite nomads, the Safavids gained the support which Shah Isma'il was then able to use in seizing political power.

Marginalized in the Ottoman state, the nomads of Anatolia often gave their support to the newly-emerged Safavid dynasty. One of the resulting rebellions, that of Şahkulu (1511–12), represented a real threat to the Ottoman state, which still had only a fragile grip on Anatolia.[12] This situation brought about a change in the attitude of the Ottoman sultans towards the heterodox religious practices of many nomads and recently settled villagers. In earlier times the Ottoman sultans had largely concentrated on expansion at the expense of their Christian (i.e. Byzantine, Serbian or Albanian) neighbours. In the process they exhibited considerable tolerance towards the heterodoxy of many of the dervish sheikhs who fought at the frontier along with their nomadic or semi-nomadic followers. This changed with the arrival on the scene of the Safavids; in the sixteenth century the Ottoman sultans became militant fighters for Sunni beliefs and practices.[13]

These circumstances probably prompted Sultan Bayezid II (reign: 1481–1512) to encourage the dervish order of the Bektashis to guide the nomads towards Sunni Islam. To this end he sponsored the enlargement of certain lodges belonging to the order, such as those located in the small town of Osmancık in northern Anatolia or else in Hacıbektaş itself. However, in order to communicate with the nomads, the dervishes had to adapt to their way of thinking, and, as a result, accepted some of the beliefs they had been sent out to combat. Moreover, heterodox dervishes – that is, those suspected of sympathizing with the Shiite Safavids – were subject to violent persecution in sixteenth-century Anatolia. Many of them sought refuge among the well-established and therefore less threatened Bektashi dervishes. In this way an order which was still more or less Sunni in character around 1500 meta-morphosed in the course of a single century into a spiritual community dominated by Shiite conceptions. Among its adherents, the mysticism dis-seminated by Fazlallâh Astarabâdî, in which letters are accorded mystical significance, was widespread. As a result, faces composed of letters of the alphabet play a significant role in Bektashi iconography.[14]

The Religiosity of the Sedentary Peoples: Islamization

Over the years most of the Byzantine peasants remaining in Anatolia turned to Islam, but few sources show just how this occurred. Neither the Seljuk sultans nor, later, their Ottoman successors made concerted efforts to convert Christians or Jews to Islam. There was nevertheless a great deal for their subjects to gain by becoming Muslims. Converts were free of the poll-tax levied on their non-Muslim neighbours, and the testimony of a Muslim carried much more weight in a court of law than that of a non-Muslim. Men with political ambitions had even more reason to consider converting to Islam. In the fourteenth and early fifteenth centuries it was sometimes possible for the minor nobility of recently incorporated Balkan states to win a military fief (timar), and thereby to enter the Ottoman ruling class, without giving up their faith.[15] However, these were positions at a local level; anyone wishing to pursue a career in the central administration had to adopt Islam and learn the

Ottoman-Turkish language. Moreover, although Christian and Jewish religious communities were tolerated, their members were not accorded a great deal of respect. Potential converts were no doubt frustrated by the requirement upon non-Muslims to wear certain clothes, or by the restrictions they sometimes faced when choosing an animal to ride, or else by the fact that they were not allowed to live near any of the many mosques.[16]

On the other hand, in many parts of Anatolia the structure of the Orthodox Church had already disintegrated during the Turkish conquests of the twelfth and thirteenth centuries. The *notitiae episcopatum*, that is, the lists of bishops who attended councils, constitute a major source on this question, even though they are often hard to interpret. Some of the bishops who appear in the lists were probably redundant because of the absence of any flock in the locality for which they had been appointed shepherd, all church activities having died out long ago. Other bishops, who did administer their sees, are easily over-looked by modern historians because fear of travelling or other considerations prevented them from attending the councils in question. Neither can we claim with certainty that the collapse of the church organization led directly to the conversion of its parishioners. There are plenty of examples which demonstrate that a religion can survive for generations in areas from which it has vanished as an organized church. Many members of religious groups which were branded heretical and therefore persecuted not just by the Byzantine state church but also (in the northern Balkans) by the Catholic hierarchy did react by turning to Islam. This may have occurred in Bosnia, for instance, in the case of the Bogomils. The Bogomils believed that the forces of evil were as powerful as God and therefore had a dualistic outlook. In the middle ages they suffered considerable persecution. However, it would be utterly wrong to assume that all Bosnian converts to Islam were therefore Bogomils.[17]

In the Islamization of Anatolia and certain Balkan territories the dervishes played a crucial part. As early as the fifteenth century it was reported that an Orthodox priest who was a friend of Hacı Bektaş had converted to Islam.[18] Quite shortly after his death, Mevlânâ Celâleddîn Rûmî was also celebrated for spreading the faith. The partly legendary biography by Eflakî describes how this famous poet and mystic pleaded for the life of a young Christian who had been condemned to death by the sultan.[19] Reprieved, the young man became a Muslim and a loyal disciple of Mevlânâ. However, Mevlânâ was also in contact with Christians who did not convert: it is reported that the founder of the Mevlevî order frequently visited the monks of a monastery outside Konya.[20]

Dervishes spread Islam not just by preaching and by their spiritual example but also simply by their presence. After the death of a well-known man of God, his followers were often convinced that prayers said at his graveside were more likely to be heard than those said elsewhere, and such places would begin to attract pilgrims. In this way dervish lodges and even villages often appeared around the graves of holy men. In some areas at least, existing saints continued to be revered and were simply reconstructed to fit the Muslim context. We should not, however, overestimate the frequency of this phenomenon.[21] In any case, irrespective of whether they arrived in an area as the leaders of Muslim settlers or worked as missionaries in a population which had not yet converted, the dervishes were far more successful in spreading Islam than the jurists and theologians (*ulema*) who were based mainly in the towns and therefore remote from their potential flocks.

Languages

Frequent links between Anatolia and central Asia from the eleventh century onwards explain why Persian was the language of Anatolian courtly and scholarly society. This language was used by educated people even in Buchara or Samarkand, even if many of them used a Turkish dialect in everyday life. Mevlânâ ('Our Lord') Celâleddîn Rûmî wrote his poems and his didactic verse narratives (*Mesnevî*) in Persian. Since the study of the master's works was the basis for spiritual activity in the order he founded, even in the twentieth century, Mevlevî dervishes learnt the language so as to participate fully in the order's ceremonies.[22] Chronicles, most notably the work of Ibn Bibi (died after 1285), were also written in Persian, and continued to be until the fifteenth century.[23]

Arabic was used as the language of theology and Islamic law, a subject taught in special schools known as *medreses*. The *medrese* as an institution was at that time still a relatively recent innovation. Among the early *medreses* were those created at the end of the eleventh century by Nizâm ul-mulk, the Vizier of the Great Seljuk Sultan Malikşâh. These new schools were vigorously encouraged by the Anatolian Seljuks and their courtiers.[24] In the former Seljuk capital of Konya in particular, there are still *medrese* buildings in existence, with ornate tilework and often with separate rooms for summer and winter.[25]

In addition, however, law and theology were taught in the mosque buildings, as had been the norm before the advent of the *medrese*. Arabic texts surviving from this period include many which institute pious foundations. Many mosques and *medreses* were inscribed with the donor's name, that of the reigning sultan, the purpose of the institution and the year of its inauguration.[26] For a very few such foundations of the thirteenth century there are also Arabic deeds of foundation. However, most of these date from the later decades and refer to the period when the power of the Anatolian Seljuks was on the wane.[27] In the fourteenth century too, Arabic was so widespread a language in Anatolia, that the North African traveller, Ibn Battuta, was able to converse with many of the locals during his journeys through Anatolia. Like many subsequent travellers he did, however, complain that his interpreter was unreliable.[28]

Among the dervishes there were also those who practised their cult in Arabic. The mystic, Ibn 'Arabî (born Murcia 1165, died Damascus 1240), for example, whose conception of the unity of all things in God was not exactly uncontroversial, campaigned for support in the Seljuk capital. The building of the dervish lodge founded by his son-in-law, Sadreddin-i Kunevî, in Konya, survives to this day. Its wonderful library, on the other hand, has not fared quite so well. This library was a source of such fascination to the Ottoman conquerors of the fifteenth century that they included a catalogue of its books in the register of foundations established immediately following the conquest, and went on to have it copied many times throughout the sixteenth century. Nevertheless, we have little idea of what happened to the library's valuable books, mostly in Arabic, in later times. Today, quite a few of them are to be found in the Yusuf Ağa Library in Konya.[29]

There is no doubt that from the very start Turkish was the spoken language of Anatolia, even in the towns. Among the earliest writings surviving in this language are some poems by the son of Mevlânâ Celâleddîn, Sultan Veled, who also dabbled in Greek verse.[30] The saint's legend by Elvan Çelebi, a dervish sheikh, written in honour of his grandfather, the leader of the Babaîs, Baba Ilyas, dates from the early fourteenth century.[31] In the late thirteenth and early fourteenth centuries there were also attempts to reproduce romantic epics from the Iranian tradition in Anatolian Turkish.[32] By the fifteenth century new genres emerged in Ottoman-Turkish literature, such as the chronicle, which from that time on became quite distinct from the legend.[33] However, the movement towards using the Turkish language in areas from which it had previously been excluded was to continue. Not until the eighteenth century did Turkish become the usual language in most social milieux for inscriptions on gravestones, mosques or public fountains; in earlier periods, Arabic and Persian were the languages favoured for such purposes. At the end of the nineteenth century, Muslim religious law was codified in Turkish, thus ending the monopoly of Arabic in all matters to do with Islamic law.[34] The attempts of politicians and literary figures of the republican period to use Turkish in absolutely every sphere of life, creating the appropriate terminology where necessary, thus form part of a long tradition.

Townspeople and Architecture

The Byzantine centres of population in Anatolia had already shrunk considerably during the early middle ages. After that period, most of them were fortified settlements rather than towns in the true sense of the word. As early as the thirteenth century it is likely that Muslims formed the majority, or at least a good part, of the population in many of the towns which were reviving under Seljuk auspices.[35] Apart from nomads closely connected to the ruling house, who therefore settled in one of the seats of the court (this probably occurred in Konya, Kayseri and Sivas, for instance), townspeople from remote regions, such as today's Afghanistan, arrived in Anatolia. It is against this background that we must see the rapid establishment of an Islamic high culture in the newly conquered lands. This culture boasted considerable achievements in poetry and historical literature from the thirteenth century onwards, and in architecture from as early as the twelfth century.[36]

Many Islamic townspeople, at least in the thirteenth century, fled to Anatolia from the armies of Genghis Khan and his sons. The Mongol campaigns mainly affected the big towns and cities of the Near East, thus for example Nishapur and Merw were looted and destroyed in 1221. Baghdad succumbed in 1258 and even Aleppo was taken.[37] However, the towns of central Asia were also drawn into the attempts of Muhammad Celâl ed-dîn Hârezmşah to block the Mongols with his army of mercenaries. All these wars created great turmoil. The mystic and poet Celâleddîn Rûmî (1207–73), whom we have already encountered, was the son of a well-known scholar in Balkh (in today's Afghanistan) who left the country, probably because of a quarrel with his ruler, and finally settled in Konya.[38]

For modern visitors to the former seats of the Seljuk court, the architecture and decoration of the all-too-few extant buildings are probably the most striking reminders of this age. As well as the *medreses* referred to above, many mosques were built. A substantial proportion of the latter still adhered to the design known as the *ulu cami* (Great Mosque), widespread throughout Anatolia in the pre-Ottoman centuries. This featured large, rectangular halls supported by columns or pillars. The prayer niche (*mihrap*) was generally located on the long side (*kibla* wall). It was frequently quite small, and worshippers might have trouble seeing it because of intervening building parts, even though the niche was frequently decorated with reliefs or colourful tilework to make it more conspicuous.[39] In many Anatolian versions of the *ulu cami*, the great hall was covered by cupolas. Smaller mosques were often to be found in complexes consisting of a mosque, *medrese*, dervish convent and founder's tomb. Sometimes, as we have seen, prayers and classes took place in the same room. These smaller mosques frequently consisted of a space covered by a simple or double dome. This form was to develop strongly in the fifteenth century, while the *ulu cami* design gradually disappeared.[40]

Caravanserais and bridges make up most of the surviving secular architecture. Caravanserais lined the main routes in the Seljuk state, connecting the capital Konya with the port of Antalya and with the major towns of the interior.[41] However, caravanserais are also to be found further east, such as in the surroundings of Malatya, reflecting the importance of trans-Anatolian routes during the Pax Mongolica which reigned over large tracts of Asia in the thirteenth century. The caravanserais invariably consist of a rectangular courtyard surrounded by buildings. These included quarters for travellers and a building, frequently monumental in form, which appears to have been intended as the stable. In the middle of the courtyard there was often a source of water, which sometimes had an upper storey containing a small mosque. Apart from the stable, the most monumental building was often the gateway. This would be richly decorated with sculpted ornamentation, including scrolls of text. These monumental entrances are also often found in the complexes of pious foundations established during the Seljuk period and its immediate aftermath. In many cases this gateway, which often housed the guards, was the only way into the caravanserai, which could therefore also be garrisoned and used as a fort. When Mongol governor Nureddin Caca wanted both townspeople and the Mongol warriors to witness the foundation of a *medrese* in the central Anatolian town of Kırşehir in 1272, he bade the two groups gather in a nearby caravanserai.[42]

Bridges built during the pre-Ottoman period are particularly valuable to the historian because of the light they often shed on long-abandoned routes.[43] Virtually no dwelling-houses have survived from this period. Only through excavations do we know something about the sultan's summer palace, Kubadabad, near the Lake Beyşehir. Apart from its foundations, parts of its decorative tiling have survived. In Konya itself, a small part of the palace of the Seljuk sultans is still visible.[44] City walls which date entirely from the Seljuk period are also rather rare. The city walls of Konya were cleared at around the turn of the century, and the Seljuk structures at the citadel in Ankara are merely additions to pre-existing Byzantine fortifications.[45] In Eski Malatya, a settlement located at the spot where Malatya stood before the 1830s, the fortifications are largely Seljuk, but they are in very poor condition, much worse than the mosques in the town. Our idea of the appearance of the larger towns of the Seljuk era is therefore rather sketchy. We have a somewhat clearer picture of the following period, that is, the years which followed the disintegration of the Seljuk state and preceded the final establishment of Ottoman rule. In south-western Anatolia this period ends around 1430. It is less certain when the interregnum began in this particular area, as Seljuk

control of south-western Anatolia was never very firm. In the small principality of the Menteşe dynasty which emerged here during those years, Peçin was
temporarily one of the major towns. In the Ottoman era, however, Peçin
succumbed to the competition of Milas, just five kilometres distant, and
dwindled away without ever actually being destroyed. The main monuments,
among the most significant of which was the Ahmed Gazi *medrese*, remained
intact. Recently, excavations have been undertaken there.[46] The citadel is well-
preserved. As was the case in many Ottoman towns of later times, only a
small, easily defendable part of the town was protected by a wall. Apart from
the Ahmed Gazi *medrese*, several caravanserais were located in the unfortified
part.

The successor town to the famous city of Ephesus, known to the Italians
as Altiluogo and to the Ottomans as Ayasoluğ, has also been excavated. It is
located clear of the modern settlement and dates largely from the Byzantine
and pre-Ottoman periods.[47] Later the rocks and silt washed along by the
Gediz Çayı made the harbour useless, and led to the decline of the town,
which had been very active even in the early sixteenth century. In central
Anatolia, Kırşehir is relatively well documented. Although, unlike Peçin or
Ayasoluğ, it was never abandoned, in the Ottoman period it did lose much of
the importance it had possessed before about 1450.[48] In fact, perhaps because
of the decline in the town's importance, many edifices dating from the
fourteenth and fifteenth centuries have survived there. Ottoman registers of
foundations offer valuable information about those buildings which have
disappeared.[49] It should therefore soon be possible to piece together a history
of the 'late medieval' town, at least in the case of Anatolia.

Political Change after 1453

Mehmed the Conqueror (reign: 1444–46 and 1451–81) inaugurated a period
of major political change in Ottoman history. Its significance goes far beyond
the conquest of Constantinople in 1453. From that time on the ruler relied
on the support of a political élite composed of individuals who had been
brought to the palace as non-Muslim youths and there raised according to
Islamic principles to ensure absolute loyalty to the ruler. Even the grand
vizier often came from this group.[50] However, since the status of these high
officials was similar if not identical to that of slaves, the ruler was able to
dismiss or even execute them at will.[51] Even so, groups of mutually loyal
individuals emerged within this élite, often based on local affiliations.[52]

Mehmed the Conqueror also introduced some radical changes to court
protocol and thereby also to palace architecture and to the organization of
public festivals. In the early years of his reign, manners were relatively

informal. It seems that well-known theologians and jurists made no attempt to hide anger or frustration when they met the sultan, behaviour which implies a degree of intimacy in their relationship with him.[53] By contrast, the court protocols of Sultan Mehmed's later years emphasize the great distance between the ruler and all ordinary mortals. The hierarchy of high officials which was introduced by Mehmed II survived in its basic features until the nineteenth century, except for modifications which were made above all in the reign of Süleyman the Magnificent (reign: 1520–66).[54]

Style and Patrons

One of Mehmed's other concerns was to restrict vastly the political influence of the old Anatolian aristocracy. He forced many of its members to emigrate to the Balkans, where such families enjoyed little political support and lost their political significance within a few generations.[55] In the final years of his reign Mehmed also took over many pious foundations, a good number of which were administered by members of long-established Anatolian families. This was a step which his successor very quickly reversed.[56] These radical changes in the political structure of the Ottoman Empire were reflected in the cultural domain. Anatolian aristocratic families were no longer in a position to sponsor works of architecture or literature. A situation arose in which the sultan, a few princes and high state officials were the only significant patrons for high culture. It is hardly surprising, then, that from about 1500 an Ottoman 'imperial style' emerged, especially in architecture. This style was consistent from Sarajevo to Damascus.[57]

At the time of Mehmed the Conqueror this unitary style was still in the process of formation. The sultan liked to commemorate the scale of his conquests, and to this end the palace he built in Istanbul included stylistic features of Iranian and Italian origin, alongside buildings of a traditional Ottoman character. The latter were meant to evoke the atmosphere of the former capitals of Edirne (Adrianopel) and Bursa. As a tilework pavilion in Iranian style, the Çinili Köşk, which still exists today, was no doubt designed to commemorate the triumph over Uzun Hasan, of the Turkoman 'Black Sheep' dynasty, who ruled great parts of Iran as well as the town of Diyarbakır in south-eastern Anatolia.[58] Much less remains of the Italianate decorations. However, the well-known portrait of the sultan by Gentile Bellini and references to the frescoes created by Italian Renaissance artists do survive. The Orta Kapu, the great palace gate, reminiscent of European medieval fortress architecture, was probably a conscious adaptation of Italian models.[59] This would have reminded the viewer of the Ottoman conquest of the stronghold of Otranto, in southern Italy, during the last years of Mehmed's reign, an event which made the conquest of Italy seem a real and immediate prospect. The Italianate motifs in the decoration of the palace appear to anticipate such a triumph. Nor were Byzantine elements neglected, as is shown by the conversion of the Haghia Sophia, opposite the palace, to a mosque and the use of the former Byzantine acropolis as the location for the new palace.[60]

This eclectic style, which Mehmed the Conqueror favoured throughout his life, must have created a degree of controversy among his contemporaries. After all, choosing such a style implied that the Ottoman sultan belonged in the line of world rulers. According to Islamic opinion, this line began with Solomon of the Old Testament. It also included Alexander (Iskender), whose biography Mehmed the Conqueror obtained for the palace library. Occasionally, he had stories of Alexander's exploits read to him. However, this particular ideal of domination, with its links to non-Muslim traditions, caused profound suspicion among some contemporary authors. The chronicler Aşıkpaşazade, for example, who belonged to a distinguished family of central Anatolia and was a descendant of the Babaî sheikh, Baba Ilyas, apparently took exception to the sultan and his unconventional new palace ceremonials, emphasizing the simple lifestyle of the early Ottoman rulers. Most of these, allegedly, had made do with just a few advisers – who incidentally came from Aşıkpaşazade's own background – and had made modest tax demands.[61] The many anonymous authors of tales about the construction and subsequent fate of the Aya Sofya (Haghia Sophia) were considerably more caustic. Written mainly during the reign of Sultan Mehmed's successor, Bayezid II, these tales stemmed partly from the Arab-Byzantine tradition, although many of them were original. Such writers portrayed Constantinople-Istanbul as an accursed place in which even Solomon (regarded as a prophet in the Islamic tradition) had fallen victim to the insinuations of his own wife, who had secretly remained an infidel. This was why the history of the imperial city was punctuated by fires, plagues and other disasters, which not even the construction of the great church, in itself a pious act, could avert.[62] The authors of such literature clearly meant to issue a warning: the Ottoman sultans must not enter the line of world rulers and thus become successors to the Byzantine emperors. In explicit terms, no alternative was suggested. However, presumably two possibilities existed: either the sultan might govern with only a minimal state apparatus as the ruler of a warlike principality doing battle with infidel neighbours, as had been the case in the early days of the Ottoman era. Or else the sultan might govern as an Islamic ruler, according to the example set by the early caliphs; obviously, the two models possessed certain points in common.[63] Such an outlook on the part of the Ottoman élite could have led to the abandonment of the largely destroyed former Byzantine capital, sweeping the ground from under the eclectic style favoured by Mehmed the Conqueror.

Istanbul as an Ottoman City

Such criticism is important for us. It shows that the policies even of the most powerful sultan, a figure who today symbolizes the fulness of Ottoman strength, were by no means uncontroversial. They were contested even in the limited sphere of the literate classes. In fact, all the things against which the sultan's critics had warned did occur. Istanbul was quickly resettled, at first as a result of Mehmed the Conqueror's coercion and later because of voluntary migration to the city.[64] In the sixteenth century the capital of the Ottoman Empire had grown to become by far the largest city in Europe and the Mediterranean area.

Immediately after the conquest and the three days of looting by the victorious Ottoman army which ensued, the sultan began with the preparations for the resettlement scheme. Previous residents were given a deadline within which they could return and reclaim their homes. In addition, however, contingents of new settlers were gathered from a diverse range of towns in Anatolia. At least the more affluent among them sometimes resisted a move which, in the short term, would harm their economic interests. There were also disputes regarding the status of abandoned houses. At first these were transferred to the newcomers as freehold property, but later their occupants were required to pay a rent to the Aya Sofya mosque foundation.

It was envisaged that mosques should form the heart of the new urban wards. Most of these mosques were founded by persons of influence at court. If the donor had sufficient means, schools, libraries, alms-houses or drinking fountains might be attached.[65] This framework for the everyday life of the people of Istanbul persisted, albeit with modifications, throughout the Ottoman era. Not until the republican period was there a thorough reorganization of the city wards.

The most important of these early Ottoman foundations was that of the Conqueror himself. As well as the mosque, it included eight *medrese*s, arranged in two rows, in which the most eminent judges and professors of the empire would henceforth be educated. There were also a hostel and a school for the recitation of the Qur'ān. Foundation income was to be derived not just from its ownership of land and buildings, but from the poll-tax (*cizye*) on the non-Muslim inhabitants of the city. The financial accounts of this foundation are therefore an important source of information about the history of Istanbul's population.[66] Many Anatolian rulers of the late middle ages regarded the creation of large foundations as a way of legitimizing their power. With much greater vigour this tradition was continued by the Ottoman sultans of the fifteenth and sixteenth centuries.[67]

The Integration of the Balkans into the Ottoman Territories

Many Turkish principalities rose and fell in Anatolia between the late eleventh and the fifteenth centuries, often surviving only a couple of generations. Among them, the Ottoman principality stands out because even in the first phase of its history it extended into the Balkans. The stronghold of Tzympe was won from the Byzantines as early as 1352, and the memory of Prince Süleyman (died 1357), a son of Sultan Orhan (reign: 1326–62), was honoured by a foundation in the Thracian small town of Bolayır.[68] Even when Timur defeated Bayezid I (reign: 1389–1402) near Ankara (1402), and destroyed his Anatolian empire, he allowed the sons of the fallen ruler to maintain control of their Balkan provinces. In doing so, Timur helped define the Ottoman state as a political construct whose *raison d'être* was the battle against unbelievers.[69] It is important in this connection that from 1361 or 1362 the town of Edirne, located close to the expanding Balkan frontier, became the official capital of the empire and remained as such until after the conquest of Istanbul.

In the late middle ages, Hungary was the most powerful state on the Balkan peninsula, and wars between the Hungarians and the Ottomans continued through both the fifteenth and sixteenth centuries. One of Mehmed the Conqueror's few unsuccessful campaigns was his assault on Belgrade, at that time a Hungarian frontier stronghold. It was finally taken in 1521 by Süleyman the Magnificent, while most of Hungary became Ottoman between 1526 and 1541.[70] The other Balkan states put up less resistance, and most of them were integrated into the Ottoman polity within a single generation. Parts of Albania were in Ottoman hands as early as 1431/32; Mehmed the Conqueror subsequently brought the whole territory under Ottoman control after breaking the resistance of Skenderbeg (or George Kastriota, which was his name as a Christian).[71]

Specialists in the field have long debated the means by which the cohesion of the Ottoman state was achieved, particularly during the severe crisis after 1402. There was a consistent flow of warriors, eager for plunder, from the Anatolian hinterland into Ottoman territory. For them, the continued expansion of the state was a matter of life and death.[72] Among educated people of the fifteenth and sixteenth centuries there was much talk of a holy war. In the legend of the Rumelian military saint, Kızıl Deli (also known as Seyyid Ali Sultan), the core of which probably goes back to the early fifteenth century, prowess in war and cruelty are writ large. These were justified by the fact that the Islamic world was winning land and subjects. In old age, Seyyid Ali Sultan founded a dervish lodge near Dimetoka (Didymoteichon in western

Thrace) and there lived out his life. On the other hand, we should not overestimate the significance of religious discourse for ordinary soldiers. Among the immigrants to the Balkans were many nomads and semi-nomads, for whom religion was certainly not the sole motivation for warfare.[73]

Thus, victorious campaigns against unbelievers but also against the Shiite subjects of the Shah of Iran, took on a major importance as a justification of Ottoman power (the Shiites were regarded as heretics). Sultan Murad III (reign: 1574–95) was strongly criticized by a chronicler because, despite the many campaigns he instigated, he did not make many lasting conquests. Even in the late seventeenth century, a war which went badly, or an unfavourable peace settlement with the unbelievers, was considered reason enough to dethrone the ruler responsible.[74] Moreover, the ideology of the war against the unbelievers was not only important among the officials active in the capital. It was probably even more significant to the governors and military personnel in the frontier regions. The material interests of both armies – that is, their desire for plunder – were no doubt crucial in the ongoing skirmishing at the Ottoman–Habsburg frontier. However, these interests tended not to be expressed directly, but were, on the Ottoman side, presented in terms of waging permanent war against the unbelievers.[75] Commanders at the frontier also were able to justify themselves in this fashion when they disregarded a ceasefire negotiated by the sultan and his viziers.

From a Balkan State to an Empire

By 1512, when Selim I, grandson of Mehmed II, acceded to the throne, the Ottoman Empire had become by far the most powerful state on the Balkan peninsula. Nearly all the smaller states of the region had been conquered, and in 1529 the army of Süleyman the Magnificent found itself at the gates of Vienna. Ottoman raiding parties began to threaten Styria and Carinthia. In 1541 the greater part of Hungary became the Ottoman province of Buda. In addition, the principality of Transylvania (Ottoman: Erdel) became, and long remained, a vassal state of the sultan's. A small part of Hungary passed into Habsburg hands; the resulting border was to remain substantially intact until the second Ottoman campaign against Vienna (1683).[76] However, in Anatolia Ottoman control at the beginning of the sixteenth century was largely confined to the west and to a few parts of central Anatolia. In the eastern part of the region several minor principalities existed, the most significant of which had been founded by the Turkoman dynasty of Dulkadır. This dynasty had immortalized itself by funding important public construction in the various urban centres of their territories. There are still mosques in Kahramanmaraş, Elbistan and Hacıbektaş which were founded by Prince Alaeddevle, his wife Güneş Hatun ('Lady Sun') and other members of the dynasty.[77] Despite the proximity of their powerful Ottoman neighbours, in political terms the state tended towards the Mamluk Sultan of Egypt, who also ruled Syria. The Dulkadır and other remaining independent Anatolian princes probably hoped in this way to protect themselves from domination by the Ottoman state, at least for a while.

However, at the beginning of the sixteenth century the Mamluk state itself was in critical condition. Like the European states of the period, Egypt and Syria were ravaged by the plagues of the late middle ages. Through a monopoly on the spice trade, the Mamluk sultans had hoped to compensate for income lost by the concomitant decline in agricultural production, a tactic which ruined the old-established long-distance merchants.[78] When the Portuguese rounded the Cape of Good Hope, the new route to the Indian Ocean led, at least in the short term, to a decline in transit trade through the Red Sea. The Mamluk sultans lost a considerable amount of their income. On top of this, the Portuguese launched attacks on the Red Sea ports, including Jiddah, the main access to the pilgrimage centre of Mecca. Lacking a navy capable of resisting these attacks, the Mamluk sultans had to turn to the Ottoman sultans for support, even though the two states had been at war during the second half of the fifteenth century. The Venetians, who depended on a well-established state in the eastern Mediterranean for the protection of their trade, quickly saw the signs of the times: at the beginning of the sixteenth century they deserted the Mamluks in favour of the Ottomans.[79]

Several prominent Mamluks also seem to have regarded the Ottoman state as the rising power in the eastern Mediterranean, and desired to come to terms with it as quickly as possible. This is probably why Selim was able to conquer first Syria and then Egypt in a single campaign (1516–17). In particular, the sherif of Mecca, whose territory depended on supplies from Egypt, surrendered voluntarily. By 1517 the Ottoman sultans governed one of the major empires west of China. In the Islamic world only the Safavids, who ruled Iran, and the Mughuls, established in India by Babur Khan in 1526, could match the power of the Ottoman rulers. In Egypt, but not in Syria, the Ottoman sultans allowed the Mamluks to continue as local administrators. Just as before, young slaves were imported from the northern Black Sea area to be given a military education and then manumitted. If the young people survived the change in climate, they had the opportunity to exercise political power in Egypt's local government and often to accumulate considerable fortunes.[80] However, their position was not hereditary, and children from their marriages to Egyptian women were regarded as 'ordinary' subjects of the sultan.

In the past, the four centuries (1516–1918) of Ottoman rule in Syria and the three and a half centuries (1517–1840) of more or less effective control

- ●   Istanbul, the Ottoman capital
- ⊡   Major regional centres (Cairo, Aleppo)
- ⊙   Minor regional centres, main ports
- •   Other towns

MAP 1 Towns in the Ottman Empire

over Egypt have been regarded as periods of decline. Accordingly, they have been given rather perfunctory treatment in the history books. Only in the last twenty years has it become apparent that, in many cases, the problems of the nineteenth century had simply been projected back to earlier times. Throughout, the national states of the Near East, when they emerged in the twentieth century, defined themselves not just in contrast to the European colonial powers, but also by distancing themselves from the Ottoman state. This was not exactly conducive to an interest in Ottoman history.[81] Moreover, French historians writing at the time when Syria was still a French mandated territory liked to see France as the 'new Rome' and to present the Ottomans, as the power France had succeeded, in an appropriately unfavourable light.

Both economic and cultural ties between the centre of Ottoman power and the Arabian provinces were closer than has previously been assumed. In Syria, a class of well-to-do families developed whose male members spoke Ottoman as well as Arabic. Members of the Ottoman administration and of its army in particular frequently remained in the province to which they had been posted and gradually became assimilated.[82] There were also many bilingual inhabitants in Aleppo. Ottoman terms relating to administrative affairs passed into Arabic, a process facilitated by the fact that the Mamluks, who belonged to a variety of ethnic groups, had communicated in Turkish among themselves even before the arrival of the Ottomans. On the Ottoman side, there was also considerable interest, particularly in the cosmopolitan city of Cairo. For this reason the chronicles of the Mamluk sultans were available in the Ottoman language as early as the sixteenth century. Somewhat later followed descriptions of the monumental architecture of the city.[83] However, even though 'anti-Ottoman nationalism' now seems less of an issue in Egyptian or Syrian historiography, cultural relations so far have been approached only with considerable caution.

In its last years, the Mamluk Empire had gained the support of the Ottoman sultans in its struggle against the Portuguese. After Ottoman rule in Egypt had become firmly established, Sultan Süleyman once again turned his attention to this issue. At stake was the control of the Red Sea and the food supply of Mecca – even in 1542, the Portuguese launched an (unsuccessful) assault on Jidda.[84] In the long term, however, the sultan probably intended to expel the Portuguese from the Indian Ocean and if possible to gain a foothold on the west coast of India for the Ottoman Empire itself. In 1538 there was a sea battle between the Ottomans and the Portuguese near the Indian port of Diu. Notable success remained elusive and, from the 1540s onwards, expansion towards the Indian Ocean was pursued with rather less vigour. Nevertheless, the rulers of the principality of Atjeh in northern Sumatra, who wanted the sultan's help in their own fight against the Portuguese, were granted military support in the form of cannon and gunners.[85] Independently of such 'military missions', Ottoman firearms specialists also seem to have found their way to the Indian subcontinent. Moreover, the Ottoman sultans made occasional pious donations to mosques on the west coast of India, for instance in the town of Calicut.[86] Since most of the merchants active in the Indian Ocean at that time were already Muslims, such donations may have been inspired partly by the desire to create a political basis for the Ottoman sultans among these people. In the end, however, it was not the Ottomans, but rather the

Mughul rulers of Delhi and Agra who brought the trade centres of western India under their control.

On both sides, the conflict between the Ottomans and the Portuguese, who had themselves experienced economic and political difficulties in the second half of the sixteenth century, was seen as a religious matter. The Portuguese kings saw themselves as the patrons of Catholic missions, and their settlement in the Indian port of Goa was soon used as the base for missionary activities in the Far East. During their expansion in southern Asia, the Portuguese kings and their officials always saw Muslim rulers and traders as their main enemies. Meanwhile, the Ottoman sultans, in their capacity as protectors of Islam, were approached by the rulers of Atjeh for support. Ottoman rulers also saw 'religion and state' (the formula used in many official documents) as indivisible.[87]

Religion, Ethnic Ties and the Structure of the Ottoman State

By the second half of the sixteenth century, the Ottoman historian and littérateur Mustafa Âlî had asked himself what the great conquests of the previous century actually meant for the Ottoman state. His answer is based on the ethnic stereotypes of his time and is of little help to us today; but it is significant that he posed the question.[88] The enduring hold of the Ottoman state on the Balkan peninsula meant that for many people of the region, Ottoman culture became the sole conceivable high culture. There were opportunities for some Albanians, Serbs or Greeks to join the Ottoman army, become Muslims and, in some cases, eminent members of the Ottoman administration.[89] However, the more successful individuals expressed themselves in the Ottoman language, and the buildings they constructed in their various native provinces adhered to Ottoman style. Those mosques which still survive in Bulgaria, Greece and Albania therefore exhibit the standard characteristics of early Ottoman architecture.[90] Dervish orders which had emerged in Anatolia quickly gained a foothold in the Balkans as well. Already in the seventeenth century there were major poets in some Balkan towns writing in Ottoman.[91] In twentieth-century nationalist historiography there has been much debate about whether Turkish immigrants to the Balkans or Greek, Albanian, Serb and Bulgarian converts to Islam played the greater role in the spread of Ottoman culture. To this question, there is no really appropriate response. Ottoman officials collected the only data now available for research into the population of that period and, for them, religion was generally the main concern; ethnic origin was only occasionally a consideration.

As a result it is possible to analyse Ottoman history only by distancing oneself as far as possible from nationalist categories.[92] There is no doubt that the cultural differences between nomads and semi-nomads on the one side, and sedentary villagers on the other, were of much greater significance than ethnic divisions. Urban lifestyle was vastly different from the customs of the countryside, at least where wealthy people were concerned. Religion was also much more important to the sense of identity of Ottoman subjects than their ethnic origin, and the Ottoman administration accordingly classified its subjects using religious criteria.[93] Similarly, the village or town from which an individual came was probably a more significant element in his/her sense of identity than language or nationality.

In addition, the fundamental difference between ordinary subjects and members of the Ottoman administrative élite determined the cultural possibilities open to inhabitants of the Ottoman Empire.[94] With a few exceptions, Ottoman powerholders were Muslims. Apart from professing Islam, linguistic ability was also a fairly important requirement for a political career, because all members of the upper class, whatever their origins, had to be fluent in the Ottoman written language, which even those whose mother-tongue was Turkish needed to learn by formal instruction. In ethnic terms, the Ottoman upper class was a colourful mixture. Among its members were 'foreigners' such as Spaniards, Italians and Iranians who had arrived as prisoners, voluntary immigrants or refugees. Among the sultan's subjects, Anatolians and Bosnians, Egyptians and Serbs all served on the same basis in the various branches of the military and the administration.[95] Although ethnic cliques did certainly exist, ethnic criteria were not decisive in gaining entry to the Ottoman upper class. This explains why Turkish nationalism developed only at the end of the nineteenth and the beginning of the twentieth centuries, much later than similar movements in the other ethnic groups of the Ottoman Empire.

PART I

Culture: How it was Created and Disseminated

3

The Economic and Social Structure of the Ottoman Empire in Early Modern Times

Urban Populations and Trade Routes in the Sixteenth and Seventeenth Centuries

In the early sixteenth century, by far the greater part of the population lived in rural areas. Towns were relatively small: Bursa, by far the most important town in Anatolia, had 8,003 taxpaying inhabitants according to the tax register of 1530–31. We may assume that each married taxpayer belonged to a family of five persons. There is no documentary basis for this, but it seems a reasonable estimate in view of the very high rate of child mortality at the time.[1] In addition, we must add a certain percentage to allow for those people who were exempt from paying most taxes and therefore not included in the registers. Among them we find prominent officials such as judges and governors, together with their respective households, but also the poorest inhabitants. Many of the latter may have been recent arrivals, who often eluded the state officials in charge of preparing registers.[2] In total we arrive at a population estimate of approximately 36,000; by the end of the sixteenth century, following a considerable population increase, the city may have been home to about 70,000 people. Most of the Balkan towns were very small; Athens was one of the major centres with 3,207 taxpayers in 1569 and thus a total population of approximately 18,000.[3] Other important Ottoman towns in the Balkans included Sarajevo, a newly-founded town for a long time populated exclusively by Muslims; Edirne, the former capital; and Salonica.[4] Edirne received many visits from the sultans even in the sixteenth and seventeenth centuries, not least because of the good hunting to be had in its surroundings. Sultan Selim II built his magnificent mosque there in 1574–75. Sofia was relatively small, and both Belgrade and Buda, the former capital of Hungary, had suffered greatly during the many wars of the fifteenth and sixteenth centuries.[5]

With the victorious campaign of Selim I in 1516–17 the Ottoman Empire gained three large cities. Two of them, Aleppo and Cairo, were among the major centres of world trade, while Damascus played an important role in the traffic between the Mediterranean area and the Arabian peninsula.[6] Moreover, Cairo had become the cultural centre of the Islamic world since the destruction of Baghdad by the Mongols (1258).[7] Teachers and students from all Islamic countries, from Morocco to Afghanistan and India, congregated in the theological schools of Cairo. The buildings of late-medieval Egypt are still a source of fascination to connoisseurs.[8] Unfortunately, no Ottoman tax register from Cairo survives, and our estimates of the city's population are therefore less reliable than those for Bursa, Salonica or Sarajevo. However, we may assume that in the seventeenth century there were about 150,000 economically active inhabitants, not counting their families.[9] Whereas Cairo profited from transit trade with India and the countries bordering the Indian Ocean, the merchants of Aleppo were engaged above all in the import of raw silk from Iran. This was then woven into valuable fabrics in Tokat, Bursa and other towns of the Ottoman Empire, and some of these silks found buyers on the European market.[10]

During the sixteenth and seventeenth centuries, merchants of the Arab world derived considerable benefit from the fact that their lines of communication were now to a great extent controlled by just one, powerful state.[11] The Ottoman Empire was not, in fact, a customs union, but the combination of calculable tariffs and a relatively efficient administration was a significant boon for many merchants from Cairo and Aleppo. Moreover Ottoman sultans were not as prone as their Mamluk predecessors, for example, to declare state monopolies on particularly profitable goods, thus restricting the gains available to ordinary merchants.

In addition, the Ottoman administration strove, with some success, to protect the great transit routes from robbers. While Ottoman caravanserais were not so magnificently appointed as the finest of the Seljuk era, there were a great many of them, and they were sturdily constructed. Smaller caravans found safety in these structures even if the travellers were not exactly comfortable.[12] Dervish convents in the vicinity of the less frequented routes were often exempted from paying taxes on condition that they offer hospitality to travellers.[13] Similarly, certain villages paid less tax in return for taking responsibility for a certain section of a route. Travellers who were robbed in a zone pertaining to such a village could demand compensation.[14]

There were, of course, instances of collusion between robbers and road guards, and, in the frontier areas between the Ottoman Empire and Iran, travellers frequently were confronted with highly problematic situations. It could be difficult to distinguish local rulers, semi-independent of both the shah and the sultan, who demanded customs duties and taxes from caravans passing through the territory they controlled, from mere highwaymen who offered no protection in exchange for their demands.[15] However, since it has become apparent to historians of the early modern period that 'war making, state making and organized crime' were also almost indistinguishable in Europe, the situation in the Ottoman Empire can hardly be considered unique.[16] If the levies were too heavy, merchants could always alter their routes and cross the land of a less demanding potentate instead. This happened quite frequently, particularly in the Ottoman–Iranian border region, where the various Kurdish princes offered merchants lower tariffs if they crossed their own territories, avoiding the official Ottoman customs stations in Erzurum and Diyarbakır.[17]

The Mediterranean as a Cul-de-sac?

There is a long-standing hypothesis, worked out by the Turkish economic historian, Sabri Ülgener (1911–83) and later developed by other scholars, according to which the political and economic well-being of the Ottoman Empire in the fifteenth and sixteenth centuries was a form of optical illusion.[18] This was a time, after all, which was in the long run prejudicial to the Mediterranean world and benefited the lands of the Atlantic coast. Only the latter profited from the riches of America, which the Genoese sailor Columbus opened up for the kings of Spain, to the great detriment of native Americans. For this reason, the economic boom in the Ottoman territories, which was at least a regional phenomenon in the fifteenth and sixteenth centuries, could not last for long. Soon the trade routes fell into disuse and the great centres declined into minor towns. In Ülgener's view and that of his successors, economic development was from then on quite impossible for the townspeople of the Ottoman realm. They therefore saw the world from a very limited perspective, not as great merchants, but as modest tradespeople, shopkeepers and the like.[19]

Recent research has uncovered evidence, however, which casts some doubt on this pessimistic interpretation. When Ülgener began his work in the 1940s, it was still thought that transit trade through the eastern Mediterranean ended once and for all with the pioneering of the new sea route from Portugal to India by Vasco da Gama (1498). In fact, a study was published which disproved this in 1940, but due to the war it was not widely circulated.[20] The truth became more generally known in the 1950s and 1960s, when the prosperity of Mediterranean trade and of Venice in the late sixteenth century became a popular topic for historical research, as did the abrupt crisis of the years around 1600.[21] The new hypothesis suggested that the circumnavigation of

Africa by the Portuguese in fact led to only a brief decline in transit trade through the Red Sea. It was the Dutch conquest of the Spice Islands in today's Indonesia which finally put an end to the Red Sea trade and condemned the eastern Mediterranean to economic stagnation. However, this explanation was also short-lived. Soon it emerged that although Venice did indeed find itself in a state of severe crisis in the seventeenth century, the merchants of Cairo continued, despite some difficulties, to thrive on long-distance trade.[22] While the spice trade with Venice had disappeared, merchants continued to meet Ottoman demand by importing considerable quantities of drugs, spices and dyes, by way of the Red Sea into Egypt. Other factors contributed to the merchants' continued prosperity. The wealthier members of the empire's population developed a fondness for Indian materials, above all cotton textiles which, despite the transport costs, were relatively cheap given their high quality.[23] In the second half of the sixteenth century, despite the dogged opposition of the Ottoman central government, a taste for coffee spread from the Yemen (where it had long been drunk) to even the most isolated small towns of Anatolia, and soon also to the Ottoman Balkans (Rumelia).[24]

Coffee provided the merchants of Cairo and Istanbul with a lucrative commercial alternative to the transit trade with Europe. Only the Venetians were unable to profit from it, as the taste for coffee did not become widespread in Europe until the late seventeenth century, and in any case the resources of Venice's hinterland north of the Alps had been exhausted by the Thirty Years War.[25] It was only in the middle of the eighteenth century, when competition to Yemeni coffee arose in the form of coffee imported from the Caribbean islands by French and English merchants, that the transit trade of Cairo declined, a crisis aggravated by the political confusion of the time.[26] Nevertheless, by reactivating their links with Iran and India, the merchants of Cairo were able to survive even the continental blockade (1806–14), which Napoleon instigated in his struggle with the British, and which devastated Aleppo's trade with Europe.[27] The hypothesis that the long-distance trade of Anatolia, Syria and Egypt was insignificant from 1500 or 1600 is thus not supported by the facts.

While from about 1760, many branches of the Ottoman economy experienced severe difficulties, even in this late period there were sectors which flourished. One of the most important was the maritime trade undertaken by Greek shippers. Since Greece was not an independent state at this time, the Greek ships of the eighteenth century should be regarded as Ottoman.[28] A few Greek ship-owners even ventured beyond the Mediterranean. Research into the port records of Barcelona in the eighteenth century has recently shown that they sometimes even engaged in American trade, side-stepping the Castilian monopoly.[29] The trade via the Balkan peninsula with Vienna and

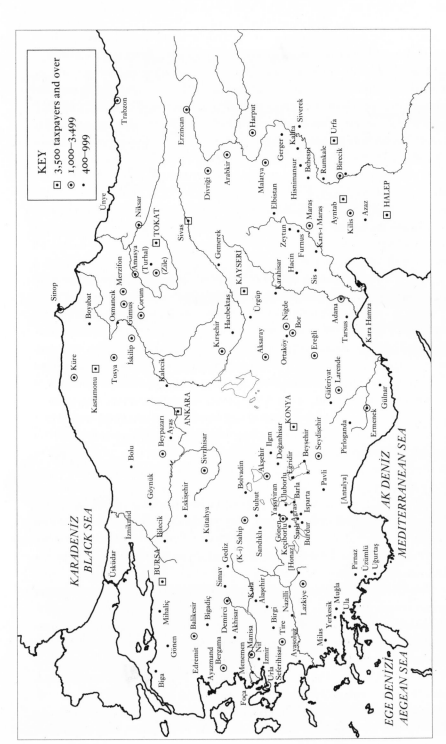

MAP 2 Anatolian towns in the second half of the sixteenth century. From: Suraiya Faroqhi, 'Taxation and Urban Activities', in, *International Journal of Turkish Studies*, I (1979–80) (data) and *Towns and Townsmen of Ottoman Anatolia*, p.13 (map)

other central European towns also flourished at this time. As a result of these relationships, the word *lipsika* entered the Ottoman vocabulary as a synonym for 'blonde'. It was probably coined by visitors to the Leipzig fair.[30]

Profits from trade financed cultural activities. In the last part of the eighteenth century those Greek, Serb and Bulgarian 'national renaissances' generally associated with the nineteenth century were beginning to emerge. Successful merchants throughout the Balkans financed schools and libraries. With literacy, the market for books grew, and printers saw an advantage in producing materials in the local languages. Moreover, the so-called Phanariots, rich Greeks from Istanbul who in the eighteenth century administered Moldavia and Wallachia (in today's Romania) for the Ottoman central government, became active patrons. Although they were foreigners in the regions they governed and usually remained in office only for short terms, they sponsored libraries, painters and architects.

It thus makes little sense to assume that the Ottoman Empire had become a cul-de-sac in terms of international trade from as early as the sixteenth century, and that it therefore lost its economic vitality. Re-examining that hypothesis over fifty years after it emerged, we can see that, like most 'great' historical models, it was a child of its own times, although of course this observation does not in itself make the hypothesis incorrect. In the years following the world economic crisis, contemporaries observed a precipitous decline in world trade and the resulting crisis in certain countries. It was then all too easy to assume that economic stagnation in the past must have arisen in a similar fashion. It is surprising only that this hypothesis has survived for so long the economic phase in which it was born.

The Ottoman Empire as Part of the European Periphery

Human inertia has doubtless been a factor, but the assumption that the Ottoman Empire declined because of a change in international trade routes can probably also be explained, at least in part, by the problematic relationship between many European and American Middle East historians and their chosen subject. A model resting on the fundamental concept of the economic and cultural stagnation of the non-European world from an early date remained attractive to many Europeans and Americans long after the end of the world economic crisis.[31] On the other hand, important aspects of this model also fitted comfortably into anti-colonial theories of economic dependence, which were developed both inside and outside Turkey. World trade did not, after all, change of its own accord; rather, this reorientation was initiated by the Spaniards, Portuguese, English, Dutch and French during the sixteenth and seventeenth centuries. An interpretation of the history of world trade which posited the enduring economic stagnation of the Near East was thus also helpful to nationalist historians of anti-imperialist convictions. They used it to highlight the distortion of economic structures established in their area of study by early colonialism.[32]

Such interpretations are based on the concept of 'world economy'.[33] It is assumed that long-distance trade always produces economic and political centres which dominate the surrounding areas. This can occur in the form of an empire, but also in the form of a system of politically equal states. Such a system has a centre, which can change from time to time without the system itself disintegrating. Thus in the seventeenth century Amsterdam was the centre of the European world economy, to be succeeded in the eighteenth century by London. Intensive manufacturing and the formation of new capital characterize the centre of the system. It is surrounded by a periphery; from the sixteenth century onwards this often meant colonies that had been conquered by force and produced raw materials for the manufacturing activities in the centre.[34] Moreover colonies also bought finished goods from the metropolis. Since their colonial status implied political subordination, these economic links represented unequal exchanges and in the long term led to the impoverishment of such territories.

In the middle of the sixteenth century the Ottoman Empire was still outside the European economic system, luxury goods constituting a major element in Ottoman–European trade. However, this changed in the second half of the sixteenth century, when the need for cereals and cotton increased in Venice and France, for example.[35] Despite all the Ottoman export bans, the relatively high prices offered by European merchants meant that a considerable proportion of the raw material produced on Ottoman territory went abroad. This in turn led to difficulties for domestic manufacturers, whose slender profit margins were decreed by the state and who therefore depended on cheap raw materials. A classic example of this are the silk manufacturers of Bursa at about 1570, who at this time still derived all their raw material from Iran. As European silk production increased, Venetian, French and English merchants began to offer prices to the Iranian raw silk producers which the buyers from Bursa could not match.[36] In the seventeenth century raw silk began to be produced in the Bursa area itself, but many historians do not consider that this could have staved off the crisis in silk manufacturing for long. Only by a piece of good luck did silk weaving in Bursa, like other Ottoman trades, recover again later. At the end of the seventeenth and throughout the eighteenth century, new horizons opened for European merchants in India and China, and the Mediterranean was reduced to an area of secondary interest.[37] Ottoman producers were thus granted another breathing space. According to such an explanation, then, European silk producers devastated their Ottoman counterparts via the pressure of their competition in a foreign market, namely Iran. On the other hand, without intensive contacts between Europe, the Ottoman Empire and Iran, Bursa would never have become a centre of silk manufacture in the first place. In terms of cultural history, the fate of the silk manufacturers of Bursa is of considerable significance, as costly, patterned silks form an important part of the Ottoman tradition in skilled crafts.

Internal Dynamics

Nevertheless, in the last twenty years it has been suggested that long-distance trade was very much less important for the Ottoman economy than had hitherto been assumed. This suggestion refers not merely to periods of economic crisis, but to the economy in general.[38] When all is said and done, relatively few people were employed in long-distance trade. Moreover, the most active merchants involved in, for example, the Aleppo transit trade during the seventeenth century, lived either in England and France or else in Isfahan. Prospects of employment and profit for native Aleppines were largely restricted to local and regional trade. A flourishing hinterland was of greater importance to the success of an Ottoman (or indeed early-modern European) town than a location convenient for international transit trade. It would doubtless be going too far to argue that long-distance trade was altogether insignificant for the prosperity of all but the few towns which had become international centres. After all, even if the natives of Aleppo, for example, profited only to a limited extent from international trade, a host of openings for brokers, landlords, warehouse-owners and camel proprietors was created along the trade routes. In addition, the Bedouins were major gainers, as they frequently demanded a protection fee from caravans passing through their territory. Nevertheless the significance of the international transit trade in pepper and other products from the Indian Ocean has been greatly exaggerated. It is certainly a mistake to blame dependence on world trade for all the political, social and economic crises to have affected the Ottoman state and its society since the late sixteenth century.

Two other factors were much more important: the manner in which tax revenue was spent by the upper echelons of Ottoman society, and political relationships with European states and economies, including the privileges which the sultan often granted to European merchants. In the eighteenth and nineteenth centuries these were so extensive that they quite evidently restricted the authority of the Ottoman state.[39] Spending a great deal of state income on financing wars was not in itself an Ottoman peculiarity: contemporary European states did the same. However, in the Ottoman case, consignments of war materials were paid for either below market rates or not at all.[40] This was a simple solution for financial administrators; given the primitive capital markets of the time, it was difficult, for example, to obtain loans from the domestic economy. During the seventeenth and eighteenth centuries the French state, for instance, frequently found itself in severe difficulties caused by its indebtedness to tax-farmers and other sources of capital. However, for Ottoman producers, in the long-run unpaid consignments were an absolute disaster, especially since the administration, in another attempt to make things easier for itself, tended to draw more heavily on the sounder businesses than on their weaker competitors. There was therefore no chance of a war boom founded on the growth in orders for armament suppliers. On the contrary, lengthy wars resulted in economic depressions, which meant that, in the eighteenth century, it was sometimes impossible to supply the armies properly. A vicious circle developed: wars burdened the treasury, and the lack of financial options encouraged those in government in their inclination to take advantage of as many unpaid supplies as possible, resulting in a considerable weakening of the manufacturers. Because of this weakness it became increasingly difficult to supply the armies and therefore to win wars. This in turn led to an increased burden on the treasury.[41]

However, this explanation of the situation begs two questions. It is true that the methods by which the Ottoman state financed its wars have not yet been researched in great detail. What we do know, however, suggests that even in the sixteenth century there was a tendency to demand supplies without paying the market price.[42] Why then did this system not prevent the Ottoman armies from winning wars in the sixteenth century? Presumably, because of the growing might of the Habsburgs and the Russian tsars, wars in the eighteenth century were more expensive for the Ottomans than they had been a hundred or a hundred and fifty years earlier.[43] Until the middle of the fifteenth century, the Ottoman state still had a relatively inexpensive administrative structure and even during the 'long war' with the Habsburgs (1593–1600) *timar*-holders not paid in cash still constituted an important share of the armed forces.[44] In other words, although wars created economic problems even in the sixteenth century, they did not undermine the viability of the manufacturers. In addition, successful wars yielded considerable spoils as well as extra tax revenue. Even though these profits went largely to the state apparatus and the military, merchants and craftsmen did benefit at least indirectly. This was because additional resources were often spent on consumer goods – a fact that may have led to local inflation but which nevertheless created a host of new economic opportunities.[45]

The second problem has to do with the reaction of the merchants and craftsmen to the Ottoman government's purchasing methods. Ottoman craftsmen were organized into guilds, useful to the authorities as organs for collecting taxes and exerting social control. However, guilds also represented the interests of the masters within their ranks. There was therefore the real possibility that these bodies would protest against the procurement policies of the Ottoman government which were so prejudicial to their members' interests. Links to janissaries and other military or paramilitary groups meant that the guilds of Istanbul, Cairo or Damascus certainly had the means to exert political pressure. Yet no such thing seems to have occurred. It is true that in the eighteenth century there was an instance of Istanbul artisans protesting against the demand that they provide services for a campaign, which subsequently failed to take place.[46] However, at present we still know too little about the Ottoman craftsmen and their political aspirations to determine how tolerant they were of war-related demands on their resources.

It might be assumed, therefore, that the integration of the Ottoman economy within the periphery of the sphere of early European capitalism, as a producer of raw materials and consumer of finished goods, took place in two stages. The first began between about 1570 and 1580, but was soon brought to a halt. After all, European expansion in America and South-East Asia was at first so much quicker than in the eastern Mediterranean, which was less accessible because it was controlled by the strong and well-organized Ottoman state. Only in the second half of the eighteenth century do we arrive at the second stage when the Ottoman Empire was finally integrated into the European periphery.[47] However, this view is one-sided and fails to take into account sufficiently the political and economic resources available within the Ottoman Empire itself. Continuing Ottoman control over the caravan routes of Anatolia, Syria and the Balkans is of particular importance in this respect, but the capacity of both Muslim and non-Muslim merchants constantly to adapt to new kinds of activity is also worthy of note. In the late eighteenth century a crisis occurred because an intensive effort, on the part of European states and merchants, to gain a foothold in the eastern Mediterranean coincided with an internal crisis in the Ottoman economy.[48]

Once Again: The Economic Conflict with Western European States and Merchants

Ottoman internal problems concern us here all the more because they have so often been neglected elsewhere. In addition, however, the activities of English, French and, to a lesser extent, Dutch merchants must also be taken into account. It is probably a mistake to see the difficulties experienced by the silk manufacturers of Bursa, as well as by other craftsmen towards the end of the sixteenth century, as the beginning of a permanent decline. Alternatively, the crisis can be viewed as a prolonged phase of economic depression, similar to the lengthy crises with which the economic historians of modern Europe are so well acquainted.[49] Several trades recovered during the following years. Indeed, in certain Ottoman territories new trades developed, such as, during the eighteenth and early nineteenth centuries, the very successful manufacture of rough woollens in the region that is now Plovdiv.[50] Plovdiv woollens were distributed throughout Anatolia and exported even as far as India, where they were used to cover the floors of tents and for elephant saddle-cloths. Not until the late eighteenth century did foreign merchants finally manage to destroy or turn to their own advantage the distribution systems of their native Ottoman competitors. Imports from Europe before this time tended to be destined for affluent customers, such as woollen goods of medium or high quality. Moreover, these customers generally lived near the centres of commerce to which the goods were imported, while a great deal of the domestic Ottoman market remained impenetrable to European traders.

This situation did not change until the defeat of Napoleon and the ensuing reinvigoration of European trade in the Mediterranean area, a trade which now took place entirely under British auspices.[51] Since many British factories of the early nineteenth century already used steam-driven machinery, production costs were relatively low, and local artisans found it increasingly difficult to compete. In addition, external wars, as well as the campaign for independence led by the governor of Egypt, Mehmed Ali (governor: 1805–48) and other internal conflicts, had greatly weakened the Ottoman central government. There was no longer any question of maintaining control over the trade routes that had remained in Ottoman hands throughout the eighteenth century. Many Ottoman trades were in deep trouble, and their plight was described, sometimes in moving terms, by European observers of the early nineteenth century. However, the crisis did not necessarily mean that Ottoman craftsmen could henceforth find employment only in remote areas or as repair specialists. Some crafts were able to adapt, such as weaving, which used imported yarn in the creation of fabrics adapted to local demands. Other professional groups arose for the first time, such as railwaymen or coalminers.[52] Nevertheless, the basic situation was that the Ottoman territories were now available to European economies as a source of raw materials such as silk and cotton, and also, until the end of the nineteenth century, cereals.[53] The trades that survived this integration into the world market now had to submit to the vicissitudes of the global economy dominated by Europe and, before long, the United States.

Life in the Countryside

At the end of the fifteenth and throughout the sixteenth century the farmers of Anatolia and the Balkan provinces lived in social circumstances that varied considerably from place to place and region to region. Nevertheless, with respect to their relationships with the Ottoman state, there were more similarities than differences. A farm (*çift*) worked by a single family or household (*hane*) constituted the usual economic unit. Additional labour, required at harvest time, probably was obtained through mutual help between neighbours, as is still the custom in certain areas of Turkey.[54]

Ottoman peasants did not own their own land; absolute ownership rested with the state, and peasants were merely hereditary tenants. Only the sons enjoyed the unqualified right of inheritance, but other family members, especially daughters, could take over the farm in the absence of sons. According to the provisions (*kanunname*) of the southern Anatolian province of Karaman, dating from the year 1584, it would be unjust to eject from a farm the family of a peasant leaving no son; in his lifetime the deceased had, after all, invested his labour.[55] Daughters did, however, have to pay a special fee in order to be granted the right to inherit, a fee also demanded of other family members such as nephews or grandchildren. The heirs were not always willing to pay; towards the end of the sixteenth century, for example, a bitter dispute ensued in a village of northern Anatolia when the family of a minor, who was about to inherit from his grandfather, resisted paying the initiation fee that was demanded.[56]

Usually peasant levies were collected by an individual granted the appropriate authority and known as *timar*-holder by the Ottoman central government. In return, the individual in question would be expected to undertake military and sometimes also administrative duties.[57] To what extent the *timar*-holder (*sipahi*) was involved in everyday agricultural business depended on local circumstances and no doubt also on his personal interests. A sultan's decree of 1648 was directed at those peasants who maintained that the *sipahi*'s only authority over them was that of levying taxes; the peasants were instructed to treat the *timar*-holder as their master.[58] On the other hand, many of these holders of tax prerogatives were kept away from the villages in their jurisdiction by their military duties. Moreover, the holders of such 'military fiefs' could themselves be exchanged by the central government at any time and moved to some remote province of the empire.[59] It was therefore difficult for them to construct a personal power base.

Nevertheless, tensions between *timar*-holders and peasants were more or less inevitable. One source of conflict concerned the peasants' obligation to transport the corn taxes that they owed the *sipahi* to the nearest market.[60] This market was often so distant that valuable working time was lost. In many provinces there was a rule that this duty should not require more than one day, but the extent to which this rule was actually adhered to is not known. Moreover, the *sipahi* might also insist that the corn be transported to a city, since the prices there were higher, even though a village market would have been nearer.[61] Another problem arose from the distribution of the harvest; most of the holders of tax prerogatives required the peasants not to collect the corn from the fields until they themselves had taken their share.[62] If a *sipahi* were delayed or, as the peasants sometimes supposed, if he failed to appear out of malice, the harvest would rot in the fields or be devoured by mice. If the villagers did not wait to clear the fields, they could expect to be fined.

Another contentious issue involved peasants seeking the consent of the *sipahi* to leave their villages to seek work in a city, or try their luck in another region. In times of population growth many holders of tax prerogatives must have granted their consent to migration in order to rid 'their' village of landless young peasants. Often unable to marry, these village boys were regarded as trouble-makers.[63] However, many peasants left their land without permission, and the *sipahi* sometimes caught up with them years later. In fact, despite such risks, migration was often possible because in case of doubt the burden of proof lay with the *sipahi*, and incomers who paid their taxes regularly were naturally very welcome among their neighbours in the towns.[64] If necessary it was possible to come to an arrangement with the *kadi*, who would decree that the person in question had lived for so many years in the city that he need not leave. Many conflicts must nevertheless have arisen from this issue, however difficult they are to discern from the dry and unemotional style of the relevant *kadi* records.

Most rural conflicts in Anatolia were, however, alleviated somewhat by the the fuzzy borders between nomadic and sedentary peoples. In many areas the peasants would move their families and animals to the high pastures in summer, while many largely nomadic groups would do some farming at their winter lodgings.[65] Thus, not only did nomads settle and become peasants quite easily, but the opposite could also occur. Most areas were very sparsely populated, increasing the options open to country people. As it was possible thus to evade the issue, conflicts between peasants and *sipahis* did not lead to the peasants' revolts characteristic of the middle ages and early modern Europe.

Mercenaries and Robbers

In Anatolia, especially in the sixteenth and seventeenth centuries, there was another option open to young men wishing to evade the clutches of their *sipahi*. Until this time, *timar* troops had been available to provincial governors for recovering unpaid taxes and garrison duty. In the second half of the sixteenth century, though, the *timar* troops, cavalrymen armed only with lance, sword and shield, came to be regarded as militarily obsolete.[66] Gradually, the

Ottoman central government replaced the *timar*-holders with tax-farmers, while many former *timar*-holders now engaged in tax-farming, money-lending and trade. Those who did not manage to make such a transition probably ended up as villagers. It is true that the speed of this change varied considerably from region to region, and that in some remote areas *timar* and *sipahi*s persisted until the early nineteenth century. Nevertheless, in general the governors now had to hire the troops needed to control their provinces at their own expense.[67]

To this end the governors employed mercenaries, who were responsible for supplying their own firearms. These mercenaries did not belong to the established group of servants to the sultan (*askeri*) who claimed a monopoly on legitimate political activity. Rather, they were mostly composed of Muslim peasants' sons. Had the central government had its way, these men would not have been allowed to arm themselves at all. However, clandestine arms production flourished, so that in fact it was not difficult to obtain weapons.[68] These irregular troops (*levend*) were generally employed only in the short term and, when not out of a job, frequently set out into the surrounding countryside in search of new opportunities. Former soldiers, who had followed their employers on a campaign and then deserted, did the same thing. In most cases these former military men showed little enthusiasm for settling back into a village community and bowing to the directives of a *sipahi*.

Yet since military life without permanent employment was extremely dangerous, the leaders of these gangs aspired to regular pay and secure positions. Indeed, several of them did manage to obtain border postings as commanding officers.[69] However, so much destitute soldiery remained that, especially in the seventeenth century, there were violent altercations between regular and irregular troops. As particularly brutal groups of unemployed mercenaries often had the best chance of attracting the attention of the governor and thus being hired, the inhabitants of the countryside would be dragged into these conflicts. Moreover, in the long run, the nature of the gangs tended to change. Initially there were small groups of unemployed mercenaries, still with links to a particular locality. They attempted to maintain these links by treating the villagers with a degree of consideration. However, as the conflict went on these groups would merge into larger units which depended much less on local support. Thus, at the beginning and end of the seventeenth century, for example, whole armies of irregular soldiers, with no ties to particular localities, were to be found in the Ottoman territories.[70] In an extreme case, one such army swept right across Anatolia from the south-east to the north-west within a few years and conquered even important towns, albeit only for short periods. Urfa fell in 1599, as did Ankara in 1603, quite apart from the many smaller towns which were also taken.[71]

In the Balkans during the seventeenth and eighteenth centuries, the roads were also infested by robbers. These, however, had developed for somewhat different reasons. Most of the rural population there was non-Muslim, and so, therefore, were the gangs of irregular soldiers. Probably for this reason, permanent employment was less of an issue: no such thing was possible, since generally only Muslims would be accepted into the established military corps. Instead, many soldiers unable to find work in the border areas turned to theft and pillage to support themselves. In any case, it is not realistic to suggest, as previous studies have, that the so-called haiduks were proto-nationalists, fighting for local autonomy.[72] Far from being 'Robin Hood' figures, taking from the rich to give to the poor, most of the haiduks attacked whomsoever they happened to come across.

Mercenaries and nomads apart, other people also left their homes periodically or because of particular crises. Inheritance disputes, epidemics, exorbitant tax demands and robberies frequently forced young peasants from their villages. Among the periodic migrants we also find itinerant workers, who sometimes covered great distances. By the end of the sixteenth century, Albanians migrated to north-western Anatolia to find a livelihood as field guards or farm labourers.[73] In the fifteenth and sixteenth centuries the Ottoman state occasionally attempted to resettle migrants, who had left their village because of some crisis, in newly conquered territory. This policy enjoyed only limited success; most migrants headed for the towns, particularly for Istanbul. A low-life subculture developed there about which we still know virtually nothing.

Estates and Sharecroppers

Although some 'estates' in the hands of non-peasants developed in the eighteenth century, particularly along the Balkan coasts, the vast majority of peasants worked family farms. Many of these non-peasant holdings, which were often quite small, belonged to members of the local administration, who had profited from their intermediary position to acquire land.[74] If the Ottoman central government demanded taxes *en bloc* from a whole province, as it often did, there was scope for profitable manipulation of the assessment of individual villages and families. Certain villages might be treated leniently and the shortfall made up from the others. In such cases the official charged with assessing the villages could expect a reward from the beneficiaries as well as winning grateful followers for himself. Further potential for profit lay in the conversion of peasant crop taxes into money – perhaps by selling them to export merchants, and forwarding the cash to Istanbul. Money-lending was also widespread, despite its contravention of the Islamic prohibition on demanding interest payments. Many members of the provincial upper classes who, particularly from the second half of the eighteenth century, also sponsored buildings and decorative painting, were thus very much market-oriented. Yet the real source of their wealth remained political.[75]

Those villagers who farmed the property belonging to the eighteenth- and early nineteenth-century rural gentry were in an altogether inferior legal position to peasants inhabiting a typical *timar* of the sixteenth century. In the earlier period, peasants at least had security of tenure so long as they farmed the land properly. This was, however, denied them, or at least limited, in those areas in which much of the land had been swallowed up by the estates of the local gentry. Peasants ended up as day-labourers or sharecroppers, and their quality of life sank accordingly. However, this process differed significantly from the 'second serfdom' introduced into central and eastern Europe from the sixteenth century onwards, to which it is often compared. For the landed aristocrats of eastern Europe who reduced the farmers on their estates to serfs could count on the support of the crown. By contrast, this was not the case in the Ottoman territories. Recognizing that the gentry was taking over farmland, the central government saw this as a problem to be dealt with at some suitable opportunity. However, the sultan always refused to grant a legal basis to the subordination of agricultural labourers to their masters.[76]

Be that as it may, the peasants of remote mountain areas had many more economic options than the tied sharecroppers of the plains.[77] Many worked as mule drivers, and as trade with Vienna and Leipzig began to flourish in the eighteenth century, many such drivers became haulage contractors or cattle-dealers. In addition, these villagers would also sell the products of local craftsmen. Trade was thus by no means the monopoly of the towns; certain sectors of rural society also profited from the opportunities which were opening up.

Town and Country

In the Ottoman realm the divide between town and country was in general much less rigid than it was in many areas of medieval Europe. Just as there were country merchants, so there were many townspeople who earned their livelihoods from their gardens and vineyards, where they often spent several months during the summer. This semi-agricultural way of life was still evident even in the middle of the twentieth century. During the late 1940s, in a medium-sized central Anatolian town such as Akşehir, most craftsmen and retailers were unable to support themselves from their businesses alone and had to cultivate their gardens. During the harvest the shops would be deserted;

only an apprentice might perhaps remain, while the owners busied themselves with their farming activities. In fact, many towns in other Mediterranean regions also possessed this semi-rural character; well into the twentieth century, many Sicilian townsmen still relied on agriculture.[78]

In cultural terms, though, the divide between town and country was clearer than it was in economic matters. Written culture, the main concern of this book, was largely confined to the towns and was accessible only to a small section of rural society. Mosques were not built in large numbers in Anatolian villages until the nineteenth and twentieth centuries. Most villagers who could read and write had probably learned to do so in the nearest town or in a dervish convent. Registers of pious foundations of the second half of the sixteenth century, which also list the existing schools, only record a very few such establishments in the countryside. Moreover, there is no evidence that large numbers of schools were founded in villages between the seventeenth and nineteenth centuries, although this did happen in many small towns. For these reasons our sources are so scanty that a cultural history of the rural population can, in general, really begin only in the nineteenth century.

Cultural Conflict and Social Conflicts

Even more important than the division between town and country was the difference between subjects (*reaya*) and the sultan's servants (*askeri*). While the sultan's servants paid hardly any taxes, they saw themselves as possessing a monopoly over legitimate political activity.[79] In general, the sultan supported the special rights claimed by his servants, although there were exceptions to this rule.[80] On the other hand, *askeri* privileges were frequently attacked by ordinary subjects. Among the most persistent were the mercenaries, who revolted many times during the seventeenth century in the hope of being included in the sultan's regular troops, with varying degrees of success.[81] We can partially explain the economic and cultural distinction between town and country by the urban residence of the sultan's servants (with the exception of the *timar*-holders). As a result of their political privileges officials possessed significant purchasing power; this was concentrated in the towns, increasing the demand for imported goods and craft products.

We have noted in the previous chapter that religious movements considered heretical by the Ottoman central authority were quite widespread. From the sixteenth century onwards, the Ottoman sultan presented himself as the champion of Sunni orthodoxy and the vanquisher of the Shiites, the latter category including both the Shah of Iran and the Anatolian adherents of a Shiite-influenced religiosity. This image of the sultan as the Defender of Sunni Islam is reflected, for instance, in the Süleymaniye, one of the great building projects of the mid-sixteenth century. However, the motif of the Sunni ruler as victor over the Shiite 'heretics' also seems to have played a part in the construction of the Sultan Ahmed Mosque at the beginning of the seventeenth century, even though by this time the religious aspect of the hostile relationship between the Ottoman state and Iran had already declined in importance. In a laudatory poem on the mosque, the author emphasizes that the building of the mosque had impressively strengthened the sultan's status relative to that of the Shah.[82]

By erecting monumental buildings even in the non-Muslim parts of the empire, the Ottoman élite liked to assert its identity amid a divergent local culture. These were generally smaller structures, however, not comparable with those appearing at the same time in Istanbul or Edirne. Yet in some areas there were so many such buildings that their mere presence had an effect on the lives of the non-Muslim townspeople. Sometimes non-Muslims were forced to sell their properties and seek new homes because of complaints that their presence resulted in insufficiently large congregations for these mosques. In some towns there were apparently also regulations stipulating that the houses of non-Muslims could not be as high as those of Muslims, or limiting the colours which non-Muslims could paint their homes. In principle, the construction of new churches was prevented, and permission had to be sought from the sultan to repair existing ones; however, repairs to existing mosques also were referred to the central administration. In practice, such rules were often flouted, and quite frequently Christian subjects were even granted permission to build new churches.[83]

Understanding cultural conflicts in the Ottoman Empire is made more difficult by widespread illiteracy among the ordinary taxpayers. Documentary evidence reflects the outlook of the upper class, a category which occasionally includes non-Muslim notables. By contrast, the opinions of peasants, nomads and poor craftsmen are available to us only indirectly, as they are presented in the writings of members of the ruling class and local dignitaries. Frequently there is an element of distortion in these reports. It is nevertheless important that we do not see Ottoman culture as free of any tensions and therefore more or less static. On the contrary: cultural and social conflicts were often played out in public. In the next chapter we shall see that, in the seventeenth century for instance, there were great disputes among scholars concerned with law and religion. These were aired in public, many inhabitants of Istanbul took sides, and the status of religious scholars within society was considerably altered as a result.

4

Images of the World and the Times

People perceive their world in a manner inseparable from the social relationships into which they are born and which they build up during their lives. In an age without newspapers or television, both Muslim and non-Muslim inhabitants of the Ottoman Empire might, for example, hear of distant events from their neighbours or from fellow members of their guild. Among the most effective disseminators were preachers and priests, who would mention such news in or after religious services. But where did this information come from? Official channels were important in this respect, and in particular the many sultans' decrees. These might order festive illuminations to celebrate a victory or, more ominously, announce a new tax. In addition, though, there were various networks consisting of Muslim jurists and theologians, Orthodox priests, or merchants of whatever religion. Some such networks extended beyond the confines of the Ottoman Empire, although this was exceptional. A typical Ottoman townsman would be involved in many such networks and gain an impression of the Ottoman world and its limits from those with contacts to the capital or to an army on campaign. Women, on the other hand, had fewer opportunities. In this chapter we shall examine the conceptions of time and place held by many inhabitants of the Ottoman Empire, with special regard to the social groups within which such outlooks arose.

Sporadic Contacts

Peasants who lived and worked in a typical Anatolian village probably had first-hand experience only of a limited area. Apart from the village itself they might know the summer pastures in the surrounding hills or mountains, and the neighbouring villages. Of special importance was the district capital, where major disputes would be laid before the *kadi*, and villagers visited the market or attended Friday mosque. Istanbul, being the capital, also played a part in the lives of many villagers. It was from there that sultans' decrees arrived, requiring the peasants to increase their supplies of timber to the naval arsenal or announcing a new tax to finance a projected campaign. Some villages also sent deputations to Istanbul to represent them in legal disputes.[1] However, the further a village was from the regional capital, the fewer contacts there would be. Even the *kadi* would be sought out less often if the journey was a difficult one.

Despite this, even in remote villages the men at least were able to find out something about the 'outside world'. In Anatolia and in some regions of the eastern Balkans the nomads often mediated these contacts, moving as they did along set routes between winter pastures located, for example, on the Mediterranean coast, and summer pastures high in the Taurus mountains.[2] These were not great distances in themselves, but since the nomads had both horses and camels they would offer their services to caravans and accompany their animals to more distant commercial centres.[3] There were also nomads who migrated over greater distances. Thus the Boz Ulus left their pastures near Diyarbakır in the seventeenth century and moved in stages first to central Anatolia, where their cattle caused considerable damage in the fields. Certain members of the Boz Ulus even reached the island of Samos, thus having covered over 1,000 kilometres within a few decades.[4] Many villagers no doubt heard of the nomads' experiences, as farmers and nomads often shared summer pastures and there exchanged news as well as produce.

Survivors of the empire's various wars were also sources of information. Some might have fought against the Safavid armies, in wars which continued from 1514 to 1639 with only the odd peaceful interlude. Or else they might have served the sultan in wars against the Habsburg Empire, which also went on virtually uninterrupted through the sixteenth century, and flared up again in the second half of the seventeenth. Ex-soldiers were certainly limited in number, as general conscription was not applied in the Ottoman Empire. Only if a major rebellion occurred would all the inhabitants of a province sometimes be called up for militia duties.[5] However, in those areas of Anatolia and the Balkans where janissaries were recruited, direct reports of the wars of the time must have filtered through. Many men who had entered the sultan's service via the 'levy of boys' (*devşirme*) – the forced conscription of youths for the Ottoman palace and the janissary troops – were by no means cut off from their former homes. On the contrary, if their careers were successful they frequently interceded for their relatives or even brought the latter to Istanbul. Presumably the fathers and brothers of janissaries got to hear something of their relatives' experiences.

Mercenaries, who were recruited in large numbers in the late sixteenth century for service as musketeers, also came mostly from farming and nomadic families.[6] Their paid service was often all too brief, and in the absence of other opportunities some of them turned to a life of crime. Bands of such men were often accompanied by village youths seeking food or adventure, and sometimes by boys who had been abducted. Even in remote areas such as Çorum in northern Anatolia such gangs were a familiar phenomenon. When robbers were captured in this area towards the end of the sixteenth century, the villagers told the court that the accused had claimed to have previously served in the Caucasus.[7] Thus even luckless, destitute brigands brought with them information about distant regions.

Prisoners of war, captured by Ottoman soldiers and sold as slaves into the interior of the empire, were also sources of information. In sixteenth- and seventeenth-century Anatolia such people were usually subjects of the Habsburg Empire, Russians, or Ukrainians. As Muslims, Iranians should not have been enslaved, although this rule was often broken. Indeed, at the climax of the Ottoman–Iranian conflict the chief legal counsel to Süleyman the Magnificent (reign: 1520–66) declared that, from the Sunni point of view, heretical Shiites should not be regarded as Muslims.[8] Many of the enslaved Russians and Ukrainians had been taken prisoner in the frontier region by the Tartars of Crimea, who owed loose allegiance to the sultan. Others had been captured by local people during an attack launched by the Cossacks on Anatolian coastal towns. In the seventeenth century even the surroundings of Istanbul were not safe from such attacks.[9] Many slaves eventually learned the local language, became Muslims and after their release settled in Ottoman territory. They would then doubtless tell the local people about life and war at the distant frontier.

In the North African provinces in particular, but also in Istanbul, there were also Spaniards, Italians and Hungarians who had joined the Ottomans of their own volition.[10] Some were motivated by religious persecution in their native land; this applied to the Calvinist Hungarians who suffered considerable repression in the Counter-Reformation Habsburg Empire.[11] In North Africa, badly provisioned and unpaid Spanish soldiers in the fortresses (*presidios*) would often desert to the janissaries. In addition, in the North African provinces, where military personnel and corsair crews contained a large share of foreigners, it was much easier for individuals to improve their social status than it was in the more rigid societies of early modern Europe, where almost everybody was tied to the estate into which he had been born.[12] All these incomers brought with them information about their places of origin, even if they only very rarely wrote about their experiences.

Interregional Organizations: Jurists and Theologians

Ottoman jurists and theologians were organized in an officially decreed hierarchy, with frequent contacts between the different subgroups. Some such men were *kadi*s, teachers at theological schools or legal counsel serving the state; others were prayer leaders, Friday preachers or institutional administrators in the pay of pious foundations. In order to be eligible for the office of *kadi*, the initial requirement was that the candidate had studied Arabic grammar, the various aspects of the Qur'ān, theology and law with a range of teachers. Law meant the religious system of justice known as *şeriat*, which was discussed only in Arabic.[13] *Kadi*s would learn the other branch of law, applied in the Ottoman Empire, namely the system of ordinance based on sultans' decrees (*kanun*), largely by experience.[14] In larger *kadi* districts, or when dealing with an area very distant from the seat of their court, some *kadi*s would appoint deputies (*naib*) familiar with local circumstances. They thus hoped to draw even remote villages into their domain.

Any young man aspiring to a successful career as a *kadi* in the period around 1600 was well advised to study at the centre of the empire. Only those who had been students at the theological colleges of Bursa, Edirne or Istanbul and had later also taught there could expect to rise to great heights. Those with sufficient luck and ability might aspire to become *kadi* of Istanbul, army judge of Anatolia or army judge of Rumelia. Both the latter positions carried with them membership of the sultan's council (*divan-ı humayun*), which played a central role in the affairs of the state until the seventeenth century. As a long sojourn in Istanbul, Edirne or Bursa was indispensable, relatively few scholars from the Arab provinces achieved eminence as judges or university teachers at the Ottoman centre. Had this not been so, the opposite might well have been the case, since Syrians and Egyptians started with the advantage of not needing to learn Arabic.

In the sixteenth and seventeenth centuries the professional progress of young jurists and theologians depended not just on their own learning and their talent as teachers, but also on the efforts of their patrons.[15] It was wise for young men to seek out such a figure soon after arriving in Istanbul. Generally, but not always, the patron would be a senior judge, perhaps a *kadi* of Istanbul or an army judge. He would ensure the progress of his protégé, since when senior judges and lecturers were promoted they would also recommend the appointment of young men recently embarked on their careers. Moreover, the patron could also commend his protégé to a pasha or even introduce him to the sultan. Such relationships generally yielded great advantages in terms of professional progress, although dependence upon a patron was accompanied by certain risks. The downfall of an army judge or chief legal counsel (*şeyhülislam*), albeit not such a frequent occurrence as the fall of a vizier, could severely affect the career of a young man associated with the erstwhile dignitary.[16]

In the course of their careers, many judges and teachers at the main schools of theology got to know one another very well indeed. There was a large surplus of qualified candidates for the positions available, so judges and teachers spent long periods in the capital between short terms of office, hoping to catch the eye of the army judges and obtain another appointment. However, in the office of an eminent judge such individuals would also encounter a host of other hopefuls. It was by no means a bad career move to seek recognition beyond the circle of one's immediate colleagues. Thus a young scholar might make a name for himself as a writer outside the academic world. In the second half of the sixteenth century the poet Baki was promoted to the post of army judge because Süleyman the Magnificent was impressed by his poems.[17] Time has endorsed the sultan's opinion; Baki is still considered one of the most important representatives of high Ottoman poetry. In his lifetime, though, Baki was much envied by his colleagues and not always regarded in a very friendly fashion.

Even a provincial *kadi* would have opportunities to maintain relationships with other judges. Minor *kadi*s were often promoted only within a certain area and would spend periods of unemployment or their eventual retirement in a town of the same region. In difficult cases the current *kadi* could 'unofficially' consult any of his colleagues residing in the same locality. Jurists and theologians were thus well known to one another and, despite bitter feuds between individuals and the associated intrigues and denunciations, there was a certain sense of solidarity.

A special kind of network emerged in Istanbul among the mosque preachers (*vaiz*) of the seventeenth century.[18] These included students of Mehmed Birgevî and later of Kadızade and Ustuvani, also known as the 'Kadızade's People' (*Kadızadeliler*). With a programme of between sixteen and twenty points according to the individual preacher, these men demanded the reversal of all innovations which dated from after the time of the Prophet Muhammad. They were particularly hostile towards the dervishes and their ceremonies, all the more so if the ceremonies were accompanied by music and dance.[19] The followers of the Kadızade attacked these innovations with particular fervour as offences against religious law. Since their way of life was much closer to that of ordinary townspeople than was the lifestyle favoured by the higher orders of the legal and scholastic hierarchy, the mosque preachers had many supporters among the inhabitants of the city. There were also many jurists and theologians who were not among the 'Kadızade's People' but who, with varying degrees of militancy, shared the preachers' reservations about the dervishes. Collected in a text resembling a catechism, the common currency of this network was the teaching of Mehmed Birgevî. When, in 1653, two theologians issued a rebuttal, the supporters of Birgevî and the Kadızade were powerful enough to have these (as they alleged) disrespectful comments regarding a pious scholar destroyed by the chief legal counsel.[20] Although the feared Grand Vizier Köprülü Mehmed Pasha banished its leaders to Cyprus in 1654, the network of the 'Kadızade's People' survived these counter-measures. In later years the sultan's teacher, Vanî Efendi, became a leading figure among the 'Kadızade's People'. It was only when he fell into disfavour after the failure of the campaign against Vienna (1683), a campaign which he had vehemently supported, that the preachers' network disintegrated.[21]

In the eighteenth century, after the end of the Kadızadeli movement, and in response to the theological dissension of the previous centuries, many new schools were built. Their founders hoped that they would help stabilize religious belief along the lines advocated by established jurists and theologians. Several of these colleges of great architectural merit can still be admired in Istanbul. They were entirely under the control of the leading members of the legal and scholastic hierarchy, who formed a kind of aristocracy resident in the capital. Edirne and Bursa thus lost the influence they had hitherto enjoyed within the Ottoman education system.[22]

Now able to bridge the long gaps between two terms in office more easily than they had been able to in the seventeenth century, the aristocratic heads of the scholastic hierarchy consolidated their position. From 1700 onwards, senior judges who, thanks to paternal influence, had won an important position while still young, were able to claim the lucrative incomes of provincial *kadis* as their pay during the periods they spent waiting for a new appointment. Someone appointed by the nominal official, often one of his young relatives, would carry out the *kadi*'s duties. There are striking parallels with the Europe of the *ancien régime*, where many clerics were also able to divert the income from a monastery or parish from its original purpose.[23]

These circumstances meant that the influence of a senior jurist or theologian in the provinces was greatly curtailed. Above all the 'middle-grade' *kadi*, who had hitherto formed an important link between the administrative centre and the provinces, had less occasion to 'cultivate' the top levels of the *ulema* hierarchy. In political terms this loss of communication was all the more serious because it was one of the jurists' and theologians' major tasks to consolidate and develop the Sunni tradition among Muslim subjects. Such scholars were the representatives of Sunni Islam, the defence and propagation of which constituted the basis for the legitimacy of the Ottoman sultans.[24]

However, the audience for the scholars' sermons and teachings was a population whose religious views frequently diverged from 'high' Sunni Islam to a greater or lesser extent. In many parts of Anatolia people followed a Shiite variant of Islam regarded as heterodox from the ruling Ottoman standpoint. Shiites were numerous in Iraq as well, and there were of course considerable Christian communities within the empire. As ties between the inhabitants of the provinces and the leaders of the legal and scholastic hierarchy loosened, the learned aristocracy lost much of its political support. This isolation was to make itself felt in the crises of the nineteenth century.

Interregional Ties: Dervishes

Many Ottoman dervishes belonged to orders which derived from a founder figure revered as a saint, and whose religious practices they often maintained for centuries. Large orders, such as the Halvetiye, would in time split into many smaller branches, which nevertheless remained very conscious of their shared origins.[25] Some of them, especially the Mevleviye and the Bektaşiye, recognized a certain lodge or convent as the centre of their order. Its leader would often have a say in the appointment of the heads of other convents.[26] The Ottoman administration also took an interest in the leadership of the central dervish lodge and without its written ratification it was impossible for the leader of any dervish community to remain in office for very long.

Some orders, such as the Ottoman (but not the Indian) Nakşbendiye, required their followers to adhere strictly to the articles of religious law. Jurists and theologians were more often among the members of such orders.[27] Other dervishes, however, believed that religious law applied only to those who had not yet achieved mystic insight, the Bektashi constituting a well-known example of this belief. Bektashi did not adhere to the prohibition against wine and allowed men and women to participate in the same ceremonies. Between these two extreme positions there were various gradations. Jurists and theologians were often ambivalent towards some dervish ceremonies, such as the sacral dance of the Mevlevîs. In spite of such tensions, however, the networks of the theologians and the dervishes were often connected.[28]

Within dervish orders, unity maintained in the course of time expressed itself through the line of succession from one dervish sheikh to another.[29] No one could follow the mystic path without the guidance of an experienced master; however, the line of descent from the founder of the order to the current sheikh might be a purely spiritual one. Often, however, there was also a hereditary line of descent because, in many lodges, sons were instructed by their fathers. Links between separate orders which saw themselves as fellow members of the same spiritual family were also presented in terms of such family trees. Moreover, it was usual to create a connection between the founder of the order and the Prophet, as well as with his nephew and son-in-law Ali.

This might have a historical basis, since there were many recognized descendants of the Prophet, or it might be founded on an 'invented tradition'.

In the political sphere, the more centralized dervish orders were responsible
for a flow of information from the provinces to the capital which was more
or less independent of the official channels. If, for example, a provincial
dignitary behaved oppressively towards the local people, the latter might ask
a dervish to intervene, who would then report back to the main lodge in
Istanbul.[30] If the sheikh had any influence at court, this procedure could be
an effective complement to an official complaint to the sultan's council. A
famous sheikh such as Mahmud Hüida'i (1543/44–1628/29) was also able to
obtain tax reductions for his home village, and although such instances were
less frequent in the sixteenth and seventeenth centuries than they had been
in the early part of the Ottoman era, they did increase the efficacy of the
dervish networks.[31]

Church Networks

For a long period Greek Orthodoxy occupied a privileged position in the
church life of the Ottoman Empire. Religion was considered more significant
than language or ethnos and, as a result, the Orthodox peoples of the Balkans
and Syria were all subordinate to the Greek Orthodox patriarchs of Istanbul.[32]
Although ethnicity was sometimes taken into account, the Ottoman bureaucracy did not regard this as a major issue. Having said that, before the
nineteenth century the organization of the various religious groups known as
millet was much less hierarchical and structured than subsequently. It is
therefore a mistake to project the bureaucratic organization of the nineteenth
century back on to the early modern period.[33]

Greek being not just the liturgical but also the everyday language in the
Greek Orthodox Church, Greek-speaking clerics had better prospects of
advancement than their competitors from other ethnic groups. Indeed, until
the eighteenth century they had a virtual monopoly on the most senior
positions in the Church. There were attempts to change this situation: while
Mehmed Sokollu, an ethnic Serb, was grand vizier, the Serbian patriarchate
of Pec was revived (1557) and a relative of the vizier appointed to it.[34]

The Orthodox Church suffered particularly from the weakness of the
links between the patriarchate in Istanbul and the provincial churches, which
resulted in a dearth of educational opportunities. Even European travellers
sympathetic towards the Greek Orthodox Church – something which was by
no means always the case – complained of the low level of intellectual training
among the provincial clergy. There were no seminaries, far less was there any
university education for Orthodox priests. Even in the seventeenth and

eighteenth centuries, would-be members of the clergy were more or less apprenticed to priests or monks, learning by rote the texts they would require for their duties. Only a small minority could study at the academy maintained by the patriarchs. This form of instruction had been widespread in late medieval Europe as well, but seemed intolerably backward to many seventeenth-century observers, in the wake of the Reformation and Counter-Reformation.[35]

For those individuals with the means to do so, it was possible to study in Venice and, above all, at the University of Padua. Until its destruction by Napoleon in 1797, despite losing Cyprus (1573), Crete (1660) and Tinos (1710), the Venetian state still possessed Greek-speaking territory in the Ionian islands.[36] For political reasons the Venetian government tolerated the existence of a Greek Orthodox colony with its own printing press in Venice itself as well as, from 1550, Greek schools in the islands. Moreover, without the always hesitant permission of the state authorities, the Inquisition was unable to operate in Venetian territory. As a result Pomponazzi's New Aristotelians were able to speculate at the Venetian University of Padua about a purely material universe.[37] Future priests may have been somewhat disconcerted by this aspect of the curriculum, but it would have been received with more enthusiasm by the Greek medical students who also often trained in Padua. A small class of laymen with an academic education, familiar with the main features of the seventeenth-century intellectual revolution in Europe, thus emerged in Istanbul. Its focus was the Fener/Phanar district, where the Orthodox patriarchate still has its see today. However, the munificence of the wealthy commercial families of Fener/Phanar, which ensured the financial survival of the patriarchate academy, did not extend to the education of provincial clergy. Links with Venice may well have contributed to the disjunction between the Orthodox intellectuals of Istanbul and the parishes outside the capital.

Cyrillos Lucaris, patriarch, except for brief intervals, from 1620 until his murder in 1638, attempted to remedy this situation.[38] Lucaris was one of those who had studied in Italy, and he also spent a considerable time in Poland as the representative of the then patriarch. There he witnessed the foundation of a Greek Catholic Church in the Orthodox Ukraine (1595). This persuaded Lucaris that the Orthodox clergy would never be able to resist the spread of the Catholic Church without the benefit of a proper education. During his term in office he not only imported books from Italy, but also oversaw the foundation of a printing press, in which endeavour he was assisted by the English envoy, Thomas Roe. In fact, the press was intended also to enable the patriarch to inform his clergy of his own point of view, which was close to the Calvinist position. This provoked the opposition of the Jesuits, who had considerable influence at the French embassy in Galata. Diplomatic steps taken by the French ambassador brought about the closure and destruction of the printing press by the Ottoman authorities in 1628.

It is certainly true that the flow of information from Istanbul to the provinces was very limited so far as theological education was concerned. However, the mere existence of the Orthodox Church granted its members opportunities to see beyond the narrow confines of their village or town quarter. Monks from certain monasteries, for example Mount Athos or St Catharine's on Sinai, journeyed through Orthodox villages to collect alms from the faithful and, as a by-product, provided information on far removed centres of Orthodoxy. These journeys were authorized by both the sultan and the patriarch, and although they took place throughout the Ottoman Empire, those in Moldavia and Wallachia, today in Romania, are particularly well documented.[39] Although both these provinces belonged to the sultan, they were ruled by Christian princes or governors. There was thus rather more latitude in church affairs here than elsewhere. Although the monks did not always receive the contributions had hoped for, their mere arrival and the news they brought with them must have awakened the faithful in many a small Romanian town to the far-flung networks of their church.

The Geographers

News spread via the networks of Muslim jurists and theologians, dervishes and Orthodox clergy ultimately filtered through to a large number of people. However, the news explicitly transmitted by such figures tended to concern the spiritual rather than the real world. Among both the Muslims and the Orthodox inhabitants of the Ottoman Empire there was also another and more worldly educated culture, in which geography and descriptions of manners and customs were of particular importance.[40] In the sixteenth century, many geographers were naval admirals and captains, who needed to produce charts in the wake of the Portuguese challenge and the newly awakened Ottoman interest in the Indian Ocean. A version of Columbus's chart of the Atlantic Ocean, which is known only in this Ottoman edition, is associated with the name of Pirî Reis (c. 1470–1554). The same author was responsible for a *Book of Maritime Matters*, which includes a series of portulan charts of the Mediterranean coasts.[41] It deals not just with the Ottoman coastlands, but also with those of France and Italy. In 1543 Ottoman and French forces together conquered the town of Nice in southern France (1543), and as a unit of the sultan's navy spent the winter in Toulon it became possible for Ottoman seamen to chart the Riviera in detail. For a time Pirî Reis was commander of the Ottoman fleet in the Indian Ocean, but in 1554 he was executed in Egypt on the sultan's orders because of perceived failures against the Portuguese.

Other naval officers delivered military reports from which information about geography and economic geography can be construed. A letter of 1516, shortly before the Ottoman conquest of Egypt, from the corsair captain, Selman Reis, vividly describes the dependence of the Holy Cities of the Hejaz on cereal supplies from Egypt.[42] Thus the Ottoman government was able to foresee that conquering Egypt would almost automatically bring with it control of the Hejaz. There were also itineraries for land routes, usually relating to military campaigns. Seydi Ali Reis documented his overland retreat to the Ottoman Empire from India after losing his ships in a battle with the Portuguese.[43] Other itineraries were included in anthologies or geographical compendia and thus made available to a wider readership. For example, a campaign itinerary of Sultan Süleyman's from the years 1533 to 1536 is to be found in a sixteenth-century anthology of official documents put together by Ahmed Feridun.[44]

Moreover, at this time special books about particular campaigns, copiously illustrated with miniatures, began to appear. Among the most famous is the work of the multi-talented historian, painter and athlete Matrakçı Nasuh, concerning Sultan Süleyman's campaign against Iraq, which at that time was still in Iranian hands (1537).[45] Many miniatures illustrate the main stopping-places of the Ottoman army; while highly stylized, the major buildings of the towns are sufficiently recognizable for the work to be a useful source for architectural history. Views of towns and landscapes as depicted by Matrakçı Nasuh feature neither people nor animals, although Ottoman miniature painters otherwise were not averse to the depiction of historical and religious figures. Instead, particularly in the illustration of Istanbul, there is an attempt to combine an accurate plan with an aesthetically pleasing panorama.[46] Another pictorial record, this time from the later sixteenth century, concerns the Caucasus campaign of Lala Mustafa Pasha in the years 1578–79. Mustafa Âlî, the author of the text, was even paid for several months to supervise work on the illustrations in the sultan's miniatures studio.[47]

Such itineraries were vital for producing maps. Many European travellers of the eighteenth and nineteenth centuries attempted to identify their position more accurately by using a compass or the stars, thereby making their itineraries more reliable. However, even if the traveller merely recorded his direction and the time he took, his itinerary could serve as the basis for a map. Thus individuals close to the historian and geographer Kâtib Çelebi, a man who had made copious use of European geographical literature in his work called 'View of the World', used itineraries and portulan charts to produce a map of Anatolia.[48] It is very obvious, however, that they possessed material relating only to a few, larger routes in eastern Anatolia, whereas they could refer to a host of intersecting itineraries for the western part. Many of Evliya Çelebi's lists of stopping and resting places, including some which he simply invented, have survived. However, although he had utilized the works of various geographers, particularly Mehmed Aşık (around 1598), his real interest lay in travel as a literary theme rather than in geographical science.[49]

It is difficult to say who had access to this bureaucratic, scientific and artistic material relating to travel and exploration. Certainly the beautifully illustrated manuscripts about sultans' campaigns were known only to a small group of high officials able to use the palace collections. Evliya Çelebi's work was hardly used before the nineteenth century. It was copied after 1700, but most copies of that time remained in the palace library and did not, therefore, become known to many people.[50] Kâtib Çelebi's 'View of the World' probably reached the widest readership. In 1732 it was even printed in Istanbul, one of the first Ottoman texts with which pioneers of the new medium experimented.[51] However, these first Ottoman printed works were far from being bestsellers, and in the first half of the eighteenth century books can have contributed to only a very few people's conception of the world.

Merchants' Networks

We know only indirectly of the communication between merchants, since virtually no personal records pertaining to them have been discovered. There was, however, a system for payments between towns which avoided the use of cash and which was verified by entry in the *kadi*'s register.[52] Regular communication between merchants was a prerequisite for such a method, since it would have been too uncertain for correspondents who knew nothing of one another. During the seventeenth and eighteenth centuries in Cairo there were many merchants from other parts of the empire, with Tunisians and Algerians well represented. Syrian Catholics became important in the second half of the eighteenth century, although they were a relatively small group.[53] In the seventeenth century the Armenian trade networks with their centres in New Julfa at Isfahan, Lwow in Poland and Amsterdam were more effective than ever.[54] Istanbul and Izmir were also involved in these networks. Raw silk from Iran imported into the Ottoman Empire was a source of profit to the Armenian merchants, yet even in the early eighteenth century, when this trade was already in decline, many Armenians appeared in the customs registers of the Ottoman frontier town of Erzurum.

It would be wrong to regard such intensive commercial contacts, even beyond the frontiers of the empire, as the preserve of non-Muslims, although this is often the impression given in history books. In the late sixteenth and early seventeenth centuries Ottoman Muslims, including Bosnians, Anatolians and merchants from Istanbul, regularly visited Venice. Some Ottoman merchants settled there permanently, serving their present and former compatriots as brokers and interpreters.[55] In the Venetian archives we find many documents concerning the trade of these Muslim merchants, and insurance matters concerning them. Muslim residents of Venice also traded with one another and constituted a clearly defined group, which was always in contact with the merchants of Istanbul.

Of course the information transmitted via these commercial networks largely concerned trade. A report might concern high demands from a tax-farmer or cheap customs tariffs being offered by a Kurdish prince of the frontier region who was keen to encourage merchants to pass through his territory. However, news regarding thieving mercenaries on a particular route, pirate attacks and bankruptcy in some distant centre of trade must also have been passed from merchant to merchant. Some such information was of course exchanged in the coffee-houses, but a good part of it was no doubt regarded as confidential and shared only by merchants who were close business associates.

A story recorded by Evliya Çelebi is illustrative of the close ties between merchants who kept certain information strictly among themselves. He reports that some merchants in Mecca negotiated prices by clasping their hands beneath a cloth and using various grips to communicate their offers.[56] When they had settled upon a price this was confirmed by another kind of hold, without bystanders being aware that a transaction had occurred at all. It was thus of vital importance to a merchant that he be part of a network extending beyond his own area, even at the risk of some business partners eventually turning into competitors.

The Nerve Centre of the Ottoman World

Due to the centralized political structure of the Ottoman Empire, all information was eventually passed on to Istanbul. As we have already observed, by the eighteenth century even the old capitals of Bursa and Edirne had largely lost their roles as centres for theological and legal education. Scholars and artists who aspired to advancement through the sultan's court had to appear in Istanbul or at least ensure that their work was made known there. Certainly, there were artists working in Aleppo, Damascus and Cairo. Local chroniclers and poets were active, and in particular there were the many masters of architecture and interior design whose work has survived there until the present day. However, it is striking how very few of the names of such master builders, interior designers, stucco-workers, wood-carvers or marquetry artists we know today. Those who wanted to make a name for themselves probably moved to the capital.

By the same token, the greatest libraries in the empire were to be found in Istanbul. In various buildings belonging to the sultan's palace there were collections of books. At the beginning of the eighteenth century Ahmed III built an additional, very elegant library of his own, in the centre of the third palace courtyard. However, such collections were made available only rarely to scholars and bibliophiles who were not members of the court. This was not the case at the libraries founded by viziers and scholars in the city, such as Ahmed Köprülü, grand vizier from 1661 to 1676. In about 1734 Grand Vizier Hekimoğlu ('the Doctor's Son') Ali Pasha endowed an elegant library in the grounds of his mosque complex, and the beautiful building founded by Ragıp Pasha before 1763 is still in use as a library today. Readers with sufficient means could also buy manuscripts in specialist shops and customers could order illustrations.

Yet in Istanbul plentiful sources of information were also available for those inhabitants who were illiterate or who had only limited access to the literary world. Much could be learned in the port, where ships bringing cereals, butter fat and other foodstuffs from the Black Sea region docked on the southern side of the Golden Horn. Here the *kadi* of Istanbul would meet the captains and merchants before laying down the price of the most important foodstuffs.[57] Information about droughts, Cossack attacks, speculation or failed harvests around the Black Sea accumulated here. No doubt much of this information was also available in the coffee-houses and wineshops of Galata. Commercial information was also exchanged in the khans of Istanbul – many of the buildings which survive today were built by sultans' mothers and important dignitaries in the seventeenth century. Where commercial news was involved, however, Istanbul had to share its privileged position with other centres. Cairo, rather than Istanbul, was the place to find out about recent developments in the trade with India. Nevertheless, Istanbul's position at the meeting point of two seas and many trade routes made it a privileged location for merchants to collect information about various markets.

People making legal representations at the sultan's court, or who wanted to complain about a provincial official also relayed information to the inhabitants of the capital. Some wealthier complainants probably appeared in person, while the inhabitants of villages or urban districts, who were pursuing some matter as a group, would pay the travel costs of the delegate who was to represent them in the capital.[58] There were so many such travellers that the central authorities sometimes suspected that the complaints were merely pretexts to enable individuals to settle in the capital. When the authorities attempted to control the rate of immigration to Istanbul, in some cases they also limited the number of people granted entry to the capital as petitioners.[59] Complainants presumably lodged in khans or sometimes with relatives. Their complaints about thieving governors and corrupt *kadi*s thus no doubt became known among a part of the population of the capital.

Diplomats and their retinues were also a source of information for certain inhabitants of Istanbul. There were many such officials, both permanent representatives and special envoys who congratulated a new sultan on his accession or else signed a peace accord. Venetian, French, English, Dutch and Habsburg diplomats apart, there were the Iranians, whose arrival was often a particularly magnificent affair. Servants and translators working for diplomats were important providers of information for the capital's inhabitants. Such persons shopped for the foreigners and both facilitated and controlled their contacts with the city's inhabitants (only a few visitors, such as the adventurous and linguistically-gifted Lady Mary Wortley Montagu, were able sometimes to dispense with such attendants).[60] The janissaries who were regularly employed to guard the diplomats also come into this category. Servants and translators tended, on the one hand, to present their masters as eminent figures in order to bask in the reflected glory. On the other, they probably did not wish to be associated too closely with the 'unbelievers' (or, in the case of Persian representatives, the 'heretics'). No doubt the stories they told their families and neighbours were coloured by these contradictory interests.

In the Course of Time

Ethnological perspectives on Ottoman social history remain uncommon. Therefore only the understanding of time prevalent among officials and courtiers can be described in any detail. One important topos in this regard is that of a Golden Age, following which humankind could only decline. This played a significant part in the scholarly world of early modern Europe as well. There were various opinions on when such a Golden Age might have begun. As the idealized image of the Roman Empire in the classical tradition of Europe shows, such a topos need by no means concern an entirely mythical age.[61]

Indeed, Ottoman writers were fond of drawing on the very recent past for their myth of a Golden Age. Very soon after the death of Süleyman the Magnificent (1566), authors of texts calling for political reform in the empire began to idealize his reign. In these tracts, a characteristic genre in seventeenth-century Ottoman literature in particular, the state of affairs which had existed, really or allegedly, around the middle of the sixteenth century soon was treated as a norm for future times. Authors such as Âlî or Koçi Beg blamed deviations from the distribution of power and other practices prevalent in the mid-sixteenth century for military defeats and political crises.[62] In the past, Ottomanist historians have often made the mistake of taking such writings at face value, of assuming that they constitute 'objective' representations of historical reality. Such uncritical readings of Ottoman sources have probably led to the assumption that after Süleyman's death the Ottoman state declined more abruptly than was actually the case.[63] Quite evidently, caution is required when dealing with the topos of a past Golden Age. Such an ideal was already to be found in Ottoman literature at the beginning of the sixteenth century, when Süleyman had yet to ascend the throne and before the empire had reached its greatest extent. Thus the pious and learned Prince Korkud (1470–1513) explained his refusal to compete (at least officially) for the throne by asserting that, in a time of decline, all rulers were forced to commit unjust acts.[64] Thus the topos of decline is significant not so much for what it says about reality but rather for its reflection of the conception of many educated Ottomans. Other authors, such as Evliya Çelebi, seem to have had a more optimistic outlook. At any rate, the traveller does not appear to have viewed the age in which he lived as a period of decline.

Prophecies, which were as widely believed in the Ottoman realm as in contemporary Europe, were important with regard to ideas about the future. This statement needs to be qualified somewhat, at least in the case of a writer such as Evliya. In his description of Vienna we find prophecies quite clearly made after the event to which they related. Either the traveller had learned of them or had invented them himself, in which latter case literary considerations were probably of primary importance.[65] If the latter was the case, it would of course be wrong to speak of naive belief.

Like Christians, Muslims believe in a day of judgement at the end of time. This parallel between Islam and Christianity may explain why Evliya Çelebi's claim to have seen a representation of the Last Judgement in Vienna's St Stephen's Cathedral is followed by a description dominated by Muslim notions about judgement day. Among the omens of judgement day was the appearance of the Antichrist, the Deccal, who arrives on a donkey as a false prophet to lead humankind astray.[66] Another indicator of the Last Judgement was still more important. This was the Mahdi, who would take over the whole world as a just ruler and prepare the way for the second coming of Jesus, which heralds the Last Judgement in Islamic eschatology. Every once in a while we encounter Ottoman rebels claiming to be this final ruler. Around 1576–77 an artisan from the northern Anatolian town of Amasya attracted supporters for such a claim.[67] A rebellion begun in 1587 by the self-proclaimed Mahdi Yahya ibn Yahya in Tripoli, in North Africa, is rather better documented. Despite Ottoman expeditions to suppress it, the revolt went on for several years, in part because the Ottoman navy reached Tripoli only in the summer, at which time of year Yahya ibn Yahya withdrew to the mountains with his supporters.[68]

Expectations and fears that the end of the world was imminent were particularly frequent towards the end of the sixteenth century, as the end of the first millennium, according to Islamic chronology, was in 1590–91. Although neither the Qu'rān, nor the tradition based on the words and deeds of the Prophet (Sunna), gives a date for the Last Judgement, even educated people in Istanbul believed that, a thousand years after the birth of Islam, the end of the world could indeed be nigh.[69] Mustafa Âlî, an eminent historian and literary figure, examined these expectations and came to the conclusion that they were unfounded, but it seems not all his contemporaries shared his opinion.[70]

Moreover, predicting the end of the world already had a long tradition at the Ottoman court. In the 1520s and 1530s, when the conquest of Vienna and even Italy seemed imminent, a certain Mevlana Isa and his circle wrote treatises celebrating Süleyman the Magnificent as the final, universal ruler.[71] Unlike the fear surrounding the year 1000 of the Hejira, these predictions were rather optimistic in tone. At court, several authors celebrated the sultan as the just ruler who would spread Islamic domination to the edges of the inhabited world. Fears of God's judgement were much less in evidence. For a time, these suggestions perhaps represented not just the opinion of the authors concerned, but the sultan's own view of himself.[72] Only from about 1550, when Süleyman's sons began to fight for the succession to the throne, without the conquest of Vienna or Rome having been achieved, did these eschatological elements vanish from the sultan's ideology of power. They were replaced by emphasis on the idea of the sultan as the representative of Islamic norms in the contemporary world.

However, perhaps the best known case of Ottoman anticipation of the end of the world was a Jewish rather than a Muslim phenomenon.[73] Sabbatai Sevi (1626–76), who presented himself as a Jewish Messiah, came from a family which had probably lived in the town of Patras in the Peloponnese until his father settled in Izmir. At the time, Izmir was beginning to thrive as a port town. As a young man, Sabbatai travelled widely through the Ottoman Empire, following the failure of his attempt to gain recognition as a Messiah by the Jewish establishment in his home town. He appeared in Egypt as well as in Gaza and Jerusalem. Sevi's messianic sermons, which incorporated elements of Jewish mysticism, caused great controversy in the small Jewish communities of Palestine. Although the rabbis of Jerusalem excommunicated him, Sevi gathered supporters, and disturbances occurred in Jewish communities. Among other things, Sevi's supporters believed in the triumphs of the 'lost tribes' of Iran and North Africa. Celebrated by his followers as the Messiah, Sabbatai returned to Izmir and at the end of 1665 he won decisive influence in the local Jewish community. People did public penance in the expectation of the impending end of the world. Sevi then travelled to Istanbul, where he sparked another prophetic movement, but he was arrested by the Ottoman authorities and banished to the small town of Gelibolu, on the Sea of Marmara. During his sojourn there, his messianic movement continued to spread. Delegates even arrived from Jewish communities in Poland. Sabbatai's opponents then complained to the grand vizier, who offered the would-be Messiah two options: either he converted to Islam or he would be executed. In September 1666 Sabbatai converted to Islam in the sultan's council (*divan-ı humayun*). Some of his supporters followed his example and formed the group known as the *dönme* (converts), which maintained its separate identity in Istanbul until very recently. Others remained loyal to their messianic beliefs and caused considerable trouble to Aziz Mehmed Efendi (Sabbatai's new, Islamic name) in his later life.

Sabbatai Sevi's story is an important indication of how much cultural common ground there was between the religions of the Mediterranean basin, even in the sixteenth and seventeenth centuries. In more recent research regarding Sabbatai there has therefore been a tendency to concentrate more on the specifically Ottoman background to his movement and to examine its relationship to anticipations of the end of the world in other religions.[74] Messianism was, it should be said, by no means unknown in the sixteenth-century Orthodox Church. There is a sultan's decree of 1565–66 which describes the activities of an unnamed monk in Thessalonica.[75] This individual required his followers to shun the market, apparently in order to do penance in view of the impending end of the world. A century or so later, many of Sabbatai's supporters exhibited similar behaviour. Since the incomes gained by local holders of tax grants (*timar*) plummeted as a result, these officials complained vocally. Thereupon the Ottoman authorities pursued the preacher, whose followers saw him as the reincarnation of Jesus.

People and Networks

The story of Sabbatai Sevi highlights the existence of rival networks among Ottoman Jews of the seventeenth century, and the very specific kinds of information which circulated within them. Sabbatai's supporters and opponents were spread throughout the Ottoman realm and beyond. Eventually the sultan intervened because of the complaints lodged by Sevi's opponents, who must have had connections at court.[76] We have encountered similar rival networks among the Muslim jurists and theologians in the case of the 'Kadızade's People' controversy. Here too the network was spread over a wide area, even if, as a result of the centralized structure of the Ottoman scholarly hierarchy, Istanbul had a central part to play.

Individuals could be involved in various networks. Many people must have had access to information via the circle of theologians and jurists as well as via the dervishes. It was also possible to be part of a network based on a common religious practice and at the same time, as a merchant, to have relationships with other merchants. In a sense the Ottoman frontiers were permeable for those involved in networks extending to Venice or even as far as Vienna, which was true of many Greek and Serbian merchants in the eighteenth century.[77] In the next chapter we shall turn to the question of how Ottoman subjects perceived the limits of their world, and what happened to those who moved out of or into the Ottoman domain.

5

Borders and Those Who Crossed Them

The Co-existence of Different Cultures

The Ottoman Empire was a state of many peoples. A variety of Christian and Muslim inhabitants of the Balkans were subjects of the sultan, and the same thing applied to the largely Muslim, Arabic-speaking inhabitants of Syria, Egypt and Iraq. Although the upper classes of these groups participated to a greater or lesser extent in Ottoman high culture, regional cultures remained very varied. In the case of Egypt and Syria, this regional culture is relatively well known today. There are studies of the 'great' architecture, but also of 'vernacular' buildings, decoration, literature and the scholarly world.[1] Moreover, the culture of the Muslim peasants and nomads of Anatolia was very different from the urban culture of the same region. Differences between town and country must be especially stressed if, as is the case in the present volume, the focus is on the larger towns. Smaller towns were often rural in economic terms, and this was probably reflected in their culture. In the course of the previous chapters, we have noted significant differences between ordinary townspeople and members of the Ottoman upper class, close to the court and so vividly depicted in the contemporary reports of Evliya Çelebi and Lady Mary Wortley Montagu.

However, in an age in which people's religion was considered much more important than the linguistic or cultural group to which they belonged, the significance of such differences was far from what it was to be in the nineteenth or twentieth centuries. Some pashas, of the eighteenth century in particular, attempted to manage 'their' province as independently as possible. In doing so they did not draw on the regional culture of the province they controlled, but in cultural matters above all they rather looked towards Istanbul. Anatolian provincial notables of the eighteenth and early nineteenth centuries were very fond of decorating the walls of their reception rooms with painted views of the mosques and seascapes of the capital.[2] In Syria there was a similar situation: at the beginning of the eighteenth century a group of influential families had emerged which continued to speak Arabic, but which had close cultural ties to the Ottoman palace and capital. Many of them spent a substantial part of their lives in Istanbul and wrote works in the Ottoman language.[3]

There were many overlaps among members of the various cultures. Thus Evliya himself belonged to the upper class, but during his travels he associated with so many dervishes, artisans, merchants and theologians from obscure places that we can use him as a guide through the urban culture of Ottoman Muslims. There were also educated non-Muslims who spoke the Ottoman language. In the nineteenth century at least there were many Armenian inhabitants of Istanbul who used Turkish both for everyday purposes and in writing.[4] A Turcophone group in central Anatolia, known as the Karamanlıs, wrote Turkish using Greek letters, and few Karamanlıs spoke Greek despite their Greek Orthodox faith.[5] Such groups thus participated in their particular religious culture, but also to a greater or lesser extent in the Ottoman urban culture of the Muslims.

Ottoman or Not? An Educated Non-Muslim

Particularly instructive is the case of the Moldavian prince, Demetrius Cantemir (1673–1723).[6] He was a son of Prince Constantin Cantemir, who governed Moldavia at the end of the seventeenth century under Ottoman sovereignty. At the age of fifteen he was sent to Istanbul to function as a kind of hostage for the obedience of his father. Except for brief intervals he lived in Istanbul from 1687 to 1691 and again from 1693 to 1710, until he himself was crowned prince of Moldavia. However, his reign lasted just a single year, due to his defection to the tsar in the war between Peter the Great and the sultan. Retreating with the Russian troops to Moscow and eventually to St Petersburg, in 1720 he followed the tsar on a campaign to the Caucasus. He died before his fiftieth birthday, shortly after his return from Astrachan to his Russian estate.

Cantemir used his long sojourn in Istanbul to study Ottoman culture, and in particular Ottoman music.[7] He also concerned himself with its architecture, designing the churches which were built for him. Above all, though, he was a writer. Ten books in various languages are extant, most of which were printed in his lifetime or soon after. Among them were two works on Ottoman music, with examples of scores, and three more about the history of his principality. His description of Moldavia was commissioned by the Berlin Academy of Sciences, to which Cantemir was elected in 1714, and which wished to find out more about a land little known in Europe.[8]

Cantemir's most renowned work is probably his history of the Ottoman

Empire, which was written in Latin but published in an English translation (soon followed by French and German editions).[9] Cantemir wrote this book after his defection to the tsar. In a certain sense, it was a justification for his action, which he did not wish to be seen as a simple case of betrayal and disloyalty by a vassal towards his sovereign. To this end Cantemir employed a philosophical model familiar in Ottoman historiography, but which he used in a quite original way. According to Cantemir, the Ottoman Empire had won its last great military victories in the late seventeenth century and had been in a state of decline ever since. From the late sixteenth century, Muslim writers had expressed similar opinions, in the hope of developing policies which would delay the disintegration of the empire for as long as possible. Cantemir, on the other hand, saw the difficulties of the Ottoman administration as a welcome opportunity to pursue his own political ambitions. By defecting, he hoped as prince of Moldavia to prepare the way for the future independence of his state, something which he claimed had become a real possibility again in the new political situation.[10] Like all such apologies, this explanation should be regarded with some scepticism. A quarrel with the grand vizier about the level of tribute demanded of him seems to have been the more immediate spark for Cantemir's change of sides.

Cantemir's account of Ottoman history is on two levels. In the main text there is a history of political and military events, arranged according to the reigns of the sultans and strongly influenced by the model of Ottoman imperial chronicles. At the end of each reign, however, there is an assessment of the character of the sultan in question, something which is absent from the Ottoman chronicles and which was inspired by European examples. Moreover, Cantemir inserts imaginary speeches by main characters at dramatic moments in the account, which he presents as verbatim quotations. This practice also goes back ultimately to the Greco-Roman tradition of historiography. In addition, Cantemir incorporates personal observations for the period which he had experienced at first hand, a proceeding found in both Ottoman and European chronicles. In the footnotes we find details about geography and particularly about individuals involved in contemporary Ottoman politics, as well as about manners and customs, idiomatic expressions and historical documents. Cantemir also sometimes finds room for gossip from the city and court.[11]

In particular, there is a great deal of information about the topography and architecture of Istanbul in the late seventeenth century, including a map.[12] Moreover, in the case of some of the capital's buildings, Cantemir not only provides historical information, but also relevant examples of Istanbul's folklore. Thus he reports that all Ottoman mosques had uniform minarets, or at least that the minarets of any one mosque were very similar, with the single exception of the Aya Sofya. Apparently the people of Istanbul thought that

B/c it is special symbolism

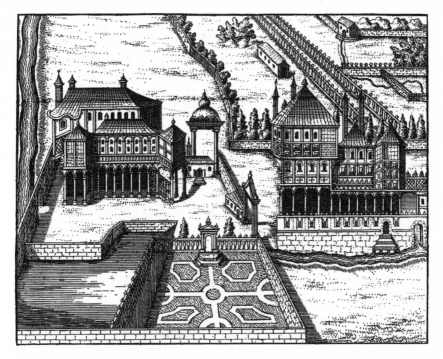

1. Palace of Prince Demetrius Cantemir

From: Demetrius Cantemir, *The History of the Growth and Decay of the Ottoman Empire* (London: John James and Paul Knapton, 1734)

Note the division of the palace complex into two parts. As in Ottoman palaces owned by Muslims, one part was probably reserved for male visitors, the other for family life. The garden gateway, which gives access to the gardens in the foreground, shows European classicist influences, although the complex as a whole is otherwise Ottoman in character.

the sultan had decreed it thus in order to draw attention to the unique quality of the great building.[13] As a student of architecture, Cantemir was also interested in the history of his own palaces in Istanbul. One of these was at Ortaköy, on the shores of the Bosphorus; after his defection it passed to an Ottoman princess. While the palace has long since vanished, the map of Istanbul prefacing his work is decorated with a vignette of the building, giving us at least an impression of its appearance.[14]

At the tsar's court, Cantemir's historical work appears to have been regarded as a compendium of politically-relevant information. A Russian translation was produced for 'official' purposes on the orders of Peter the Great, but never published. Cantemir's own position seems more ambivalent.

In his work he sides with the Orthodox Church and, less obviously but nevertheless perceptibly, with the tsar, whose subject he had now become and to whom he was indebted for his new princely rank. In his description of the Ottoman–Habsburg war of 1683–99, which almost entirely dominates the pages dedicated to the sultans of those years, his sympathies are quite clearly on the side of the Habsburgs. 'His Most Christian Majesty' (Louis XIV) and his diplomats are the subjects of frequent ironic asides because of the Ottoman–French accord.[15] In religious matters Cantemir also regards Islam as the great enemy, differing little from European authors of the same period who wrote about the Ottoman–Habsburg conflict.[16]

However, Cantemir had first-hand experience of the political life of Istanbul, and he often appears to admire the structure of the Ottoman state. This is apparent in his sympathetic treatment of Süleyman the Magnificent and, with a few reservations, of Selim I.[17] Even when describing the political processes of his own age, a period which he had already defined as a period of decay in the very title of his work, he finds many positive aspects. Thus he mentions the bonus payments due to soldiers when a new ruler took the throne, and discusses the suggestion that they motivated the soldiers to bring about the fall of the sultan as often as possible in order to obtain more money. He argues that in fact the rule was by no means destabilizing for the Ottoman state, since the sultan's awareness that he could so easily be toppled by the soldiers generally persuaded him not to abuse his power in a tyrannical fashion.[18]

Cantemir is similarly subtle in his analysis of the powers of the grand vizier, who was able to behave as a ruler for as long as he had the trust of the sultan.[19] As a result, the sovereign could distance himself from a measure which was unpopular among soldiers and other subjects by blaming it on the vizier. Despite his power, the grand vizier had no choice but to remain loyal to the sultan. Due to widespread awe for the House of Osman, he could not hope to become sultan himself even if he managed to topple the present ruler. Nor did the grand vizier have anything to gain from a coup and the arrival upon the throne of someone who was often young, and always inexperienced. New sultans regularly dispensed with viziers who had been disloyal to their predecessors. By throwing all responsibility on to the current grand vizier, the sultan could survive most eruptions of popular discontent. Only if the sultan did not avail himself of this tactic, or did so too late, did he have to fear for his own position. This was what happened to Sultan Mustafa II in 1703, when he was reluctant to break with his mentor, Sheikh Feyzullah.

An influential Turkish historian of the present day has said that during Cantemir's time in Istanbul the future defector functioned as a mediator, enabling educated Ottomans to become familiar with European culture.[20]

Cantemir was indeed a friend of the then Grand Vizier Rami Mehmed Pasha, himself an important literary figure, and of other members of the Ottoman élite who took an interest in history and the arts. In the last years of his life, after the death of his first wife, it seems that Cantemir became deeply nostalgic for Istanbul and Ottoman culture and that he tried to communicate the Ottoman outlook in Europe. All his life, then, he was an ambivalent figure. Perhaps this human interpretation of Cantemir's eventful career is the most convincing of all.

It remains to be discovered whether Cantemir was simply a unique figure or whether the story of his life reflects more general truths about his time. We do not really know whether Cantemir's defection from the Ottoman sultan to a rising opponent and competitor was typical of the behaviour of educated non-Muslims at that time. Generally, the intellectual life of non-Muslim Ottomans has been examined against the background of the nation to which they are said to have belonged, but which in fact often arose only long after their death. Cyrillos Lucaris has been of interest to modern historians as a representative of the educated Greek clergy (see Chapter 4). Cantemir's work has been examined above all by Romanian scholars, who see his books and musical compositions as a part of their national cultural inheritance.[21] These are by no means entirely invalid approaches, since the Greek language and cultural tradition were indeed of central importance to Greek Orthodox clergy of the seventeenth century. Cantemir, meanwhile, demonstrates in his works on the history of Moldavia that his succession to the region's governorship was more than a matter of chance; he really did feel that he belonged there. In another sense, however, research which is limited by national borders has been unhelpful to our understanding of many non-Muslim Ottomans with intellectual interests. Such a view does not admit of the 'Ottoman' element within their works. Neither can an approach which stresses unduly the Greek or Moldavian aspects of their identities do justice to their involvement in a cosmopolitan, European context. A whole book could be written on this topic; here we must content ourselves with merely alluding to the problem.

The Frontiers – or How Some Ottomans Regarded Foreigners

In the last chapter we presented the 'real' Ottoman Empire, the one experienced by its inhabitants, as a plurality of overlapping networks. In many cases the political frontiers also marked the extent of the networks. Only commercial networks were different, in that they extended to foreign centres of trade such as Tabriz, Vienna or Venice. From the second half of the sixteenth century, the frontiers which were uppermost in the minds of the Ottoman Empire's inhabitants were probably those with the Habsburg possessions in the west, and with Safavid Iran. In Africa south of Egypt, in Yemen and in the steppes of southern Russia and the Ukraine before the late seventeenth century, there were no organized, substantial states beyond Ottoman territory. As the Ottoman documents of the late sixteenth century show, it was a long time before the expansion of the tsars in the steppes began to be perceived as a danger.[22] By contrast, conflicts were frequent at the Habsburg–Ottoman and Iranian–Ottoman borders. These wars posed a considerable threat to the peoples of the frontier regions and were a constantly recurring financial burden on the central provinces. Only for the soldiers and their commanders was war a lottery which might sometimes produce a winning ticket.

There is little evidence of what workers and taxpayers thought of the wars which affected their lives. We do know, however, that some people attempted to avoid the financial obligations these wars placed upon them. There were often quarrels between guilds about which guild was assigned to which other as its 'helper'(*yamak*). Such a 'helper' had to do its bit to help pay the senior guild's taxes.[23] If it were necessary, guilds would also equip a master to accompany the army and supply those goods required by the soldiers. This could also cause disputes between masters of guilds. If such a case were brought before the *kadi*, accusations would only be made about a rival guild, not about a vizier, still less about a sultan. However, in 1730 things were different: the guildmasters of Istanbul had been required to contribute to the preparation of a campaign, the start of which had been postponed over and over again. The resulting discontent grew into a revolt which cost the sultan his throne and the grand vizier his head.[24] Perhaps one of the purposes of the extravagant craftsmen's processions in Istanbul before a campaign, of which there are several seventeenth-century descriptions, was to exhibit, amid all the pomp, the unity between the sultan and the guildmasters, thereby averting any discontent.[25]

What did a young, intelligent officer, a future interpreter with a talent for languages, make of life at the Habsburg border? How did he see the war which officially lasted from 1683 to 1699 but which continued as an apparently unending series of frontier skirmishes? This we can discover from a book which its editors entitled *The Life and Adventures of Osman Ağa*.[26] In 1688 the author became a prisoner of war and overcame numerous obstacles to obtain the ransom demanded by his captors. However, his treacherous master did not release him even then. Instead, he was conveyed into the interior of Austria, where he found himself in the service of Count Schallenberg, learned the confectioner's trade, visited Vienna and travelled with the count to Italy and Hungary. Finally in 1699, after the Treaty of Karlowitz, Osman Ağa was able to flee to Ottoman territory. In the process he occasionally disguised himself as an imperial Habsburg officer, a role which he was able to play convincingly as a result of his linguistic prowess. Other adventures during Osman Ağa's escape included a dangerous journey down the Danube and an equally hair-raising crossing of the newly-determined frontier.

In the early years of his captivity, Osman appears to have seen himself basically as the helpless victim of recurring ill-fortune, exemplified in the episodes of his capture, exploitation and kidnapping. All his efforts to protect himself appeared to be in vain. Nevertheless, this probably largely accurate conception of his circumstances did not persuade him to give up the struggle. On the contrary, he was constantly on the look-out for the right opportunity to achieve his long-term aim of defeating the odds and returning home.[27]

With this idea in mind, Osman Ağa resisted all his master's attempts to persuade him to change religion and remain permanently in his service. He was prepared to risk his life to return to his home, the town of Temeşvar (Timisoara). For all that, he was capable of making subtle observations of the people whom he encountered in the course of his adventures. Osman Ağa was quite prepared to admit that even people on the opposing side might behave humanely. Despite his many harsh experiences, his general attitude was by no means petulant or defensive. His greatest scorn was reserved for those who broke their word and for soldiers who left their unit in order to murder and plunder on their own account. His concise descriptions of the desolate landscape and semi-destroyed settlements bear impressive witness to the horror of war.[28] His experience of the division between the Christian and Islamic world is the basis for Osman Ağa's whole account. Nevertheless, when he finally returned home he did not attempt to leave all his experiences in Austria behind him. Osman Ağa worked for the rest of his life as an interpreter and intermediary, wrote a book about the history of the 'Germans' and later, when the currents of the time swept him to Istanbul, earned his living as interpreter to the Habsburg envoy.[29]

An artless treatment of first-hand experiences is also characteristic of another author who wrote about his time as a prisoner of war in the second half of the seventeenth century. He was an Egyptian janissary named Süleyman, who, after his capture towards the end of the seventeenth century, was assigned to a French nobleman.[30] His master took him to France, where he assisted him in learning the building trade. With the appreciation of a master builder, the janissary observed the French fortresses and the Louvre. In the account he wrote after his return, the author notes that at first he had hesitated to describe his experiences lest he be accused of displaying undue sympathy towards the unbelievers. Only after his officers had set his mind at rest on this matter did he decide to go ahead.

As one might expect, the tale by the Egyptian janissary is based at least partly on the common literary topos of travel literature as a vehicle for criticism of the author's own society. This topos was also very popular in European literature of the seventeenth and eighteenth centuries.[31] Moreover, it is a definite feature of Evliya Çelebi's work. In his accounts of his visits to Chios and Vienna, Evliya describes how carefully the unbelievers looked after their churches and libraries and comments that Muslims would do well to follow their example.[32] His descriptions of the flourishing towns he claimed to have seen on his journey from Buda to Vienna, and which actually appear to be largely of his own invention, are probably designed to do more than just add interest to his report. Probably they were also intended to contribute to the topos of the industrious unbelievers and encourage his compatriots to take a leaf from the Austrians' book.

Evliya's description of Vienna – there is, incidentally, an excellent translation into German available – can also help us to understand how Ottomans perceived their frontiers, especially if we compare this work with the reports of the many Habsburg envoys to Istanbul.[33] Both Evliya and the Habsburg ambassadors have commented on attempts to uphold the reputation of the relevant sovereign by dogged one-upmanship in matters of ceremonial detail, and other diplomats were no strangers to these experiences either. Evliya describes such disputes with a certain irony. Thus, he reports the refusal of the Ottoman ambassador to have the janissary band play at the presentation of gifts at the Viennese court, simply on account of the fact that the Habsburgs had requested it. This despite the fact that, shortly before the Habsburg request was received, the ambassador himself had ordered that an Ottoman military band should play.[34] Looking beyond such matters, Evliya's account is on two levels. On the one hand, much space is devoted to recollections of the siege of Vienna by Sultan Süleyman. Throughout Evliya's report recur the adventures of Voyvoda Kasım, one of Süleyman's semi-mythical commanders, along with the heroic deeds and death of an anonymous Circassian soldier in the siege of 1529.[35] In the context of these tales of derring-do, the hope is expressed that the Ottomans will one day succeed in conquering the city. It is in this light that we should understand Evliya's portrayal of the Habsburg emperor as the very quintessence of ugliness, although the unfortunate ruler is described as clever. It has to be conceded that the features of many Habsburgs also did not quite live up to the European aesthetic ideal of the time.[36] Be that as it may, Evliya is somewhat cautious in expressing his hopes that Vienna might one day be taken by the Ottomans, fearing that the buildings of the imperial city which he so admires would never survive a war unscathed.

Indeed, one of the characteristics of Evliya's account is its attention to the beauty of buildings and paintings, especially in his descriptions of the Imperial Palace and St Stephen's Cathedral. However, the Ottoman traveller did have difficulties with those features which were unfamiliar to him from Istanbul churches, such as the rib-vaulting of the cathedral, which he misconstrued as domes. Evliya admitted that, as well as buildings, gardens and paintings, the dexterity of Viennese doctors and surgeons represented a positive side to life among the unbelievers. He recounted several anecdotes about the wounds and sicknesses they were able to cure.[37] Our traveller also found praise for the merchants, and he mitigated a critical comment about flirting in public by conceding that there were, after all, many good-looking people in the area.

Among all these positive points, the question of the religious divide is articulated only occasionally. We do not get the impression that for Evliya the arts and skills of the Viennese were devalued because the artists, doctors and craftsmen were unbelievers. There is little hint of the topos which is so frequent a feature of European travel literature about the Ottoman Empire, namely that the people 'beyond the divide' were incapable of achieving anything worthwhile because they followed a 'false' religion.[38] Evliya certainly believed that the Viennese were following a 'false' religion, but this by no means caused him to consider them barbarians.

It seems, then, that Evliya viewed the skilful unbelievers as potentially valuable additions to the Ottoman state and that this made it seem worthwhile to look at them in detail. Evliya himself came from an artistic family – his father was a court goldsmith – and as a young man he had received a musical education. For these reasons alone buildings and pictures, as well as the music which he heard in Vienna, were bound to impress him.[39] More than this, however, Evliya's 'urban' identity probably contributed to his generally positive assessment of Vienna. For this traveller at least, culture as we understand it today was inconceivable outside towns. The Viennese proved their affection for their town by maintaining it, adorning it with beautiful buildings and keeping it clean, and this in itself endeared them to Evliya.

Access for Foreigners to Ottoman Culture

At both the Ottoman–Iranian and Habsburg–Ottoman borders there was a sort of cultural 'no man's land'. This zone was crossed fairly frequently and in both directions. During the Ottoman–Safavid conflict in the sixteenth century, Iranian Sunni jurists and theologians entered the country, and some went on to become senior Ottoman state officials. Mirza Mahdum, for example, who had been a teacher to the future shah of Iran, Ismail II, died as the *kadi* of Mecca, after having achieved the rank of *kadi* of Istanbul in 1586.[40] There was a particularly large influx of Persian-speaking immigrants in the second half of the sixteenth century, when certain regions of the Caucasus and western Iran came under Ottoman control, some of them briefly, some for extended periods. Two factions formed in the Ottoman bureaucracy at that time. On the one hand there were the 'Rumelians', members of various ethnic groups of the Balkans selected for court service after forming part of the well-known levy of boys. On the other, there were the immigrants from Iranian territory.[41] Mustafa Âlî, the Ottoman bureaucrat and historian who observed the rise of these potential rivals with a degree of irritation, believed that the Ottoman court should be extremely selective in appointing foreigners. He saw the infiltration of formerly Iranian soldiers and bureaucrats as a potential threat to the solidarity among state officials and in particular to their loyalty towards the sultan.[42]

Things were rather different at the Ottoman–Habsburg land border, where those taken prisoner by the Ottomans were non-Muslims. Unlike the Iranians, they could therefore legally be enslaved and used as servants in households or as workers on the estates belonging to the sultan's great foundations in the surroundings of Istanbul. Many prisoners would be taken after successful Ottoman campaigns, and they were correspondingly cheap as slaves. In their journey together through the Ottoman territories in the mid-sixteenth century, Busbecq and Dernschwam encountered many such people.[43] If a prisoner's freedom were not bought by his relatives, his chances of ever leaving the Ottoman domain were not very great. Some of them attempted to flee, but the odds against eluding recapture were considerable. In many Anatolian provinces there was an official who was responsible for recovering escaped prisoners and stray cattle. There were substantial fees in such cases, and as a consequence the local official would detain any suspects to verify their identity. Freed slaves could apply for and receive a document to confirm their status and protect them in the event of such checks. Some European slaves succeeded in being bought by a consul or ambassador, in whose service they would eventually leave the empire. However, this could cause problems, as the Ottoman authorities often sought to prevent the departure of workers who, moreover, were Muslims or at least potential Muslims. A sultan's decree of 1587 refers to a convent in Athens where the nuns were allegedly hiding female slaves and assisting them to escape. Now the local authorities were to put an end to this.[44] Some prisoners also may have doubted that after so long an absence they would receive a warm welcome home. Goods might in the meantime have been taken over by their relatives, and a wife or fiancée might well have assumed the death of her partner and married somebody else.

Many slaves therefore probably attempted to make the best of their situation and build a new life for themselves. To do this they needed to win the trust of their owner or, if this were impossible, to bring about their sale to another (they hoped) more sympathetic proprietor.[45] Such owners often released a slave after periods which varied in duration, either in exchange for performing some special service or as a pious act.[46] In the fifteenth and sixteenth centuries, weavers and textile merchants in Bursa often promised their slaves freedom once they had woven a set quantity of material.[47] Such a promise, delivered in front of witnesses, was binding and could not be revoked unilaterally by the master. Others promised that when they died, their slaves would be freed; in this case too, their word was binding. If an owner recognized that a female slave had borne him a child, she would be automatically released after his death according to religious law. Many individuals were therefore enslaved only for a certain period. There seem to have been very few second-generation slaves who spent their entire lives in bondage. Nevertheless, the fate of individual slaves depended entirely on the character and intentions of their owner. Hans Wild, a mercenary from Nuremberg who travelled throughout the Ottoman Empire between 1604 and 1609 as the slave of various merchants and military officers, reports that he was finally bought by an Egyptian janissary commander. Unlike his previous masters the Egyptian treated him well, offered him opportunities to earn money, and gave him his freedom a year later.[48]

Between Cultures: Sailors and Corsairs

Such former slaves doubtless spent their whole lives between two cultures. However, there are few descriptions of how they coped with their situation. Among the seafarers and corsairs there are better-documented examples of people who belonged to more than one culture. Their outlooks are expressed, for example, in the story of a gaoler-captain of the seventeenth century.[49] Known in Ottoman as *deniz levendleri* ('freebooters of the sea'), the heroes of this tale waged their own guerrilla war on Christian ships, particularly those of Malta. Any members of the captured crews who wished to join them were received with open arms. If these new shipmates later converted to Islam their decision would be greeted enthusiastically as an opportunity for celebration. However, even seamen who had not (yet) converted were welcome on board if they proved their skill and boldness, as did the hero of the gaoler-captain story.

In this world it was an accepted fact of life that one had to beware of all the established powers, including the Ottoman state. When the officers of the corsair ship in the story were summoned to the pasha of Cyprus, they suspected that a trap lay behind the flattering words of the invitation, and made themselves scarce.[50] In all probability, this provincial governor was motivated mainly by political considerations. He would not have wanted the corsairs' behaviour to lead to conflict with other states. However, cultural differences were also involved; thus a provincial governor happily allows his 'wayward' son to sail off with the corsairs.[51]

Even with the Algerian and Tunisian seamen, who shared their own background, the gaoler-captain and his friends could not maintain amicable relations for long. As demonstrated by many records in the archives of the Spanish and Papal Inquisitions this instability was a characteristic cultural trait of Mediterranean seamen and corsairs. After having served aboard an Ottoman corsair ship, many seamen returned to the Inquisition's domain voluntarily or under duress, namely after they had been taken prisoner by Maltese or Spanish patrols. Those who had taken up arms against Christians, something which entailed a degree of volition, would be treated more harshly than those who had merely manned an oar in a galley. If the prisoner persuaded the court that he had converted to Islam under pressure from his master, he might be treated leniently, as the judges accepted that, in such a situation, slaves had few alternatives.[52] On general principles however, a person appearing before the Inquisition's court was well advised to conceal as best he could the extent of his cultural acclimatization among the Ottomans.

Even so, it is clear that many individuals appearing before the court had opted for the Islamic world without coercion and also (in some cases) returned home of their own choice. In the second half of the sixteenth century and during the seventeenth, the frontier was easier to cross at this level of the 'ordinary people' than it was at the level of high culture. Certain Spanish and Calabrian fishermen who settled in North Africa were aware of this fact and exploited it to move back and forth across the front-lines.[53] The very specific society of the *deniz levendleri*, who incidentally developed their own *lingua franca* based on a mixture of Italian and Greek expressions, constituted a transit zone between Ottoman and Catholic Mediterranean culture.[54] This frontier society is reflected with similar vividness in the Ottoman story of the gaoler-captain and in the testimony of former corsairs and galley slaves before the courts of the Spanish and Italian Inquisitions.

'Educated' Border Crossers

As well as the fishermen, farmers and soldiers, about whom we generally have little in the way of evidence, there were people who had received an education in their native country before they crossed the border. Sometimes they took this step of their own volition; in other cases, they arrived as prisoners of war who ultimately converted to Islam and stayed. One famous example from the seventeenth century is that of Ali Ufkî. From a Protestant noble family, he was born aound 1610 in Lwow, then in the kingdom of Poland, as Wojciech Bobowski.[55] When writing in Latin and Italian, he sometimes used the pen-name of Albertus or Alberto Bobovius/Bobovio. Presumably as a young man, Bobovius was taken prisoner by the Tartars and taken to Istanbul. Shortly after arrival he was brought to the sultan's palace.

His age suggests that he was a schoolmate of Evliya Çelebi's although Evliya does not seem to have mentioned him by name.

Similarly to the young Evliya, Ali Ufkî, as he was known after his conversion to Islam, chose music as his 'main subject' at the page school, his instrument being the dulcimer (*santur*). It seems that he had already received a thorough grounding in this art while still in Poland, because soon after starting his musical education at the palace he began to notate the melodies he had learnt. He reports that originally he did this for his own benefit, in order to remind himself of anything he might have forgotten.[56] Soon the other pages in his classes began to ask him for help whenever they did not remember the melodies they had been taught. Ultimately, Ali Ufkî became director of music of the page choir, spending a full nineteen years in the palace. A composer in his own right, he also notated about three hundred of the melodies which were to be heard in the Topkapı Palace in the first half of the seventeenth century.[57]

Ali Ufkî had many friends both among the intellectuals of Istanbul and among the educated foreigners who were resident in the Ottoman capital at the time. He worked closely with the Ottoman scholar Hüseyin Hezarfenn (*c.* 1600–*c.* 1679), whose sobriquet of 'the man of a thousand skills' alludes to his interest in numerous branches of learning.[58] Ali Ufkî also knew Antoine Galland, who first translated *A Thousand and One Nights* into a European language. Galland also gave the French Enlightenment figure Pierre Bayle the information about Ali Ufkî which Bayle included in his encyclopaedia.[59] Throughout his life Ali Ufkî apparently maintained his ambiguous position between two religions and two cultures. He wrote Ottoman poetry and a famous description of the Topkapı Sarayı, as well as setting an Ottoman version of the Psalms to music and translating the Old and New Testaments into the Ottoman language. A modernized version of Ufkî's Bible translation is still in use among Turkish-speaking Christians of today.[60]

Another educated central European who settled among the Ottomans was Ibrahim Müteferrika (*c.* 1674–1745), originally from the Transylvanian town of Koloszvar (Cluj). He may have been educated at a Latin school in his native town.[61] He himself reports that even at this time, before he entered the Ottoman domain, he had secretly studied books hostile to the doctrine of the Trinity. He was probably referring to the works of the Unitarians, who had been active in Transylvania while this principality was within the Ottoman orbit. Probably the Ottoman authorities regarded the Unitarians, who were persecuted in most European countries, as a counter-force against the pro-Catholic zeal of the Habsburgs. Moreover, the rejection of the Trinity did represent genuine common ground between the Muslims and the Unitarians. This at any rate is how Ibrahim Müteferrika appears to present the situation in his still-unpublished autobiography.[62] At least until there is proof to the contrary, it seems wisest to accept this version rather than the alternative ones, which suggest that he converted to Islam as a Calvinist prisoner of war.

We know neither what Ibrahim's name was in Transylvania, nor how he developed his knowledge of Ottoman language and culture. Nevertheless, we do know that after arriving in Istanbul he quickly made a name for himself in the Ottoman bureaucracy. In 1715 he was sent to Vienna to negotiate with Prince Eugen. In later years he was liaison officer to Rakóczi Ferenc, who came to the Ottoman Empire in 1717 to help construct a French–Ottoman alliance against the Habsburgs and for Hungarian independence. In this connection Ibrahim Müteferrika also wrote a military work, advocating the modernization of the Ottoman army along the lines of the European model.[63]

For our purposes, though, Ibrahim is important not so much as a diplomat and writer on military matters, but rather as a scholar and as founder of the first printing press specializing in Ottoman books. After completing an early work he took no further part in religious polemics. As laid down in a sultan's decree, his printing press was not to publish any kind of religious works. Instead, Ibrahim Müteferrika concentrated on history and geography, printing the *Imperial Chronicles* of Naima (1655–1716) and of Mehmed Raşid (died 1735).[64] For many of these works, Ibrahim Müteferrika provided his own commentaries and he took a particular interest in the publication of maps.

For and Against the Art of Printing

It has long been a matter for debate among Turkish, European and recently also Tunisian scholars, why the printing of Ottoman works began only in the eighteenth century. A series of religious, aesthetic, socio-political and ultimately economic factors played a part in this. From 1588, when Murad III (reign: 1575–95) issued the necessary decree, it was explicitly permitted to import and possess non-religious books published in Europe using the Arabic alphabet.[65] However, Ottoman customers generally showed very little interest in printed books. Thus, although there was much demand for a certain work by Ibn Sīnā (Avicenna, 980–1037), it proved impossible to sell this text in print, even at a lower price than was being demanded in Europe.[66]

Many Istanbul bibliophiles regarded the Arabic characters generally used in Europe as decidedly unlovely. This problem was aggravated by the fact that many printers there based their typefaces on North African models, which were seen in Istanbul as foreign and unattractive. Concern about the survival of calligraphy was also a factor. This had evolved to the status of a high art-form in the Islamic middle ages and was widely practised in early modern Istanbul.[67] Many Ottoman scholars and literary figures no doubt were sensitive to the threat which ugly-looking printed texts posed to this highly-regarded art.[68]

Another problem resulted from the many errors contained in a high proportion of printed texts. European printed versions of the literary classics of Islamic civilization, not least because of the linguistic deficiencies of their publishers, were often peppered with mistakes. Of course, readers of that time would have been familiar with manuscripts containing errors, but the same problem in a new type of book, which was in any case regarded with a degree of suspicion, would have seemed a more serious matter. A further consideration was the possibility that once the art of printing was introduced the Qu'rān would eventually be printed. This did indeed occur in the late nineteenth century.[69] As the Word of God, the Qu'rān had been carried down through the ages in very careful copies, and making these copies was regarded as a way of earning religious merit. From a religious point of view, then, it seemed unacceptable that the holy text should be subjected to error-strewn duplication through the printing press. Moreover, the printing of the Qu'rān would mark the end of a significant way of achieving religious merit among literate Muslims; as soon as there were sufficient printed copies available, copying by hand would lose its purpose.

Printing also had the drawback of arriving in the Muslim world as a 'Christian invention'. This seemed less important where innovations in weaponry or seafaring were concerned, as in such cases it could always be argued that the inventions of the unbelievers would increase future successes against them in war. Of course, not all educated Ottomans saw the problem of cultural contacts and imports in such narrow terms. Evliya's remarks about the organ music he encountered in his visit to Vienna show that he respected organ-makers and players simply for their skills and the beauty of their work.[70] On the other hand, neither did Evliya suggest introducing organ music to the Ottoman Empire. For many people, including Ottoman Christians, the 'foreignness' of printed books remained a problem for a considerable time. Thus a Jesuit missionary wrote in 1652 that he preferred to work with hand-written tracts, since printed matter was instinctively regarded as 'Frankish' even by Ottoman Christians.[71]

Moreover, by no means all literary figures and theologians were convinced that the spread of reading was a good thing. In the Ottoman Empire, just as in many other non-industrial societies, there was a conception that a frank debate about certain problems might be tolerated so long as only a few, well-educated people participated in it. This was how many of the mystics who indulged in bold speculations, highly suspicious to most rulers and theologians, had been able to save themselves from persecution. There was, after all, no Ottoman equivalent to the Inquisition, which aimed to discover the most secret beliefs and practices of the faithful. In the Ottoman world, the philosophies of small groups and the communications between their members, either oral or in very cryptic written form, did not cause the authorities to intervene so long as no public nuisance was caused. In the comments attributed to them by Lady Mary Wortley Montagu, some Ottoman dignitaries sound almost like freethinkers. Such remarks belonged within a 'private' sphere of cultivated gentlemen and, sometimes, ladies.[72] Certain literary figures and dervishes may well have feared that their already limited freedoms would shrink even further if knowledge were to be obtained chiefly from printed books, which were generally available and thus heavily censored.

At least until well into the seventeenth century, the Ottoman bureaucracy also looked on printed books as a potential source of conflict. This is clear from the reaction to the Calvinist tracts which the Orthodox patriarch Cyrillos Lucaris had printed in Istanbul in 1627.[73] The grand vizier and his advisers probably feared that unpredictable political consequences might develop from conversions of the Orthodox to another Christian denomination. However, the doubts regarding printed books which resulted from such considerations were by no means spontaneous. In the early seventeenth century there were papal as well as Calvinist attempts to woo Orthodox believers. At a time when the tensions caused by the Reformation and Counter-Reformation exploded into the Thirty Years War, the French ambassador noted that he had taken care that the consequences of an expansion of Calvinist influence be made abundantly clear to the grand vizier.[74] Thus the measures taken against printing presses were based only partly on an aversion to printing itself.

As well as these political and religious-cum-cultural arguments against printed books, there was also an economic consideration. Thousands of people lived by copying books, even if the claim made by Luigi Fernando Marsigli, a Habsburg general and scholar, that there were 90,000 copiers in seventeenth-century Istanbul is clearly a considerable overestimate. Moreover, founding a printing press was expensive. The first machines had to be imported from Europe, and training the printers, who were highly qualified craftsmen, also had to be paid for. Due to these financial obstacles, Ibrahim Müteferrika's printing press occasionally foundered even during his lifetime, before doing so completely after his death. After a few more false starts in the late eighteenth century, continuous printing began in Istanbul only after 1800.[75]

Religious and Cultural Conflicts Among Ottoman Mulsims

So far we have looked at transitions, intercultural debate and the more-or-less successful communication between Islamic and Christian civilizations, both at the level of Istanbul's high culture and at that of the 'ordinary' people along the empire's various borders. Clearly, contemporary individuals did perceive an antithesis between the Christian and Islamic worlds whenever they thought about the issue in the conventional terms of their particular religious culture. However, as we have seen, the Ottomans of the seventeenth and eighteenth centuries were often involved in a relationship with the 'other side' which had little to do with such abstract principles.

Some bitter cultural conflicts, however, had nothing to do with the antithesis between the Christian and Islamic worlds, but rather with antagonisms within Islam itself. Thus, until the early sixteenth century there were dervishes in Anatolia and other parts of the Islamic world who led ascetic lives which challenged the practices of ordinary townspeople in general and those of jurists and theologians in particular. As to the piety of 'established' men of God, it seems to have been viewed by these ascetics (few of them put their thoughts into writing) as mere worldly vanity.[76] The 'real' ascetic saw himself as dead before his physical death. Begging (or at least not working) and retreating to deserts or cemeteries were other features of this form of piety. In the first centuries of Ottoman power, the sultans tolerated and sometimes even patronized these ascetics. However, following the start of the wars against the Shiite Safavids (1514), the Ottoman sultans saw themselves more and more as the defenders of Sunni Islam, as it was represented by jurists and theologians. This led to brutal repression of those dervishes who did not adhere to the religious laws and conventions of urban society, even though by no means all such ascetics were Shiites. Only by seeking the shelter of a recognized dervish order could they protect themselves from this persecution, and most of them chose the Bektashis.[77]

We do not know how these dervishes, seen by many researchers as 'antisocial', reacted to their persecution. However, we do know that members of another heterodox group within Anatolian Islam actively incited the conflict rather than simply suffering the consequences. Such behaviour is memorably evoked in the poems ascribed to Pir Sultan Abdal and his circle. Our knowledge of the author is confined to a few pieces of information disclosed in his poems. There is also a dirge in which a daughter of the poet functions as the speaker (the poetic first person).[78] Pir Sultan Abdal describes himself as a radical supporter of the shah of Iran, whom he perceives as a religious figure, and from whom he will never allow himself to be separated. Brought before the Ottoman governor Hızır Pasha in 'bloody Sıvas', Pir Sultan Abdal steadfastly refuses to renounce his loyalty. A legend also claims that the poet was offered an amnesty if he would sing three songs which did not relate to the shah.[79] Pir Sultan Abdal rose to the challenge, and wrote three texts including a call to the shah in every stanza. He then accepted the news of his death sentence bravely, even joyfully.

If the story is based on fact, it probably took place in the sixteenth century. However, even if it is pure fiction, its survival right up to the present day demonstrates the depth of the cultural conflict between the Ottoman élite and the dissident peasants and nomads of Anatolia. Today known as Alevî, these people were called 'red heads' (Kızılbaş) after the ceremonial headgear of their leaders. Religious conflict apart, a political challenge to the Ottoman sultan was also involved. Far from being celebrated as the defender of Islam, this ruler was denounced as the representative of a purely worldly power, to whom no pious person could or should offer allegiance. This attitude also explains why even in the 1960s and 1970s, some of the songs of the poet hanged so long ago in Sıvas became popular among Turkish leftist students.

Towns, Nomads and Sedentary Peoples

Kızılbaş/Alevî political loyalty to the shah of Iran, one of the sultan's main opponents, was certainly the main reason for the violent persecution to which these dissidents were subjected in the sixteenth century. In addition, however, it was probably significant that most Kızılbaş were villagers and nomads, although they were also represented in medium-sized towns such as Amasya, Tokat or Sıvas. In particular the nomads were systematically excluded from political power in the Ottoman Empire. Although they were expert with horses and weapons, they were only occasionally used as soldiers from the sixteenth century onwards, probably because the sultans feared that they might desert to the Safavid enemy at a critical juncture. Because of the nomad marginalization, most members of the Ottoman upper class would have had little contact even with their leading and princely families. Once again, the traveller Evliya Çelebi was an exception to the rule. He spent some time at the court of the Kurdish prince of Bitlis.[80]

Evliya did not miss the opportunity to describe in detail a world which was very foreign to his readers in the capital. However, he had less sympathy for the Bedouins whom he encountered in the course of his pilgrimage to Mecca (1671–72). As a member of a caravan which reached the Holy Cities only after many trials and tribulations, he did not appreciate Bedouin attempts to exploit the turmoil of the times. At the time the Ottoman ruler was waging war on Poland. This, in the eyes of Bedouin leaders, seemed a good opportunity to extort protection money from pilgrims, even though the central government regularly subsidized them with money and goods. Evliya applied various unfriendly epithets to the Bedouins and reports with obvious satisfaction that the commander of the caravan had arranged for the execution of some of their leaders in Medina.[81] It appears that many Ottoman Muslims believed that Bedouins lost their status as Muslims when they robbed pilgrims and extorted money from them. No thought was given to the possibility that the Bedouins also believed they were pursuing valid interests.

Women Who Crossed Borders

If we consider the networks and borders which have been discussed in this and the previous chapter, it might seem that women lived in isolation, did not participate in any networks and never crossed borders. Of course this was not the case. The problem is simply that fewer traces survive of the networks in which women were involved. Nevertheless, in the next chapter we shall examine aspects of their social relationships and cultural activities, at least where the women of the Istanbul upper class are concerned.

Some women, freely or under duress, are known to have entered or left the Ottoman domain. Demetrius Cantemir took his family with him when he moved to the Russian Empire. Both his wife and his sixteen-year-old daughter died shortly after this change in climate and culture.[82] There were also women among the prisoners taken by the Ottomans, and most of these spent the rest of their lives within the Ottoman cultural domain. Most were employed as domestic servants to Ottoman masters, or they might belong to a genteel lady. (The distinction is significant, as slaves belonging to an Ottoman woman could not be touched by her husband.) Quite frequently, women who had been slaves were remembered in the wills of their former masters or mistresses, or benefited from the establishment of a foundation. Such instances testified to the integration of these women within their owners' families. Sometimes owners would also free their female slaves in order to marry them.[83]

Some freedwomen rose to considerable eminence; such women were to be found above all in the sultan's palace. After completing his training in the Topkapı Sarayı the Spanish nobleman Gutierre Pantoja, first a page and then a senior officer in the Ottoman navy, obeyed custom by marrying a former palace servant (see Chapter 6). He reports only that she was named Alime and was a Russian or a Ukrainian; he does not even mention her Christian name. By the time Pantoja came to describe his life as an Ottoman to the court of the Inquisition, she had long since died.[84] Other former slave girls of the palace were more fortunate. Hurrem Sultan, for example, who even achieved formal marriage to Sultan Süleyman the Magnificent (reign: 1520–66), was also a former Russian or Ukrainian slave.[85] Some prominent Ottomans were quite open about their slave background. Fatima (Fatma), the wife of a senior Ottoman state official, told her friend Lady Mary Wortley Montagu that talking about her mother's past as a foreign slave caused her no discomfort at all.[86]

Of course there were also Ottoman women captives in the service of aristocratic European families, particularly in the Habsburg domain. Compiling archival evidence of the lives they led would be a worthwhile project, but it has not yet been undertaken. From the report by the Temesvar soldier Osman Ağa, we know that some such women took control of their own destinies: there were two women among his companions on his dangerous flight back to Ottoman territory.[87] Women who crossed the divide between the Ottoman domain and the states of the Christian kings in either direction also crop up in the biographies narrated to the courts of the Inquisition. A great deal of work remains to be done on the matter of female border crossers, but our picture of them could become much clearer in the future.[88]

6

Women's Culture

Only in the last twenty or thirty years have Europeanist historians turned their attention more fully to women as historical figures. Until the 1970s the historians of the Ottoman realm also largely neglected women. One of the major questions which then arose concerns the material goods possessed by women. 'What did Ottoman women do with their property?' also remains a favourite topic among historians of Ottoman women.[1] Underlying this concern with property is the fact that Ottoman women – in law, at least – retained control of their property even after they married, unlike most European married women who gained control of their property only in the nineteenth or twentieth century. Similarly, women were subjects of the empire in their own right as soon as they reached puberty. Again unlike many European married women, they could therefore complain to the *kadi* about any injustice suffered – and also, of course, be accused or sued by others. In the towns, where there was relatively easy recourse to law, women did take advantage of their legal rights. However, many of them must have found themselves at a disadvantage in the law courts. There would have been informal pressure from their male relatives, and religious law limited considerably women's ability to bear witness themselves.[2]

Thus, most of our sources of information about Ottoman townswomen between the sixteenth and early nineteenth centuries come from the records of the *kadi* courts. Looking for other sources requires a good deal of imagination. Until recently, historians dealing with the European middle ages and the early modern period often conceded that the history of women did in fact belong within any comprehensive social history, but protested that unfortunately there was a dearth of the necessary sources. Growing interest in women's history has, however, brought a great deal of new material to light.[3] Historians of the Ottoman realm must now overcome similar difficulties. In recent years, greater attention has been paid to Ottoman women and more sources have indeed emerged, such as letters, diaries and personal household documents. Moreover, the rise of feminist movements in Turkey itself is likely to produce important research in the near future.[4]

Wives

In Ottoman society it was rare for anyone to remain unmarried all their lives. Marriages were arranged by parents, although young men were sometimes able to escape such arrangements if they were not to their liking, by moving elsewhere. Young girls and women had fewer options. There are very few references in the *kadi*s' registers to women who agreed to elope, and only slightly more to women who pleaded that they had been married as minors and now, having come of age, wished to dissolve the marriage. According to religious law it was possible for a Muslim man to marry a non-Muslim woman, although the opposite was not permitted and the children of 'mixed' marriages were considered Muslims.[5] Such marriages were quite common, particularly in frontier districts or in areas with a large non-Muslim population.[6] In the Peloponnese at least, Orthodox Christians at times entered their marriages in the *kadi*'s register, although neither religious law nor the sultan's regulations required them to do so.[7] We can only speculate about their motivations.

Despite all the impediments, there are examples of Ottoman women who played an active part in representing the family interests even while their husbands were alive. We know of an action brought by a Christian woman who lived in a village near the central Anatolian town of Kayseri in the mid-eighteenth century.[8] Her son-in-law had very probably murdered her daughter, and there was also a dispute regarding certain valuables. Whatever the facts of the matter, the plaintiff took the issue as far as Istanbul. Another case, involving a Muslim woman from a family of the central Anatolian élite, dates from the same period.[9] In connection with some unfathomable affair, the woman's husband had been arrested and she as plaintiff campaigned actively for his release. Clearly, some energetic women did find opportunities to step out from the shadows of their male relatives. The ways in which they contrived to do this would be worth investigating in their own right.[10]

Recent studies of the Ottoman institution of marriage have shown how much the significance of polygamy had previously been overestimated. It is hard to provide figures, as we do not have a complete list of all the inhabitants of a town, both male and female, with appended information concerning their personal status. However, it is clear enough from the evidence of all the inheritance cases brought before the *kadi*, the records of which fill many pages in the registers, that polygamy was relatively uncommon.[11] In the complete lists of heirs which form an important part of the relevant documents, there are few references to two wives, although widows were each entitled to a part of the inheritance and thus were bound to show up in the inheritance records. This finding has been confirmed so often that we must regard monogamy as the norm for the families of Anatolian townswomen.

Divorces were more frequent, and the husband could divorce his spouse unilaterally and without explanation at any time. We also know that some marriages were dissolved on the initiative of the woman. In such instances the husband would expect to be more or less handsomely remunerated for his consent. At the very least, any woman who desired divorce because (to use the official expression) 'there is a lack of good understanding between us' would have to give up the financial benefits which normally would have accrued to her at the termination of her marriage.[12] If the divorce were instigated by the husband, the wife had the right to a sum of money, agreed at the time of the marriage, and three months' alimony. Often, a woman seeking divorce would agree to pay her husband an additional sum of money. This form of separation was thus available only to affluent women.

In the early eighteenth century, polygamy was rather frowned upon among the well-to-do families of Istanbul described by Lady Mary Wortley Montagu (1689–1762). The wife of the English ambassador reported that the husband of one of her friends had recently taken a second wife. As a result, he lost his moral standing among his first wife's women friends and his first wife herself refused to allow him into her room.[13] Such attitudes perhaps stem from the fact that many women of eminent families regarded the marriages of Ottoman princesses as their model. High officials who were offered the hand of a princess in marriage had to separate themselves from their previous partners, both wives and slaves. Their marriage to the princess would remain monogamous.[14]

Attempts by eminent Ottoman ladies to impose monogamy on their husbands must have followed from the special circumstances of the eighteenth and early nineteenth centuries, when the princesses exercised a particularly strong influence on Istanbul high society.[15] Exceptional cases apart, princesses had not possessed this standing in the sixteenth century, nor did they do so under the neo-absolutist regime of Sultan Abdülhamid II (1876–1909). A study of the institution of Istanbul marriage from 1880 onwards, based on quantitative data, has shown that, by this time, polygamy was virtually confined to palace society and to religious officials. It hardly existed among the merchants and artisans.[16] Unlike ordinary townswomen, ladies of superior rank thus appear to have enjoyed only limited success in their attempts to impose monogamy.

Some marriages between Ottoman princesses and senior officials seem to have been happy even though neither the bride nor the groom had any part in arranging them. Evliya Çelebi reports that his relative, Melek Ahmed

Pasha (1588–1662), was heartbroken when his wife, Princess Ismihan Kaya, died giving birth after about fifteen years of marriage.[17] Interesting is the widower's furious response to the grand vizier's attempt to console him by promising soon to arrange his remarriage to another princess: 'I hope you die before you do any such thing.'[18] Whether the story is true or not is irrelevant for our purposes. Even if Evliya invented it, the storyteller came from the same social background as the story's hero, and his interpretation of Melek Ahmed Pasha's marriage is thus as interesting as the relationship itself.

If there were conflicts between a vizier and his wife, the husband could always remind 'his' princess that he, after all, had not chosen her. Evliya is unique in having recorded for us, albeit in somewhat romanticized form, the kind of recriminations which an eminent married couple of the seventeenth century made to one another in a crisis.[19] The story begins with the princess demanding more money from her husband, the very same Melek Ahmed Pasha who had eventually remarried despite his previous objections. Melek Ahmed Pasha complained that his wife was old and ugly; both of them were probably in their sixties at the time, the pasha perhaps even older. He also makes the point that he had been married without being consulted; indeed, without even having been present at the event. According to Evliya, the quarrel ended with the pasha leaving his palace and assuring his relative, the narrator, that he had no intention of ever casting eyes on his wife again. We know of several Ottoman princesses of the eighteenth century who hardly ever saw their husbands.[20] It is a matter for conjecture how often conflicts of the sort described by Evliya played a part in such separations.

Love and Affection

It must have been very difficult for young people from high-ranking families to meet potential partners from their own social class. Among the 'ordinary' people in the towns, on the other hand, the cramped circumstances of their everyday lives doubtless created certain opportunities. Young people among the peasants and nomads could encounter one another more easily, at work in the fields, gardens or pastures. From which social class, then, came the list of lovers' symbols described by Lady Mary Wortley Montagu? This list relates to a collection of small objects in a purse, each object representing a declaration of love. At the beginning we encounter a small pearl, which apparently means: 'You are a pearl amongst the fairest.' A clove signifies: 'You are a clove, but you do not endure (fade quickly), you are a rosebud, but cannot be tended (kept), I have long loved you, but you know nothing of me.' A hair means: 'You are the crown upon my head'; and grapes (presumably the ones described as 'black' in Turkish) mean: ''My two eyes' (still used today as an expression of affection). A piece of gold wire, on the other hand, signifies: 'I am dying, hasten to me.' As a postscript to the letter there is a little pepper: 'Send me (us) a true message!'[21]

Lady Mary's information came from her female friends in Istanbul, following her request for examples of Ottoman love-letters, partly because she had been asked for them by the women with whom she corresponded in England. However, this does not necessarily mean that the symbols of love which she describes really came from the upper echelons of Istanbul society. It is quite conceivable that Lady Mary's Ottoman friends, eager to do her a favour, asked for information from the tradeswomen who sold jewellery, materials or even slaves in the harems of prominent families. Servant girls employed at the public baths might also have provided information. At any rate, the symbols would then be more likely to have come from the world of artisans and merchants. Moreover, tradeswomen were sometimes non-Muslims, representing a possible point of contact with yet another section of Istanbul society. All these symbols could be used by illiterate couples. However, since many women even in the upper classes were restricted to the spoken word, this fact does not in itself tell us in which section of society the lovers' symbols were used.

Surprisingly enough, conventional 'love-letters' survive in the archive of the Topkapı Palace. Perhaps the most famous such examples are the seven letters which Hurrem Sultan (Roxelane) wrote to Süleyman the Magnificent while the latter was away leading his armies. At least the earlier ones were penned by a secretary, since Roxelane still had an insufficient command of the Ottoman language.[22] These texts were therefore not entirely private between the two correspondents. Moreover, we do not know whether the verses which adorned several of the letters were composed by the sultana herself. But according to the editor of the letters, Roxelane did eventually become so fluent in Ottoman that she was capable of producing such verses.[23]

Despite the parts played by secretaries and possibly by eunuchs, the letters do convey a flavour of the familiar atmosphere between the two. Thus Hurrem Sultan conveys greetings from other members of the harem and herself sends a greeting to an unnamed pasha.[24] Prince Mehmed reports, no doubt under orders, what Roxelane has already written: that she can hardly endure the absence of her beloved master any longer. This is followed by a brief reference to the book which the prince was currently studying with his tutor.[25] With time, Roxelane shifts from the formal form of address to the informal one; unfortunately we know nothing about the background for this switch. In later letters, the sultan's wife offers Süleyman her advice.[26] Süleyman's replies do not survive, but he does seem to have dedicated a laudatory poem to Roxelane; connoisseurs rate the sultan as an entirely respectable poet.[27]

When a pasha of the eighteenth century married a princess, he might dedicate verses to his bride. Sometimes he had written them himself, sometimes he had commissioned them from an established poet. Lady Mary Wortley Montagu recorded such a text, both in a literal translation and rendered in her own, elegant English verse.[28] In it, the poetic voice is that of Ibrahim Pasha, the bridegroom, who has so far been forbidden by the sultan to see his new wife and is being driven to despair by his longing for her. There have been few studies of the ways in which members of the Ottoman upper classes displayed and expressed affection, and we thus have yet to discover whether this poetic declaration of love was Ibrahim Pasha's own idea or whether such verses were common.

Social Life Among Women

In this area our information is mainly about women of the upper class, references to the wives of craftsmen and merchants being few and far between. Even Evliya, who wrote about virtually every aspect of Ottoman life, has little to contribute. We learn from the writings of Lady Mary Wortley Montagu that the ladies of Istanbul high society in the early eighteenth century paid each other extended visits. This was easier for those who did not live in the sultan's palace and who were therefore not subject to the latter's stringent etiquette. An acute observer, the English ambassador's wife quickly perceived this difference. Thus she writes that the widow of Sultan Mustafa II (reign: 1695–1703) was keen to show herself in her best light in social situations, but that her lack of experience meant that she was not quite sure how to do so. By contrast, Lady Mary's friend, the beautiful wife of the senior assistant to the grand vizier (kâhya), was most adept at social matters and Lady Mary believed that she would have held her own at any European court.

As well as visiting each other's homes, Ottoman townswomen met one another at the baths. Lady Mary again provides us with the earliest first-hand description of such social encounters. Only in the nineteenth century did many female European visitors attend the baths, viewing them as part of a social ritual without which the experience of Istanbul would have been incomplete.[29] The significance of visits to the baths is underlined by the outfit which eminent women took with them on such occasions, which was carried by a servant.[30] Among their bathing accessories were embroidered towels and high, wooden pattens, often inlaid with mother-of-pearl, which allowed them to walk on the wet marble of the bath-houses without getting their feet damp. Parts of such an outfit can be seen in a miniature by Buhari, an Ottoman painter of the eighteenth century.[31]

Picnics were very popular in the seventeenth century and remain so to this

day. They offered another opportunity for social contact and, no doubt, for
cultivating personal friendships among women. Towns were all surrounded
by open country, planted with trees; often there was a sacred tomb in the
vicinity. Visiting such tombs allowed women to combine religion and social
contact. In Istanbul at the start of the eighteenth century, the valley of
Kâğıthane, at the far end of the Golden Horn, was a favourite destination,
often referred to by European travellers as the 'sweet waters of Europe'.[32]
Thanks to the enthusiasm on the part of European visitors we have several
illustrations of parties of ladies enjoying picnics. Some of the pictures appear
to have been painted by Ottoman miniature painters to meet demand from
Europeans.

Excursions to public spaces apart, there were private gardens with summer-
houses in which the warmer months were spent.[33] If there were any fruits or
vegetables they would be dried or used for making jam, something which was
no doubt regarded as women's work. Lady Mary is virtually our only source
of information about the conversations among well-to-do ladies at social
occasions. Her knowledge of the Ottoman language meant that, in the later
months of her stay, she was able to take part in such conversations. Often the
ladies seem to have talked about pregnancy and children; Lady Mary reports
that her friends regarded it as a great misfortune when they became too old
to procreate.[34] If she is to be believed, it seems to have been almost a matter
of social honour in her circle to become pregnant, simply in order to prove
one's youth. On the other hand, Evliya reports that Princess Kaya initially
avoided her husband's attentions, believing her friends' prophecy that she was
destined to die in childbirth. Concerns about the dangers of pregnancy and
giving birth, which did indeed later claim Kaya Sultan's life, seem therefore
to have been greater than the generally optimistic Lady Mary assumed. As the
inheritance lists of Bursa townspeople demonstrate, the high rate of child
mortality ensured that the number of surviving sons and daughters was not
especially large.[35]

Jewellery and Clothes

Inventories compiled prior to the division of an inheritance also tell us
something about the clothing and jewellery of townswomen. Lady Mary
Wortley Montagu was enchanted by the beauty and value of the jewels with
which the Istanbul ladies of her acquaintance adorned themselves.[36] However,
for our purposes the estate inventories of the female inhabitants of Bursa,
most of whom were probably the wives and daughters of artisans and merchants, are of more interest. By no means every woman's estate included
items of jewellery. Among those who could afford such luxuries there was a

marked preference for earrings, generally of gold or silver.[37] More affluent women often had earrings incorporating pearls; more popular than any other jewels, these were probably imported from Bahrain. Bracelets were also common; they were always made of gold and were sold in pairs.[38] Necklaces, which had little Qur'ān or amulet caskets, seem to have been less popular, as were rings, and in the women's estates which have so far been examined there are hardly any references to jewellery worn in the hair.[39] However, well-off female inhabitants of Bursa often had a belt made with copious amounts of precious metals. As well as silver belts, there were belts made of fabric fastened with a silver or gilt buckle. Such fabric belts were often richly adorned with silver and gold thread, and sometimes embroidered sashes were also worn around the waist.[40] Gold and silver embroidery was also found in other items of clothing as well as in pillowcases and other household textiles.

Relatively few such items have survived, and most of the examples to be found in museums either belonged to the sultan's family or were made, or at least re-created in their current form, only in the nineteenth century. Yet it was in 'everyday' jewellery above all that craftsmen tended to repeat certain motifs from one generation to another. Thus, there are earrings from the nineteenth and twentieth centuries which are clearly reminiscent of early Byzantine examples.[41] For this reason, despite the limitations, it is possible to gain an impression of the jewellery owned by an eighteenth-century towns-woman.

We know from modern ethnological studies as well as from everyday experience that at their weddings Anatolian brides are given jewellery which can, if necessary, be sold later to ensure the newly-founded family's economic position.[42] Today, these gifts are generally bracelets, and we can assume that this was also the case in early eighteenth-century Bursa. The fact that the bracelets were always made of gold supports this theory. Even Ottoman princesses sometimes used jewellery as a form of savings and would melt it down when required.

So far as men were concerned, both Ottoman and European observers were well aware that clothing expressed the social status of the wearer.

2. Miniature from the Hazine manuscript, 1517 (Library of the Topkapı Sarayı, Istanbul).

Registration following the selection of boys for the sultan's service. The youths in the foreground are dressed in red and are being guarded by a janissary (front left, with cane). In the background, on the right, are the boys' families, who are also being held back by a janissary officer. Note the attempt to reproduce the various costumes of the Christian subjects.

Similarly to most rulers in medieval and early modern Europe, the Ottoman sultans desired to maintain a stable and clearly defined social order. This aim underlay the clothing ordinances, often issued and equally often ignored by the subjects. Equally the social status of a woman was to be discernible from her apparel. Thus, in 1564 it was decreed that non-Muslim women must wear skirts made of angora wool or a mixture of silk and cotton (*kutnu*), probably manufactured in Bursa.[43] This means that there must have been regional differences in costume, as it would have been impossible to obtain the specified cloth in every corner of the empire. Ottoman observers themselves perceived a sort of folklore of clothing. Thus, Evliya does not fail to mention the materials of the coats and veils worn by the women of different towns when venturing outside their homes. In the case of the women of Mecca, he even described their perfume.[44]

Evliya's descriptions of female clothing are followed by the standard formula 'they move with great modesty'. This relates to the most important function of women's clothing with regard to the male observer: that of demonstrating the modesty of the woman by obscuring her. In fact, the ideal woman would have been entirely invisible. Particularly in the eighteenth century, sultans often legislated in this spirit, and their decrees also drastically restricted the few remaining opportunities women still had to go out on to the streets and squares.[45] Even embroiderers' shops, which women were fond of visiting, were once closed down in the wake of such an initiative.

Clothing and jewellery were thus worn largely for the benefit of other women; otherwise these items would be seen only by members of a woman's immediate family. Apparently the former aspect was important, at least in the upper class; an exotic visitor such as Lady Mary was received by the ladies of Ottoman high society 'in full array'.[46] We can imagine that a woman's companions would scrutinize her dress with an eye to modesty, costliness and elegance, and that word would then spread through the networks in which women were involved.

A well-to-do woman (in this, as in so many other matters, we know very little about the poor) typically wore a loose-fitting shirt (*gömlek*), made of fine cotton or silk.[47] This was worn beneath the gown (*entari*), which both in the upper class and among wealthier townswomen was often made of velvet or silk. For the less well off there were cheap silks and cottons, known as *beledis*. Often, embroidered veils were fastened to a fez or hood with a brooch, creating an elaborate headdress. A jacket (*dolaman*) was worn as an outer garment, essential in winter in the underheated houses. Outdoors, women wore a loose coat, called a *ferace*, in the sleeves of which there was space to conceal their hands.[48] Their faces were hidden behind two cloths attached to the headdress leaving only a slit for the eyes.

3. Mecca pilgrim in white veil, late eighteenth century. This veil was often preserved by its owner throughout her life, just as men kept the clothes they wore for their pilgrimage.

From: Mouradjea D'Ohsson, *Tableau général de l'Empire Ottoman*, vol. 3 (Paris: L'Imprimerie de Monsieur, 1790).

In many areas, non-Muslim women dressed like the Muslims. Whether or not they left their face uncovered depended on the area and sometimes on the individual's status in life. In the Balkans and in Istanbul, non-Muslim women generally tended to leave at least part of their face visible, although there were exceptions. In Athens, young, unmarried women wore veils and only the married ones showed their faces.[49] Among the Armenians in eastern Anatolia and in the Caucasus, women wore veils like the Muslims. However, there were also areas in which European observers report seeing elaborate regional costumes among non-Muslim women as early as the sixteenth and seventeenth centuries. Evidently, these were not obscured by a coat. Around 1700, when the French botanist Pitton de Tournefort visited the Greek islands, he described the costumes of the female inhabitants and even added engravings to his work, illustrating the items of clothing individually.[50] In an Ottoman miniature of the sixteenth century, there are veiled Christian women as well as some *décolletés*.[51]

Women Who Headed Households and Earned Money

Unmarried women who lived alone were rare in Ottoman towns. However, widows quite often chose not to enter the household of a male relative. In the Balkan provinces in particular, Ottoman tax regulations accorded a special status to a woman managing her deceased husband's farm.[52] In the central Anatolian trading town of Tokat as well, around 1640 there were many households for which the tax collectors entered the name of a woman. They, too, must therefore have been recognized as the heads of their households. A widow received only a small part of her husband's estate, the lion's share going to the children of the deceased. On marrying, the husband had to pledge to his wife a sum of money in the event that he divorced or predeceased her, which in the case of death, had to be paid before the rest of the estate could be divided.[53] Careful husbands or fathers sometimes gave money to their wives or daughters during their own lifetimes, or nominated them as administrators of a family foundation from which they then drew a salary.[54] However, even these incomes were often insufficient and many widows probably sought to remarry as quickly as possible. If this were not possible and there were children to care for, the woman would have to find some way of earning money.

There were limited opportunities available. Things were easiest for the woman who had a cash sum which she could lend or otherwise invest. Some women, no doubt from merchant backgrounds, even became involved in trade.[55] Some invested their money as 'silent partners'. This could be done via the partnership contracts known as *mudaraba*, which involved the silent partner entrusting her money to a travelling merchant. However, the Bursa registers of the seventeenth century also contain a record of a warehouse belonging to a woman merchant. She must have been trading on a substantial scale, although she may simply have inherited the business from her merchant father.[56] Women trading on a smaller scale were more common, supplying affluent women with textiles and jewellery, as well as bringing with them the latest news. There are several estate inventories in the Bursa registers of the early eighteenth century relating to women who possessed an above average quantity of costly textiles, often printed or embroidered.[57] Some of these women may just have been particularly fond of needlework. However, we can assume that others were tradeswomen, particularly those who owned a large number of shawls or wrappers (bohça). Tradeswomen would generally transport their wares in such cloths, and were known as 'the woman with the wrappers' (bohçacı kadın).

There was little chance of a widow who had to support herself finding a position as a servant in a well-to-do household, because many affluent women possessed slaves. Often acquired while still very young, these girls would eventually be granted their freedom and allowed to marry. Another factor was a custom which persisted until the early twentieth century and which in Ankara can be traced back as far as the sixteenth. A poor family would send a daughter to become a servant in a wealthy household when she was still a young girl. There she would be brought up and supported while carrying out duties which varied according to her age. When she was ready to marry, the family which employed her would provide her dowry. At the beginning of her service it would have been agreed whether her parents or the family for which she worked were to select her husband. In most cases this agreement seems to have been an oral one, but occasionally it would be entered in the kadı's register.[58]

Adult women who needed to earn money, and who did not have enough capital to become small-scale traders, thus had to resort to manual work. As in many parts of early modern Europe, women were not generally admitted to guilds, and this made it even harder for them to gain a foothold in such a trade.[59] However, it is noticeable that many of the looms on which mohair was woven in Ankara during the seventeenth century were located in homes rather than in workshops. It seems likely that in such cases the craftsman's wife would, as a member of his family, assist him in his work, if she were not a weaver herself.[60] Women, some of whom were in the pay of a merchant, were engaged above all in spinning mohair yarn.

Piety and Theology

Poetry and elegant conversation, both held in high esteem by the ladies of Istanbul's high society in the eighteenth century, require a certain level of education. In the Ottoman upper class of the seventeenth and eighteenth centuries, education was above all a religious matter. The number of women who read religious books and were able to discuss their contents seems to have been greater than a first glance might suggest. It is true that, even in the sultan's palace, apparently not all the slave girls being brought up there were taught to read and write.[61] Nevertheless it would be a gross simplification to suggest that the culture of Ottoman women was an exclusively spoken one. Thus, for example, the seventeenth-century diary of the Istanbul sheikh and mosque preacher Seyyid Hasan contains a note to the effect that he had borrowed a book from one of his sisters, a Turkish translation of an anthology of canonical statements by the Prophet Muhammad.[62] Elsewhere, Seyyid Hasan also refers to a 'spiritual conversation' he has had with his sister.[63]

Right from the start of Islamic history, men did not have a monopoly on handing down the authoritative traditions associated with the Prophet. For example, a series of traditions which were recognized as canonical derived from 'Ayşa, the young wife of the Prophet Muhammad, and many scholars of the Islamic middle ages have attested to the significance of female authorities in this field.[64] Having said that, women were not permitted to study religious law or to become judges, although many scholars believed that, within certain limits, there was no purely theoretical or legal obstacle to women judges.[65]

Şeyhülislam Feyzullah's writings contain an example of a learned woman of the seventeenth century. The writer was a tutor to Prince Mustafa, whose career blossomed in the late seventeenth century when his former student acceded the throne as Mustafa II (1695). At this time it was accepted practice among the members of the Ottoman upper class, as it was in early modern Europe, for an individual who attained high office and influence to lend a helping hand to the careers of his family members. However, Feyzullah immediately appointed several of his very young sons to positions in the scholastic hierarchy and, as Şeyhülislam, interfered with matters which, in the Ottoman world of his time, were traditionally reserved for the viziers. He thus made many enemies, who engineered his dismissal and murder in 1703.[66] Shortly before this dismal end to his own and his sons' careers, in 1702, the Şeyhülislam wrote two small works in which he described the history of his family, his own career, and the beginnings of the careers of his sons. Since Feyzullah includes information about the women of the family these works were probably meant for domestic use.[67]

Pirî Hanım, Sheik Feyzullah's maternal grandmother, is of particular interest for our purposes. She studied the traditions of the Prophet, the interpretation of the Qur'ān and accounts of the life of the Prophet Muhammad, not just with her husband, but with other scholars, sheikhs and holy men.[68] She also took an interest in hagiology. No doubt the environment into which Pirî Hanım married was particularly conducive to religious studies; her husband was both a dervish sheikh and a (Sunni) legal counsel in Ganja (Azerbaijan), which was at that time ruled by the Safavids. Her husband seems to have been supportive of her studies, since otherwise she would certainly not have had access to any teachers. Since, judging by his title, her father did not belong to the sphere of scholars and dervishes, she must have had fewer opportunities to study when she was growing up.

Without doubt there were other women like Seyyid Hasan's sister and Pirî Hanım in the world of the theologians and educated dervishes. The more we investigate informal literature written for a small circle of readers, the more we learn about such women. One particularly interesting case, regarding a female mystic, has only recently come to light. Asiye Hatun lived during the seventeenth century in the Macedonian town of Skopje.[69] Her milieu was that of the Halvetiye order, which was also influential in Istanbul. However, she did not content herself with visiting holy tombs and listening to recitations of religious texts like most of the pious women around her. Rather, having apparently enjoyed a good education, she cast around for a sheikh able to introduce her to the *zikir*, the meditative recitation of the various names of God. Among the Halvetîs this was how people were initiated into the mystic way of life, and it would have been unthinkable to attempt this project without the guidance of an experienced master. However, Asiye Hatun faced particular difficulties; as a woman, she could not simply go ahead and seek out the sheikh whom she had chosen. She therefore obtained spiritual guidance through correspondence. Among other matters, in the letters she wrote she described her dreams. 'Her' sheikh – in fact there were two, since Asiye Hatun eventually decided that the old sheikh could help her no further and therefore chose a new spiritual guide – interpreted the dreams of his disciple just as he would have done for any male student.[70] Unfortunately, the letters written by the two sheikhs have not survived, and neither have the originals of those from Asiye Hatun. However, the would-be mystic made copies of each of her letters – or they may have been her drafts – and kept them in her cabinet. After her death they were preserved by her family, ultimately finding their way into the library of the Topkapı Sarayı, where they remain to this day.

Thus at least Asiye Hatun's descendants, and probably some members of the palace staff as well, considered her letters to be valuable and interesting.

Asiye Hatun's possible failure to marry, an unusual phenomenon in Ottoman society, also shows that her wishes tended, in certain matters at least, to be respected.[71] In one of her letters she suggests that she could imagine marrying only her sheikh, but no such opportunity appears to have arisen.[72] Celibacy for ascetic reasons is repeatedly rejected in Islamic tradition, but it did occur, above all among those who dedicated themselves to mysticism.[73] Thus, if Asiye Hatun, as seems to have been the case, remained unmarried of her own free will, her family must have felt a degree of reverence for her religious aspirations. Such a reaction was not in itself unheard of; we have seen already that Şeyhülislam Feyzullah spoke of his learned and pious grandmother with considerable respect. Of course, we know about the intellectual endeavours only of those women whose families showed them such understanding; nobody wrote about the others.

Much ambivalence can be discerned in the letters from Asiye Hatun to her sheikh. It was usual in the relationship between master and disciple for the disciple to accept all the master's demands. In this respect at least, then, Asiye Hatun's suggestion that she could imagine marrying her sheikh certainly made sense: after all, obedience was also expected of a wife. However, there were matters on which the mystic differed from her master. Thus, at one point her sheikh suggests that she has reached the stage in her endeavours at which she can move on from meditating on a certain name of God, to another one which was regarded as more difficult. Asiye Hatun's reaction to the good news is rather cool, a reaction which persuaded a modern editor to publish her texts under the title *The Hesitant Mystic*. The editor identifies this self-critical attitude as a typically feminine way of reacting to her own talents.[74] Perhaps, though, the female dervish's rejection of praise was more of a 'modest gesture'. Be that as it may, the fact that the mystic was bold enough to challenge the 'way' chosen for her by her sheikh shows that she was by no means short of self-confidence. She had expressed her personal opinion on a matter of considerable significance and thereby insisted that she was the best judge of the state of her own soul.[75]

Access to the Arts: Women Poets

We do not know how many women were involved in creating the songs written in everyday Turkish and performed by professional singers. There are many examples of poetry in dialogue, above all love lyrics, in which the woman has a part to play. There also survives a famous dirge in which the daughter of Pir Sultan Abdal laments her father, hanged in 'bloody Sıvas' (see Chapter 5).[76] While the number of female poets writing in the formal literary language is limited, they have existed in every age. However, a woman with a poetic imagination needed both more luck and more organizational talent than a man if she was to make something of her gift. First, she had to learn the Persian language in order to study the classics of Near Eastern lyric poetry. Such studies were a part of any well-to-do young man's education, but few women had studied literature. Moreover, the would-be poet had to familiarize herself with the work of her contemporaries. Since these were not available in printed form, she had to obtain manuscripts and find a way into poetic circles. Both of these, and especially communication with living poets, were difficult and could be managed only if the woman poet had an understanding and supportive family.[77]

Particularly important was the role of the father. One of the most famous Ottoman women poets never married, which would certainly have been impossible without the consent of her father. Mihri Hatun, whom we shall discuss here despite her having lived before our period (c. 1470–after 1515), was the daughter of a *kadi* of Amasya, himself a recognized literary talent.[78] As a descendant of Baba Ilyas, one of the leaders of the Babaî revolt (see Chapter 2), Mihri Hatun belonged to a family of theologians and educated dervishes, where literary activity was an established tradition. Mihri Hatun was also fortunate enough to have access to the literary circles which had formed around Prince Ahmed (1465–1513), who resided in Amasya. At his court this son of Bayezid II had gathered a host of literary figures, who also came to be well known in Istanbul. At first, however, the capital remained inaccessible to Mihri Hatun, and her poems 'replying' to the works of the poet Necatî provoked a sharp response from this colleague and competitor.[79] The poet herself suggested that she was not taken seriously by her male colleagues and composed a concerted, if brief, defence of talented women.[80]

Despite all the obstacles she faced, the poet did eventually establish herself. In the later years of her life her name appeared on the lists of literary figures who were honoured with gifts by Sultan Bayezid II (reign: 1481–1512). Clearly, she had become known in the capital, in part, no doubt, because of the efforts of Prince Ahmed.[81] Her collection of poems (*divan*) survives, a further indication of her renown, since many *poetae minores* are today represented only by odd verses in anthologies. She also features in the collections of contemporary poets' biographies.[82] In the Ottoman Empire, as in other Islamic cultures, these collections were produced by virtually every generation. Inclusion meant that a writer had a reputation among his or her contemporaries. Mihri Hatun, moreover, fell in love with several members of the literary circle of Amasya. She broke with literary convention by naming names when referring to these romances in her poems. All her biographers agree, however, that her relationships remained platonic. It seems that the poet always adhered to current morality and etiquette.

Hubbi Hatun was a notable female poet of the sixteenth century.[83] However, she is less famous than Fitnat, whose 'real' name was Zübeyde (died 1780). Fitnat lived in Istanbul, the daughter and sister of two Şeyhülislams. She too must have received her education before she left her father's house: the biographers report that her husband, descended from the family of Şeyhülislam Feyzullah (murdered in 1703), was remarkable only for his obtuseness.[84] As well as her literary work, Fitnat was well known for her ready wit, and her name also appears in collections of anecdotes. In these dialogues, Fitnat and some male literary figure fire poetic insinuations at one another, and do not shy away from erotic innuendo.[85] Most of these tales are probably apocryphal.[86] However, the mere fact of their existence shows how difficult it was for a woman poet to operate within the limits imposed by religion and convention; many of Fitnat's contemporaries obviously found her literary activities difficult to accept.

Access to the Arts: Women as Patrons of Architecture

Since women had control over their own fortunes, they were able to establish pious foundations. In mid-sixteenth-century Istanbul, 37 per cent of all officially recorded founders were female. However, this does not mean that women constituted a similar proportion of the building patrons.[87] Most women established only small foundations, consisting of a sum of money or a house which might benefit an existing mosque. Due to their limited means, they were not in a position to erect new buildings, and did not have to seek an architect and make all the other decisions which were the responsibility of a patron awarding a building contract. However, there were exceptions to this rule, and sultans' mothers, princesses and ladies of the court did construct mosques, fountains and other edifices. Some of these still adorn Istanbul today, such as the complex founded by Süleyman's wife, Hurrem, and the two mosques known by the name of Mihrimah Sultan (1548 and 1565). From a later age, Şebsefa Kadın's and Zeyneb Sultan's mosque complexes are worthy of note (built in 1787 and 1769 respectively).[88]

Another aspect of the princesses' involvement in architecture has been almost forgotten because the buildings in question no longer exist: the summer palaces on the shore of the Bosphorus.[89] During the eighteenth century, members of Ottoman courtly society were keen to escape the constricting etiquette of the Topkapı Palace and spent much time in newly-built or converted palaces beside the Bosphorus. Many Ottoman princesses of the eighteenth century were assigned a palace at birth, or at least on the occasion of their engagement or marriage, both of which would take place during their childhood. In such palaces the harem area would be particularly

sumptuous, often considerably more magnificent than the *selamlık* reserved
for the husband and his male guests. After all, the vizier or governor who had
been chosen to marry the princess did not belong to the sultan's family, while
in certain circumstances during this period, the princesses represented the
authority of the sultan.

Some princesses took a keen interest in the architecture and decoration of
their palaces. Even when there was no major rebuilding, cushions, carpets
and curtains would be changed to suit the taste of each new owner, certain
rooms would undergo alterations and, above all, the building would be re-
painted. In the damp air of the Bosphorus the brightly coloured paints used
for the houses of eminent personages did not last for long. When a princess
died, her palace would immediately be reassigned to another, who would then
instigate her own set of alterations. Thus, the buildings described by European
travellers did not necessarily reflect the taste of the period in which they had
originally been built, but rather the current style of the time in which the
traveller was writing, up to the late nineteenth century.[90]

Access to the Arts: Textiles

Even today examples of Ottoman embroidery, kilims and carpets fill museums
and private collections both in Turkey and abroad. Women played a major
part in the production of these items. Written sources testify to this, although
the relevant documents are tantalizingly few in number. Moreover, in the
nineteenth century, many women were employed in the textile sector, and it
seems unlikely that the division of labour between men and women was
fundamentally different in the seventeenth or eighteenth century.[91] In about
1550, the French traveller Nicolas de Nicolay reports that two hundred girls
were learning needlework at the sultan's palace. Since the Frenchman cannot
have had any reliable sources of information about the sultan's harem this
figure was probably based on hearsay.[92] In the early eighteenth century, Lady
Mary Wortley Montagu described the embroidery skills of the women slaves
of Sultan Mustafa II's widow. As was customary among well-to-do Ottoman
ladies, this royal woman surrounded herself with many young servant girls,
the older ones apparently teaching the younger recruits the skill of embroidery.[93] However, adult Ottoman ladies also practised this art. Pietro della
Valle, an Italian nobleman and traveller, was married to an Ottoman Christian
and thus had a certain insight into the world of seventeenth-century women.
This author described the skill of Ottoman embroiderers, particularly the
works executed on transparent material which could be viewed from either
side, thus perhaps corresponding to the shadow embroidery popular in Europe
at the beginning of the twentieth century.[94]

Embroidery with gold thread was also much admired by della Valle, although a modern specialist in this area believes that this was produced mainly by men.[95] Male embroiderers sold their work in shops or were commissioned to produce items for the palace. According to Evliya Çelebi, writing in 1638, there were about ninety such men in Istanbul alone, although this author's figures are not always very reliable. As we have seen, visiting these shops was a favourite recreation for the women of Istanbul in the eighteenth century.

Rather than meeting the needs of just their own households, certain female embroiderers also worked on commission. A report addressed to a lady of the harem documents the existence of such women, who in this case had been commissioned to embroider counterpanes for the palace.[96] In fact, the embroiderers rejected the commission because the needlework required was too delicate. During the seventeenth century there was a special market in Bursa where women could sell work they themselves had produced, without paying tax.[97] Embroidery was no doubt prominent among such work. Other needlework was sold by tradeswomen who supplied affluent harems with luxury and consumer goods. In the Habsburg parts of Hungary and at Christian courts in south-eastern Europe, the embroidery skills of sixteenth- and seventeenth-century Ottoman women were also highly prized. Some members of the nobility attempted to obtain such women as slaves for their own residences. Eminent Christian women also sometimes corresponded with Muslim ladies about embroidery patterns or attempted to learn such patterns from their Turkish maids.[98] Unfortunately, it was very rare for earlier examples of the textile arts to be dated or signed.

A few European illustrations of the eighteenth century show how female embroiderers worked.[99] However, these illustrations must be interpreted with care, since the painter or sketcher is unlikely to have had the opportunity to see the interior of an Ottoman harem. They may have been fortunate enough to watch professional embroiderers at work, among whom there were many non-Muslims. No doubt these women were then portrayed in the costumes of elegant ladies. In such illustrations there is a horizontal frame, on which the material to be embroidered is stretched; the contraption thus resembles a table. Such embroidery frames were among the typical attributes of a woman as early as the fifteenth century: a tombstone from this period shows a female figure crouching before such a device.[100]

And Those of Whom We Know Nothing ...

'Anonymous was a woman' is a statement which has become something of a rallying cry in feminist literary criticism.[101] In the Ottoman domain, too, all we can say about certain anonymous female artists is the claim that they must have existed. Among the most important are the carpet and kilim weavers. They were active in the nineteenth and twentieth centuries, but also, without doubt, in earlier times as well.

Perhaps one day it will be possible to write another chapter in this vein, dealing with female singers and musicians. In the sultan's palace, the maids of the harem as well as the pages were involved in choirs and musical performances. In the eighteenth century at least, music was one of the arts which ladies of Istanbul's high society would have taught to their slave girls if they displayed the necessary talent.[102] Generally, amateur performances seem to have been less popular than they were in nineteenth- and early twentieth-century Europe, and concerts by specialists were preferred. We do not yet know how these musicians were trained or whether the foremost among them were 'lent' from one genteel harem to another. However, no references to musical instruments have yet been found among the hundreds of estate inventories which have been examined. Therefore the instruments must have belonged to the musicians, and no inventories relating to musicians' estates have yet been discovered.

It is clear, then, that plenty of Ottoman women could see beyond the day-to-day business of family life or, in the case of the wealthier ones, that many of them were not content merely with clothes, women friends and sweets. This conclusion may at first appear trivial. After all, Ottoman culture was an ancient high culture with long literary and artistic traditions. Thus, we would expect some of the numerous women who lived in the sixteenth, seventeenth and eighteenth centuries to have felt the urge for 'men's education, art, wisdom and honour' and to have been successful in pursuing their ambitions.[103]

However, two factors have combined to cause this female contribution to Ottoman culture to be forgotten. First, all patriarchal cultures, not excluding our own, tend in one way or another to exclude female achievements from the general consciousness. Second, a particular image of women is implicit in the conception of the 'exotic Orient', which is already apparent among nineteenth-century painters such as Delacroix (1798–1863). This image is negative and misogynous, but it survived for a long time and above all in purportedly scholarly literature. Women appear in it as passive beings, about whom there is little beyond their erotic radiance which is worthy of note. The voyeuristic tendency of men, or rather scholars, leads to the exaggeration of this erotic aspect and to the 'passive, oriental woman' becoming a symbol of a foreign culture. This symbol can be taken to imply that Near Eastern society, seen as feminine in character, is a passive phenomenon which to be dominated by an outsider, who is, of course, a man. Active women who exhibited artistic interests do not fit such an image. These stereotypes are the products of utter fantasy, and this has been amply demonstrated by historians – particularly women – in many areas, and it is to be hoped that this chapter has shown that they are equally unhelpful in looking at Ottoman culture of the early modern period. To quote Mihri Hatun: 'You say women have little understanding and that you do not listen to them for that reason. Yet Mihri, who prays for you [and wishes you well], explains – and clever and mature people confirm it: a talented woman is better than a thousand untalented men, a woman of understanding is better than a thousand stupid men.'[104]

PART II

The Arts

7

Architects, Pious Foundations and Architectural Aesthetics

If the French writer Victor Hugo is to be believed, in Europe the medieval period was an age of architecture. Hugo believed that the great sacred buildings of the period, in particular, were validated by the large number of people for whom they were significant and who visited them in the course of their everyday lives.[1] Admittedly, the symbolic content of a great cathedral, for example, could have its full impact only on those who had received the necessary education.[2] However, many levels of significance were accessible to the ordinary member of the congregation if he or she looked closely at stained-glass windows, frescoes or capitals. This public character was an important prerequisite for architecture's development as an art. According to Hugo, architecture lost its leading role only with the arrival of printed books, which quickly turned literature into the art with greatest resonance in the general public. Victor Hugo saw two contrasting ages: the middle ages without printed books but boasting great architecture, and a modern era in which architecture was much diminished in importance and literature took over as the leading art.

These theories are also of interest to cultural historians dealing with the Ottoman Empire. Until the eighteenth or even the early nineteenth century, architecture appears to have been the most prestigious of the Ottoman arts. Sultans, princesses, viziers and, in the eighteenth century above all, local magnates commissioned countless mosques, palaces, theological schools, dervish convents, drinking water fountains and alms-houses. Significant sums of money were spent on these buildings. Just as in pre-nineteenth-century Europe, in the Ottoman domain many of the most important monuments were dedicated to the worship of God. They were not merely open to the faithful in a physical sense, but also relatively easy for them to appreciate. Unlike in literature, esoteric symbolism was relatively unimportant in architecture, although it was by no means completely absent. Ottoman architecture can thus also be said to have enjoyed a particularly marked influence on the general public in the so-called classical period (*c.* 1450–*c.* 1680). This furthered the development of the art of architecture in just the manner identified by Victor Hugo.

Our retrospective judgement of the particular significance of Ottoman architecture is no doubt partly the result of chance. We are less able to appreciate classical music of the seventeenth century because only a small proportion was notated and has thus survived. However, many Ottomans of the sixteenth and seventeenth centuries equally appear to have regarded the architecture of their age as something special, something which stirred their imaginations. Thus, a host of poems, legends and tales revolved around the great buildings of Istanbul. Byzantine buildings as well as Ottoman mosques were integrated into the imaginative world of the people of Istanbul in this way.[3] Evliya Çelebi, the traveller who dedicated a substantial part of his ten-volume work to his native city of Istanbul, bears witness to the force of the fascination exerted by architecture on the minds of educated Istanbul inhabitants in particular.[4] This mythology of buildings and their construction was a part of the everyday culture of Ottoman townspeople. On the other hand, no evidence has yet emerged to suggest that they attempted, as did Victor Hugo, to create a hierarchy of the arts with architecture explicitly at its head.

No books were printed in the Ottoman language and on the sultan's territory until 1726, and even then they remained uncommon until the second half of the nineteenth century.[5] Moreover, as in contemporary central Europe, the distribution of books and news sheets was often severely affected by censors' directives. However, at least by the beginning of the twentieth century and probably somewhat earlier, Ottoman literature overcame these difficulties to emerge as the art with the greatest general resonance. By the mid-twentieth century, poems, novels and satirical short stories written by Turkish authors were read not just by their compatriots but also, through translations, reached an international public. Simplifying things somewhat, we might say that in the nineteenth and early twentieth centuries Ottoman society moved, as Europe had, from an age dominated by architecture into a period in which literature was pre-eminent. In this chapter we shall investigate why architecture was so very influential in the sixteenth and seventeenth centuries.

Official and Vernacular Architecture

In Ottoman towns there existed two classes of building. Monumental architecture was built of stone with occasional decorative features using bricks. In the eighteenth century particularly, bricks were arranged in horizontal bands to add colour to the light grey quarried stone of the building. Such monumental edifices generally had domes which were sheathed in lead or, until the fifteenth century, sometimes tiled. In monumental buildings it was considered very important that ashlars should be regular. If dressed stone was reused from older buildings, it was because such spoils were considered valuable, antique material with a high symbolic content, rather than because they were cheap and readily available.[6] In some cases fayence was an important decorative element: inscriptions were often in blue and white, and in the fifteenth and sixteenth centuries above all there were often large decorative features. Depending on the current style, these might be abstract designs or realistic floral motifs.

Art historians have used the stylistic changes in monumental architecture to identify several clearly demarcated periods. In addition to the 'classical' mid-sixteenth-century style of Sinan's time, they dwell on the experimentation of the great architect's later years, for which his students may have been partly responsible. In the eighteenth century, many Ottoman architects integrated decorative elements of European provenance into their structures, pending the development of an eclectic style in the middle of the nineteenth century.

Apart from this 'official' style there was a vernacular type of architecture, using whatever materials were locally available. Stone buildings were constructed only where no cheaper materials existed. In Egypt or Aleppo, for example, there was very little timber at hand; or else in certain regions, the local stone was particularly soft and easy to work, such as in the tuffaceous landscape of Ürgüp, near Kayseri in central Anatolia.[7] Timber was the most popular material for vernacular buildings in Istanbul. Many wooden buildings were colourfully painted, but many owners no doubt allowed their houses to fade to the brown or black colour with which we are familiar from surviving wooden buildings of the late nineteenth and early twentieth centuries. In the interior of Anatolia, where timber was usually more expensive because no water-borne transport was available, a sort of half-timbered construction was common. While the framework was of timber, the filling would be of air-dried clay or baked bricks. If timber was in even shorter supply, such as in Konya, houses would be built entirely of clay and clay bricks, with wood used only for the supporting elements and the ceilings. If the house was vacated, the supporting beams would be removed, leaving just a pile of clay. This was illustrated in the experience of the inhabitants of the town of Malatya in 1838–39, when they were ordered by the sultan to make their town available to a troop of Ottoman soldiers for the winter.[8] When the inhabitants returned from their houses at the garden settlement in which they had spent the cold season, they discovered that the troops had used the supporting beams of the houses as fuel during the bitter winter, leaving nearly the whole town in ruins. They thereupon decided to move permanently to their garden residences and founded the modern town of Malatya at the site of the former summer settlement of Aspuzi. In the dry steppes the houses often had flat roofs used as terraces in summer. In the wetter regions of the coastal forest land, roofs tended to be slightly inclined and covered with shingle or tiles.

Although the official and vernacular building styles were so distinct from one another, it is not always easy to determine when each of the two was applied. Mosques and theological schools were usually built in the 'official' style, but so were humble kiosks used to supply passers-by with drinking water, if they had been commissioned by a sultan, a member of the sultan's family or a provincial governor. In the eighteenth century, even lesser provincial magnates had buildings constructed in this way, especially in Egypt. On the other hand, the palaces of Ottoman dignitaries often seem to have been built in less grand a manner, despite the fact that they sometimes served not merely as dwellings but also as administrative offices.[9] However, wooden and half-timbered buildings often fell victim to fires, earthquakes and other disasters, and often they were torn down to make room for new constructions. This is why so few examples of the many viziers' and governors' palaces in Istanbul and the larger provincial centres have survived until today.

Some mosques and other religious buildings were constructed in the 'vernacular' building style of the local area. In Ankara there are still small, rectangular mosques with tiled roofs and flat, wooden ceilings.[10] These only changed slightly between the fifteenth and eighteenth centuries, while 'official' architecture was characterized by a succession of styles. Building contractors made use of columns and other types of dressed stone from any older buildings they came across. If necessary, a column which was too short might be set upon a pedestal, while if it was too long, it would no doubt simply be shortened. Most dervish convents were built in the vernacular style at least from the seventeenth century onwards; it seems that many were in fact simply enlarged dwellings. There are very few exceptions indeed of which we know or which still survive in some form. Among the most notable of these major dervish lodges are the main seat of the Mevlevî order in Konya, with domes over the living quarters, and above all the central monastery of the Bektashis between Ankara and Nevşehir. Both of these were built in the 'official' style.[11] In such cases, there is generally evidence of endowments from governors and even sultans.

Architects and Their Careers

Official architecture and vernacular construction also differ in that we very often know the architect responsible for official buildings, whereas this is never so in the case of buildings in the vernacular style. Yet even of most Ottoman architects only the name and the approximate career dates are known. In a few cases chroniclers wrote about them, as in the case of Atik Sinan (Sinan the Freedman). This was the man responsible for the great mosque and school complex which Mehmed the Conqueror ordered built at the site of the former Byzantine Church of the Apostles.[12] Disagreements apparently ensued between the architect and Mehmed II about the use of the antique columns which can still be seen today in the mosque's courtyard. The sultan reacted by having his architect arrested, and Atik Sinan's death in prison provoked strong criticism of the sultan from some contemporaries. We are much better informed about another Sinan, the sixteenth-century architect responsible for the Şehzade, Süleymaniye and Selimiye mosques (completed in 1548–49, 1557 and 1574–75 respectively). He can be considered the originator of the classical style of Ottoman architecture.[13] Even in the sixteenth century, many catalogues of his works were produced, differing from each other in matters of detail. In his old age, Sinan also dictated a short autobiography to one of his friends. His successor, Davud, is known only from a few references in chronicles and official documents.[14] There is, however, a fairly comprehensive biography of Mehmed Ağa, the builder of the Sultan Ahmed Mosque (Blue Mosque), probably written by a member of his household. The author, a certain Ca'fer Efendi, was an uncritical admirer of his master. Not only did he celebrate Mehmed Ağa's most important designs in verse, but he also attempted to transfigure the less successful periods of his hero's life in the manner of a saint's legend.[15] There is good archive material available for several architects of the eighteenth century. An estate inventory recently has come to light for one lesser-known architect of that period, giving us an insight into the property which might be amassed by such a personage and into the strategies leading to his success.[16]

Ottoman architects were thus by no means anonymous craftsmen, totally constrained by their obligations to their guilds and the orders they received from the sultan's bureaucracy. On the contrary, they were often men of influence. Sinan, the builder of the Süleymaniye, was permitted by his patron to incorporate his own mausoleum into the great complex which he had built for the ruler on a hill overlooking Istanbul. Sinan, who came from Ağırnas near Kayseri, was able to extend quite significant privileges to his relatives.[17] Admittedly, the great builder was exceptional; his fifty years in office as architect to the sultan demonstrate the point. A more humble, provincial architect would have been much less self-confident. In the 1630s the master involved in the great restoration of the Kaaba in Mecca seems to have been worried mainly by the possibility that he might subsequently be held responsible for any mistakes.[18] He does not seem to have exerted any political influence, not even at a local level.

In his early career Sinan, the architect of the Süleymaniye, had been a janissary officer responsible for building bridges. He had completed only a few mosques before the sultan entrusted him with the construction of a large complex in honour of a prince who had died while still young.[19] We know little about the architectural training of Mehmed Ağa, who built the Sultan-ahmed Mosque. He probably spent many years working for and with Sinan, although in his biography he appears as an already accomplished master.

Most architects employed by the central government were trained in the team of palace architects. This organization can be traced back to the early sixteenth century.[20] Unlike the members of most organs of the Ottoman central administration, architects working for the sultan did not necessarily have to be Muslims. Plans for buildings which had been commissioned by the sultan or members of his family would be approved and submitted by the senior architect. This practice was responsible for the large number of buildings attributed in the catalogues of works ascribed to Sinan. The contributions of his students, many of whom were talented artists in their own right, cannot be determined with any accuracy, but they were certainly substantial. If a building was to be constructed outside Istanbul a (probably fairly young) architect would be entrusted with supervising the site. As a result, most buildings constructed in the provinces in the sixteenth and seventeenth centuries differed but very slightly from the style favoured in the capital.[21] However, the lists of Sinan's works show that, in his day at least, most Ottoman building projects were located in or around Istanbul.[22]

Architects in the Provinces

The Ottoman word *mimar* designates not just architects but also building technicians of more modest status. Dwellings were generally designed by the owner together with a carpenter or mason rather than by a graduate of the corps of sultan's architects. In Istanbul at least, as well as in the pilgrimage city of Mecca, there were directives which we would today associate with the 'Surveyor's Office' and which regulated the design of new houses.[23] Upper storeys were not allowed to lean into the street, and there were limits on the size of the stone benches in front of the houses, often used for selling goods. Those responsible for building contracts and architects had to find out about such regulations, consulting the *kadi*'s register if necessary. Directives were generally issued in the form of sultan's decrees and would be entered in the register by the clerk of the court. These regulations were often ignored, particularly when substantial additional expense would be incurred in adhering to them.

In many towns of the Ottoman Empire from the early seventeenth century onwards there was a 'municipal architect' appointed by the central government to represent the sultan's chief architect, whose office was in the capital.[24] He was charged with supervising all those craftsmen involved in the building industry. In many places private building operations were prohibited until approval had been granted by the 'municipal architect'. Sometimes the latter would also set standards for the materials to be used in construction. This was the case above all for stone. Municipal architects also supported the *kadi* in resolving disputes concerned with construction and buildings. Thus, if a house were to be divided among several heirs, this official might specify which rooms corresponded to each heir's share of the inheritance. Municipal architects were also tax-collectors, receiving the taxes paid by building craftsmen. Above all, their role was to enable the central powers to exert bureaucratic control over the provincial towns. It is difficult, however, to determine how successful the average official was in this regard.

An Institutional Framework for Building Activity: The Pious Foundation

Apart from citadels, palaces and a few town houses, most Ottoman monumental architecture served religious or charitable purposes. As well as large mosques, in which public prayers were held together with Friday sermons, there were smaller houses of God, generally pertaining to a particular town quarter, in which the faithful could perform their ritual Islamic devotions five times a day. In larger towns there were schools offering courses in theology and religious law to prepare future *kadi*s for their duties. Schools in which children were taught to read, write and recite the Qur'ān were housed in smaller, but often quite ornate, buildings. Public libraries contained significant collections of manuscripts. The larger dervish convents consisted of a hall for the order's ceremonies, the tomb of the convent's founder, which sometimes had an attached mosque, the sheikh's residence, and often a large kitchen which prepared food both for the dervishes and for the many visitors. Other large hospices operated independently from any dervish convent. In Istanbul these were used as sultans' guest-houses, in which dignitaries visiting the capital on business could stay for short periods. For the widows of deceased officials, the kitchens in these hospices also supplied food, while distributing the surplus among the poor. Sometimes the foundations included hospitals, but they were greatly outnumbered by less expensive projects such as the so-called *sebil*. These were pavilions, often very elegant in appearance, at the edge of the streets, where passers-by would be served with drinking water free of charge. Today many of these small kiosks are used by vendors of newspapers, sweets and soft drinks.[25]

In institutional terms, all these buildings were pious foundations (*vakıf*). As early as the seventh and eighth centuries of our era, the framework for such foundations was enshrined in Islamic law, thus pre-dating the emergence of the Ottomans.[26] Endowments could be made to any religious or charitable end, with the beneficiary either a specially-created institution or else a long-established one. Whatever was endowed then belonged to the foundation for ever. If a benefactor wanted to make doubly sure of this, he or she might instigate legal proceedings demanding the return of the property, only to be informed by the *kadi* that this was impossible. This judgement would be recorded in the register, confirming the validity of the foundation's status. A document would also be drawn up defining precisely the nature and purpose of the endowment and naming those who should profit from its establishment. Since those named were often family members, some foundations were conceived at least partly in order to keep a certain property within the family without its being divided among a multitude of heirs.[27]

Pious foundations could be established by men or women, the only requirement being that the benefactor was a free adult, and had sole ownership of the landed properties or other items endowed. Fields and pastures, which were the property of the state according to Ottoman sultanic law (*kanun*), could be endowed only if the sultan explicitly consented.[28] This restriction was important, since land was the first requirement for many foundations. Land was needed for building on and was also a significant source of income to support the foundation's activities. Many sultans granted their relatives and prominent officials the privilege of dedicating tax income from whole villages to a foundation; indeed, the sultans' foundations themselves depended largely on agricultural taxes.[29] However, the legal status of the peasants who lived in such villages was unaffected and they remained answerable directly to the sultan.

Ordinary subjects unable to obtain the sultan's special permission to endow agricultural land might donate houses or gardens which they owned in full. There were also scholars who gave their books to a foundation's library, a practice which has led to the survival of many manuscripts. In the Turkish parts of the Ottoman Empire, and particularly in Istanbul, it became common in the sixteenth century to donate money to an existing mosque, which would then lend it at set levels of interest (generally 10–15 per cent) after collateral had been pledged.[30] Along with other revenue items, interest payments were used to maintain the mosque. This practice was regarded as controversial, for many jurists did not believe that the value of money was stable enough to serve a foundation which was intended to exist for eternity. Moreover, it constituted a flagrant breach of the prohibition against charging interest, enshrined in Islamic law.[31] However, the controversy among theologians does not appear to

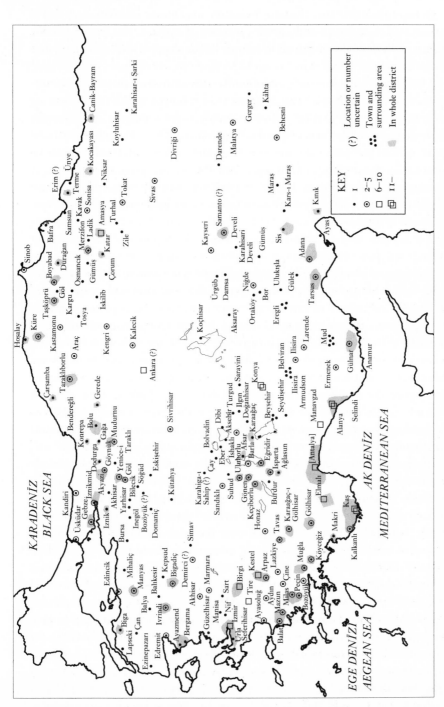

MAP 3 Friday mosques in Anatolia (*c. 1520–35*) *Source:* Suraiya Faroqhi, 'A Map of Anatolian Friday Mosques', in, *Osmanlı Araştırmaları,* 4 (1984) p. 173.

have prevented most benefactors from donating money in this way. In the
second half of the eighteenth century there were so many foundations lending
money in the Anatolian textile town of Bursa that they filled voluminous
registers.

More affluent townspeople, and Ottoman administrators in particular, were
fond of endowing shops, baths, bazaars and caravanserais.[32] Shops belonging
to foundations were used by craftsmen with hereditary tenure. Many foundations demanded that tenants agree in advance that any repairs and new
constructions passed to the foundation at the end of the tenancy, without
compensation being paid. However, often the tenants were in the stronger
position, particularly when, following a fire, the foundation lacked the means
to construct new buildings and was forced to let its land cheaply to those who
promised to build on it.[33]

A hereditary tenant would pay a substantial initial sum, but the subsequent
annual rent was generally low.[34] Sons had the right of inheritance, and in
some places so did daughters. Many craftsmen were able to achieve a secure
hold on their shops by using a foundation in this way. However, in the second
half of the eighteenth century, the situation changed. Because of a series of
lost wars, the Ottoman government found itself in severe financial difficulties
and responded by trying to squeeze income out of the foundations. In fact,
property belonging to a pious foundation was untouchable according to Islamic
law, but the government by-passed this by 'freezing' the foundation's income
and seizing the rest for the state coffers. Since, in addition, the eighteenth
century was a period of currency depreciation, many pious foundations
suffered such severe losses that they became moribund. In particular, they
were often unable to maintain their buildings.

Many foundation administrators attempted to limit the damage by demanding higher rents from their craftsmen tenants. The latter responded by
declaring their tools and shops to be a special type of property which could
be sold only within their own guild (gedik, which might be translated as
'master's place').[35] Property was sometimes designated in this way even before
1750, but it became very much more common in the difficult years which
followed. Kadis were often inclined to accept the claim that a shop was a
gedik. No doubt one of their considerations was that itinerant craftsmen and
traders without a shop of their own tended to be unreliable taxpayers. Thus,
in Istanbul at least, many craftsmen were able to protect their interests against
the foundations. This development did have a negative side: lack of money
meant that many pious foundations were unable to function properly and due
to the need to acquire a gedik, the economic life of the towns became very
much less flexible.

Foundations would lease larger properties, such as commercial buildings (khans) at public auctions to the highest bidder, who would in turn sublease to individual tradespeople. Public baths were also sometimes run in this way. The main lessee would employ the necessary personnel, such as the guards who protected a khan or the servants who kept public baths clean and looked after the customers. However, the strong position of the main lessee did not prevent some subtenants from settling more or less permanently in a khan and altering the rooms to suit their own requirements. In the Syrian trading centre of Aleppo, it was customary for English or Venetian merchants to rent a khan as a group. Such a khan might remain in the hands of the same merchant organization for centuries. European consuls also used khans for their offices.[36]

Apart from the large foundations, the principal sources of contracts for Ottoman monumental architecture, there were also many smaller ones, consisting of a single house or shop. These buildings were constructed in a 'vernacular' manner using currently available materials. They did not differ from houses or shops in private ownership, and indeed it was quite common for a craftsman to turn his house or shop into a pious foundation.[37] His descendants could then profit from the foundation on the condition that every year they said a certain number of prayers for the founder's soul. Similarly, a woman might specify that her house should pass into the ownership of a foundation for the benefit of her freed slaves, thereby ensuring that her former servants would have a roof over their heads in their old age. Due to the proliferation of pious foundations of all sizes, a large part of the land in the centres of the main towns was not available for purchase. A foundation might exchange its property, but never sell it.

Thus the fate of both monumental and 'vernacular' buildings was closely tied to that of the pious foundations, both commissioned buildings and ensured that they were maintained. In case of money shortages or quarrels among the administrators, the buildings often, of course, suffered neglect and gradually decayed. Virtually every significant new construction in densely populated towns depended on transactions between foundations. On the other hand, until well into the nineteenth century establishing a new town also implied the institution of one or more new pious foundations.[38] Once the requirements for the development of a town were present in the form of mosques, schools, a covered market and a few shopping streets, the inhabitants generally soon followed.

Patronage

In the late fifteenth century and throughout the sixteenth, the sultans, the members of their family and senior officials were by far the most significant sources of building contracts. Young men with ambitions to become celebrated architects had to seek a place in the official corps of architects (*hassa mimar-lari*). Once they had attracted the attention of various patrons they would be introduced to the sultan, who could give them the opportunity to undertake larger projects.[39]

However, this collaboration was by no means entirely free of friction. In some hitherto rather neglected passages of the autobiography which Sinan dictated in his later years to his friend Mustafa Saî, the 'Ottoman Michelangelo' describes some of the difficulties in the patron–artist relationship between Süleyman the Magnificent and his architect. Conflicts began with a bridge over the Pruth which Sinan had constructed while he was still a janissary officer. Sinan did not believe that the bridge should be fortified, a view which resulted in his being accused of fearing that he might be appointed as the commander of the new fortress. Such an appointment would, of course, have detained him in the remote frontier region for an extended period. Sinan thus accepted gratefully the suggestion that he 'retire' from his janissary career and work instead for the sultan's corps of architects.

We do not know if the sultan supported or even knew about the accusations levelled at Sinan in this matter. However, there is no such uncertainty regarding another episode, which took place during the construction of the Süleymaniye complex (1550–57). A few eminent personages had used various pretexts to pursue the construction of their own residences, causing delays in the work on the mosque.[40] These led to doubts being voiced about the architect's competence. It was suggested that his central dome was unstable and that he himself was both lazy and over-emotional to the point of obsession. In a towering rage, the sultan himself appeared at the building site and threatened Sinan with the same fate which had befallen his unfortunate namesake, architect to Mehmed the Conqueror. (Incidentally, this story is an interesting indication of the fact that, at Süleyman's court, it was believed that Mehmed II was responsible for the demise of his architect.) Sinan responded by promising that the mosque would be finished within two months. At the court this promise was widely seen as madness, yet Sinan stuck to it even when the sultan himself offered him the opportunity to retract it. Sinan kept his word and the keys were indeed handed over two months later, but this is less interesting for our purposes than the brutal honesty with which Sinan and his biographer presented the celebrated architect's relationship with the Ottoman ruler. At several points there are allusions to the difficulty of asserting oneself in the jungle of bureaucratic intrigue. We are shown how the sultan allows himself to be influenced by Sinan's enemies and threatens his able subject with execution. Sinan's eventual triumph made fools of his enemies, but even the sultan cuts a less than brilliant figure. It is also noteworthy that Mustafa

Saî included this tale in his account even though he was writing at a time when the Süleymanic era was already regarded as a 'golden age'.

Particularly interesting is the role of women as patrons. Because religious law (*şeriat*) allowed a married woman to remain in control of her fortune, it was entirely possible for upper-class women to commission a mosque or *medrese*. It was a woman who gave the great Sinan his first opportunity to build a mosque, and female members of the ruling family acted as patrons from as early as the fourteenth century. Nefise Melek Hatun was married to a member of the Karaman dynasty and there is still a *medrese* bearing her name, built in 1388, in the southern Anatolian town of Karaman.[41] In Ottoman provincial towns, such as Tokat, Manisa or Trabzon, mosques were built and named after the mother of an Ottoman prince who lived there for a while.[42] However, we do not know to what extent the former palace women were themselves involved in these constructions. Possibly the mosques were simply built in their mothers' honour by the imperial princes.

Among the female members of the Ottoman dynasty of the sixteenth century, Hurrem Sultan, known in Europe as Roxelana, seems to have taken a particular interest in the construction of buildings serving religious and charitable purposes. A large complex consisting of a mosque, *medrese* and other establishments was built for her by the architect Sinan.[43] In Mecca, Medina and Jerusalem hostels and alms-houses were founded in her name, although some of them were built only after her death. Later the sultan's mother, who headed the ruler's harem as the Sultana Valide and often exercised political influence, emerged as an architectural patroness. Thus the Yeni Cami at the Golden Horn was begun by the Sultana Valide Safiye in 1597 and completed, after a lengthy interval, by the Valide Turhan in 1664.[44] However, most foundations set up by the mothers of sultans and other female members of the dynasty were located on the Asian side of the Bosphorus, in Üsküdar.[45] The Sultana Valide Safiye even endowed an institution in Cairo; however, this may have been due to coincidental circumstances, since the mosque was originally built not by her but by one of her eunuchs.[46]

Many viziers of the sixteenth century also emerged as important architectural patrons, both in Istanbul and in their particular native towns. Thus the Grand Vizier Mehmed Sokollu (died 1578) built an architecturally interesting combination of mosque and *medrese*, decorated with tilework from Iznik, in the capital. In addition, he built a bridge over the Drina in his home region.[47] Less prominent but still successful Ottomans who had come to court through the levy of boys also instigated building projects in their home towns. Sinan, the chief architect from the Kayseri area, built a fountain in his native village,[48] and there are many other such examples. In this way the inhabitants of even some very remote places were reminded that one of their own had risen to a

senior position in the service of the sultan, thus indirectly at least consolidating
their links to the Ottoman centre.

In the case of Egypt, the involvement of dignitaries in building projects
other than those ordered by the Ottoman central government has been studied
more closely than anywhere else. Until the beginning of the nineteenth century,
the local government there was run by the Mamluks, in whose hands political
power had lain since the middle ages. The Mamluks were brought to Egypt
as young military slaves, mainly from the Caucasus in what is now southern
Russia. Their everyday language was Turkish even though they were often of
Circassian or Georgian rather than Turkish ethnic origin. Since Islamic law
prohibits enslaving Muslims, we can assume that they were all of non-Muslim
background. After converting to Islam, completing their education and
becoming accustomed to the Egyptian climate, the Mamluks acted as military
rulers over a civilian population. From 1250 onwards the rulers of Egypt also
came from their ranks; a new sultan emerged after political struggles, often
fought out with arms in hand, between the strongest groups of Mamluks.[49]
Following the Ottoman conquest in 1517, the central government in Istanbul
appointed its own governors for the new and valuable province. As there were
no more sultans of Egypt, most armed conflicts between the Mamluks lost
their *raison d'être*. However, the recruitment of future Mamluks in the
Caucasus for service in Egypt continued, although Syria, which had also been
ruled by the Mamluk sultans until 1516, was separated and placed under
direct Ottoman control. While the central government in Istanbul demanded
an annual tribute from the Egyptian Mamluks, the most powerful among
them still had sufficient resources to indulge in active patronage. After all,
these military men and tax-farmers paid less and less in the form of tributes
after about 1660–70, and increasingly used monies meant for state projects for
their own purposes.

Both the leading Mamluks of Cairo and wealthy merchants built magnificent dwellings, some of which survive.[50] In the sixteenth century many
Cairo patrons took their lead in architectural terms from Istanbul. However,
in the eighteenth century, by which time effective power had passed from the
governors appointed by the central administration to Mamluks and locally
recruited soldiery, a style peculiar to Egypt became popular, which reincor-
porated elements from the Mamluk architecture of the middle ages.[51] Indeed,
from time to time texts come to light reflecting the objections of the Ottoman
central government to inordinately expensive Cairene building projects, and
making clear the ambitions which those wielding local power hoped to further
via their involvement in patronage.[52]

In addition to the Muslim patrons there were also non-Muslims, who had
varying degrees of authority according to their political position. At the court

of Mehmed the Conqueror, figures such as the historian and panegyrist Kritobulos, who was a Byzantine Christian, and the scholar George of Trebizond, were able to find official support. We also know of influential non-Muslims at court in the sixteenth century. Respected Christians with this kind of background could become patrons by supporting churches and monasteries.[53] Monks from monasteries within Ottoman territory were generally allowed to seek subsidies in Christian areas. St Catharine's Monastery of Sinai, to take just one example, made active use of this permission.[54] In the sixteenth century, Meteora monasteries were built on steep mountains in what was then Ottoman Thessaly, and in some parts of Greece and Serbia, neo-Byzantine architecture and painting flourished for a considerable time.[55] By the eighteenth century, Greek families from the capital, who provided interpreters for the sultan's council and acted as provincial governors in Moldavia and Wallachia (in today's Romania), had become important patrons for Greek culture.[56]

What a Patron Needed to Consider

We know that several Ottoman sultans took a keen interest in the buildings they commissioned. This interest is particularly well documented in the cases of Mehmed the Conqueror (1451–81) and Süleyman the Magnificent (1520–66). Buildings helped legitimize the rulers, above all in the eyes of the upper class within their own empire, but probably also in the eyes of foreign Muslims if, for example, the buildings were erected in Mecca and were thus visible to Iranian or Indian pilgrims.[57] Mustafa Âlî, the historian and literary figure, cited the buildings constructed by Süleyman the Magnificent immediately after his conquests as evidence of the greatness of the ruler. He believed, however, that only victories over the unbelievers gave a sultan the right to patronize architecture.[58]

Before the ruler approved a large building project, he would often demand to see the designs. These consisted of plans and sketches, sometimes also of three-dimensional models.[59] A magnificent model of the Süleymaniye (completed in 1557) was particularly famous, and was kept or copied after the completion of the building. In 1582, when Prince Mehmed, later Mehmed III (reign: 1595–1603), was circumcised, a Süleymaniye model was borne along in the ceremonial procession.

As well as visual designs, the sultan's treasury also demanded cost estimates. These have tended to survive better than plans and elevations. In such documents, materials such as stone, lead or tiles were listed together with their prices. There would also be an estimate of how many days' work would be involved, differentiating between the work requiring qualified masters and that which could be undertaken by unskilled or trainee workers.[60] If the project involved repairs, there was often a clause indicating that the estimate was valid for a repair undertaken as soon as possible. If work was delayed, higher costs could be expected.

If estimates were difficult, as in the case of the domes which still adorn the gallery of the Great Mosque in Mecca, it seems that construction was begun on a trial basis.[61] A limited number of domes were built and these provided a basis for calculating the cost of the originally planned total of 400–500 domes. It appears that the sultan decided that the project was too expensive, as only 152 domes were finally built. On the completion of a project, more accounting was done. If less money had been spent on material or labour than had been anticipated, the financial administration quickly reduced the budget allocation retrospectively.

However, before beginning construction, the person initiating the project had to acquire the necessary land.[62] This aspect was of particular importance in the case of pious foundations, in which the patron or patroness was attempting to bring blessings upon his/her soul. For this, land and materials had to be acquired by legitimate means. The problem was that by the middle of the sixteenth century Istanbul, within the Theodosian city walls, was already full of pious foundations. As we have seen, land for a new foundation could be acquired only via complex exchange deals which increased costs. Women from the ruling dynasty were perhaps in a more difficult position than the current sultan when they wished to acquire land for building on.[63] Some building patrons and patronesses avoided these problems by constructing their foundations in less populated areas, such as on the Asian side of the Bosphorus in Üsküdar, which was still an independent town at that time. In the second half of the sixteenth century, pious foundations proliferated there; the population of Üsküdar grew as a result and gradually it was integrated into the city of Istanbul.

One fundamental decision which the patron or patroness had to take related to the use of expensive materials for decorative features. 'Classical' Ottoman architecture is characterized by the harmony of its proportions, the diversity of spaces and the overall pattern of its façades, as well as by its attention to detail at a technical level. Expensive marble, gilt and even gold or silver features were the exception, being used, for example, in the mausoleums of celebrated Islamic holy men and in particular at the tomb of the Prophet in Medina. In the foundation deeds for the Süleymaniye, Süleyman the Magnificent explicitly stated that he had opted for a spacious and solidly-built mosque and had largely refrained from costly decoration.[64] Thus the amount spent on decorative features depended not just on the available budget, but on the character of the building. Moreover, certain architectural forms were reserved for the sultan, such as mosques with more than one minaret. Clearly, in addition to religious, aesthetic and financial considerations, the decisions of the patrons also had a political relevance.

The Procuring of Building Materials

Due to the high costs of land transport, even the sultans resorted to using quarries close to the Sea of Marmara for their Istanbul building projects.[65] Quarried stone (*küfeki*) or the marble of the Marmara Adası could be shipped directly to the capital. However, transporting blocks of stone on barges, which were difficult to steer, was so laborious that such work was treated as a punishment, like rowing aboard galleys. Once the blocks of stone had arrived in Istanbul, they were loaded on to carts and drawn by oxen or horses to the hilltops where many great sultans' mosques were built. Bricks were produced outside the city, as was the lime used for making mortar.[66]

Sultans and viziers often considered that buildings in the representative, official style, built in areas where transport problems made construction particularly difficult, were good for the prestige of the ruler. Thus, soon after Ottoman dominance had been established, the flat ceilings of the Great Mosque in Mecca, dating from the Mamluk era, were replaced by small domes. These were apparently viewed as something peculiarly Ottoman, and thus justified the additional expense involved in transporting the materials to the Hejaz.[67] Sometimes transport problems were regarded as a factor which positively increased the value of a building. This was why three of the four great columns to be used for supporting the central dome of the Süleymaniye were obtained from so far away. One or two columns came from Baalbek in Syria and another from Egypt.[68] Transporting them laboriously over such great distances was no doubt meant to highlight the extent of the empire ruled by Süleyman the Magnificent, but also to draw attention to the technical resources at his disposal. In papal Rome similar ideas seem to have obtained at this time. In 1586 an Egyptian obelisk, which in fact had already been in Rome since ancient times, was erected in St Peter's Square amid great celebration.[69]

Although Ottoman monumental buildings were of stone, large quantities of timber were required at the construction site, not just for doors, windows, panelling and pulpits, but also for the scaffolding. Even if the wood used for this last purpose could be reused after the completion of the building, it had nevertheless to be procured. Moreover, the Ottoman conquest of Egypt in 1517 led to an increased demand for timber in Cairo.[70] During the middle ages, Cairene dwellings and the palaces of Mamluk dignitaries had all been built entirely of stone. However, after the Ottoman conquest, the Egyptian upper class developed a taste for ornate wooden ceilings, of the kind produced until very recently in some parts of Anatolia. Probably, the prestige attached to styles of building favoured by the Ottoman conquerors was responsible for the rapid spread of wooden ceilings, while the scarcity and high cost of timber positively contributed to their attractiveness. As a result of the increased demand, timber was sometimes smuggled in from Anatolia; for the Ottoman government attempted to reserve the limited resources available for the needs of the capital and, in particular, for the naval arsenal.[71]

Procuring iron and lead could also be a complicated process.[72] Iron was required for window lattices as well as for the brackets which held together the large blocks of stone used in Ottoman monumental buildings. Ottoman architects also sometimes included iron reinforcing bars in the transverse arches which supported a dome or semi-dome. Although this was not a particularly elegant solution, it did contribute to the strength of the construction. Lead was used mainly for the sheets with which the vaults and domes were covered on the outside. Seen from above, the lead makes Ottoman buildings look like a blue and grey sea of domes.

Lead often occurs naturally together with silver, and it used to be obtained in the Balkans. However, when American silver appeared in the sixteenth century, it lowered the value of silver in the Mediterranean region and the Balkan mines became unprofitable. Many were abandoned. Thus, locally produced lead became scarcer, and from the seventeenth century onwards domes were sometimes covered with imported lead. Most iron for civil buildings came from the town of Samoko in what is today southern Bulgaria. There it was smelted in small blast furnaces.[73] Before a major building project such as the Süleymaniye, the Ottoman treasury had to advance funds to the furnace owners so that they could adequately expand their capacity. This procedure could cause problems for the local *kadi* whose responsibility it was to find the sound businesses required. He also had to answer for any losses caused by blast furnace masters who took the proffered credit but then failed to deliver any goods. Iron was either transported on the river Maritza (Meriç) to the Sea of Marmara or else brought to Istanbul with caravans. From there it was sometimes dispatched to distant destinations. Thus the iron required for the major alterations to the pilgrims' mosque in Mecca, ordered in the second half of the sixteenth century by sultans Selim II (reign: 1566–74) and Murad III (reign: 1574–95), came from Samoko.[74]

Architectural Aesthetics

There was hardly any literature concerning architectural theory in the Ottoman domain. However, we can learn how contemporaries reacted to buildings from some descriptions of famous structures. We shall now examine the description by Ca'fer Efendi of the Sultan Ahmed Mosque, which today features as the Blue Mosque in the itinerary of every visitor to Istanbul.[75] Evliya Çelebi's description of St Stephen's Cathedral in Vienna is also instructive, but in a different way. Evliya's response to a building belonging to a barely familiar artistic tradition gives us an understanding of the aesthetic ideals of an educated Ottoman.[76]

When beginning his biography of the architect Mehmed Ağa, which incidentally contains a small but valuable dictionary of Ottoman architectural terminology, Ca'fer Efendi pays conventional homage to God, the Prophet Muhammad and the first four caliphs. In the praise of God, the whole of creation appears as a mosque, with a high vault, ornate lamps, brilliant wax candles, brightly-lit windows and high arches. God is extolled as the architect who has created such a magnificent building 'without sketches, without mathematics and without analogy' (probably for calculating the proportions).[77] This motif of the creation as architecture also occurs in a poem dedicated to the Sultan Ahmed Mosque, in the first lines of which the sky is described as a vault, the rainbow as the prayer niche (*mihrap*), the sun and moon as shining candles and Mount Sinai as an ornate pulpit. Here, too, God is praised as an architect, although Ca'fer Efendi places less emphasis on the majesty of God than on the majesty of the sultan, 'God's shadow'. He praises the founder, Sultan Ahmed, for building the mosque, in his generosity and beneficence, at a formerly deserted place, inhabited only by owls.

In line with a topos already familiar from the Süleymaniye, the mosque under construction appears as the temple of Solomon, the ruler and prophet.[78] To praise the ruler is inseparably linked to praising the mosque, since in the following prose section the fourteen balconies of the minaret are interpreted as standing for the fourteen sultans to have reigned up to and including the current ruler, Ahmed I. In another poem the mosque is described as the 'commander-in-chief of the army of mosques'. This is another allusion to the sultan, whose title of caliph extols him as 'commander-in-chief of the faithful'. Similarly, Ca'fer Efendi relates the sultan to another image centrally important to him, namely that of the mosque as a heavenly rose garden.[79] The same image is used for the sultan's good deeds, while, in the good wishes with which he closes, Ca'fer Efendi expresses the hope that the heart of the sultan should bloom like the bud of a flower.

Images of the heavenly garden, with its roses and nightingales, go back a long way in the architectural aesthetics of the Islamic world. In the text which Ca'fer Efendi calls his 'Spring Poem', he likens the licking flames of the mosque's lamps to tulips and the stream of water within its fountain to a nightingale in its cage. His poetic imagination associates the sultan's private box, which was in an elevated position, with the outstretched branches of a plane tree, while the columns are described as the trunks of palm trees.[80]

4. The Sultan Ahmed Mosque, Istanbul. The many annexes to this great
foundation are missing from this late eighteenth-century European engraving.
From: Mouradjea D'Ohsson, *Tableau général de l'Empire Ottoman*, vol. 2
(Paris: L'Imprimerie de Monsieur, 1788).

However, this garden is not a physical reality but a product of the human
imagination. This allows the poet to celebrate the artistry of the architect,
whose 'rose garden' is complete and perfect. Similarly to the heavenly garden,
the mosque is elegantly constructed and the architect has built it in a place
of unsurpassable beauty. Moreover, the mosque has a symbolic significance;
in fact, according to Ca'fer Efendi, the whole work of art is a great symbol.
In addition to the symbolism of human creation as an image of God's creation,
of praise of the ruler and of the motif of the heavenly garden, Ca'fer Efendi
introduces a musical element. As an observer familiar with music, the author
interprets the building using musical terminology.[81] Since Mehmed Ağa, the
architect responsible for the Sultan Ahmed Mosque, had been a practising
musician in his youth, such an interpretation seems entirely convincing.
Unfortunately, we do not know if, and to what extent, the sultan was familiar
with these symbolic aspects of his mosque.

Religion and aesthetics go hand in hand in this homage to the Sultan
Ahmed Mosque. By contrast, Evliya Çelebi, who is describing a non-Muslim
building, first has to deal with the problematic issue of the relationship between
its religious and aesthetic aspects. The traveller describes St Stephen's
Cathedral in superlatives. He claims that nowhere in the world has 'such a
massive building and so venerable a work of art been constructed', and that
this 'nowhere' includes the Islamic world.[82] One important element in his

appreciation of the beauty of the cathedral is the costliness of its construction. Thus Evliya describes (or rather, invents) the sixteen columns made of rare and costly minerals, that allegedly support the church. He also extols the cathedral's treasures – its monies and books – while in his description he adorns the domes, by which he meant the vaults, with a shining mosaic. This too was a figment of the author's imagination, influenced by his familiarity with Byzantine churches. Another aspect which attracted him was the opulent fashioning of the cathedral, and he asserted that no two of its many kneeling chairs were quite identical.

Music plays a central role in Evliya's praise of the cathedral as well.[83] Here, however, unlike in the case of the Sultan Ahmed Mosque, musical harmony is not used as an analogy for architectural harmony. Rather, Evliya is concerned with the beauty of the sound of the organ and the technical skill involved in using the instrument. It is conceivable that Evliya's informants told him something of the high status of the organ in contemporary European culture.[84] If this was the case, such respect for the organ would certainly have coincided with Evliya's own outlook. He was very fond of referring to real or invented technical achievements in his travel narratives.[85] Interestingly, Evliya's description of the organ also touches on a religious aspect. He refers to the prophet Davud with the wonderful voice, who, as David of the Old Testament, was also regarded in Europe as the patron saint of musicians. Evliya was well aware of this fact. He also alludes to Jesus, 'the spirit of God'. Yet he stresses immediately that the organ itself has nothing to do with anything supernatural, but rather with an entirely human art. It seems very much as though Evliya is here referring to a conception of beauty common to followers of all three monotheistic religions. The same may be said of his discussion of the works of art in St Stephen's Cathedral. A depiction of paradise impresses him so much that 'on catching sight of it [paradise] one wants nothing more than to give up the ghost immediately and enter the Abode of the Blessed'. On the other hand, Evliya regards an image of hell as a powerful exhortation to be penitent, just as those who commissioned such illustrations would have wished them to be seen.[86]

In Evliya's description, music and painting are integral parts of a 'whole work of art', the framework of which is the architecture of St Stephen's Cathedral. This is why he always returns to the matter of the building itself after digressions concerning the organ or paintings. Evliya also sees the cathedral, including its spire and its imagined inhabitants, not just as a structure which is complete in itself, but as a scene of ongoing activity. He refers to religious services as well as to pious and scholarly lectures, debates, music-making and religious asceticism. Victor Hugo would have appreciated Evliya's description.

8

Town Life: Urban Identity
and Lifestyle

Ottoman towns were not governed by any specific municipal law, town halls and mayors being innovations of the nineteenth and twentieth centuries. This has led earlier historians to assume that for most townspeople it was a matter of indifference whether they lived in Istanbul, Bursa or Ankara. Allegedly the inhabitants of the Ottoman Empire defined their identities by belonging to a certain religious community, rather than to a certain town. Admittedly, the significance of religion and of religious communities in particular should certainly not be underestimated, as the latter played an important role even in non-religious activities, such as in tax collection and in resolving disputes. From the traditional theory we may easily gain the impression that the inhabitants of the Ottoman Empire, living in small, starkly divided communities, cared little for their towns. It is sometimes claimed that only the religious and the private, family spheres were important; that is, the mosques, churches and synagogues on the one hand and people's homes on the other. In such a social structure, so the argument runs, there was no room for a real sense of urban identity.[1]

Modern historians would considerably modify such an assessment. Religious identity was certainly important, but it by no means excluded other loyalties. Today it is even thought that the sharp divisions between the different religions and denominations, and the political disputes which went with them, were more a product of the time after about 1770, when traditional groups became politicized in the wake of increased European interference.[2] This changed understanding is partly the result of our taking a more critical view of the manner in which colonial powers acted upon Near Eastern social structures than was usual some fifty years ago. Partly, however, the change reflects a changed understanding: institutional phenomena such as mayors or municipal budgets are no longer seen in such absolute terms as they were a generation or two ago.

Today we tend to look less for evidence of town privileges and more for the cultural expression of an urban sense of identity. That there was Ottoman interest in the concept of the town as a whole is evident from the townscapes, of which there are so many among sixteenth-century miniatures. In these illustrations there is a clear attempt to reproduce the topography of a town in such a way as to make it distinct from any other. There were many such pictures of Istanbul in particular. The tradition begins with the famous Matrakçı Nasuh view from the sixteenth century and continues with the many illustrations of Istanbul which adorned well-to-do provincial homes in the eighteenth and nineteenth centuries.[3] Many goods were also named after the towns in which they were really or allegedly produced. This shows that the reputation of a town was bound up with the reputation of its artisans. At least at certain times, dervish saints could also become symbols of towns, as Pirî Baba did in Merzifon.[4] A town could even become renowned for the beauty of its young people.[5] It seems reasonable to conclude, then, that mayors, municipal law and a town hall are not prerequisites for a sense of urban identity.

Town Quarters

Ottoman towns were divided into quarters, which were generally inhabited by between five and a hundred families, sometimes more, as in Aleppo.[6] Typically, town quarters would be home to between thirty and forty families. These units collected certain taxes levied on their inhabitants and often consisted of people sharing the same religion, ethnic group or denomination.[7] However, 'outsiders' quite frequently settled in a town quarter, causing its original character to change over time. Often neighbours were related to each other, directly or by marriage. The inhabitants of a town quarter attempted to control those who entered and left it, so large through roads suitable for carts were relatively scarce. In troubled times the populations of certain town quarters even erected gates to seal themselves off from one another. Usually there were numerous blind alleys which were considered public streets only to a limited extent. Divided inheritances led to complex, interlocking patterns of housing in which the passage of large loads and sewage disposal both presented major difficulties.[8]

These town quarters were able to demarcate themselves so clearly from the outside world because many artisans and merchants did not work where they lived. In the larger towns in particular, there were often 'business districts' consisting of khans, covered markets and frequently of shopping streets financed by pious foundations. Few people lived permanently in such districts.[9] Unfortunately, we have no information about how long artisans and

merchants spent travelling to work each day. However, since most towns were
small by our modern standards, their journeys were probably not very long.
Istanbul was an exception in this respect: in the eighteenth century it was
already so large that it was no longer practicable to cross the city on foot.
However, in Üsküdar, Galata and Eyüp there were secondary centres which
meant that most people would not have had to travel too far to work. Moreover, the Bosphorus, Golden Horn and Sea of Marmara were all busy with
water-borne traffic.[10] As a result, the Bosphorus villages were integrated into
the capital as early as the eighteenth century.

The Market as an Integrating Factor

Other factors, particularly business links, counteracted the tendency towards
isolation in any given town quarter. Buyers and sellers of both sexes would
meet in open markets and in shops. Everyday essentials were available not
just in the centre, but in the residential districts as well, although the inhabitants tended to be unenthusiastic about the establishment of too many
shops and workshops in their midst.[11] Yet bakers and vendors of perishable
foodstuffs had to be near their customers. The same was true of the public
baths, which many people visited regularly. Only the most affluent could
afford a bath-house on their own property.

Women probably visited the shops of the town centre only on special
occasions, but more frequently they went shopping in their own town quarter.
We know of many complaints lodged against boorish individuals who harried
passing women in eighteenth-century Aleppo.[12] These complaints suggest
that women were able to pass through the streets of 'their' town quarter as
and when then liked. As well as paying visits, shopping would have been one
of the main reasons for leaving the home, although no doubt servants and
children often ran errands. Certain shops were preferred by female customers.
In Istanbul, as we have noted, the embroiderers' shops were popular, probably
supplied in part by women working at home. We have already encountered
the women's market in Bursa, and, for a while, a similar institution functioned
in Istanbul. In Eyüp, the small religious centre before the gates of Istanbul,
it was the shops of the cream vendors which attracted women in the sixteenth
century.[13] Markets and shops thus helped integrate women into urban society,
even if this caused misgivings among many contemporary observers.

There were also pedlars who plied their trades in the residential quarters,
supplying ordinary foodstuffs and, particularly, water. Town quarters located
on hilltops, such as those occupying the citadel at Ankara, did not have any
wells or fountains. A long trek to the next public source of water was the only
alternative to having water delivered – in this respect, Ankara was no different

from many European towns until well into the nineteenth century. Some pedlars no doubt distributed news as well as wares; the exent to which they talked to housewives and servants depended on local customs and individual personalities; the potential existed, at any rate.

Retailers in the residential districts had to obtain their wares either from farmers and gardeners in the surrounding area or from wholesalers based in the town centre. News was often diffused via such relationships, especially news concerning droughts, blocked trade routes, failed harvests and prohibitive taxes. Thus, the links between the inhabitants of each district and the local traders, as well as those between the traders and their suppliers, constituted a counterweight to the isolationism characteristic of many town quarters. In this way, then, everyday trading relationships helped turn a collection of small residential areas into a town or city.

Vernacular Architecture

We know much less about dwellings, even those which belonged to wealthy people, than we do about monumental architecture. Fires, earthquakes and general decay have destroyed most such buildings. Even those structures which have survived from the eighteenth century tend to have been so radically altered that it is very difficult to discover the original form. Moreover, it was not the custom to inscribe dates on dwelling-houses, even though this was standard practice on even minor public buildings. This is why a date inscription from the seventeenth century, discovered a few years ago on a wooden house in the port town of Mudanya on the Sea of Marmara, caused a minor sensation.[14]

Only a single family lived in most Anatolian houses of the sixteenth and seventeenth centuries. This is apparent simply from the small size of the dwellings. In Kayseri at the beginning of the seventeenth century, houses with one or two rooms accounted for nearly 60 per cent of the homes documented in the *kadi*'s registers over a period of several years, and, in fact, the number of tiny dwellings may have been even higher.[15] Yet houses were relatively cheap compared to horses, textiles and other goods, so that it is unlikely that families had to squeeze into intolerably small spaces. Generally the house would belong to the husband and father of the family, who would pass it down to his sons and daughters, while the widow benefited to a much lesser extent. Members of the family would sell their shares of the house to one another, so that eventually the dwelling would end up in sole ownership again. However, there were some instances of married couples acquiring a house together, and of female home owners.

Most surviving dwellings were the homes of influential families, the so-called *konaks*, which often had magnificently decorated reception rooms. There are still some eighteenth-century summer residences beside the Bosphorus, among which the property of the Köprülü vizier family is particularly well preserved.[16] These villas were built partly over the water, allowing boats, which constituted the main means of transport for the occupants, to be moored at the lower level. Cairo also had a well-to-do villa district around the Birkat al-fil, or 'Elephant Pond', and another, called Azbakiyya, where wealthy Mamluks lived in the eighteenth century. In areas where building in stone was the norm, a few *konak*s from the fifteenth and sixteenth centuries have survived, such as for example the Gübgüboğulları house in the central Anatolian town of Kayseri.[17] Aleppo, Damascus and Cairo also boasted opulently decorated residences, some of which remained in the same family for many generations.[18]

Different regional styles can be clearly identified in vernacular buildings. Thus the flat-roofed, one- or two-storey houses of the Kayseri area, with their carved decorations surrounding doors and windows, are quite unlike the houses of Ankara, just 350 kilometres away. There the old town consists of two- or three-storey half-timbered buildings, and carvings are more likely to be found inside the houses than on their façades. Ground floors, which were used for storage and the servants' quarters, had relatively few apertures, but the upper levels had many windows overlooking the street; screens and balustrades ensured that passers-by and neighbours could not see into the house.

Although 'vernacular' or anonymous building was more conservative than 'great', official architecture, styles did change even in the 'vernacular' sector. Above all, the multi-storey houses of Istanbul seem to have been much admired by wealthy provincial house owners. In Ankara, multi-storey houses largely replaced single-storey buildings during the seventeenth century, no doubt under the influence of Istanbul dwellings.[19] From the second half of the eighteenth century onwards, painted vedutes, highly prized at the time in the sultan's palace and among senior dignitaries, suddenly began to appear in the houses of the provincial élite as well.[20] Although countless of them were destroyed by fire (and, in the last fifty years, countless more have been demolished by property speculators), many examples of this form of decoration still survive. Thus, we must consider even 'vernacular' buildings in regional styles to be implicated in a historical process of change.

Most of the plans we know of for dwelling-houses, other than palaces, date from the nineteenth century.[21] Late Ottoman architects, and especially their colleagues from the early republican period, documented sizeable numbers of Ottoman homes. Their records are the all more valuable because many of the houses for which they provided plans and sketches fifty or seventy years ago no longer exist. For older dwelling-houses we have to make do with the lists of rooms which are to be found in many deeds of sale.[22] Only in places such as Aleppo and Cairo, where stone was currently used, is it possible to compare descriptions with surviving buildings.[23]

Most houses in seventeenth-century towns such as Ankara or Kayseri were rather cramped. Generally, only a single room was heated by an open fireplace. In winter, families therefore had to live together more closely than in summer. In many areas, they would either move to a lighter, better ventilated upper storey during the warm season, or, in areas where flat roofs were usual, use the roof terrace as living and sleeping quarters. Unlike European houses of the early modern era, it was unusual for rooms in Ottoman houses to communicate directly with one another. Rather, the rooms were accessible only from a hall or veranda which, during the summer, provided the stage for a great deal of family life.

This arrangement was partly the result of the absence of distinct living and sleeping quarters in Ottoman houses. Bedding would be stowed away in chests or built-in cupboards in the morning and the room then arranged for use during the day. Only in the larger houses was the kitchen clearly divided from the living quarters.[24] Thus, all the rooms were multi-functional, except for the wing known as the *selamlık*, which in the homes of the wealthier Istanbul and Anatolian families was reserved for male guests of the householder. In the *selamlık* there would be a reception room (*divanhane*), sometimes with a niche where a servant could prepare the coffee inevitably served to visitors.[25] If there was sufficient space, the *selamlık* would be a separate building beside the stables and servants' quarters in the complex's entrance courtyard. By contrast, the family resided in a second courtyard, which only female visitors would be allowed to see. However, in less affluent households a room had to be vacated to allow the householder to receive guests from outside the family.

Few town houses had gardens, but there were sometimes trees or ornamental plants in the courtyard. Well-to-do people also possessed ornamental ponds with fountains. However, contact with nature was largely restricted to a period of *villegiatura* during the summer months. Most of the more affluent families had gardens and vineyards outside the town, and unless robbers made the area unsafe, they would move to their summer residences during the warmer part of the year. Shopkeepers and artisans also established themselves in the garden settlements, leaving the town more or less deserted in the summer. This was a time for relaxation, above all for women. Since trees and shrubs obscured private areas and the inhabitants of such settlements tended to be related to one another or at least were long-standing acquaintances, the precautions taken to hide women from male strangers in the town were unnecessary here. Summer settlements were seen as a virtually private domain.

This is evident from a sultan's decree of the years 1568–69, according the inhabitants of the small Anatolian towns of Divriği and Arabgir the right to pay certain taxes as a lump-sum.[26] Tax-collecting strangers were no longer to disturb the townspeople during their summer sojourn in the countryside.

A 'Textile' Culture

We know more about the furnishings of Ottoman houses than we do about their architecture, although most records and surviving objects belonged to wealthy families. During the day the rooms were made habitable with cushions and carpets. A distinction was made between the large, flat cushions for sitting on and those used for leaning against; cushions reflected the affluence of the household.[27] In Bursa, a town famous for many centuries for its silk manufacturing, the standard cushions at the beginning of the eighteenth century were made of a coarse silk or cotton material which it was possible to weave at home. In houses belonging to wealthier townspeople, there were more elaborate cushions of brocade and velvet.

Nobody set foot in the living quarters in their street shoes, and the floors were covered by rugs. These might also adorn divans. Regarding the use of rugs in Ottoman households, some information comes from the inventories of an area which formed a part of the Ottoman Empire only between 1541 and 1699, namely Hungary.[28] Hungarians usually specified the location of carpets entered in testaments and estate inventories, information which is absent from inventories compiled in the Ottoman core provinces. However, we should not assume that the Hungarian aristocrats who, according to the customs register of the Transylvanian town of Braşov, imported Anatolian carpets, had an entirely 'Ottoman' lifestyle.[29] In their dwellings, Anatolian carpets were combined with European-style furniture; textile hangings on the walls of the fortified, very 'medieval' stone houses of the Hungarian aristocracy made them seem a little cosier. For this reason, walls were often decorated with numerous rugs and carpets; one room – and not, it seems, a very large one – in the castle of Szentdemeter, contained a grand total of seven such pieces.[30] Carpets were also indispensable in the houses of well-to-do townspeople; in Braşov the town council presented each of the patricians' daughters with a carpet when they married. In Calvinist churches a carpet covered the communion table, while Catholic priests often placed this item on the steps to the altar. As table coverings were subject to less wear and tear, more rugs and carpets have survived in Calvinist churches.

Carpets were also frequently donated to mosques, from where they were occasionally stolen. A text of the late sixteenth century concerns a carpet thief whose fellow townsmen tried to get rid of him by proposing that he be drafted as a forced settler and sent to Cyprus.[31] Donated carpets were not necessarily new: in some places it was customary to cover the body of a deceased relative with a household carpet, which would then be passed on to the mosque after the burial. Some mosques, such as those in the Ottoman towns of Sıvas and Divriği, accumulated large collections of donated kilims and carpets.[32]

However, most of these textiles were worn out through everyday use and finally discarded. As a result, the number of carpets preserved until now in museums and other collections bears no relation to their original abundance. Today it is hardly possible to conceive of the riches which must have existed in the Ottoman domain. In fact, during the sixteenth and seventeenth centuries Ottoman carpets were numerous in many parts of Europe as well, particularly in Italy, England and the Low Countries. These were depicted in paintings, above all from the fifteenth century onwards (but occasionally even earlier), and since pictures have survived much better than carpets, we may use them to reconstruct much of the history of carpet weaving and of the carpet trade with Europe. A recent monograph dealing with the period from 1540 to 1700 takes account of almost a thousand examples of Dutch carpet illustrations alone.[33] By contrast, only three oriental carpets which have been in Holland since early modern times have turned up in today's Dutch collections, a stark indication of the rate of wear and tear.[34]

Of course, the depictions by Mantegna, Lotto, Holbein or Jan Steen are not a representative sample of the items to be found in an affluent Ottoman household. The carpets encountered by these painters were either diplomatic gifts to the Signoria of Venice or the king of England, or items which had been produced in carpet-making centres such as Uşak or Kula, no doubt with an eye to the export trade.[35] There is little evidence from before the nineteenth century that Anatolian carpet weavers modified their designs to suit the tastes of their European customers. But since it could be difficult to find ready buyers for carpets in Europe, not least because of the high prices, it seems likely that European importers preferred 'standard patterns' which had already found acceptance and which they could be sure of selling.[36] Thus we must assume that a history of carpet styles based on paintings from, above all, Italy and the Low Countries gives only a considerably distorted picture of what was happening in the Ottoman carpet centres.

Pictures do, however, have one great advantage over surviving carpets: it is possible to date them relatively accurately. Thus we can counter a prejudice rife among carpet connoisseurs. All too often it is assumed that all old carpets are consummate in both technical and aesthetic terms. However, if we take into account examples which can be definitely dated via illustrations, we find that, even in the fifteenth, sixteenth and seventeenth centuries, carpets were produced which were crudely knotted and poorly designed. In particular the Dutch masters recorded such defects with their customary ruthless precision.[37] Equally, respectable examples of the carpet-maker's craft can be attributed to more recent times, which have generally suffered from a 'bad press'. Radio-carbon dating has made great strides; yet often this method will only allow us to establish a two-hundred-year limit within which the carpet in question must have been manufactured.[38]

In the period which concerns us here, that is, the second half of the sixteenth and the whole of the seventeenth century, the carpets decorated with animal motifs which feature commonly in earlier illustrations had largely fallen out of fashion in Europe.[39] Instead, buyers preferred 'Lotto' carpets – so called in honour of Lorenzo Lotto (1480–1556) who depicted many of them in his paintings.[40] Such carpets are characterized by a strong contrast between the border and the central field. In early versions the border was decorated with a design known as the 'cloud-band', which can be traced back ultimately to Chinese models. In later examples, we often find a cartouche pattern dominating the central field. There was originally a more or less ornate arabesque design. However, in later variations, the arabesques were often modified so as to resemble a *kilim* pattern. It is this contrast between the borders and the internal pattern which makes 'Lotto' carpets easy to recognize.

Another type of Ottoman carpet of which both original examples and seventeenth-century illustrations (mostly Dutch) survive is known as 'Tran-sylvanian'. Many such carpets came from Anatolia, probably from the area around the western Anatolian town of Uşak, and acquired their name because they frequently decorated churches in Transylvania.[41] Like Muslim prayer rugs, they show a niche pattern; this is often repeated at both ends of the carpet, so that no religious function is apparent and the middle ground appears to be enclosed at its corners by quarter medallions. An Ottoman *şeyhülislam* of the early seventeenth century did in fact once attempt to prevent the production of carpets with prayer niches and other Islamic religious symbols. He declared that such items were improper, as they were frequently sold to unbelievers who were not supposed to own objects of Muslim religious signifi-cance.[42] However, as the surviving carpets and those illustrated in paintings prove, the ban was unsuccessful.

Anatolian carpets were generally decorated with abstract designs, unlike their Persian and Indian counterparts, in which animals and lifelike botanical motifs were prominent. It has sometimes been suggested that this difference was due to the fact that the Islamic prohibition on figurative images was taken more seriously in the Ottoman realm than in the neighbouring empires. However, such an explanation seems questionable, since illustrations of animals and people formed an integral part of courtly Ottoman miniatures. Outside the palace milieu, seventeenth-century ceramics also show figurative designs. Moreover, lifelike illustrations of flowers were typical of Ottoman ceramic decoration of the sixteenth century. Unfortunately, due to the extreme scarcity of textual evidence regarding Ottoman carpet weaving, the true explanation remains obscure.[43]

Woven rugs (*kilim*) belonged in every household, whether home-made or bought from a weaver. Some of the motifs featured in such pieces had a very specific significance in regional folklore. By selecting the appropriate motifs, a young girl could, for example, inform her parents that she wished to marry.[44] Although interpretations of such motifs draw only on studies of nineteenth- and twentieth-century folklore, it seems likely that a similar, older tradition existed. As well as carpets for sitting and resting upon, most adults possessed a prayer rug, decorated with a prayer niche and reserved for religious purposes. Few prayer rugs were particularly valuable, although the material from which they were made did depend on the affluence of the owner.

Pieces of felt constituted a cheaper form of floor covering and were produced in various thicknesses. They might feature pictures or else embroidered decorations. In the eighteenth century, they were often named after the Rumelian town of Yanbolu, where they were produced in large quantities.[45] Quilts were used as bedclothes, and were generally stuffed with cotton. In some Anatolian towns there are still artisans called *hallaç* who prepare cotton for this purpose. When somebody has been badly beaten, he is said to have suffered like cotton in the hands of the *hallaç*. The upper side of these quilts was often shiny and silken; satin, brocade or the products of simple domestic looms (*beledi*) were the preferred materials. Even today, Turkish quilts often have a shiny, monochrome upper material showing off the motifs depicted by the quilt-maker's needle, while the sheets are basted to the underside of the quilt. We do not know whether this was already customary in the eighteenth century or even earlier, but it seems likely. Most sheets in eighteenth-century Bursa appear to have been made of cotton, and rather fewer of linen. Only the very wealthy sometimes had a sheet made of fine, slightly crinkled silk (*bürümcük*).

Household Equipment

Large and high tables were unknown. Food would be placed upon a mat known as the *sofra*, often made of leather, and trays of wood or metal were also used. Even today the word *sofra* is still associated with meals, although the item itself has not been used for many years in most urban households; guests are invited not to table, but to the *sofra*. Dishes were generally made of copper and lined with tin to prevent poisoning. Specialized artisans moved from one village or town quarter to another, renewing the tin linings. These cooking utensils were valuable commodities and the more affluent families would possess whole sets of them. Some owners would have a few show-pieces gilded or engraved with their name and title.[46] Large cauldrons had symbolic significance: when the janissaries rebelled they refused to accept the food provided for them by the sultan and upset the cauldrons. A large cauldron survives in the central Anatolian dervish lodge of Hacı Bektaş, which had links with the janissaries. According to its inscription, it had been presented by the élite troop and was used mainly for festive occasions.[47] Large dervish convents were expected to provide a bowl of soup for arriving guests, and the cauldron, on the boil day and night, became a symbol of hospitality.

Most food was eaten from large bowls or pots, serving a group of people. Coffee cups and their metal holders were the main individual items. Such cups, and the pots in which coffee was made at the beginning of the eighteenth century, were to be found in the legacies even of very poor people. At this time they were also rarely absent from the kit of the travelling merchants or artisans who died unexpectedly in a Bursa khan. Ordinary coffee drinkers used pottery cups, mostly from the town of Kütahya in western Anatolia where everyday and ornamental vessels are still made. Wealthier individuals generally had a cup of Chinese porcelain. As early as the seventeenth century so many of these vessels were imported that apparently the fine pottery of Iznik, which we so admire in present-day museums, could not compete and vanished from the market.[48] Most people owned only individual cups, not whole sets. When an inheritance inventory contains many such cups, the former owners tended to be persons who had required them for professional purposes, such as the barber from eighteenth-century Bursa who seems to have offered his customers coffee while he cut their hair.

Few clay pots and earthenware bowls for everyday use have survived. Excavations in urban areas have turned up large quantities of fragments, but these have not been considered worthy of closer attention. On the other hand, museums have large and small dishes, jugs with matching wash-basins, and other pottery items which were used in wealthy households. Some exceptional pieces are dated or have their owners' names painted upon them. A jug which was made in 1510 bears the name of an Armenian named Abraham from the town of Kütahya.[49] Such items, produced for customers with plenty of money, display a clear historical development. In the fifteenth century, abstract designs predominated, derived from the style of Timur's court (lived 1336–1405). In the sixteenth century, however, floral patterns became more popular, especially those featuring carnations and tulips. Around the middle of the century, the colour red began to be used for the first time.

In top quality pieces, the areas painted in red produced a clear relief. Larger-scale compositions based on identifiable representations of flowers were to be found decorating walls in palaces and mosques and also on show-piece items of tableware. The technical quality of Ottoman pottery declined in the seventeenth century. Nevertheless, attractive depictions of ships, animals and sometimes people continued to be produced.[50]

During the sixteenth century the small town of Iznik in north-western Anatolia was famous for its pottery. However, during the same period, there seem to have been masters of the art in Kütahya as well. Moreover, the latter managed to survive when the pottery trade of Iznik collapsed during the seventeenth century. In the eighteenth and nineteenth centuries a less sophisticated, but very colourful branch of ceramics also flourished in Çanakkale, near the Dardanelles. Masters of this tradition also turned their hand to free-standing sculptures of considerable size. In Ankara's Ethnographic Museum, for instance, there is an impressive statuette of a camel from Çanakkale.

Built-in cupboards or chests were used for storing clothes or household items. In wealthy Kayseri houses, a whole wall of the main room was often equipped with niches, some of them fitted with doors.[51] Bedding was placed in the larger spaces, while the smaller shelves housed books and caskets or might be used for lamps. Many inventories mention the boxes and caskets in which smaller objects were kept. Chests were normally made and sold in pairs. The more exact stock-takings discriminated between chests with and without feet and between those made of wickerwork and the others, not described but probably made of planks.

If the elements of the typical Ottoman domestic room were very different from what was typical in early modern northern Europe, there were similarities with other Mediterranean societies. The French historian Fernand Braudel once noted that in early modern times it was far more comfortable to spend the winter in the Low Countries or the German lands than in Rome or Naples.[52] Although the winters are often cold, heating appliances were rare in the Mediterranean region and in Ottoman Anatolia or the Balkans, and in the winter life must have been hard. While living quarters and kitchen were equipped with fireplaces, the damp chill of the Bosphorus no doubt penetrated the houses once the wood of doors and windows had warped.[53] Some theological schools tried to conserve heat by having very small windows or even none at all. This, however, merely obliged the teachers and students to spend more time outside, even in winter. In addition to fireplaces with their tower-like chimneys, some of them decorative rather than functional, there were also charcoal braziers which warmed the townspeople without producing too much smoke. These braziers often had a cover under which people could warm their feet, although such covers could easily catch fire or cause the brazier to be upset. In Istanbul and Bursa, where houses were built of wood, many of the countless devastating fires probably started in this way. However, if it is possible to generalize – at least for the Mediterranean parts of the Ottoman Empire – from data relating to Bursa in the early eighteenth century, such braziers were to be found only in the better equipped households.

Comparisons: Common Ground and Regional Differences

A comparison between Egyptian or Syrian domestic culture with what we know so far about Istanbul and Bursa shows that even across the great expanse of the empire the great cities shared a common domestic culture.[54] In none of the three areas was there much heavy furniture. Bedding was stowed away in built-in cupboards or niches when not in use, allowing the same rooms to be used during the day for living quarters and during the night for sleeping in. In all three regions cushions were used for seating, although the material with which they were covered varied from region to region. In hot climates, woollens were probably avoided, especially during the warmer part of the year. Using public baths for the maintenance of bodily hygiene and as social centres for women was also common to the townspeople of Syria, Egypt and Anatolia or Istanbul.

Certain fundamental priorities equally were shared by the inhabitants of Ottoman towns, such as maintaining control over access to residential districts and ensuring the privacy of the living quarters. If at all possible, male guests were, for this reason, received outside the family quarters. In all three regions, blind alleys were popular, for they facilitated control over access to the neighbourhoods and set the latter apart from the thoroughfares open to all comers.

Here, however, the differences begin. In Anatolian towns 'non-public' roads (*tarik-ı hass*) were relatively uncommon, as most blind alleys seem to have been regarded as public streets. By contrast, in Aleppo there were many more roads controlled by their inhabitants.[55] Living quarters in Cairo and Istanbul were often located in the upper storeys, with many windows offering a view of the street outside.[56] In Aleppo, where dwelling-houses were nearly all single-storey buildings, the outside walls lining residential streets tended to be bare of windows.[57] Instead, Aleppo homes had windows overlooking their court-yards, which were to be found in virtually every house. However, in Ankara, Kayseri and Cairo, courtyards were frequently dispensed with. With space at a premium, courtyards in the great city of Cairo evidently distinguished the homes of affluent inhabitants from more modest dwellings, to which access was via a stairwell.[58] Thus, shared priorities by no means necessarily resulted in common architectural forms.

When constructing a house it was important to ensure that none of its windows offered a view of the inside of a neighbour's dwelling. People who failed to adhere to this rule were quite frequently summoned before the *kadi*. However, the limited amount of space available made compromises necessary. Even if neighbours could not see directly into one another's homes, the *kadi*'s registers of Ankara, Bursa, Aleppo and Cairo make it clear that townspeople were generally well informed about their neighbours' affairs.[59] A good deal of information was clearly exchanged at the baths, in the cafés and by women visiting each other at home. Thus, it would be quite wrong to think that each house was sealed off from its neighbours. What we know of the domestic architecture of Aleppo, so different from the layouts of Cairo or Istanbul, might seem to support such a conclusion, but it would be an unrealistic one.

Similar nuances emerge when we look at how the houses were used. In Cairo during the Ottoman era it was usual to conjoin a large, multi-functional living space with rooms intended for specific purposes such as toilets, sleeping niches or kitchens. Such clusters constituted more or less self-contained apartments.[60] A large house would hold several of them, which a testator might bequeath to various members of his household. It was thus a straight-forward matter to receive male guests from outside the family by allocating them one of these apartments. Given this arrangement, in eighteenth-century Cairo structural divisions between men's and women's quarters, of the kind found in large houses in Istanbul for example, were not customary, and the appropriate terminology (*selamlık*, *harem*) was equally absent.[61] However, a study still needs to be undertaken of the houses of Istanbul, based on material from the *kadi* registers, to confirm whether residential patterns in Cairo really differed as substantially from those of the capital as would currently appear.

All in all, the houses of Ottoman townspeople had to fulfil very similar requirements right across the length and breadth of the empire. Until the nineteenth century, even non-Muslims did not have a domestic culture distinct from that of the Muslims. If Jews or Christians could afford to do so, they would build pleasant homes for themselves in the particular style of the region.[62] Moreover, Muslims and non-Muslims quite frequently sold houses to one another, which would indicate a basic similarity across religious divides. The absence of clearly demarcated ghettos was probably a significant factor in the standardization of domestic culture.

However, similar functionality by no means implied complete consistency of form. Regional differences were inevitable, depending on the climate and the available building materials; above all, though, differences stemmed from distinct architectural traditions. In the case of Cairo, which has a particularly well-studied architectural history, continuities have been identified even from the Egyptian dwelling-houses of the Pharaonic age.[63] In Anatolia, too, continuities stretch back into the distant past, namely the Turkish domestic architecture of central Asia on the one hand, and the Anatolian architectural traditions of antiquity and the middle ages on the other.[64] In addition, the buildings of the imperial capital, Istanbul, often set the standards for wealthy townspeople in the provinces. Yet elements of Istanbul's architecture combined in many different ways with local traditions. We are still in the process of untangling these interwoven threads in order to get a better idea of the complex whole.

A Plea on Behalf of Ottoman Urban Culture

Art historians have tended to emphasize aspects of the lives of Ottoman townspeople which hark back to the nomadic past of the latter's ancestors. The design of some dwelling-houses, the fondness for garden settlements, the scarcity of furniture and the preference for easily transportable textiles have all been interpreted in this light.[65] Moreover, the great mobility not just of the rural dwellers, but also of the townspeople has attracted attention. If robbers made the streets unsafe or a tax-collector made excessive demands, it was not uncommon for a whole town quarter to be deserted by its inhabitants, many of whom would move to quite distant places.[66] At the beginning of the seventeenth century there were complaints that the small Black Sea town of Varna was being overrun by refugees from eastern Anatolia, who seem to have traversed the Black Sea in its entirety.[67] 'Istanbul's streets are paved with gold', says a popular phrase, and although, in the eighteenth century, the Ottoman authorities erected roadblocks to halt the flow of incomers to the capital, Istanbul remained the chief destination for all those who were dissatisfied with conditions at home.[68]

Nevertheless, it would be wrong to infer from the mobility of so many townspeople that their culture was not truly urban. The misunderstanding goes back to the Europeans writing about their travels in the sixteenth and seventeenth centuries whose impressions have influenced even twentieth-century ideas of Ottoman towns. Western and central Europeans often found it difficult to comprehend how these towns, which were so foreign to them, actually functioned. This is particularly evident from the travel diary of Hans Dernschwam, a pensioned chief clerk to the Fugger (the German mercantile and banking dynasty), who accompanied Ferdinand I's ambassador from Vienna to Istanbul and thence to the northern Anatolian town of Amasya.[69] Dernschwam's conception of a town was derived from the appearance of places such as Augsburg or Nuremberg: densely populated and with multi-storey stone houses. By contrast, the low buildings of sixteenth-century Anatolian towns seem to have struck him as rather rural. Only Istanbul, with its many old and new monumental buildings, made a deep impression on European observers. As early as the sixteenth century the painters Pieter Coecke van Aalst and Melchior Lorich visited the Ottoman capital in order to 'draw from life' there.[70] Most Anatolian and Rumelian provincial towns attracted little interest from European travellers.

Partly as a result of the tendency of Turkish historians perhaps to over-emphasize the nomadic early history of Ottoman culture, and of most European travellers' neglect of provincial towns, the urban component in Ottoman culture has been consistently underestimated. Yet closer examination shows that this culture was in fact very strongly urbanized. Thus in the second half of the seventeenth century the travel writer Evliya Çelebi wrote a ten-volume work dedicated almost entirely to the towns of the Ottoman Empire. Of the countryside, the author was really interested only in the roads leading from one town to another, and the Bedouins, robbers and rebels whom one might encounter while travelling on them.[71] Evliya indulged in etymological speculations about the names of towns and felt compelled to say something about their founders; this shows that he saw Ottoman towns very much as historical units. If, as was not infrequently the case, he did not know who had founded a particular town, he did not shy away from invention. For example, he tells us that the founder of the town of Muğla in south-western Anatolia was a prince by the name of Muğlu Bey, otherwise completely unknown to historians.[72] However, it would have been pointless to invent such stories if educated Ottomans had not had a sense of both the value and the historical continuity of their towns.

9

Ceremonies, Festivals and the Decorative Arts

Dervish Convents and Dervish Ceremonies

We cannot lay claim to any understanding of Ottoman architecture and domestic culture without knowing how, by whom and for what purposes mosques, palaces and kiosks were used. There exist, for example, rooms in the annexes of the great Ottoman mosques of the fifteenth century which may have been intended as accommodation, since they contain not very functional fireplaces and built-in shelves. Some experts believe that these often sumptuously-appointed rooms housed visiting dervishes.[1] This begs the question of which dervishes were eminent enough to lay claim to such exceptional quarters. Would these dervish sheikhs occupy the rooms on a permanent basis, or would they have to make room for others after a few months? We can only speculate. We may hypothesize, furthermore, that the disappearance of this type of building in the early sixteenth century was connected to the lower esteem in which dervishes were held by the sultans and other powerful patrons of the time, now that many of them were suspected of heterodoxy.

In fact, it was after death that many dervish sheikhs perhaps exerted their greatest influence on religious architecture. The tomb would be enclosed and a dome might be constructed over it, attracting pious visitors wishing to present their entreaties to the saint. Sick people, women unable to bear children and, more recently, students worried about their exams all tied – and sometimes still do tie – scraps of material to the railings of the mausoleum or to a nearby tree in order to draw themselves to the attention of the saint.[2] Often trees, rocks or fountains beside which the pilgrims performed their devotions became parts of the shrine. At the tomb pious visitors would light wax candles, the soot from which would gradually accumulate over the course of many years on the walls and ceiling of the mausoleum. Wealthy visitors would donate metal candelabra or carpets for the floor. And as we shall see, the destruction of many shrines in the nineteenth and especially in the twentieth centuries was also a symptom of changed religious practice. Jurists and theologians in the 1920s and 1930s decried the lighting of wax candles and the tying of scraps of material as reprehensible superstitions. After the banning of the dervish orders in the newly created Turkish Republic (1925), many saints' tombs were completely destroyed. That many of them have been reconstructed in the last ten years is a new twist to the story.[3]

Although cults often arose around the actual tomb of a saintly dervish sheikh, they could also originate in other ways. Sometimes a cult developed around a saint who had lived in the distant, hardly remembered past, in which case various places might claim to house his remains. Seven places supposedly possessed the tomb of Sarı Saltuk, a warrior probably active in thirteenth-century Dobruja.[4] There were also instances, reminiscent of parallel episodes in medieval Europe, of the remains of a saint being 'found' at some politically opportune moment. Thus, the remains of Eyyüb Ansari, an associate of the Prophet, who was said to have lost his life in the seventh-century siege of Istanbul by the Arabs, were 'discovered' during the Ottoman conquest of Istanbul in 1453. This invention enabled the Ottoman sultan, who had few links with early Islamic history, to present himself as fulfilling a mission going back, indirectly at least, to the Prophet himself.[5] Above the grave, a shrine was erected which highlighted this connection between the sultan and the Prophet's associate. In later centuries, it was at this spot that a religious dignitary would buckle the sword of Sultan Osman on to a sultan who had newly ascended the throne.

Although dervishes settled around holy tombs, the latter's designs demonstrate that veneration of the tomb was by no means the only ceremonial function of the dervish lodge. Members and followers of the order would gather in a room generally known as the *meydanevi*. In the case of the Mevlevîs, this room was a substantial one, since it had to accommodate large numbers of dervishes performing the cultic dance, and space was also required for a small orchestra.[6] Moreover, the order's ceremonies were open to non-members so that, in larger convents at least, room had to be left for the audience. In the case of the Bektashis it was necessary to be recognized at least as one of the order's sympathizers and followers in order to be admitted to the ceremonies. However, in some places a large proportion of the inhabitants regarded themselves as descendants of the saint who had originally founded the convent, and in such cases a large number of visitors could also be expected. If there were many women among them (as there often were, particularly at Bektashi convents) a special building was sometimes constructed for them, such as the so-called 'bread-house' at the Hacıbektaş convent.[7]

However, even the kitchens of dervish communities were not purely functional spaces. Ottoman sultans sponsored dervish convents only partly because
of the saintly reputation of their founders. Their main consideration was the
hospitality which dervishes offered to travellers.[8] This hospitality was particularly important along routes with little traffic, where there were no hostels
open to the public (khans) and where travellers were by and large left to their
own devices. However, the dervishes' hospitality became a ritual in its own
right, as the traveller Evliya Çelebi did not fail to observe; he regularly
mentions the soup offered him in the convents.[9] Extravagant kitchen buildings,
covered by domes and distinguished by ornate chimneys, highlighted the
ritual of feeding guests. The Mevlevîs even went one step further. Here the
dervishes responsible for the kitchen, namely the cauldron master and the
cook, were also the masters of novices, responsible for allocating duties in the
lodge. When a candidate presented himself he was obliged first to undertake
menial duties such as collecting firewood. Later he would be sent to the
market to buy the convent's groceries and other everyday items. And if it was
finally decided to admit the dervish to the order, the sherbet maker – who
would serve sherbet in honour of the new member – the cook and the master
of novices all played central roles.[10]

Festivals of the Sultans' Court, Celebrated in Town

Many court festivals took place within the walls of the sultan's palaces at
Istanbul and Edirne or, in the eighteenth century, in the enclosed grounds of
the great villas on the shore of the Bosphorus, but they are not relevant to
our purpose. More pertinent are the great festivals ordered by a sultan and
celebrated not just in the palace, but in the whole of the capital and often in
the larger provincial towns as well.[11] Apart from some records in Ottoman
chronicles, the eyewitness reports by Evliya Çelebi provide valuable information concerning these festivals, as do those by European travellers. It is true
that few of the latter spoke the Ottoman language, and that they must
therefore have overlooked or misinterpreted certain features. In particular,
their language difficulties must have prevented them from understanding the
political message articulated in specific festive episodes. However, certain
festivals constituted the highlights of the Istanbul visits of these travellers
(many of whom had some connection with a diplomatic mission) and they
therefore described them in great detail. Of course, foreign visitors saw only
the public parts of Ottoman festivals, that is the episodes taking place in the
city's streets and squares or in the outer courtyard of the palace.

Court festivals of the most elaborate sort were celebrated when a prince
was circumcised.[12] Still magnificent but somewhat less elaborate were the

weddings of Ottoman princesses.[13] By contrast, the weddings of sultans themselves were public events only up to the fifteenth century, when the Ottoman sultans were still marrying princesses from neighbouring and rival dynasties. Although no details are known, magnificence was *de rigueur*; the wedding of Mehmed the Conqueror to Sitt Hatun, the Dulkadır princess from eastern Anatolia (1449), lasted three months.[14] From the sixteenth century onwards, though, there were no longer any remotely equal dynasties in the lands surrounding the Ottoman Empire with whom the dynasty could have exchanged princesses. At this time sultans started generally to take slave girls as their concubines. Even when the ruler married a freed slave or the daughter of a dignitary, as sometimes did happen, the occasion was not marked by a public celebration, and neither were the weddings of those princes who had not yet acceded to the throne.

Circumcision celebrations, on the other hand, were very public occasions. Since one festival was usually arranged in the honour of several princes, the ages of the children being circumcised could vary considerably. In 1675 two sons of Mehmed IV were circumcised amid impressive celebrations; Prince Ahmed (who was to ascend the throne in 1703 as Ahmed III) was then two years old, while the future Sultan Mustafa II was twelve.[15] In the first days of the circumcision festivals the children often accompanied the sultan to somewhere outside the city, where they were allowed to see the festive decorations prepared in their honour. For each of the princes to be circumcised (and for each princess about to be wedded) there would be the wooden poles or pyramids known as *nahıl*s, copiously decorated with real or artificial flowers and fruits, often gilded or silver-plated. Apparently the *nahıl*s were intended as fertility symbols. Generally, one large and several smaller *nahıl*s would be dedicated to each child. In addition, so-called sugar gardens were manufactured, in which trees, kiosks and other decorative objects were modelled in sugar. These objects cannot all have been edible, since many of the substances used for colouring them were toxic. However, when one considers how expensive and rare a commodity sugar was until the nineteenth century, it becomes clear that these gardens represented a form of conspicuous consumption.[16]

From the accounts pertaining to various stages in the preparation of the 1720 festival, we can gain an insight into the activities 'behind the scenes'. For making *nahıl*s and sugar gardens, for the foodstuffs to be served at the festive banquet, for equipping festival stewards and torch carriers, purchasing copper utensils and new clothing for the palace pages, 20,100 *guruş* were set aside; this sum also covered presents and administrative expenses, yet it probably fell far short of the total spent on the festival.[17] The list of purchased items could hardly be more varied: included in the cost of producing the *nahıl*s were purchases of paper, charcoal for heating and for the foundry

5. From the festival book illustrated by Levni, showing the circumcision feast of
1720 (Library of the Topkapı Sarayı, Istanbul). Four obelisk-like structures (*nahıl*),
decorated with flowers and architectural ornamentation, were erected in the grounds
of the Eski Saray.

furnace, flax, willow twigs, flowerpots and wooden pails. There is even a sheep in the list; this was to be sacrificed to win God's blessing for the work in progress.[18] Adhesive, to the tune of 18 kilograms, was procured for a wide variety of purposes, while for the colourings which illuminated the flowers and fruits of the *nahıl*s and sugar gardens there was indigo, named after the city of Lahore, today in Pakistan; 15 kilograms of costly saffron were also acquired.[19]

On each of the fifteen days over which the 1720 festival was spread, there were banquets for the various state dignitaries, and the lists of provisions for these occasions have also survived.[20] Meat soup and lamb were planned as the meat dishes; these seem to have been decidedly spicy, as the list includes 118 kilograms of pepper! However, this may well have been a clerical error. Cinnamon and cardamom were also consumed in considerable quantities, although this involved but a few kilograms. However, over 52 kilograms of saffron were used, representing real extravagance. This spice cost the same by weight as cardamom and cinnamon imported from South-East Asia, although it was cultivated in nearby northern Anatolia. Large amounts of saffron were probably required to colour sweet dishes, particularly those made of rice. Equally luxurious was the relatively small quantity of mastic which appears in the accounts: 1.28 kilograms cost 1,000 *akçe*. *Baklava* was served as one of the sweets. There were probably also candied chestnuts, still a speciality of Bursa: 64 kilograms of chestnuts and 4,153 kilograms of sugar are listed. Some of the sugar was probably used to candy the many other fruits provided for the guests, such as almonds (519 kilograms), raisins, dates, apples, nuts and apricots. Or it may have been needed to sweeten the juice of 2,817 lemons, as well as the pitchers of lemon juice also acquired by the sultan's kitchen. For making the *baklava*, 12,088 kilograms of honey were needed.

However, the greatest use of sugar and perhaps also of honey was in the production of confectionary figures. These came in various sizes,[21] but could generally be carried upon a tray on the head. Birds and fish were the most popular, but there were also lions and leopards, as well as mythical figures such as mermaids.[22] Like the sugar gardens, these figures were coloured. However, we know that at the end of the procession the sugar birds, fishes and mermaids were distributed among the subjects and soldiers, so it seems likely that only non-toxic colouring agents were used. These figures appear to reflect a certain taste for the exotic which was shared by many members of the Ottoman upper class with their counterparts at early modern European courts. There were in fact many Jews among the confectioners, descendants of immigrants from Spain and Venice, who were thus no doubt familiar with many decorative motifs of the European Renaissance.[23]

Among the other ingredients used in the festival kitchens, the most notable is the large quantity of butter fat (13,404 kilograms), compared to which even the amount of flour recorded seems relatively modest. A good part of the butter fat would have ended up in the fillings of the various types of *baklava* and in rice dishes; the lists refer to over 236 *keyl* (1,745 kilograms) of rice.[24] However, some of the rice, which was explicitly described as being of high quality, was probably also used for the sweet called *zerde*. This was provided for the many boys whose circumcision festival was arranged by the sultan, as a charitable gesture together with the princes' celebration. Yoghurt and vegetables are major items in modern Turkish cuisine; and the festival accounts confirm that the same thing was true in the eighteenth century. As well as the thick cream (*kaymak*) still used in many modern Turkish desserts, the accounts mention 209 dishes of yoghurt and another 300 kilograms of the 'loose', variety, probably supplied in bags. Rather like modern *torba yoğurdu*, this type had already lost a large part of its water content. Among the vegetables feature 39,437 aubergines and about 1,000 kilograms of pumpkins, as well as a large quantity of okra, quite apart from 302 bundles of parsley and other aromatic herbs. Unfortunately, it is not clear whether the vegetables were served warm, with a small amount of meat, or whether they were eaten cold. However, since mention is made of only a little olive oil, it seems more probable that they were mostly served warm. Until now no record has been found of the large quantity of bread which must have been consumed.[25]

Artisans' Pageants

Among the major attractions in circumcision festivals, as well as in the solemnities marking the departure of the Ottoman army for a campaign, featured large parades of artisans. Various guilds of the capital (and, in at least one case, those of Edirne as well) would file past a kiosk where the sultan was seated. This was known as the 'parade kiosk', and as the different guilds passed, they would hand costly presents to the ruler. Such pageants were also recorded for posterity in literature. In 1582, when Sultan Murad III's son, later to become Mehmed III, was circumcised amid particularly splendid celebrations, the event was described in a 'festival book'.[26] Many miniatures from this volume illustrate in great detail the parades of the artisans which marked the occasion. Literary descriptions of this event, however elaborate, tended to be based mainly on the prosaic lists of participating artisans which were put together for practical, organizational purposes. Evliya Çelebi probably drew on such a text from the year 1637 for his description of the artisans' pageant in the Istanbul volume of his travelogue.[27] Other authors, such as Evliya's contemporary, the Armenian scholar Eremya

6. Confectionary animals. From the festival book illustrated by Levni
(Library of the Topkapı Sarayı, Istanbul).

Çelebi, also wrote about the guild parades, although none in as much detail as Evliya. Finally, we have the 'festival book' which the writer Vehbi was officially commissioned to write for the circumcision of Ahmed III's three sons in 1720.[28] This text was also illustrated with miniatures by Levnî, the great Ottoman artist of the eighteenth century. Oddly enough, the many Europeans who witnessed the Ottoman festivals paid relatively little attention to the pageants of guilds.

Evliya records 1,109 guilds, divided into 57 groups. Each group consisted mainly of guilds whose members were engaged in closely related tasks. These groups seem to have been more than just a means by which Evliya made his enumeration easier, since Eremya Çelebi refers to similar units. According to Evliya, most of the groups of guilds were led by a court servant, who was responsible for supplying the palace or the army with the goods produced by the artisans he preceded. Thus the kasap başı, responsible for the provision of meat, led the butchers, as well as the makers of cheese, yoghurt and candles. An official known as the 'chief merchant [to the court]' was at the head of the guilds engaged in marine transport: seamen and ships' carpenters as well as the captains and merchants who sailed over the Black Sea and the Mediterranean.[29] By these pageants, the Ottoman central government attempted to integrate into the structure of the state those artisans who, though rather poor, maintained links with the troops stationed in the capital and therefore could rebel if discontented. Unfortunately, no contemporary source describes how these measures were received by the artisans in question.

Many guilds did not merely file past the sultan, but rather created tableaux vivants which were drawn on carts or carried through the streets on the artisans' shoulders. Ottoman miniatures feature such showpieces much more often than they do actual shop scenes, and presumably the aim was to create visually attractive scenes. Modern historians of the theatre regard these scenes as the indigenous beginnings of dramatic art. An elaborate device was often foregrounded to attract attention, for example the glass-furnace, surrounded by working glass-blowers, which featured in the pageant of 1582.[30] The cook-shop owners used a kitchen oven, with finished dishes upon it, as the centre-piece of their scene. In 1720, even a three-dimensional model of a Turkish bath was brought along to enable the bath attendants to show off their trade.[31] As well as the working process itself, products of the trade were also presented. Thus the weavers of costly materials either carried the appropriate bales before them, or bore banner-like illustrations through the streets, to exhibit the intricate patterns of their materials.

In particular, these festive self-portrayals by Ottoman artisans celebrated technical skills, either by displaying masterly pieces of work, or by virtue of the simple fact that the young craftsmen produced usable goods as they were

7. Janissaries and artisans on the At Meydanı (Hippodrome). From the festival
book covering the circumcision festivities of 1582. The float is evidently being
pulled and pushed by men.

jolted along on a moving platform.[32] This emphasis on craftsmanship formed part of the sense of identity of Ottoman guild masters, who thus set themselves apart from outsiders who were really or allegedly incompetent. Not just in their pageants, but also in the petitions which on occasion they sent to the Ottoman government guildsmen defined themselves as possessors of skills. In response the administration was keen to strengthen the position of guild masters in relation to their unorganized competitors, who were difficult to control and even harder to tax. Some festival floats clearly depicted the hierarchical construction of shops and workshops, as the masters were distinguished from their assistants by their more costly clothing. Without doubt, the masters and the officials had a shared interest in maintaining this hierarchy, and the guild pageants gave expression to this consensus.

In some artisans' pageants, members of the state apparatus also appear, such as the various grades of jurists and theologians. This broadened the pageant into a depiction of Ottoman society in general, orchestrated by the sultan's officials. There were also parades involving mainly the more senior officials, at which the subjects were mere spectators.[33] One such parade, in 1720, was described by members of the Habsburg diplomatic mission. Among the participants were the supreme commander of the artillery, the Ağa of the janissaries and the various palace and chancellery officials, along with theologians and sheikhs. In this distinguished company the barbers responsible for the many boys to be circumcised together with the princes appeared rather as outsiders. One small detail shows clearly that certain parades were indeed self-portraits by the state hierarchy which underlined its pre-eminence over the lower orders. Carpenters accompanied the floral decorations (*nahıl*) which formed the high points of these pageants, with orders simply to demolish any projecting structures on the houses impeding the passage of the procession and the large, bulky *nahıl*s in particular. However, the house owners were at least immediately paid compensation.[34]

As well as representing the overwhelming and somewhat intimidating might of the Ottoman state, the pageants also contained a carnival element (Terzioğlu, 1995). The Austrian diplomatic report mentions that between the janissaries and the *Çavuş* in the 1720 parade of Ottoman officials, there was a 'mascherata' of men who had smeared oil over themselves. They beat back the 'common people', that is, the spectators, when these crowded too close, using dummy clubs filled only with air. In this report the participants in the 'mascherata' are thus portrayed as stewards, but we know from other sources that these men also functioned as clowns. The combination of the two roles at least meant that fun was poked at the lower officials of the state, who would have been all too familiar to the townsmen who were policed by such personages in everyday life.

8. In the foreground is a giant, two-headed puppet. Note also the lambskins decorating the mock 'shop' in the background. From the commemorative book illustrated by Levni (Library of the Topkapı Sarayı, Istanbul).

There was yet more room for the comic element in the guild parades. According to the miniatures illustrating the circumcision festival of 1720, the participating artisans carried with them puppets which were larger than life-size. These represented bearded men in long caftans, some wearing headgear decorated with tassels.[35] One of them bears on his shoulders an object which resembles an outsized pumpkin. In another miniature there is a Janus-faced figure, on the left a beardless youth and on the right a man with a black beard. In this illustration the young man wears a tight-fitting cap, from under which a little hair shows only at the temples. The older man, by contrast, has a cap decorated with a tassel, with a flap projecting from the front. It is quite different from the headgear worn by the human participants in the pageant. The young figure holds in his hand a small puppet dressed in red, probably meant to represent a boy. At least one of the men armed with muskets accompanying this double figure has his face blackened, as may several of his comrades. This scene was possibly meant to depict the stages in a man's life – but why, then, is there no depiction of old age?[36] Although the portrayals of age in early modern Europe have been thoroughly researched, nothing is yet known of Ottoman treatment of this theme.

Festive Structures, Fantasy Architecture and Fireworks

As in European festivals of the Renaissance period, Ottoman celebrations featured 'edifices' of plywood and tent canvas, hung with silks and velvets and placed upon barges, in order to provide a special setting for the occasion. Marquees were particularly popular.[37] Such temporary structures made it possible to hold large receptions and banquets without being restricted by the limitations of the Topkapı Palace in terms of either space or etiquette. However, the tent also had a symbolic value in the Ottoman cultural domain, as it was associated with victorious military campaigns and memories of the early, conquering sultans. For Ottoman dignitaries the tent was emblematic of their position; a vizier who had fallen from favour would have his guy-ropes cut. This symbolic role explains why the tents were often so sumptuously appointed. Unfortunately, the tents erected for the great circumcision festivals have not survived, so we are left only with descriptions and a few miniatures. As well as the tents, whole pavilions were constructed to give eminent spec-tators a comfortable view of the performances. At the circumcision and wedding festival held by Mehmed IV at Edirne in 1675, such a building was constructed in the immediate vicinity of the palace, in order to enable the ladies of the harem to watch without being seen.[38]

According to some miniatures, when a sultan returned to the capital from a campaign, the streets were lined with costly fabrics to provide a colourful

9. Acrobats on the At Meydanı (Hippodrome). In the foreground is the obelisk dating from Byzantine times and the snake column, both of which have survived. The sultan is observing the scene from a bay window of the former Ibrahim Paşa Palace (today the Museum for Islamic Art). From the festival book covering the circumcision festivities of 1582. (Library of the Topkapı Sarayı, Istanbul).

backdrop for the ceremonial procession.[39] Unfortunately, we do not know who supplied these textiles and saw to it that they were fixed in position. Was it the townspeople themselves, or did the materials come from the palace stock? It is also conceivable that some textiles might have been borrowed from the weavers' guilds. It was in fact common practice to borrow from the artisans of Istanbul whenever existing palace stocks of pots, bowls and cauldrons were insufficient for some large banquet.

In many pageants, models of buildings were displayed. Apart from the model of a Turkish bath which featured in the artisans' parade of 1720, the best known example is the model of the Süleymaniye Mosque, which was carried through the streets in the festival of 1582 (see Chapter 7).[40] This was already twenty-five years after the completion of the Süleymaniye, so it seems unlikely that the model had originally been used during construction to illustrate the design for the donor, Sultan Süleyman, and for architects and officials in charge of the building project. From among the great mosques of Istanbul the Süleymaniye was probably chosen because even shortly after his death in 1566 Süleyman the Magnificent was already revered as the representative of the 'golden age' of Ottoman power.

In addition to model mosques and baths, models of fortresses were often carried in pageants. One miniature, illustrating the parade of 1720, shows such a model, borne on a four-wheel, spokeless cart drawn by an elephant. In this shaky vehicle there was a three-storey model: 'soldiers' peeped over the battlements, which were guarded by canon, while in the background was the castle's lofty, magnificently painted donjon.[41] In the lower storey a painting of two horsemen can be made out. They are carrying a light device which appears like a net for birds or butterflies. On the higher part of the tower there is another painting of two, apparently unarmed, horsemen, at whom several men on foot are levelling their muskets. In the foreground, half obscured by the battlements, there stands a figure with an elaborate headdress and scimitar. Next to the cart, men armed with muskets are running along the street. They are aiming at the castle from all sides, creating copious amounts of 'powder-smoke', while up on the highest battlement a show fight takes place. This seems to be the enactment of a story which has yet to be identified, possibly the capture of a fort in the Peloponnese, which had recently been wrested back from the Venetians. It is worthy of note that the model fortress is decorated with painted figures of probably about a quarter life-size. Apparently the restrictions on representing people and animals, otherwise taken very seriously in the Ottoman domain, were considerably relaxed for the duration of the festival.[42]

Festive structures were also a feature of the war games which often marked victory or circumcision celebrations in the sixteenth and seventeenth centuries.

10. A tower has been drawn up on wheels and is being defended against its 'attackers' amid clouds of gunpowder. Note the painted marksmen on the upper part of the tower and the model of a galley in the foreground, decorated with tree branches. From the festival book illustrated by Levni (Library of the Topkapı Sarayı, Istanbul).

A model of a castle would be constructed for this purpose from wood and canvas, equipped with model cannon and manned by persons wearing uniforms reminiscent of those worn by Hungarian or Habsburg troops.[43] This model, bearing the name of some fortress recently fought over in Hungary or elsewhere, would then be stormed by Ottoman troops and conquered in a show battle. This game was probably nothing new to the European observers invited as guests, as similar show battles were also popular at festive occasions in European countries, particularly in Spain. Such events often ended with the burning of the model fort, which had been prepared beforehand to ensure exciting visual effects.[44]

This leads us to the other way in which light was used for briefly projecting fantasy architecture into the real world, that is, the town illuminations known as *donanma*.[45] These might be ordered by the sultan to celebrate the birth of a prince or princess, but were also a part of the victory celebrations after the capture of a town or stronghold. Houses and, in particular, mosques were illuminated by rigging lines to the balustrades of the balconies from which the muezzins called to prayer. Attached to these lines were glass receptacles in which wicks burned, steeped in oil and protected by a lid from the effects of wind. Those who could afford these multi-coloured glasses were able to create colourful patterns with them if they chose.[46] Even today such decorations are rigged to the minarets of Turkish mosques for religious festivals, even if in the age of illuminated advertisements they no longer have quite the same effect as in the past, when the setting sun left towns in complete darkness.

Festival days were often brought to a close with firework displays. In the Ottoman Empire the Egyptians were thought to be particularly adept at making fireworks, and indeed they dismayed many pious individuals with their habit of celebrating successfully completed pilgrimages to Mecca with firework displays.[47] On the other hand, the Europeans resident in Istanbul in the seventeenth and eighteenth centuries regarded the Turks themselves as masters of the art. There are even records of Jewish firework specialists. At the circumcision festival of 1720, one of them fell a victim to an offended chief eunuch, who had the firework master executed on account of a technical mishap.[48] In addition, the organizers of Ottoman festivals sometimes hired European firework masters; the glamour associated with anything or anybody new and exotic probably explains the special reputations enjoyed by foreign specialists in the Ottoman Empire and abroad.

Ottoman and European Festivals

Pageants in which the social hierarchy was manifestly represented were as common in the Ottoman domain as they were in the European late middle ages and Renaissance, and they continued to be celebrated into the eighteenth century. Both cultures also shared the tendency to depict the social hierarchy with a touch of the grotesque, making it acceptable by means of parody.[49] However, in the Ottoman domain there was much less of the carnival-like and unrestrained element which was typical of European pageants until state and church expurgated 'offensive' parts in the seventeenth century, and finally managed largely to put a stop to public festivities altogether. This is why European observers of Ottoman public festivals, all of whom belonged to the nobility or the bourgeois élite, often praised the restraint and high level of order demonstrated, as they saw it, by the public.[50] It seems that, in the eyes of many European visitors, the discipline which was still to be instilled in the subjects of their own countries already existed in the Ottoman realm. Yet the clowning of the festival stewards and the texts of some puppet-plays show that the weaknesses and absurdities of their rulers were not necessarily taboo to Ottoman townspeople either.[51]

The acrobats' displays which were often a part of Ottoman pageants were also a feature of festivals during the period of the European Renaissance, as were the firework displays which brought them to a close. Even the practice of decorating the route of a parade or procession by hanging out the finest materials available was to be found in both cultures. Miniatures illustrate the tradition in the Ottoman domain, while many Renaissance paintings show the same custom in Europe. In both the Ottoman Empire and in the European Renaissance, the building of fanciful structures and the creation of *tableaux vivants* were typical elements of public festivals.[52] These common features no doubt explain why European observers were so fascinated by Ottoman celebrations; after all, in many respects these festivals coincided with the expectations of the foreign guests. Since the basic pattern was familiar, they were able to admire the artistry of a particular performance or mock the poor quality of another. Similarly, the keen interest Sultan Ahmed III (reign: 1703–30) took in French gardens, palaces and courtly pastimes may be seen against the background of a common festive culture.

The Relationship between Ruler and Subjects as Expressed in Festivals

Our sources, be they Ottoman or European, describe almost exclusively festivals commanded by the sultan. Even if, in Cairo or Damascus for example, senior officials played a central part in a festival, they took care to emphasize that they occupied their eminent positions only as loyal servants to the sultan. Their letters, diaries, travel accounts and 'festival books' reflect the enthusiastic interest of both European and Ottoman writers in the sultan's festivals. By

11. Firework display beside the sea at night, with a fireworker in the foreground.
From the festival book illustrated by Levni (Library of the Topkapı Sarayı, Istanbul).

contrast, they had very little to say about the festivals of Ottoman subjects. The two phenomena are closely related. Our sources are not 'impartial'; if they had been penned by Ottomans, they form part of a discourse in which the sultan's might was exalted. In the case of European observers, the basis was the whole conception of monarchical power. These texts thus reflect Ottoman society in a manner which is doubly refracted. First, the ruler and his officials ordered that the guilds, for example, should form themselves into a pageant, the basic characteristics of which were without doubt determined largely by those wielding political power, and only to a much lesser extent by the artisans themselves. Moreover, the authors describing these events tended to write from the same perspective, legitimizing the rule of the sultan or, if European visitors, referring to the ideal of absolute monarchy.[53]

Except at those festive parades in which the sultan returned to his capital after a victory in battle, he was almost always a spectator at celebrations and performances. In this respect the Ottoman sultans differed from absolute monarchs in Europe, such as Louis XIV, who often played appropriate parts in mythological ballets as a young man.[54] However, the role of spectator did not mean that Ottoman sultans were inconspicuous at festivals – quite the contrary. In the miniatures illustrating the two great festivals of 1582 and 1720, the ruler's tent or balcony from where he and his pages watch the performances by artisans and entertainment artists often forms the centre of the composition.[55]

In the festivals ordered by the sultan, the exchange of gifts was an important element. Most of our information relates to gifts presented by senior officials and foreign envoys. However, there was also a similar exchange between the sultan and his subjects. In the accounts relating to the festival of 1720, the gifts from various guilds are enumerated. These were of substantial material value and must have placed a considerable burden on the artisans, who were often quite poor. Unfortunately, few documents have yet been found which reflect inter-guild disputes about the apportionment of costs. For his part, the sultan gave the guilds presents of money to express his satisfaction with their offerings.[56]

Little has yet been discovered about how the inhabitants of the capital reacted to the sultan's festivals. We know of only one, distinctly negative reaction. In 1730 a revolt by the janissaries, who had support among the artisans of Istanbul, led to the murder of the Grand Vizier Damad Ibrahim Pasha, renowned for his architectural patronage, and ultimately to the fall of Sultan Ahmed III. Senior Ottoman officials then ordered the demolition of the kiosks in the garden of the former ruler's new palace-construction, Sa'adabad. Located at the Golden Horn and partly inspired by French models, this complex had been the site of many court festivals.[57] It seems that the destruction of these kiosks was one of the concessions made to the rebellious soldiers in order to persuade them to return to their barracks. Perhaps the buildings caused offence because they were seen as a foreign innovation, copied from the unbelievers. However, the monies spent on their construction probably made the new buildings unpopular among many Istanbul artisans in much the same way that St-Cloud or the Petit-Trianon were resented at the end of the *ancien régime* in France.[58] Moreover, the nature of the festivals celebrated in Sa'adabad may well also have been of significance. These were neither palace ceremonies of the old style, nor public rejoicings in the manner of the circumcision festival of 1720, but rather private festivities, confined to the sultan's circle of favourites and princesses. Possibly this new form of festival was regarded as far more offensive by the artisans and soldiery of Istanbul than the older type of courtly celebration to which they had become accustomed.

The Subjects' Festivals

On the two great feast days of the Muslim calendar it was no doubt usual for people to visit one another and exchange sweets, as well as to present children with new clothes. The Prophet's birthday was also a festive occasion. As to life-cycle festivals, drawings showing Istanbul life recorded the processions in which a bride, invisible in her curtained baldachin, was brought to the home of her bridegroom; such images were much sought after by European customers in the sixteenth and seventeenth centuries. Circumcisions were also celebrated.[59] Particularly from the eighteenth century onwards, foreign visitors described the popular picnics on the shores of the Bosphorus or at the Golden Horn. According to Evliya Çelebi, many larger towns had *mesires*, park-like landscapes, to which excursions were made.[60] Groups of men and women separately enjoyed such outings, sometimes combined with a pious visit to the mausoleum of a saint. Ceremonial visits to dervish convents were another kind of festive occasion for families involved with a given dervish order.

Ottoman sources have more to say about the festivals celebrated by the sultan's subjects which gave rise to real or alleged disorder and incurred the wrath of the authorities. One of the most important functions of any festival is the relaxation or even temporary suspension of everyday restrictions. Although public festivals in the Ottoman Empire were very civilized occasions compared with their counterparts in early modern Europe, even here there was certainly a loosening of constraints. Eyewitness reports suggest, for instance, that during the great festivals ordered by the sultan, male inhabitants of Istanbul were able to amuse themselves in the taverns of Galata without special precautions being taken to exclude Muslims.[61]

On the other hand, when it cames to activities not organized by the authorities, Ottoman sultans and officials seem to have been as mistrustful as the
absolutist bureaucracies of early modern Europe. Thus, a sultan's decree of
1564–65 prohibited the parades with which the artisans of some Anatolian
towns welcomed home pilgrims from Mecca. Similar parades marked the
conversions of Jews or Christians to Islam.[62] Although these occasions appear
unexceptionable in religious terms, the way in which the artisans literally beat
their own drum, against a backdrop of flags and festive illuminations, seems
to have made the authorities in Istanbul wary. In the North African provinces,
where the grip of the central powers was laxer, such processions remained
part of town life.[63]

Other festivals were banned because Sunni Muslims in the service of the
Ottoman state regarded them as heretical, although it is by no means clear
that the participants themselves shared this opinion. At the end of the sixteenth
century janissaries and future janissaries, often newly-converted Muslims,
were fond of attending a festival in the small central Anatolian town of
Seyitgazi.[64] This festival, combined an annual fair, was loosely connected with
the local dervish convent. Dervishes probably accompanied the festival-goers
as they wended their way through the streets, making music. From the
Ottoman administration's point of view, it was particularly obnoxious that
music was played even in the courtyard of the mosque itself. However, in the
short term at least, attempts to get rid of the festival were unsuccessful.

In 1572, the Ottoman authorities thought they had uncovered another
form of 'heretical' festivity. An annual fair was held, in a small town of
Thrace, together with a church ceremony.[65] In the sultan's decree the annual
fair is mentioned before the ceremony; a European observer would doubtless
have seen things the other way around. Both Christians and Muslims took
part in a procession, which involved exhibiting a 'board' (probably an icon),
decorated with silk and silver, presumably in honour of the local church's
saintly patron. However, the participation of Muslims suggests that a fertility
ceremony for cattle and land was also involved. For the Ottoman authorities,
the idea of Muslims taking part in a Christian ceremony was as objectionable
as the festival which marked the occasion, in which Sinti or Roma were also
involved and which was doubtless not always very restrained. The Christians
were instructed to restrict their worship to the confines of their church.
However, the real threats were directed at the Muslims, who were to be
referred to Istanbul for punishment if they did not comply with the directives
of the ruler.

A festival celebrated by African slaves and freedmen, which has been
documented for the second half of the sixteenth century in the province of
Aydın on the Aegean coast of Anatolia, provoked a similarly negative reaction.[66]

In this case, however, the authorities did not suspect heresy, but took exception to the way in which funds for the festival were come by. It seems that the Africans would collect money from slave-owners. Menacing scenes developed if the requested money was denied them, causing those affected and other well-off persons to complain about extortion.

In addition, there were occasional directives prohibiting, on the grounds of public morality, the swings which were exceptionally popular at festivities of every kind. These may have represented attempts on the part of the sultan to strengthen his political position by espousing the beliefs of a religious group known in the early seventeenth century as the Kadızadeliler (followers of the *kadi*'s son; see Chapter 4), but which also attracted supporters in later times. Some rulers, however, may just have been trying to strengthen their control over their subjects' celebrations. Exceeding certain otherwise customary limitations was acceptable if the sultan himself was staging the festival, but not if some group of subjects themselves decided on the occasion for these transgressions. A good example of this principle was the presence of women as spectators at festivals. Mehmed III is said to have positively demanded that they witness the celebrations marking his return to the capital after the victory of Mezökeresztes (1596).[67] Similarly, at the circumcision festival of 1720 a large terrace was made available to allow women to take part in the public banquets organized by the ruler.[68] However, apart from at festivals which had, like these, been sanctioned by the sultan, the presence of women in public spaces was regarded with considerable misgiving.[69]

While the festivals organized by the sovereign were the most spectacular and magnificent among Ottoman festivals, they also may have provided an outlet for tensions between the ruling classes and the general population. Since both foreign and Ottoman observers always accepted, indeed amplified, the sultan's projection of himself, traces of such conflicts are rather difficult to find. It would, however, be naïve to assume that all the subjects of the empire – slaves, women or country people regarded as heretics, for example – accepted unconditionally the 'official version' of the social hierarchy as it was presented in the sultan's festivals.

10

Readers, Writers and Storytellers

In our survey of the everyday culture of the Ottoman Muslims we have looked first at aspects of architecture and interior decoration, that is, at town quarters, houses and domestic furnishings. Our consideration of festivals has introduced us to the plastic and graphic arts and simple forms of theatre. We shall now turn to literature. In line with the general intent of this book, we shall be dealing not with courtly or scholastic literature, but rather with the forms in which the everyday world of, above all, the townspeople was reflected. Everyday modes of literary activity are particularly relevant, since the Ottoman state administration, which had a major influence upon the development of the town and only rarely surrendered the initiative at public festivals, had a much less significant role in the literary field. This is true at least in so far as writers did not hope, via their literary activities, to win an official appointment. There were in fact many authors who did hope that their works would qualify them for an official career, but to us they will be of only marginal interest.

In the sixteenth and seventeenth centuries there were cases of theologians and poets being punished or even executed on account of their books or poems.[1] However, in an age when only very few books were printed, there was not yet a formally appointed censor's office invested with the authority of the state to collect and pulp books, or to comb through texts for certain 'forbidden' words. Books with a small readership were rarely copied and have survived only as unique examples, if at all. Under certain circumstances, it was quite possible to write not for learned fellow scholars at the theological schools or for the sultan and his courtiers, but for oneself or for a small circle of friends and relations. This intimacy lends the everyday mode of literary production its particular charm.[2]

Nevertheless, even writing for a small circle of readers did depend on some degree of institutional support. As we shall see, dervish convents brought young people into contact with written culture. This was achieved by means of teaching and libraries, but also by reciting literary texts before a group of listeners – usually men, but sometimes also women. Moveover, following the mystic path enabled some townspeople to speak about themselves and about their dreams. We shall therefore begin by looking at the arts of reading, writing and narrating in the context of the dervish lodges and their members.[3]

The Problem of School Education

We do not know what percentage of the urban population was literate, and there is no documentary evidence to help us fill this gap in our knowledge. However, it would certainly be wrong to believe that access to 'high culture' was restricted to a small number of people at court and scholars versed in religious law, while all the rest of the inhabitants of the Ottoman Empire were restricted to an orally transmitted 'folk culture'.[4] In the towns there were many schools, financed by pious foundations or by payments from private individuals, in which pre-pubescent boys, and sometimes also girls, learned to read, write and recite the Qur'ān.[5] Religious education was the principal aim of these schools. In the countryside they were rare, but not completely absent. Thus, at the beginning of the nineteenth century, the Bektashi convent of Abdal Musa, not far from the small town of Elmalı in south-western Anatolia, even had two rooms dedicated to its school, one for the winter and the other for the summer.[6]

Only a small proportion of the students who had completed a basic education could then have progressed to a theological school (*medrese*) to learn religious law, taught in Arabic, and study theology. Even fewer young people could afford private tuition in order to learn Persian, regarded as the language of literary education. A basic command of Persian equally made it easier to learn the official Ottoman language. Literary Ottoman was interspersed with many loan-words and grammatical constructions taken from Persian, many of which did not feature in the everyday language of even the educated classes.[7]

What did people take with them from the 'children's schools', as these institutions were called to distinguish them from the *medrese*s, which were intended for older pupils? Those who had attended such schools were certainly literate, even if they could not generally understand texts written in the more elevated styles of official Ottoman. Thus, when looking more closely at the written culture of the Muslim townspeople, we become involved with a cultural zone which did not belong to the culture of the *medrese*s and the court, but which was not transmitted by purely oral means either. An analogous phenomenon is to be found in the European history of the Renaissance and the baroque era. At a time when the learned world was using Latin and when

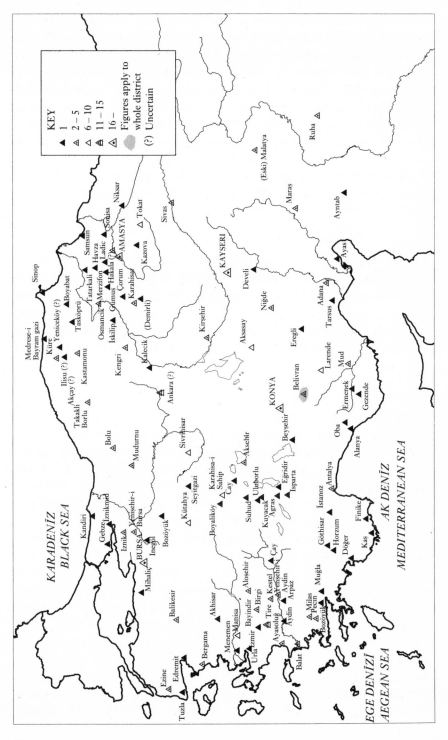

MAP 4 Medreses in Anatolia (c. 1565–80)

court culture was based on Italian, and subsequently on French, there were
many people in the towns able to read and write in their native tongues, but
who did not speak a foreign language. These people read almanacs and saints'
legends in the Catholic areas and the Bible in Protestant ones, as well as the
many broadsheets available at annual fairs and from pedlars.[8] It is more difficult
to define the reading matter of the Ottoman townspeople because, until the
second half of the nineteenth century, there were very few printed books.
However, manuscripts of the Qur'ān in particular were available at a modest
price, at least in eighteenth-century Bursa, and there are occasional references
in estate inventories to 'books in Turkish' or 'a Turkish poem'. Access to
written culture was clearly wider than it might initially appear.[9]

Dervish Convents: A Way into the World of Books

Dervish convents offering interested townspeople access to written culture
were widespread. Larger towns might well have more than twenty of them.[10]
Not many dervishes lived in such lodges on an ongoing basis. In general, the
permanent residents were limited to the superior or sheikh and his household,
and, at least in the case of the Bektashis, those members of the order who
had taken a vow of celibacy.[11] Others would appear each day for devotional
purposes and to carry out their kitchen, storeroom and household duties.
Since we do not know a great deal about the everyday lives of the dervishes,
it is not possible to determine whether perhaps some members of the order,
with no families nearby, would spend the night in some quiet corner of the
lodge. Moreover, there were also people who were associated with the order
as families. The male members would have an 'ordinary' occupation, but met
in the evening or on holidays to participate in the religious activities of the
order. When prayers and recitals had been completed, a convivial social
gathering might ensue. Women would visit the tombs of venerated saints in
order to beg for the blessings of childbirth and good health. Women were also
admitted to the religious ceremonies of the Bektashis and the allied Alevi
communities of central Anatolia.[12]

Many dervish convents belonged to a recognized order, which might, or
might not, be hierarchically structured. Among the Mevlevîs and the Bektashis,
there was a central convent, whose superior (sheikh) nominated the sheikhs
of the other convents before they were officially appointed by the sultan. In
fact, in most convents the rank of sheikh was passed down through the
founder's family, and there was thus only a limited choice of candidates. At
least in the fifteenth century there were occasional examples of female sheikhs;
at least one such woman followed in the steps of another female sheikh as
superior of a convent.[13] In some cases, women were involved as administrators

of the pious foundation, having inherited their status by virtue of belonging to the founder's family. Such women could have a powerful say in things, since they had control over the finances. Sheikhs and foundation administrators influenced the cultural activities of the institution by obtaining donations of books and persuading prominent authors to make extended visits, or even to join the convent lodge.[14]

Larger convents would have a library of books donated by dervishes and other devotees of the saint. Undoubtedly the most famous example is the main convent of the Mevlevî dervishes in Konya, the library of which has survived to the present day. Published as a book, the catalogue runs to three hefty volumes, including treatises of Qur'ân interpretation and great collections of the sayings of the Prophet Muhammad, such as those put together by Buharî and Muslim.[15] The great Islamic theologians and mystics, such as Gazalî, 'Attar and, above all, Ibn 'Arabî, are each represented by several manuscripts.[16] In addition, the Mevlevî library possessed an important collection of poetry texts – after all, the order had been founded by Mevlana Celaleddin Rumî, one of the medieval 'classics' in the Persian language. Among others, the catalogue lists Camî, Hafız and Sa'dî, as well as Ottoman poets such as Kaygusuz Abdal and Süleyman the Magnificent.[17]

What makes the Mevlevî collection unique, however, are the texts relating to Anatolian mysticism. These include, of course, the writings of Mevlana Celaleddin Rumî himself, which were the subject of intensive study by generations of Mevlevî dervishes.[18] The library also contains many examples of the writings of his descendant, Divane ('The Madman') Mehmed Çelebi, an inspired mystic who travelled through Anatolia at the beginning of the sixteenth century and is said to have once made a pilgrimage to Mecca accompanied by a group of Mevlevîs and Bektashis.[19] Persian, the language of Mevlana ('Our Lord'), was cultivated particularly in Mevlevî convents. Some dervishes doubtless read the Persian poets of the thirteenth and fourteenth centuries in order to prepare themselves to understand the works of the order's founder. These religious-cum-literary studies were aided by the commentaries to Mevlana's writings, such as the work of Yusuf Sineçak. Şahidî, who lived in the fifteenth and early sixteenth centuries and included autobiographical sketches in one of his mystic treatises, was also represented in the library.[20] Many Mevlevîs also seem to have taken an interest in authors writing in the mystical tradition but who did not belong to their own order. Thus the Mevlevî library contained work by the seventeenth-century mystic Niyazi-i Mısrî, whose inspired preaching had been received with both awe and revulsion by contemporaries. Probably less controversial was the commentary to a work by the mystic Farid al-Din 'Attar authored by the Celvetiye dervish, Isma'il Hakkı.[21]

By contrast, the chroniclers, otherwise among the most widely diffused Ottoman authors, were poorly represented in the collection of the Mevlevî dervishes. Nevertheless, the library is a treasure-house for modern historians. Thus a work which survives as a unique example in the collection has been discovered and published, namely a life of the dervish sheikh Baba Ilyas, who was killed in an anti anti-Seljuk rebellion of Anatolian nomads in the thirteenth century. This biography was written by Baba Ilyas's fourteenth-century descendant, Elvan Çelebi, and constitutes one of the oldest surviving texts in Anatolian Turkish.[22] Elvan Çelebi's verse narrative also provides a counterbalance to the works of the other chroniclers, most of whom wrote from the Seljuk sultans' point of view.[23]

Many other convents had libraries which have since been scattered. However, a list survives which was made in 1826 and details the literary treasures of the Bektashi lodge known by the name of Abdal Musa.[24] This was one of the most important Bektashi establishments, but even today the area in which it was located is remote and rural. Amassing its collection of nearly 150 manuscripts thus must have required a great deal of time and effort. There were more copies of the Qur'ān than of any other text, and the library also contained a treatise on the correct pronunciation of the Holy Book. There would certainly have been a need for this, given that, for the dervishes, Arabic was a foreign language learned only at school. Intriguingly, there is also a work in the library by Mehmed Birgevî, a rigid adherent of *şeriat* law and hardly a friend of the Bektashi dervishes, who were regarded as non-conformist.[25] Multiple copies existed of Mevlana Celaleddin Rumî's works and other texts from the pre-Ottoman tradition of Islamic mysticism. *Belles-lettres* in the Persian and Ottoman languages were also well represented. There were collections of poems by the Persian poets, Hafız and Camî – the latter was esteemed by his contemporary, Mehmed the Conqueror – but also by Bakî and Fuzulî, both important poets of the sixteenth century, in addition to a work by the eighteenth-century poet Nabî.[26] Romantic love stories such as 'Hüsrev and Şirin' or 'Yusuf and Züleyha' were also available. However, the list does not name the writers, so we do not know if these were the Persian originals or versions in Ottoman Turkish.[27]

In order to appreciate this literature, a knowledge of Persian was required, conveyed by Persian–Turkish grammars and dictionaries. Texts covering Arabic grammar were also available to assist students of the Qur'ān. Those interested in the poets' biographies were able to consult a reference work on the subject. Other branches of knowledge, such as medicine, were rather poorly represented. Probably for practical reasons the dervishes seem to have evinced a more serious interest in law books. As well as compendia on the Hanifite school of *şeriat* law, there was a collection of legal pronouncements and another of sultans' ordinances.[28] Anatolian hagiology was represented, including the legendary biography of Hacı Bektaş, the patron of the Bektashi order, although such works were fewer in number than might be expected in one of the main Bektashi convents.[29] Despite the difference in size the basic conception behind the libraries of the Mevlana and the Abdal Musa convents seems to have been rather similar. A well-founded literary education was aimed for, defined in terms of the established Ottoman understanding of education. By no means did the libraries of major dervish lodges limit themselves to reading matter associated with 'popular culture', such as hagiology and religious lyrics in the local language. The libraries of the larger dervish convents, even those located in the countryside, should therefore be regarded as furthering the classical, literary high culture, even if that was by no means their only achievement.

Dervish Convents and Founders' Legends

Nevertheless, both the Mevlana convent in Konya and the Abdal Musa convent did possess several works of hagiology, and we must assume that these texts were written and copied by dervishes. An example from a late period, the end of the nineteenth century, is well documented. In 1895 a certain dervish, about whom little is known, copied the biography of Seyyid Ali Sultan, also known as Kızıl Deli, and donated his manuscript to the main Bektashi lodge in the small town of Hacıbektaş, near Ankara.[30] However, he did not find the original text of the biography sufficiently elegant, and therefore couched it in the Ottoman literary language of his time. His interventions are particularly easy to identify, since we also possess another, less 'literary' version of the same text. We thus have to assume that the hagiology which survives today – often, indeed, only in the form of nineteenth-century manuscripts – is not in its original form.[31] After all, the biographies were copied, not principally for philological or literary reasons – although such concerns were by no means alien to many educated *ulema* and bureaucrats – but rather for religious motives. There was a desire to have a permanent source of reference regarding the life of a venerated saint and convent founder. Since the visitors to the larger dervish lodges always included persons familiar with 'classical' Ottoman literature, there would certainly have been a demand for biographies written in the literary as well as the everyday language.

Let us look at the manner in which the dervish convent of Pirî Baba in Merzifon created the life story of 'its' saint, which survives in two, slightly variant, seventeenth-century versions.[32] Merzifon is a town in northern Anatolia, not far from the Black Sea. As evident from the large baths, founded by Sultan Mehmed I (reign: 1413–21) the town was already significant in the early fifteenth century. There were baths in existence during the lifetime of Pirî Baba, whenever that may have been, and the saint lived for a time in the boiler-house. He was regarded as a 'divine fool', and had given up his original craft of shoemaking. Among other things, he predicted to pregnant women that they would bear sons. According to Pirî Baba's legends, his presence in the baths even during the periods when they were reserved for women, caused the reigning sultan to order an investigation of his case. However, the saint's miracles, or prophecies, ultimately convinced the ruler. According to one version of the story, this encounter between the monarch and the saint led to a generous contribution from the sultan which financed the building of the lodge. Another version has it that Pirî Baba rejected these donations, in line with a tradition among holy men. Both versions agree that the convent was founded only after the saint's death. However, a connection between the deceased Pirî Baba and the founding of the shrine, which still exists today, was established by the claim that shortly before his death, the saint personally sought out the site of its construction.

Thus the biography of Pirî Baba belongs to the category of founders' legends. The miracles which the saint accomplished during his lifetime turned a shoemaker of village background into a personality renowned even in the towns. His fellow citizens seem to have held him in such high esteem that they used him in their battle of prestige with the neighbouring and more important rival town of Amasya, for a while the sultan's residence.[33] The uneducated 'divine fool' put to shame a learned member of Amasya's *ulema* and even, eventually, the sultan himself. Unfortunately, it is not possible to determine when these stories first began to circulate. The events mentioned in the legend suggest that Pirî Baba died in the middle of the fifteenth century, but experience shows that historical details in hagiographical texts are not always reliable. However, it is certain that the lodge already existed at the beginning of the sixteenth century, by which time Pirî Baba was no longer alive.

Both surviving versions of the legend date from the seventeenth century, and it would be interesting to discover whether the local notabilities whose names are cited in connection with the lodge's construction did not perhaps belong to this later period. This is certainly conceivable in the case of a certain religious teacher named Hoca Ibrahim, to whom the more detailed version of the Pirî Baba legend is credited. The second, shorter version comes from the traveller Evliya Çelebi, who probably picked it up during his visit to Merzifon in the mid-seventeenth century.[34] Unfortunately, Evliya does not say whether the tale was told to him, or whether he had access to a manuscript. However, as he writes for an urban audience in the remote Ottoman capital, Evliya is much less interested in the legend of the founding of the convent and the roles played by local dignitaries than in the picturesque aspects of the story, such as Pirî Baba's life in the women's baths. Moreover, he sees Pirî Baba as predicting Ottoman victories, and in particular the conquest of Istanbul, a theme which is referred to only incidentally in the 'local' version of the story.

Pirî Baba's legend is a particularly valuable source of information about the world of small-town artisans; few other texts tell us much about these people's outlook on life. Other hagiological texts are set among the country people and nomads of central Anatolia, such as the legend of Hacı Bektaş.[35] Kızıl Deli, or Seyyid Ali Sultan, is the hero of a legend dramatizing the warfare which bought the Balkans into the Ottoman Empire. It is thought that the original version of this particular founder's legend dates back to the fifteenth century. After many adventures in battle the hero retreats to a hermitage close to Didymoteichon (today in Greece; Dimetoka in Ottoman), which supposedly formed the core of a lodge which existed into the nineteenth century.[36] First and foremost, Seyyid Ali Sultan was a warrior for his faith, and at the start of the story, his religious legitimacy is emphasized. He is sent to do battle in the Balkans by Hacı Bektaş, who was already very much revered at that time. However, the biography survives only in nineteenth-century manuscripts. It is thus impossible to trace the history of the text and to discover whether perhaps the religious motifs and the references to the Ottoman sultan were later additions. Set in the period when Kızıl Deli was in his prime, the main part of the work deals chiefly with battles against, and victories over, the unbelievers, while religious themes are inconspicuous. It is conceivable that the story is a relict of the heroic sagas of the conquest period.[37]

Much hagiology has survived anonymously, and often nothing is known about those few authors named in the texts, such as Hoca Ibrahim, the purported author of the life and legend of Pirî Baba. Sometimes, however, the presumed author of a saint's legend may have developed a second persona by writing in the Ottoman literary language as well. For example, it seems likely that such a fifteenth-century figure, known as Tall Firdevsî, or Firdevsî the Lengthy on account of the length of his work, played a significant part in the creation of Hacı Bektaş's biography.[38] One of the best known examples of Ottoman hagiology, this book contains so many thought-provoking stories, some possibly of Buddhist provenance, that it is an enjoyable read even for the non-specialist.[39] However, at least the last sections of Hacı Bektaş's vita once again concern the founding of a major dervish lodge. The ambitious architecture and wealth of its votive offerings set this foundation apart from the humble central Anatolian village where it was located. Pilgrimage and population growth today have allowed Hacıbektaş, named after its patron saint, to develop into a small town

According to the vita of Hacı Bektaş, his mausoleum was built by a legendary architect named Yanko ibn Madyan. This latter personage was also credited with great Byzantine buildings in Istanbul, which during the lifetime of Firdevsi had been in Ottoman hands for only a few decades. As late as the seventeenth century this fabled personality cast his shadow over Evliya Çelebi's account of the Ottoman capital.[40] Yanko is said to have crowned a long and successful career as an architect by converting to Islam, finally being buried at the entrance to the shrine. In fact, although Yanko ibn Madyan seems to have become a harmless enough legendary figure by the time in which Evliya was writing, in the context of late fifteenth-century Istanbul he was far more controversial. Stories about Yanko ibn Madyan were used by anonymous authors to denounce Mehmed the Conqueror's choice of Istanbul as the new capital.[41] This decision and Mehmed the Conqueror's claim to be the legitimate successor to the Romano-Byzantine emperors were regarded by opponents of the 'imperial project' as nothing less than portents of the imminent end of the world.[42] It is even possible that the story of Yanko's conversion was conceived to undermine the 'anti-imperial' discourse, arising as it did at probably about the same time as the apocalyptic legend of Yanko ibn Madyan, the godless founder of a cursed capital. If the author of Hacı Bektaş's vita really was Firdevsî, then it is significant that the latter apparently was close to the court of Sultan Bayezid II (reign: 1481–1512), even if his poetry was not particularly appreciated in the palace.[43] The legend of the founding of the central Bektashi convent thus creates connections with Mehmed the Conqueror's son and successor. Recently, researchers have asserted that this part of the story is by no means invented.[44] Sultan Bayezid II was known for being devout and is said to have urged the Bektashis to help spread urban Islam among Anatolian nomads and semi-nomads, whose conversion was as yet rather superficial. An unexpected consequence of this policy was that, in the course of time, the Bektashis came to adopt many of the beliefs of the rural peoples they were supposed to be redeeming.

The Telling of Autobiographical Tales

Until now we have seen how dervishes and those around them recounted the stories of their patron saints and the founding of their convents. However, among the dervishes it was also easier than elsewhere to formulate personal life stories. Until very recently it was thought that, until the second half of the nineteenth century, first-person narratives, which so often include auto-biographical elements, were rare in the Ottoman cultural domain.[45] This was often explained by the claim that until the cultural shift of the mid-nineteenth century, individuals were not accorded sufficient value in Ottoman culture for first-person stories to seem worth telling. However, in the last few decades more and more texts have come to light in which a first-person narrator is employed sporadically or continuously, and the traditional argument therefore has to be revised.[46] New outlooks are also apparent in recent research regarding first-person narration in the European Renaissance period. Today it is no longer assumed that people need to see themselves as autonomous individuals in order to consider that their own experiences merit recounting.[47] Rather, they sometimes view themselves as members of particular social groups, which by no means requires a sense of individuality. This change in theoretical perspectives on first-person narration probably gave considerable impetus to the search for Ottoman texts in this genre.

There were also some first-person narrators from outside the dervish milieu. Osman Ağa, for example, who recounts his unfortunate experiences as a prisoner of war in the Habsburg Empire, was not, so far as we know, connected with any dervish order (see Chapter 5).[48] However, first-person narration is so common among the dervishes and their associates that some sort of connection between the two phenomena seems likely. After all, following the mystic path and discerning its different stages did involve a certain amount of introspection and a concern with the state of one's own soul, which may well have provided a basis for first-person narration.

The Diary of an Istanbul Dervish

One particularly striking example of a first-person narrative from a dervish milieu is the diary written by a member of the Sünbülî order, named Seyyid Hasan.[49] Seyyid Hasan, who wrote between 1661 and 1665, does not actually name himself. However, he says so much about his friends and acquaintances, and particularly about other Sünbülî dervishes, that it has proved possible to identify him. Seyyid Hasan was in his early forties when he wrote the diary – he sometimes noted his birthday. During the years in which he was writing it he did not work and held no official position. He thus lived '*bourgeoisement*', as French contemporaries would have put it – off his own means. Unfortunately, he has little to say about the financial side of life. Later he became the sheikh of the Ferruh Kethüda convent, but after his appointment soon ceased to keep his diary. The position of sheikh in this particular institution was a stepping-stone towards the leadership of the main convent of the Sünbülî order, but the diarist remained in the former post, humble enough in itself, until the end of his life. We do not know why his career failed to develop any further. In addition to his activities as a dervish, on Fridays he preached in a mosque. In 1688 he died of the plague in Istanbul, aged almost seventy. As far as we know, Seyyid Hasan hardly ever ventured outside Istanbul in the course of a life which was lengthy by contemporary standards. In this respect, although his position made him a marginal member of the *ulema* hierarchy, he differed from those specialists in religious law who elected to become *kadi*s or professors and spent their careers travelling back and forth between the places where they officiated and Istanbul, the source of all appointments.

When Seyyid Hasan began the diary, the plague was raging in Istanbul, and his wife was one of its victims. His account of this catastrophe is entirely dispassionate. He reports that he returned home after a lengthy absence to find his wife already close to death.[50] He mentions the details of the funeral ceremony, such as the alms customarily given to make amends for the dead person's omissions, and the sweet known as 'soul helva', which was served in remembrance of the deceased.[51] In the weeks which followed, a death is mentioned on nearly every page; women and children were particularly affected. Seyyid Hasan took part in the funeral processions and mentions whenever a respected sheikh of his own order officiated at the funerals. In between, he describes excursions into the surroundings of Istanbul with friends, particularly to Alibeyköyü, then a popular summer resort. In the Islamic domain, and therefore in the Ottoman realm, it was considered a religious offence to flee from an area when plague broke out, as so many of at least the wealthier inhabitants of contemporary Europe tended to do.[52] There is little sense of panic in Seyyid Hasan's sober accounts of deaths and funerals, and he did not confide to his diary any other thoughts he may have had concerning the epidemic.

Seyyid Hasan's diary is interesting above all for the insight it grants us into the activities of a member of the Istanbul 'upper middle class'. Since Seyyid Hasan did not need to work and therefore to spend long hours in a business or workshop, he had plenty of time to meet people. Social contact took place in the dervish lodge or in group excursions, on which Seyyid Hasan was often accompanied by his son.[53] Horses were lent and borrowed on such occasions, and each returned animal conscientiously recorded.[54] Istanbul's great business quarter with its khans, many of which were built in Seyyid Hasan's lifetime, does not seem overmuch to have attracted the author and his friends. Visits to private homes were much more frequent. Since Seyyid Hasan's acquaintances were mostly, no doubt, as comfortably off as he was himself, their houses probably had parts reserved for men in which a guest might sleep. Seyyid Hasan also visited his relations; he mentions sleeping in his mother's home, for instance. She must therefore have lived separately from him, in her own home or perhaps with another of her children. He also refers to meetings with his sisters; since the diary was a private one, there was no reason not to mention the women of the family.[55]

Seyyid Hasan had received a religious education, although he does not, unfortunately, record whether he graduated from a *medrese* in his youth. It seems likely that he did so, since the position of a preacher required theological knowledge. This knowledge could, however, be acquired in the family or in a dervish convent.[56] Writing does not seem to have been a problem for him, and he sometimes mentions reading religious works in the Ottoman language.[57] We do not know how good his Arabic was. However, he and people like him evidently constituted a reading public for which religious works were composed in Ottoman or else translated into that language. His reading habits might be likened to those of well-to-do Frenchmen of the same period, who learned Latin at school without becoming scholars.

Practising Mystics as First-person Narrators

Although Seyyid Hasan was a dervish, his diary was by no means concerned with spiritual experiences. It is true that the author refers to a sheikh of his order simply by the latter's honorary title of 'the Beloved and Respected', but we learn little of this man's spiritual status.[58] This is worth mentioning because other sixteenth- or seventeenth-century dervishes, for instance Mahmud Hüda'î, wrote in quite a different mode. Mahmud Hüda'î penned his diary in Arabic from 1577 to 1578 while he was studying with the celebrated mystic Üftade.[59] Unlike the personal records of Seyyid Hasan, this work seems to have been intended for circulation among dervishes; Üftade had founded a new order known as the Celvetiyye. This is probably why the diary has survived in a number of manuscripts and was translated into the Ottoman language in the second half of the nineteenth century.[60] Readers turned to this work partly because of the information it provided about the person of Üftade and the tales it contained about his miracles. But many readers probably valued this diary because of the respect they felt towards its author. During Hüda'î's lifetime, Sultan Ahmed I granted the birthplace of the sheikh, the small central Anatolian town of (Şerefli) Koçhisar, an exemption from certain taxes in honour of the sheikh's spiritual merits. Even European diplomats used Mahmud Hüda'î as a mediator when they wished to pursue some matter at the sultan's court.[61] One reason why the diary's renown proved so enduring was that it contained many descriptions of dreams. As was usual among dervishes, Hüda'î told his dreams to his master, and on this basis, the master would draw conclusions regarding the spiritual progress of his disciple. However, some readers found the descriptions of dreams irksome and had copies made in which they were omitted.[62]

Despite the large readership enjoyed by the diary among outsiders, it does appear to have been a genuine diary and not literary fiction. Thus it includes references to Hüda'î's family life; like most dervishes, he was a married man.

On one occasion Hüda'î recounts telling Üftade that his wife was in labour, and that his sheikh responded by wishing the couple well. Later on the same day, after a baby girl had been born, he returned to the sheikh, who provided the name for the child. A year and a half later she became seriously ill, and Hüda'î's esteemed sheikh gave him an amulet to protect her against the evil eye, which did not, however, have the desired effect.[63] There are also some references in the diary to the family life of Sheikh Üftade himself.

Hüda'î's records show the spiritual filiation which led from Hızır, Üftade's mystic master, via Üftade himself to Hüda'î.[64] The latter would have considered himself a legitimate dervish sheikh by virtue of his being a student of an important spiritual leader, and in time he too became a famous master. Probably the spiritual status of the two dervish masters elevated these personal notes into a devotional book.

From an earlier period, probably the first half of the sixteenth century, dates the fascinating autobiography of the poet and Mevlevî dervish, Şahidî. It is included in a treatise by Şahidî on his order master, the enthusiastic and inspired Divane Mehmed Çelebi, who made a deep impression on the writer.[65] Later leaders of the Mevlevî order seem to have attempted to suppress this work as far as possible, since its author freely discloses that Divane Mehmed Çelebi allowed those around him to drink wine and use narcotics. For our purposes, Şahidî's story of his own youth, before he had joined the dervishes, is of greater importance. Although his family came from the minor town of Muğla in south-western Anatolia, many of its members did not exactly enjoy a peaceful small-town existence. One grandfather had fought in the Balkans and there carried off and married a non-Muslim girl. Later he lived for a time in Egypt, probably before it came under Ottoman control. After many adventures, one son from this marriage, the writer's father, finally returned to Muğla. Not long afterwards he became a disciple of a Halvetî dervish, who sent him to Iran to further his education. Again Şahidî's father eventually returned to Muğla and there became the successor to his sheikh. However, his wife, who played an important part in the life of her son Şahidî, was not associated with the Halvetî order; rather she was a follower of the Mevlevîs. Şahidî lost his father at an early age to the plague; indeed, two sisters and a brother perished likewise and in the same night.

Şahidî describes in detail how he rejected his mother's decision to apprentice him to an artisan who had been friendly with his father. Instead the young man went to Istanbul and studied there at a *medrese*. He writes of the worldly life led there by him and his fellow students, and of the plague, which could claim the life of vigorous young men in a matter of days or even hours. Disillusioned, he finally returned to Muğla without having completed his studies. He goes on to tell of his search for a spiritual leader, mercilessly exposing the weaknesses of the various sheikhs he encountered. He felt drawn towards the Melametîs, a mystic movement whose adherents led a worldly life in order not to let themselves be drawn into temptation by the awe in which the general population held real or alleged ascetics. Finally he came across the Mevlevî sheikh Divane Mehmed Çelebi, who himself displayed clear tendencies towards the Melametiyye. This encounter influenced Şahidî's development into a notable writer, whose works – except for the one here retold – were frequently read among the Mevlevîs.

Şahidî apparently tells his tale as a story of conversion, a genre with which, following the appearance of Augustine's *Confessiones*, the Christian world was also familiar. For a long time the writer sought the right path, finally finding it with the help of his sheikh.[66] Şahidî probably hoped that his work would win supporters for the enthusiastic, inspirational wing of Mevlevî mysticism. This was well represented in the early Mevlevî order, alongside a conformist, more 'civilized' element.[67] Perhaps Şahidî's book did indeed fulfil its author's intentions, until the Mevlevîs of the seventeenth century took fright at the anti-dervish Kadızadeliler and suppressed the book.[68] It is noteworthy that Şahidî does not only describe the encounter with his sheikh, but also gives us a vivid picture of his family background and youth. It would appear that Şahidî's unswerving search for the right path made his personal story 'relevant' not just in his own eyes, but in those of his readers among the dervishes.

Evliya Çelebi: A Visitor to the World of the Dervishes

Seyyid Hasan's diary is a collection of notes in chronological order without literary pretensions, and in the tales by Hüda'î it also seems that the contents took precedence over the form for both the author and his readers. Things are less straightforward in the case of another first-person narrative of the time, the ten volumes in which Evliya Çelebi (*c.* 1611–after 1683) recounted his travels. Not many contemporaries would have granted his work much literary merit, as can be deduced from the small number of surviving manuscripts.[69] However, since the middle of the nineteenth century, Evliya's star has risen considerably. Studies of parts of his great travel narrative appear nearly every year, some of them finding room for praise of his writing style; indeed, the present volume could hardly have been written without his monumental work.

Evliya's father was a goldsmith serving the sultan's court. His mother was related to the Grand Vizier Melek Ahmed Pasha, who took Evliya with him on trips and also supported him in other ways.[70] Despite these connections, Evliya never showed any interest in a career in the Ottoman administration. Only occasionally did he take on minor tasks, when they offered him the opportunity of visiting regions he had not previously seen. His first journeys led him along the Black Sea coast of Anatolia. Later he crossed the Anatolian peninsula and Syria by all the main routes. He spent some time at the court of the Kurdish prince of Bitlis, who ruled more or less independently under Ottoman overlordship. Officially, Evliya was there as the prince's guest, but in fact he was more of a hostage.[71] Later Evliya came to know the Balkans and he wrote at length about Greece, Serbia, Bosnia and Hungary, quite apart from his great description of Istanbul, a city he knew better than anyone else.[72] However, this indefatigable traveller did not often venture outside the Ottoman Empire. He reports some journeys to the Caucasus and in Azerbaijan, both of which were in Iranian hands at the time. Moreover, he describes in some detail a diplomatic mission to Vienna, where he travelled in the suite of the vizier, Mehmed Pasha. Following the battle of St Gotthard an der Raab (1664; see Chapters 5 and 7), the latter was to negotiate a peace settlement with the Habsburgs. This was how Evliya came to be mentioned in the Viennese state archives.

Evliya wrote in the educated everyday language of his time, avoiding most of the Arabic and Persian terms characteristic of standard literary Ottoman. However, he was entirely fluent in Arabic and had also mastered the Ottoman literary language. Moreover, Evliya had a sensitive ear, as his transcriptions of foreign languages and dialects show. During his stay in Vienna in 1665 he accurately identified and reproduced the peculiarities of the Viennese dialect.[73] He must, therefore, have made a conscious decision to write in the everyday language of educated people and not in the standard literary idiom. This spirit of innovation is also apparent in his defiant selection of the first-person mode, which went against the conventions of contemporary geographical literature. We know, however, that Evliya was thoroughly familiar with and indeed drew upon the works of scholarly geographers, in particular the sixteenth-century author Mehmed Aşık.[74] However, he often takes very little trouble to represent accurately what he has read, and it is clear that he did not see himself as a learned geographer. The poetic licence with which he treats his sources may be seen as a gesture of independence, for the accurate use of texts was generally instinctive to Muslim scholars, educated as they were to quote precisely the religious and legal opinions they were taught.[75] Evliya seems to be well versed in the oral narration of his time, and he expertly discusses the major Istanbul storytellers in the first volume of his travel book.[76] However, this does not necessarily make Evliya a 'popular' author. Listening to oral narratives was an established pastime among the Ottoman upper class, and storytellers were even sometimes invited to the palace.[77]

Evliya took a particular interest in dervishes and holy men, but he does not seem to have been an active member of any particular order. Rather, he would pay his respects to whichever local saints and mausoleums he happened to come across on his travels. This eclectic attitude was by no means uncommon among the members of the Ottoman upper class. We have Evliya's wide-ranging interest to thank for an enormous amount of information about dervish convents of various orders. As an example, let us look at his description of the convent of Abdal Musa, the library catalogue of which we have already encountered. According to Evliya's description, the convent was located in the middle of a vineyard or garden, surrounded by a high, fort-like wall made of sun-dried bricks.[78] There was a dome over the mausoleum, protected by a cone-shaped outer roof made of wood. The saint's remains rested beneath, amid a host of calligraphic votive inscriptions; it seems that the ceiling was similarly adorned. Evliya tells us that visitors came from all over the Islamic world, and many of them left beggars' bowls and musical instruments to commemorate their visit. In a similar spirit, Evliya himself left behind a couplet of his own composition to mark the occasion of his visit. He was also impressed by the functional buildings of the convent, and in particular by its kitchen in which, it was said, the fire had never been allowed to die since the foundation of the shrine.

According to this traveller, the paved square in front of the Abdal Musa convent had been created by means of one of the saint's miracles. This, then, is yet another legend about the founding of an institution, albeit in a reduced form. When the dervishes complained about the mud at the entrance to the convent, the saint responded by leading them, in the name of God, in a festive procession to a nearby mountain, accompanied by the sound of drums and flutes. After a short prayer, Abdal Musa demanded of this mountain 'in the name of the noble forebears' (probably a reference to the family of Muhammad) that it provide the stones needed for paving the muddy area. Each stone was to be the size of the body of a donkey or horse.[79] A massive earthquake then occurred, and, as the dervishes prayed, countless stones flew through the air. Next morning the route was neatly paved to a distance of 3,000 paces. No doubt Evliya himself found this pavement, the regularity of which he likened to the art of calligraphy, to be a boon on his arrival and departure.

Here as at other points in his account Evliya figures as a devout visitor to a saint's tomb and dervish convent. Our traveller often asked dervish sheikhs to bless an item of headgear, which he would then carry with him for the sake of its beneficial effects.[80] It would, nevertheless, be going too far to see Evliya's text mainly as an account of the 'pilgrimage of life'. This is evident from the fact that the author did not undertake the pilgrimage to Mecca until he was in his sixties, despite the obligation on every Muslim with the means to do so to make this journey.[81] Evliya writes that he decided to travel to Mecca only when his father and his teacher appeared to him in his dreams to upbraid him for his negligence.[82] However, Evliya's particular interest in saints and their mausoleums does enable us to set his self-portrait in the context of dervish culture. This was a traveller who perceived the space within which he moved – the towns and roads of the Ottoman Empire – to be full of mausoleums of saintly men, and he incorporates the stories he heard or read in dervish convents as building blocks into his own tale. This method was by no means uniquely his; many exponents of Ottoman narrative art had connections with dervish convents at some point in their lives.[83]

In this author's narrative, the first-person voice is conspicuous. Evliya does not generally describe his emotional responses to buildings or even to dervish ceremonies. But his accounts of good food, historic towns, pleasant strolls, attractive women and well-built men all communicate the pleasure he took in the good things in life and invite the reader to share that pleasure with him. Even when describing a mausoleum with its attendant votive gifts, he never for an instant allows us to forget that it is he, Evliya, who is recounting the scene for us. Sometimes he mentions an inscription with which he has marked his passing, sometimes he refers to a conversation he has had at the place he is describing. Evliya was profoundly impressed by many dervish saints and they helped shape his world, yet he defined himself in basically secular terms. He saw himself as a member of the Ottoman upper class and above all as a traveller. In this latter role his ambition was to have visited even the remotest spots in person, and sometimes his imagination had to fill in the gaps left by his experience of reality. Unlike Mahmud Hüda'î, Evliya, for all his piousness, presents himself above all as a man of this world.

First-person Narration, Dervishes and Everyday Portrayals of the Self

Among upper- and middle-class Ottoman Muslims of the sixteenth, seventeenth and eighteenth centuries, the self as a theme of diaries and autobiographical texts was by no means as exceptional as was believed until recently. Moreover, in this field a great deal remains to be discovered as library catalogues are still often inadequate. Often first-person accounts therefore emerge only by accident.

It is also worth noting that many of the authors of these 'informal' texts were not prominent participants in the literary or political life of the capital. A former officer and future interpreter such as Osman Ağa, a sheikh from a minor dervish convent such as Seyyid Hasan, a Mevlevî sheikh in a small, remote town, and a soldier of rather modest status in Egypt: all these figures considered their personal experiences to be worth recording. Even Evliya

Çelebi can be included in this category.[84] Despite his eminent relatives, he would have been seen by his contemporaries as a person of lesser status, given that he held no significant office; his literary fame began only about a hundred and fifty years after his death.

This all points to the beginnings of a cultural change from about the second half of the seventeenth century, one which was to manifest itself in some of the poetic output of the following years. An increasing emphasis on everyday life and an interest in the experiences of 'ordinary' people became discernible, although at first these trends were far from dominant. The dervish convents, some of which had cultivated such tendencies as early as the sixteenth century, played a special part in the creation of an interest in intimate matters. With their libraries and their interpretations of a canon of religious texts, the dervishes made the 'classical' literary education of the time accessible to a fairly wide circle in the towns, and sometimes a few privileged countrymen as well. In doing so, they also gave a certain number of people the means to express themselves in a socially acceptable manner. By reciting the legends concerning the founding of convents, dervishes and their supporters came to see themselves as members of a group which made a spiritual life possible, and within the context of which a former shoemaker's apprentice could put the learned *ulema* to shame. For all their humility towards their sheikh, people following the mystic path, often outside the educated classes, acquired a greater confidence in their own judgement. The search for the right path and the right sheikh led a *medrese* pupil, later to become a dervish, on to the roads of the empire and drew public attention to the differences of opinion among dervish sheikhs in the depths of provincial Anatolia. Even the experiences of women, whose access to written culture was quite limited, came to be regarded as valuable in this context. Dervish culture was not, of course, the only factor which led to the rising level of self-consciousness, above all from the second half of the seventeenth century onwards. Nevertheless, the importance of this culture should not be underestimated.

11

Food, Drink and Sociability

Large banquets were the centrepieces of circumcision festivals in the sultan's family, as well as of many other festivals and ceremonies at the Ottoman court. However, even though much of the available evidence concerns courtly meals, eating is an everyday activity and Turkish cuisine enjoys a great deal of popularity outside the country. Thus it is worth taking a closer look at the routine aspects of food culture. However, we shall be dealing almost exclusively with food prepared for fairly large groups of people, or at least for a single esteemed guest. This might mean meals consumed at home, or food served in the guest-house of a pious foundation or in a dervish convent. This is because the evidence available about food culture in the sixteenth, seventeenth and eighteenth centuries nearly all relates to catering for guests.

In relation to the culture of eating and drinking, the first matter to address is that of its material basis, namely the available foodstuffs. This basis depends, of course, on the kind of agriculture possible in each area, or, particularly in the cases of Istanbul, Mecca and Medina, on the maritime trade which made it possible to obtain provisions from distant regions. However, Ottoman attitudes towards various victuals are also important. Which were reserved as luxuries for special occasions, which were favoured as staple foods, which were used only as emergency rations during periods of shortages? Traditions, which had developed in an environment which had long since vanished from the Ottoman towns, were often significant in this context. Thus, in sixteenth-century Anatolia olive oil was often used in lamps, and less often for cooking, for which butter fat was preferred.[1] This predilection, which changed gradually but comprehensively in the end, probably arose in the steppe, among a sheep-breeding people.

As we do today, seventeenth- or eighteenth-century Ottomans associated social prestige with certain foods. The degree of social prestige accorded a particular foodstuff not only affected the demand for it, but also might influence the way in which it was prepared. Thus, in the Ottoman Empire of the sixteenth century, meat was definitely a high-prestige food. According to the sultan's administration, many officials present in the capital had the right to meat at affordable prices, and this had to be obtained for them by political means if the market could not deliver.[2] However, since meat remained scarce, the habit seems to have developed of serving it minced or mixed with vegetables.

Table etiquette, or rather, since we are dealing with Ottoman customs, the etiquette associated with the mat known as the *sofra*, constitutes another facet of our topic. Who would eat with whom, and in what circumstances? Particularly relevant in this regard is the division between men and women. Most of the information we have relates to meals at which only men were present. Thus the account by the English aristocrat, Lady Mary Wortley Montagu, is of particular value; she visited Edirne and Istanbul at the beginning of the eighteenth century as the wife of the English ambassador. As a high-born lady, she was invited to eat with the wife of the grand vizier and other eminent Ottoman ladies, and described what took place at such occasions.[3]

Bread, the Staff of Life[4]

In Anatolia at least, virtually all bread was baked using wheat. Barley bread must therefore have been consumed mainly in emergencies and although rye was cultivated, references to rye bread are very rare.[5] Evliya reports that the Kurdish farmers in the mountains around Diyarbakır baked bread from red millet.[6] There were various types of wheat bread. White bread was the most esteemed, and many variants crop up among Evliya's descriptions of the local food specialities of Anatolian towns.[7] In houses without baking ovens, a flat, unleavened loaf was baked in the ashes of the fireplace. At the beginning of the fifteenth century, Ruy Gonzales de Clavijo, a Spanish envoy on his way to Timur's court, came across this type of bread in Anatolia.[8] If fuel was in short supply, a reserve of unleavened bread could be baked and dried, and then moistened before use. Sheets of dough akin to present-day fila pastry formed the basis for croissants and envelopes filled with meat or vegetables and cooked in fat or in the oven. This was the dish known as *börek*, which occurs in seventeenth-century menus and is still often eaten today.[9]

A register of Istanbul prices from the year 1640 mentions only one kind of basic bread, which was probably the loaf called *fodla*.[10] A miniature in the 'Festival Book' of 1720 shows the bakers of such loaves at work.[11] Two types of sweet bread were also available. One was described as 'coarse', while the other was prepared using a considerable quantity of fat. There were three types of bread rings, one of which was sweetened and another sprinkled with sesame, probably similar to the *simit* which are still sold on the streets of modern Turkey. Two types of prepared *börek* were available, as well as a triangular pastry, similar to puff-pastry. Finally, there were *gözleme*, an unleavened bread prepared using a little fat, and which takes its name from the bubbles of air which develop during baking (*göz* means 'eye') and which is still a popular picnic food.[12] Together with these types of bread, the register also refers to a dish called a 'morsel' (*lokma*). Today this consists of a small ball similar to a cream-puff, dipped in syrup, but among the Mevlevî the same word was used for a type of pilaff mixed with vegetables.[13]

With the exception of the 'coarse' sweet bread, all these pastries cost two or three times the price of the standard loaf. They were therefore probably consumed above all during festivals and on the excursions to the picnic grounds which townspeople made in their leisure time. Around the middle of the sixteenth century the Habsburg envoy, Busbecq, praised the moderation of the Anatolian country people, who allegedly made do with salt, garlic, an onion, yoghurt and bread.[14] It has to be taken into account, however, that he intended his description to put his own compatriots to shame. The janissaries fared rather better than the peasants; at the end of the sixteenth century a special tax was introduced in order to provide them with meat.[15]

Noodles, Wheat Gruel and Rice

As well as bread, staple items included wheat and millet gruels. Today, various types of noodle have replaced such gruels, but no evidence has yet been found of the existence of most of these noodle types in seventeenth-century Istanbul. However, the Istanbul price register of 1640 does include variants of vermicelli (*şehriye*) from Istanbul and Cairo, the first of which was further divided between 'white' and 'black' types.[16] These were probably eaten mainly in soups, just as they are today. Vermicelli may have been a relatively new dish at that time, as the kitchen accounts from sultanic guest houses and dervish convents of the sixteenth century seem to mention only soups with wheat rather than noodles.[17] In his description of Bitlis, in eastern Anatolia, Evliya Çelebi refers to a dish called *mahiçe*, consisting of pasta boiled in broth, which must have been similar to modern noodle dishes or filled pastas.[18]

Evliya Çelebi came across wheat gruel in Mecca in about 1670, for example, where it had not yet been superseded by rice. He extols the fortifying qualities of the gruel, which allegedly also gave the early Islamic heroes their strength for the battle against the unbelievers. He claims, in addition, that the ladles and other cooking utensils dated from the time of the Prophet.[19] However, he also encountered gruels in other places, such as Diyarbakır and Bitlis.[20]

Rice was still something of a luxury in the sixteenth century, since only a limited quantity was produced in Anatolia, around Boyabat and Tosya, and in Rumelia, around Plovdiv. However, rice was by no means unfamiliar among the wealthier classes, as is apparent from the accounts compiled by the administrators of certain foundations used as official hostels. There is even evidence from the second half of the sixteenth century that rice was consumed in dervish convents in provincial Anatolia, where the standard of life must have been rather more modest. In Diyarbakır there was a dish made of rice and melons, spiced with cinnamon and cloves.[21] However, rice was so valuable that it was often 'stretched' by being used in soups and deserts. When he fell ill in Antalya at the start of the seventeenth century, Hans Wild, a former prisoner of war from Nuremberg, was given a rice soup by some charitable townsfolk. According to the 1640 register of prices from Istanbul, a rice and chick-pea soup, prepared with lemon juice, was available commercially, probably in cook-shops.[22] Although Evliya does not mention it, by the second half of the seventeenth century rice was already widespread in the Hejaz. This was because Indian rulers sent large quantities to Mecca, where they were distributed as alms or sold; in the latter case the proceeds were used for charitable gifts. It seems, therefore, that by about 1670 rice had already begun to replace wheat in the Arabian peninsula.

Meat and Fish

In Anatolia and Istanbul, meat usually meant mutton or lamb, although the island of Chios was, according to Evliya Çelebi, famous for its tasty beef. Beef was eaten mainly in the form of dried meat seasoned with garlic and known as *pastırma*, which appears in two varieties in the Istanbul price register of 1640.[23] Poultry seems to have been consumed only in small quantities and was very expensive. Pork, as well as being forbidden to Muslims, was (and still is) regarded as rather disgusting. Moreover, one of the ways in which Muslims set themselves apart from the 'unbelievers' was by the fact that they did not eat pork. By contrast, in the Balkans, where Christians lived together in substantial, self-contained groups, neither pig breeding nor the consumption of pork was prohibited; indeed, a tax was levied on the breeders by the Ottoman exchequer.[24]

In the countryside meat was eaten only very rarely, at weddings and other celebrations, or if an animal were injured and had to be slaughtered. In the towns poor people would have had even fewer opportunities to enjoy meat. However, the Istanbul register of 1640 does list a few possible ways of eating meat without spending too much money. As well as *pastırma*, which was consumed in paper-thin slices, there was a type of mutton sausage; and in special cook-shops, prepared sheep's heads and trotters were available.[25] The Ottoman authorities set the price of forty large morsels of baked liver at one *akçe*, which was equivalent to the price of 150 *dirhem* (462 grams) of bread.[26] This would appear to have been 'good value for money'. However, the situation in Istanbul was not typical: the large number of sheep brought to the city to supply the needs of the upper class and the military meant that there was also a larger quantity of the less esteemed types of meat on the market.

Evliya's descriptions of provincial Ottoman towns give us an insight into popular meat dishes, as he sometimes went into great detail about how a certain dish should taste when properly prepared. Thus he claims that sheep's trotters *à la mode de Kütahya*, a rather unpretentious dish, should be white and clear and taste like bone marrow.[27] He is evidently referring to a type of jelly, rather like aspic. In various towns of western Anatolia Evliya came across a variety of kebab, cooked slowly in earth ovens, as well as loaves of bread filled with meat.[28] Local specialities in the eastern Anatolian town of Bitlis included roast partridges, partridge pies and pilaff garnished with partridge.[29] We must take into account that here Evliya was staying at the court of a local prince and therefore probably encountered festive and luxury dishes more often than ordinary foodstuffs. It is interesting, nevertheless, that Evliya does not mention any famous meat dishes from Edirne, where the court was often to be found, but where the traveller seems to have spent his time largely among townspeople.[30]

Istanbul was in the special position of having its 'own' supply of fish. At certain times of the year, fish pass in great numbers through the Bosphorus, where angling remains popular today, and the nearby Black Sea also offers good fishing. Fresh fish were known by poetic names such as coral, silver fish, sea rose, black eye and lark, or they might also have a Greek name.[31] In the 1640s, fish could be obtained for 3–4 *akçe* each during the appropriate season. Some fish were processed to make *pastırma* or steeped in vinegar. In terms of its food supply, the plentiful availability of fish gave Istanbul a distinct advantage over the towns of inner Anatolia.

Trabzon, at the eastern end of the Black Sea, was another good place for seafood. Evliya Çelebi even describes the cries by which the fishmongers attempted to attract customers.[32] Above all, he tells us about the folklore which even then surrounded the anchovy, a fish caught commonly in the Black Sea. It was held to be a remedy against every ailment, while fumigation using anchovy heads was alleged to drive out snakes and other vermin from the home. The inhabitants of Trabzon prided themselves on the 'forty', meaning many recipes using this fish. As we might expect, it was fried, served in soups and sauces, and made into a filling for *börek*. It is rather more difficult to imagine how the sweet known as *baklava* might have been prepared from or with anchovies, even if Evliya acclaims the anchovy as a fish which does not smell fishy. It is possible that the dish in question was flat and lozenge-shaped like a sweet *baklava*, and consisted of something similar to puff pastry with an anchovy filling.

Evliya must have been inordinately impressed by this fish, as he uncharacteristically includes a complete recipe for it.[33] It requires a pan made of fire-proof stone (probably something akin to the soapstone we use today). The anchovies are cleaned and skewered, ten to each skewer. A mixture of parsley, celery, onions and leek is strongly seasoned with black pepper and cinnamon and cooked in a pan. Then the anchovies and vegetables are stacked in layers in the soapstone pan, beginning with a layer of fish. Olive oil is added and the result cooked slowly for about an hour, probably on a low heat. The traveller considered this to be a treat for feast days.

Fruit and Vegetables

Kitchen accounts from dervish convents in provincial Anatolia list expenditure on meat, which seems to have been used to 'season' soups and vegetables.[34] However, rather uninspiring daily fare, dominated by bread and soup, was enlivened by fruit and vegetables wherever the climate was suitable. Where they could not be grown, fruit and vegetables were often obtained from elsewhere. Thus, to mention an example from the last decades of Ottoman history, the English writer and explorer Charles Doughty, who visited the Arabian peninsula in 1876, reports that in Jiddah, frequented by Ottoman pilgrims and soldiers, fruit and vegetables were brought in from the oasis of Taif.[35] They were transported on the backs of camels, although their condition must have deteriorated considerably as a result. Price lists include spinach, onions, cabbage, carrots, rape, lettuce, leek and vine-leaves, but there are few details regarding varieties and quality. In his description of Bitlis, Evliya refers to *cacık*, better known today by its Greek name, *tzatziki*, a summer dish consisting of cucumbers, garlic and yoghurt.[36]

By contrast, there is a great deal of literary evidence regarding attitudes towards fruit. An acquaintance of Prince Cem (1459–95), a son of Mehmed the Conqueror, reports that during his European exile the prince was very fond of melons, grapes, apples and pears. A geographical text of the seventeenth century relates that in the town of Malatya in south-eastern Anatolia, fruit growers cut out the letters of various words and sayings in paper. These pieces of paper were then stuck to the semi-ripe fruit, and remained green or yellow while the rest of the fruit ripened to its natural colour.[37] When we remember that most peasants would have been illiterate, it becomes clear just how much trouble was taken to produce such *de luxe* fruits. Evliya Çelebi repeatedly mentions fruit among the most notable products of Anatolian towns. He observes, for example, that in the town of Kütahya, in western Anatolia, there were twenty-four sorts of pear, seven sorts of juicy cherries and also grapes, although the latter were of poor quality.[38] He praises the citrus fruits, figs, almonds and pomegranates of the Aegean coast.[39] Further south, in the warm, humid climate of Adana, Evliya mentions sugar-cane as well as citrus fruits and figs, and in Diyarbarkır he becomes positively lyrical in his appreciation of the melons.[40] In the chapter devoted to Bitlis, south of Lake Van, he reports finding eleven types of pear.[41] In Edirne, at the other end of modern Turkey, the seventeenth-century traveller comes across blushing peaches, and is particularly struck by the many varieties of quinces, which are still grown around the town.[42]

Evliya is not alone in his enthusiasm for Turkish fruit. The Istanbul dervish Seyyid Hasan interrupts his accounts of the funerals of relatives and acquaintances who had perished in the plague to describe a basket of fruit which he had been given.[43] This contained two sorts of pears and also two types of grapes, the names of which he mentions. Seyyid Hasan took evident pleasure in describing these fruits in detail. Osman Ağa, in the early eighteenth century, also wrote about fruit. He reports that a military expedition in which he took part made an unplanned, one-day halt in the town of Lipova, where the cherries had just ripened and could be bought very cheaply in the market. The troops paused to take full advantage.[44]

Sweets

Presumably the popularity of fruit was related to the general taste for sweet things, and both fruit and sweets were characteristic of Ottoman cuisine in the sixteenth and seventeenth centuries. In sixteenth-century foundation accounts, large quantities of raisins and currants are mentioned; these, incidentally, were equally popular in contemporary England.[45] Honey and a grape syrup were also used for sweetening. Cane-sugar was imported in small quantities from Egypt and Cyprus, but it was a considerable luxury.[46] The Istanbul price register of 1640 lists four different sorts. There was doubly refined sugar, basic cane-sugar, and a sugar described as 'vegetable', of which a white, 'good' variety and a cheaper one were available.[47] In addition, sugar mixed with spices, such as cinnamon, cloves and aniseed, was sold in front of the Istanbul bazaar, probably at the very place where herbs, spices and household remedies are still traded today. It is possible that this was not crystallized sugar but rather something such as the bonbons which are today know as akide şekeri. There was also a tree resin, named sakız after the island of Chios from which it came. It was a state monopoly and in the seventeenth century mostly constituted a source of revenue for the sultana mother.[48] Evliya

Çelebi states that it was punishable by death to withhold even a tiny quantity from the state.[49] However, since the price register of 1620 lists three types of *sakız*, this much sought-after resin, whose name is still used for ordinary chewing-gum, must also have been available on the open market.[50]

Fruits and sugar were used to make the jams which are today known as *reçel*. They differ from European-style jams in that they are not jellied. Evliya claims that at the court of the prince (khan) in Bitlis he was treated not just to lemon, rhubarb and pear jams, but also jams made out of wild carrots, blackcurrants and nutmeg.[51] There was also a wide variety of drinks made from sweetened, diluted fruit-juices, which were indispensable at celebrations. In the town of Bitlis, Evliya came across sherbets made of pomegranates, apricots and rhubarb, as well as a drink made from poppies and perhaps valerian.[52] As well as being used for sweets and drinks, fruit was stewed to make the compôtes which Evliya cites as the specialities of several towns. In western Anatolia, the town of Tire produced a compôte made of stewed cherries, which those who could afford it liked to eat with ice. Ice was obtained in the mountains; in the case of Istanbul, the source was the Uludağ, or Bithynian Olympus; well insulated, it could be stored in cellars. Busbecq also mentions the many compôtes made of dried fruits; it seemed to him that at festive occasions in the Ottoman domain, the table was filled mainly with sweets.[53]

Trays of *baklava* were among the dishes offered to every group of guests at the circumcision festival of 1720.[54] Around the middle of the seventeenth century, this delicacy, which requires a great deal of preparation, was also to be found in as remote a place as Bitlis.[55] It is possible, however, that it was served mainly at the khan's court and less in the homes of the townspeople. In Istanbul, nevertheless, by the mid-seventeenth century, *baklava* was a familiar dish. It is not named in the price register of 1640, but the grills and trays needed for preparing and serving *baklava* do occur.[56]

Apart from the different types of sweet bread which we have already encountered, there were local varieties of the sweet known as *helva* in many towns of the Ottoman Empire. *Helva* might be made from a wide range of ingredients, and could also be a natural product; in Diyarbakır a sort of manna was popular, gathered from the leaves of certain trees.[57] In Edirne *helva* appears to have been perfumed with musk; it may have been that the sugar mixed with musk, which was available in Istanbul, was used in the preparation of such a sweet.[58] The Istanbul register mentions 'white' *helva*, about which no further details are given, as well as other varieties, one made with honey and almonds, and another with sesame. Two further types were known by rather curious names: a 'Frankish-style' *helva*, whose composition remains unknown, and a 'soap-style' *helva*, probably named for its appearance.

When compiling the 1640 register, the Ottoman bureaucrats were evidently determined to be comprehensive, and they even listed the stirring-spoons and ladles which were vital for producing sweets.[59]

Helva was particularly important in the ceremonial life of the urban populations. Evliya Çelebi describes a 'soul *helva*', which was served in the name of the deceased as a last good deed.[60] Anatolian artisans would gather in winter to eat *helva*, the ensuing conversations being known as *helva sohbetleri*.[61] This was a diluted and somewhat secularized relic of a ceremony which we first encounter in the writings of the poet and founder of the Mevleviyye order, Mevlana Celaleddin, and which was common among guild members in the fifteenth and sixteenth centuries.

There are various explanations of the ceremony's significance. They are known to us from a text which originated in the Ottoman artisan milieu of the fifteenth century. This contains several, slightly divergent, accounts. In the first story the *helva* ceremony is derived from the reconciliation between Adam and God. This reconciliation is said to have taken place after the expulsion from paradise, when Adam admitted his guilt and recognized the greatness of God. There is a second traditional account in the same text, which complements the first rather than contradicting it. It refers to the Prophet Muhammad, who was said to have arranged a *helva* ceremony shortly before his death for members of his family and the closest of his associates.

A third tradition, recorded in the same text as the first two, relates the *helva* ceremony to an event in the life of the Prophet's descendant, Zayn al-'Abidin. Two artisans supposedly saved him from certain death, which was possible only because one of the two rescuers sacrificed his own young son. As can be gathered from the surviving texts, the *helva* ceremony was originally a part of an initiation rite by which Anatolian artisans of the post-Seljuk and early Ottoman periods were initiated into the Fütuvvet, a religious-cum-mystic men's association. Probably the custom, alluded to above, of distributing *helva* for the salvation of the deceased, is also connected with the idea of the innocent child sacrificed to save the Prophet's descendant.

In its simplest form, the *helva* prepared at these ceremonies consists of dates and milk. According to the tale of the *helva* ceremony held by the Prophet, a more complicated type is mentioned, which contains oil and grape syrup as well as the dates. At the memorial ceremony for the artisan's dead child, when both the rescuers of the Prophet's descendant are appointed as leaders of their respective guilds by heavenly intervention, the most elaborate form of all is prepared. Flour, oil, honey and saffron are all added to the dates. Occurring in all three versions, the dates are evidently a key element. However, since they are virtually impossible to grow in Anatolia, the ceremony must have arisen and developed in a commercial centre, possibly with links to Egypt.

There was also great ceremonial significance in the eating of another sweet, namely *aşure*. Today this consists of a type of pudding enriched by raisins, currants, almonds, nuts, haricot beans, wheat granules and pistachios. Often the pudding is perfumed with rose-water and garnished with pomegranates.[62] A similar mixture was probably used in the sixteenth century, although, even now, the flavour of *aşure* varies considerably depending on what is available to the person making it. A good proportion of the raisins and currants which appeared in the accounts from sultans' hostels and pious foundations was no doubt used in preparing these puddings. *Aşure* was, and still is, prepared and distributed on the tenth day of the Islamic lunar month of Muharrem, in remembrance of the death of the Prophet's nephew, Husayn, at Kerbela. Imam Husayn has a particular importance in Shiite theology, but the custom of preparing *aşure* is by no means restricted to Shiites, and Sunnis also practise it. In pious foundations, great quantities of the sweet were prepared and distributed. Even today, many housewives who have made the dish send samples for their neighbours to taste. In the dervish convent of Hacı Bektaş there was a tradition that the great cauldron, presented by the janissaries to their patron saint's convent, had only ever been used for the ceremonial preparation of *aşure*.[63] If a foundation became impoverished and was forced to reduce its expenditure on food, it would try at least to continue distributing *aşure*.

Beverages and Dairy Products

Water was very much appreciated by those who valued good food and drink, and, in the seventeenth and eighteenth centuries in particular, benefactors of modest means often decided to offer their fellow citizens a refreshing drink of water. To this end they had small, elegant kiosks constructed, from which free water was dispensed.[64] In his description of Diyarbakır, Evliya commends the water from a certain spring and, above all, from the river Tigris, which at that time had evidently not yet become polluted by the sediment from the mining activities to the north of the town.[65] The traveller was particularly impressed by the crystalline clarity of the water, both in liquid and in frozen form. This water was also said to aid digestion, and to neutralize the surplus bodily fluids which people of that time blamed for illnesses.

At the court of the khan of Bitlis there was probably a wider variety of beverages available than anywhere else, with the exception of the sultan's court. As well as the sweet sherbets which we have already come across, Evliya Çelebi mentions tea, in what is probably one of the earliest references to what has since become a national drink in Turkey. Presumably the tea came from China, either by way of Russia, or by the long route via South-

East Asia and the Hejaz, which was how substantial quantities of Chinese porcelain reached the Ottoman Empire.[66] People also drank fennel tea and *salep*, a winter drink made out of the roots of a type of orchid, which is still popular today. Water was also thickened to a soup-like consistency with other substances such as rice flour and consumed hot. Milk was also esteemed; Evliya extols the quality of the milk in Diyarbakır, and it was served to guests at the court of Bitlis.

Butter fat was one of the most widespread dairy products, as its durability made it suitable for transport over long distances. Butter fat consumed in Istanbul usually originated on the northern coast of the Black Sea. However, Ottoman authors have not written much about butter fat although the fat used in cooking affects the taste of an entire cuisine. No evidence has yet been found of fresh butter eaten with bread as is the custom today, but we know that many Istanbul women, and no doubt men as well, enjoyed eating cream, which was sold in special shops.[67] Cheese is not often mentioned. However, when Seyyid Hasan had to set off in order to see his sick wife before she died from the plague, he did not omit to refer to the piece of *kaşkaval* cheese which he took with him, wrapped in bread, to eat on the way.[68]

Putting Together a Menu

There is less information about the composition of whole meals than about individual dishes, but even the smallest scraps are worth collecting; as an eighteenth-century French master of the culinary arts once said, a poorly conceived menu spoils the effect of the food.[69] His older contemporary, Lady Mary Wortley Montagu, reports that at a formal invitation to a festive meal from a sultan's widow, every dish was brought to the *sofra* separately, and that, on another occasion, the soup was the last dish to appear.[70] Evliya Çelebi provides us with some information about breakfasts. On his visit to the court of the khan of Bitlis, a sweet pastry was set before him each morning, together with a large number of jams and fruits candied in syrup.[71] Evliya does not mention any beverages, but Seyyid Hasan's diary records his drinking coffee at the start of the day.[72] This was not always a family occasion, but sometimes took place in the part of the house reserved for men, and guests might also be invited.

Moreover, the best available information on menus comes from Seyyid Hasan's diary, in which he often described what was served at the gatherings of his friends. It seems that, in this 'middle-class' environment, food was expected to be both tasty and plentiful. Thus Seyyid Hasan informs us that a dinner might consist of seventeen dishes without its being a very special occasion. Apart from three sorts of meat cooked in sauce, 'sweet', 'sour' and 'normal' (meaning without any special characteristics), the guests were served stuffed onions and zucchini, spinach, pilaff and pasties (*börek*). Several sweets also appeared, namely *baklava*, milk pudding and two sorts of compôte. Afterwards, coffee was probably served, although it is not actually mentioned in the diary.[73] From this example and others, it is clear that well-to-do families of Istanbul frequently treated themselves to hearty meals even in everyday life, and not just to celebrate weddings or major religious festivals. This is another reason why food and drink legitimately occupy so much space in a book dealing with everyday culture.

Coffee, Wine and Tobacco

Prince Cem, son of the conquering Sultan Mehmed II, considered that spiced wine was not really wine at all, and he drank it even though he otherwise abstained from alcohol. At the court of the khan in Bitlis, a boiled wine was served, which was acceptable because its alcohol content had been eliminated by the heating process.[74] There is no mention of conventional wine being available there, but Evliya does seem to have come across it elsewhere. Apart from the wine or arrak known as 'lion's milk' available in Izmir, Evliya mentions another, which he does not name. This was served in a monastery on the island of Chios, and supposedly produced hardly any signs of inebriation.[75] Evliya appears to have been informed about a church festival on this island, along with the associated annual fair. At this occasion the non-Muslims would drink enthusiastically, while the few Muslims on the island armed themselves in order to ward off any sudden attacks. Even non-Muslims, however, were not permitted to drink in public where and whenever they liked. In the mid-sixteenth century, when Busbecq and Dernschwam visited the ageing Süleyman the Magnificent (reign: 1520–66), the ban on wine was enforced much more strictly. At that time, the public sale of wine was prohibited and even the legation often found it difficult to obtain any.[76] Stricter and more tolerant periods went in cycles. In the seventeenth century, when the hard-liners known as the Kadızadeliler enjoyed a great deal of influence for a time, prohibitions were enforced more rigidly than in other, more tranquil times.

These prohibitions were directed above all at those Muslim subcultures in which drinking wine was a part of life. Except when renewed prohibitions drew attention to the issue, the existence of such subcultures was probably accepted by 'respectable' townspeople as an unfortunate symptom of an imperfect world. Prominent among these regrettable social minorities were the mercenaries (*levend*), who were recruited for military campaigns from the second half of the sixteenth century onwards. They also constituted the armed force used by provincial governors to collect taxes.[77] Corsairs and pirates formed another such group. When, in the course of a seventeenth-century story, the eldest son of a pasha runs away to join the corsairs, his father observes that this is just the right career for such a wine-quaffing ruffian.[78] It was regarded as a more serious matter if a theologian and jurist, who should have known better, were known to drink 'like a mercenary'.

Finally, many dervishes, particularly the Bektashi, believed that their elevated spiritual status absolved them from religious law and its prohibitions. There are whole anthologies of 'spiritual jokes' originating from the Bektashi milieu and dealing with the problematic relations between the representatives of Islamic law and the dissident dervishes. Unfortunately they are of limited use to cultural historians because it is so difficult to date them.[79] Normally the joke is at the expense of some hypocritical, overbearing theologian and jurist whom the Bektashi provokes by enjoying wine or arrak before his opponent's very eyes. From an inventory of the Bektashi convent of Abdal Musa, dating from 1826, it is clear that certain Bektashis produced their own wine. Thus, in their stories, real wine must have been meant, and not the 'inebriation of the soul' which leads the devotee to God and is a common metaphor in Islamic mysticism.[80] In a less elevated mode, the dervishes of Abdal Musa owned a vineyard on the coast of south-western Anatolia, together with a wine-press and barrels.

Coffee was, as we already know, widespread and popular in the early eighteenth century. From the second half of the sixteenth century onwards it was consumed both at home and in cafés.[81] There is a note from the Ottoman sultan, dated 1567, complaining that the soldiers stationed in Cairo were not at their posts.[82] When they were required, they had to be sought out in the coffee-houses. At that time coffee was an innovation which pilgrims returning from Mecca had brought to Egypt from the Yemen, where coffee had been drunk throughout the middle ages. A *kadi*'s register of about 1600 mentions a coffee-house in Ankara. At about the same time, coffee roasting was taking place in other towns as well. This was probably a state monopoly, since such enterprises were bestowed as tax-farms.[83] Towards the end of the sixteenth century, when this beverage was still virtually unknown in Europe, coffee was popular even in remote Anatolian villages. At any rate, the owner of a few minor tax privileges in a village in the district of Çorum apparently believed that there was money to be made by mortgaging his right to collect taxes and buying coffee with the proceeds.[84]

Until the middle of the eighteenth century, the Yemen was still the only area in which coffee was cultivated, and the merchants of Cairo did very well from the transit trade.[85] At first the trade consisted of imports to Egypt itself and to Anatolia and Rumelia; not until the second half of the seventeenth century did French and Dutch merchants also become interested in the coffee bean. Coffee, as well as Indian cotton materials, dyes and drugs, enabled the merchants of Cairo to survive the Dutch irruption into the Indian Ocean, and the resultant monopoly on certain spices, much more comfortably than their Venetian trading partners.

However, in the seventeenth century, drinking coffee was frequently pro-hibited by sultans' decrees, forcing cafés to close.[86] Some theologians saw coffee as analogous to wine, despite the different physiological effects they produced. For others, the fact that coffee could not be proven to have existed at the time of the Prophet and the first caliphs was enough to persuade them that it was a deplorable innovation. No doubt another factor was that for urban males, especially the poorer ones, cafés very quickly became meeting places; the conversations which took place in coffee-houses could not easily be monitored by state officials. However, wholesale merchants importing coffee sometimes must have profited from prohibitions. When they were able to smuggle contraband past customs farmers, many purchasers must have been prepared to pay high prices.

By contrast, the Ottoman state was, up to a point, fairly tolerant of the use of opium, mostly in the form of pastes containing the drug. In 1584 there was some concern before Özdemiroğlu Osman Pasha was made grand vizier about the rumours of his predilection for opium, but the appointment went ahead nevertheless.[87] In some Anatolian towns of that period the sale of pastes containing opium or similar substances was a source of income for the state.[88] Evliya Çelebi reports that in the town of Afyon-Karahisar, in south-western Anatolia, both the artisans and their wives took opium; it was the fact that the women did so that particularly amazed him. In the area of Isparta and Afyon-Karahisar, the poppy was cultivated as early as the sixteenth century.[89] If Evliya has painted a reasonably reliable picture, the artisans probably obtained their supplies from these nearby fields. Evliya claims that in some places the men spent their time in the cafés because their own as well as their wives' use of narcotics caused domestic disputes.

Tobacco smokers, on the other hand, were frequently faced with con-siderable difficulties. Since the tobacco plant originated in America, it must have reached the Ottoman Empire via Europe, either from Italy or over the Habsburg–Ottoman border. Encounters with the weed in the Hungarian frontier region were probably of particular significance, since janissaries, who often fought in that area, contributed significantly to the spread of tobacco smoking. A decree from 1637, issued by Sultan Murad IV – also known for his banning of wine and coffee – documents this connection. The text concerns janissaries and cavalrymen who had acquired the habit of 'drinking smoke'; even today, pipes and cigarettes are 'drunk' in Turkish. We also learn that tobacco was thought to be cultivated illicitly in a small village in the rural province of Beyşehir, far from any main roads. This was now to be investigated and those responsible punished.[90]

Sultan Murad IV's prohibitions and executions did not prevent the spread of tobacco. This is clear from a book by the historian, geographer and bibliographer, Katib Çelebi (1609–57), written after the death of Sultan Murad in 1640. From his own experience the author reports that the prohibitions served only to drive smokers underground. Although Katib Çelebi did not smoke himself and considered the habit harmful – but for a few, medically proven exceptions – he supported a jurist who had recently declared that smoking was legitimate. In this decision the primary considerations were practical. Katib Çelebi did not like bans which were unenforceable, and could not see any overwhelming grounds for declaring tobacco illegal in religious terms. In such cases of doubt, he believed that the best policy was to protect people from sin by making allowances for their weaknesses.[91]

Eating and Drinking: Sociability and Ritual

Many descriptions of banquets and other occasions on which meals were shared with guests relate to the world of the court; there are relatively few from other levels of society. Lady Mary Wortley Montagu describes a meal to which she was invited by the grand vizier's wife, and mentions the friendly conversation she enjoyed with her hostesses before the meal.[92] This required the help of an interpreter, a Greek lady, since at this time Lady Mary was not yet fluent in the Ottoman language. While the hostess urged Lady Mary to try each dish, this was impossible due to the sheer variety of dishes on offer. Otherwise Lady Mary was an enthusiastic gatherer of new experiences, including culinary ones, and seems to have thoroughly enjoyed herself. At the end of the meal, coffee was served, and two slave girls perfumed Lady Mary's hair, clothes and handkerchief. Probably from her interpreter, she learned that this was considered to be a special courtesy. Afterwards, the slave girls belonging to the grand vizier's wife played various instruments and danced, occasioning apologies from the hostess for their lack of expertise. She explained that since she herself had largely renounced worldly amusements, she had not taken much care about training the girls.

Lady Mary also describes an invitation to afternoon coffee which she received from the wife of an eminent official, the grand vizier's *kâhya*.[93] Her hostess received her sitting on a sofa, with her small daughters at her feet. She rose in honour of her guest, a courtesy which was not always extended to foreign ambassadors visiting the grand vizier. Lady Mary was given the place of honour in the corner of the room. Here too, the slave girls danced to lute and guitar music, and it appears that some of them delighted Lady

Mary by their singing. On this occasion, the whole room was perfumed with fragrances before coffee was served. Conversation continued during all this time. When they left, Lady Mary, her interpreter and her servants were all presented with embroidered cloths, more or less elaborately decorated depending on the status of the receiver. The ambassador's wife and the wife of the *kâhya* seem to have taken a spontaneous liking to one another, so it is possible that the friendly atmosphere of this visit was not due simply to the rules of polite behaviour.

Lady Mary's accounts give the impression that the dishes she was offered were new and strange, but that matters of etiquette and ceremony were not very different from what she was accustomed to. This might be because a *de facto* aristocracy had emerged in the Ottoman Empire from the late seventeenth century onwards, although hereditary nobility as such was unknown. Military and civil bureaucrats with court connections, as well as eminent theologians and jurists, made up the elite of the capital.[94] In their manners, these aristocratic ladies and gentlemen were both comprehensible and sympathetic to Lady Mary, who herself was a member of the English nobility. This affinity adds a certain charm to her descriptions.

Women would gather in the homes of their female friends and acquaintances for meals, music and conversation (see Chapter 6).[95] For the male inhabitants of the towns there were also public meeting places, among which the cafés we have just encountered were particularly popular. Evliya Çelebi reports that there were seventy-five cafés in Bursa in the middle of the seventeenth century. At such places storytellers practised their art, and their performances were apparently of sufficient quality to attract even educated, well-to-do men to the cafés.[96] Evliya is particularly enthusiastic about the storyteller Kurban Alisi Hamza, who, he claims, had no equal throughout his lifetime, while the narrator Şerif Ali was famed for his account of the classical Persian epos of Firdawsi. Unfortunately, we do not know whether Şerif Ali recited the original or an Ottoman version of this text. In the Emir's café, which was the most prestigious one in Bursa at that time, dance performances were also held. Evliya noted that in Bursa even the *boza* taverns, which served a lightly fermented millet beer, were considered to be a 'school of knowledge', and this impressed him as an indication of the high level of culture current among the townspeople.

We do not know for certain whether or to what extent there were inns in which drinking companions of various religious beliefs would gather. Süleyman the Magnificent had caused all inns to be closed down, but they seem to have reopened under his successors.[97] In the seventeenth century, Murad IV (reign: 1623–40) was well known for his furious persecution of taverns and drinkers. Yet it is in his reign that the narrative artists (*meddah*) set the stories of Bekrî Mustafa, an enthusiastic tavern-goer, who is said to have encountered the sultan on his nocturnal excursions and managed to win him over by the wit of his responses. Evliya Çelebi, who was a contemporary, also mentions this figure, and Bekrî Mustafa's posthumous fame is reflected in the stories recorded by the Wallachian prince and scholar, Demetrius Cantemir, in a historical work which he wrote in the early eighteenth century.[98] These stories describe how the drunkard, renowned in his city, introduces the sultan to wine and thereby achieves greater honour than others achieved by their virtuous behaviour.

As is apparent from the Istanbul price list of 1640, in the Ottoman captial it was possible to buy many prepared, 'ready-to-eat' dishes. This proves the existence of cook-shops; moreover, the 'living images', which featured in the great artisans' pageants of 1582, show that these places not only prepared 'take-away' food, but also had long tables for those wishing to eat on the premises.[99] Some shops specialized in roasting meat, the ancestors, perhaps, of today's kebapçıs. However, these kebapçıs seem mostly to have served only modest clienteles; those who could afford it would have their meals prepared at home.

Some cook-shops were meeting places for dervishes. In his diary the sheikh Mahmud Hüda'î (1543/44–1628/29) mentions the Bursa dervish, Hızır, the teacher of the diarist's own master, Üftade. Hızır apparently came from Moldavia and arrived in Anatolia via the levy of boys. While Hızır was working for a family of Anatolian peasants, as future janissaries had to during their training period, his feet became frostbitten, and his master expelled him from the household, considering him a 'useless extra mouth to feed'. Eventually the boy reached Bursa, where he worked in a kebapçı's shop and managed to amass a modest fortune, no doubt providing food for the odd disciple. Hızır's reputation as a dervish and source of spiritual nourishment very likely contributed considerably to the reputation of his cook-shop.[100]

Food Culture

It may seem surprising that so much space should be devoted to the culinary arts in a book dealing with the involvement of Ottoman townspeople in culture. However, as we have seen, social contacts were connected with the enjoyment of the arts, and constituted a significant element of life not just at court, but among the more affluent townspeople as well. Shared meals – separate ones for groups of men and women – were, in turn, an indispensable part of social life. At the very least, guests would be offered coffee or sherbet. Moreover, since the 'higher' arts were often practised in a social setting, it is also important to examine festive meals. We have noted that well-to-do women would oversee the training of their slave girls in music and song. These musical performances, which usually followed an elaborate meal, were opportunities for the hostess to show off her taste and organizational talents to her guests. *Mutatis mutandis*, this also holds true for the hosts in male society.[101] At such occasions the banquet, together with all the compliments presented by those involved, would represent the centrepiece of a carefully staged 'complete work of art'. It would therefore be an unwarranted act of abstraction to separate the musical or literary offerings from this framework. It is unfortunate that the many European men who attended Ottoman banquets from the fifteenth century onwards were so much less perspicacious than Lady Mary with regard to such matters.

However, quite apart from the performances which accompanied them, meals were in themselves significant cultural and social events, in which social distinctions were made manifest and, at the same time, reaffirmed. This certainly applied to the court banquets, where the dignitaries ate at different *sofra*s according to their rank; work remains to be done on the extent to which rank was manifested among well-to-do townspeople. Who, for example, would Seyyid Hasan invite and by whom would he be invited? Was there a set hierarchy governing invitations and the returning of visits? It was not for nothing that Seyyid Hasan tended to enumerate the people with whom he shared the *sofra* more often than he described the food that was served.

Social distinctions also played a part in the invitations to meals issued by Ottoman ladies. Lady Mary, ever alert to differences in status, noted that the Ottoman aristocracy of her time was ready to respect those foreigners who were of high social rank in their own countries.[102] However, there seem to have been fewer considerations of protocol involved in inviting the wife of an ambassador than in invitations extended by the grand vizier to her husband, or by the grand vizier's *kâhya* to a foreign dignitary. This situation probably explains why, in her descriptions of the meals to which she was invited, Lady Mary had more to say about those present as individuals.

PART III

Cultural Change

12

Crises and New Beginnings, 1770–1839

The last quarter of the eighteenth century was a traumatic period for the Ottoman upper class, just as it was for the Muslim townspeople of many regions of the empire. The first problem was that between 1760 and 1770 a long period of economic prosperity drew to an end in Anatolia and many parts of the Balkans, as well as in Egypt. This period had commenced in the early eighteenth century, with the end of the long wars against the Habsburgs and Venetians in 1718. In the past, historians have tended to regard the whole of the eighteenth century as a time of crisis both for the state and for Ottoman society, but this is not accurate as far as the economic situation is concerned. Far from it: in the first half of the eighteenth century many Anatolian towns recovered from the damage they had suffered during the military rebellions of the seventeenth century.[1] Some branches of the Ottoman economy, such as the various textile industries, enjoyed a strong upturn in their fortunes from the beginning of the eighteenth century. In Tokat, for example, the manufacturing of printed cotton materials developed, while the older tradition of mohair weaving in Ankara had by no means disappeared. On the Aegean island of Chios, silk materials were produced. The capital required for this was probably supplied in part by the profits from merchant shipping.[2]

This meant that the depression was all the more dramatic when it arrived. To aggravate matters, a lengthy period of peace was followed in 1768 by a new war against Russia. The economic depression made it ever harder to pay for the necessary military equipment and win battles. After the Treaty of Küçük Kaynarca (Kainarji) in 1774, a first wave of Muslim refugees arrived in Istanbul. These were Tatars who were fleeing their native land because of Russia's increasing influence over the Crimea.[3] The disquiet caused by the lost war and the economic depression was all the more pronounced for the fact that so few people had expected such a set of reverses after enjoying prosperity for so long.

The Causes of the Crisis

The problems of the period after 1760 may be traced back to a series of factors, many of which are connected directly or indirectly with the increased pressure the developing capitalist economies of Europe were exerting on their Ottoman counterpart. For example, until that time Cairo had benefited substantially from the export of coffee, both to the other Ottoman provinces and to Europe. However, in the second half of the eighteenth century the *café des îles*, grown by African slaves in the Caribbean islands, began to compete successfully with the Yemeni coffee traded in Cairo.[4] Moreover, the beginnings of industrialization in England were already making themselves felt in the last quarter of the eighteenth century, although it was not until after 1815 that domestic producers were hit by the full force of this competition. The production of red cotton thread in the small Greek town of Ambelakia, for example, had flourished precisely because of the heavy demand from mechanized weaving-mills in England, but when spinning also came to be mechanized from 1800 onwards, the market for this semi-finished product suddenly contracted.[5]

Equally significant were the effects of the wars conducted by the Ottoman Empire during the second half of the eighteenth century, first against the armies of Catherine II of Russia and later against revolutionary and Napoleonic France. Equipping the armies and keeping pace with the strategies and tactics evolved in these wars cost more money than the Ottoman state, with only a partly monetized economy, had at its disposal. This led to tax policies which weakened in the long term the competitiveness of many branches of the economy. Indeed, it was common practice for the Ottoman authorities to demand goods and services required by the military from artisans, and to pay for them either far less than the market value or not at all.[6] This saved the state from running into the kind of debt which helped break the absolute monarchy in France in 1789, but it made capital accumulation in the trading sector almost impossible. The easiest option for the Ottoman financial administration was to draw most heavily on the most competitive enterprises. The exorbitant demands created by the wars often forced such firms out of business altogether, or at least drastically to cut back their production. After several lengthy wars in the second half of the eighteenth century, many branches of the Ottoman manufacturing economy were completely stagnant.[7]

The export of cotton materials from Ayntab (Gaziantep) is a good example of the damage caused by war. This trade flourished until 1778–79, only to succumb all the more dramatically to the crisis. In the first half of the century, new enterprises had sprung up in the area around Aleppo, despite a severe crisis in the city itself. Since the seventeenth century, Indian cotton materials had won a significant market share both in Europe and in the Ottoman Empire, and these printed cottons were very successfully copied in Gaziantep.[8] Some of the prints found their way to Marseille, where samples have survived to the present day. Probably clashes between the Ottoman Empire and Iran in the frequently disputed region of Iraq brought about the crisis. Failed harvests and exceptional cold in Syria, which caused great hardship for the weavers, exacerbated the problems. These were hardly being overcome when, from 1792, the French revolutionary wars put an end to the export trade altogether.[9]

Resistant Sectors

However, even during the time of crisis which began in the 1760s, there were several branches of the economy and even whole regions which were only lightly affected by the general malaise. The first two-thirds of the eighteenth century had also been a time of booming trade. During this period, many non-Muslim Ottomans managed to break out of the role of broker or middle-man for European merchants and become active on their own account. There were active colonies of Greek and Serbian merchants in Vienna and other towns of the Habsburg Empire; being Orthodox and, worse still, subjects of the sultan, these were regarded with a degree of unease by the Habsburg authorities, but they became very active nevertheless.[10] There were even better opportunities to be had in the port of Trieste, which was in Habsburg hands at the time. The government in Vienna did its best to encourage international trade through this town, a project which seemed all the more realistic as Venice had by then declined to a regional port for northern Italy. The Habsburg administration even attempted to persuade some merchants to set off for China from Trieste, albeit without success.[11]

Greek ship-owners and captains were able to take advantage of discounted duties in the newly-built port.[12] In the Black Sea, which was closed to non-Ottoman ships until 1774, Greek shippers, as subjects of the sultan, already enjoyed a long-established position. Even after the Ottoman defeat in the war of 1768–74, when the Black Sea was opened up first to Russian and then to other vessels, Greek shipping, now flying the Russian flag, was able to maintain its position. Odessa was founded in 1794 to serve the export of cereals from the south of the modern Ukraine, which was conquered by the Tsars during the eighteenth century.[13] It too became home to many Greek merchants, who developed active associations. The 'Philike Hetairia' (Friendly Society), the organization responsible for the Greek Revolution of 1821, was founded in 1814 in the Crimea, a region ruled by the Russians.[14] Greek merchant shipping flourished mainly at times when French competition was diminished by wars,

such as during the Seven Years War (1756–63), the American War of Independence (1774–83) and, above all, during the wars sparked off by the
French Revolution and Napoleon's campaigns (1792–1814).[15] During these
wars some Greek ships even joined the English forces as privateers. War-
induced booms enabled the Greek ship-owners to weather relatively unscathed
the economic crisis which at the end of the century befell many sectors of the
Ottoman economy.

The prosperity of Ottoman trade and manufacturing until about 1760 also
prepared the way for the nationalist movements of the nineteenth-century
Balkans. A more urban and stratified society emerged, a process which has
been well studied in the case of Bulgaria. In the seventeenth century, towns
such as Ruse, Sofia and Vidin were home to a small number of affluent
people, most of whom were connected with the Ottoman administration, and
who were set apart from the general population of subjects, largely undiffer-
entiated in economic terms.[16] This began to change in the eighteenth century,
when some traders managed to join the ranks of the affluent. In the nineteenth
century, this society became even more diversified, and an initially small
group of educated lay people emerged.[17] The textile traders prospered particularly. They processed locally-produced wool to make coarse cloth, often
using peasants from the surrounding areas as part-time 'distributors', finding
a market for their wares even in the depths of Anatolia. Elegant residences
in Balkan towns still bear witness to the affluence of the most successful such
merchants.[18] They were also active sponsors, supporting churches and schools,
and from 1806 wealthy merchants helped to found the first printing presses
producing Bulgarian books.[19] Without these 'sponsors', the 'national resistance' in nineteenth-century Bulgaria could not have happened.

Decentralization and Local Rulers

In so far as the technical limitations of the time allowed it, the Ottoman
state during the sixteenth century was governed directly from the centre of
power, and to a degree this continued in the seventeenth century. However,
from after 1600, the increasing shortage of money meant that governors
were no longer allocated any resources for local administration. Instead, they
were expected to finance themselves by levying taxes on their subjects.
However, since governors were often deposed, and were frequently absent in
any case, they would appoint local tax-collectors, who often achieved a
considerable level of power. Other families gained influence by controlling
the assessment of individual villages and town quarters for the taxes which
were levied as a lump sum on the subjects of each province. This role
offered opportunities for various illegal or semi-illegal money-making ruses.

In the eighteenth and early nineteenth centuries, several affluent provincial families acquired quite large areas of land, though this was not a prerequisite for power.

In the second half of the eighteenth century, many areas were controlled only nominally by the sultan. Thus, the Tuzcuoğulları ruled the eastern coasts of the Black Sea, the real power in central Anatolia was in the hands of the Çapanoğulları, and on the Aegean coast it was the Karaosmanoğulları who controlled the export of cotton and cereals. Such local magnates were also to be found on the Balkan peninsula, where some of them managed to gain control over whole provinces. In 1808 a coalition of these magnates was even granted official recognition of their power at state level. However, soon afterwards Sultan Mahmud II (reign: 1808–38) embarked on a long and ultimately successful war of attrition against these 'Lords of the Valleys' (derebeyi), as the Ottomans called them. Only the families of land-owners without political ambitions were able to survive the campaign. For this reason, the magnate residences still existing today tend to be those of minor provincial dignitaries rather than those of the greatest power-holders.[20]

Cultural Repercussions: The Pious Foundations

Ottoman pious foundations, such as the many mosques, theological schools, dervish convents and libraries, which together constituted one of the most important pillars of Ottoman cultural life, were not immune from the effects of the economic and political crisis. Islamic religious law guaranteed that the property of a pious foundation was untouchable for eternity. However, in reality things worked out rather differently. In the eighteenth century, pious foundations were often left with just a minimal sum, the level of which the state could determine more or less at will, while the rest was confiscated for the war-chest.[21] The adminstrators of pious foundations might increase the rents of foundation-owned shops to compensate for the shortfall, but this tended to produce a reaction from the artisans affected, who themselves felt the effects of the economic crisis.[22] In Istanbul at least, artisans were often able to have their shops and the tools they contained legally defined as the necessary equipment of a master craftsman. This meant that they could then be sold only to members of the same guild. This new legal development enabled many masters to survive, but meant that the guild structure became much less flexible than it had been before.

Many foundations thus found themselves unable to make good the drop in their income and maintain their services. Indeed, many of them literally collapsed, because no money was available for structural repairs. Disputes between members of the founder families about administrative and supervisory

posts exacerbated the other problems. In the twentieth century much was
written about how foundations were abused by private individuals, and it is
true that this did often occur. However, we should not overlook the fact that
the Ottoman state had actively helped to erode the viability of many pious
foundations from as early as the eighteenth century.[23]

The Sultan's Family and Leading Officials as Architectural Patrons

The construction of monumental buildings did not grind to a halt despite the
problems between 1770 and 1838. Even during this period, members of the
sultan's family and leading officials built mosques and libraries, albeit somewhat smaller and more modest ones than those of earlier times. In fact, in the
most successful examples the moderate size of the building contributed to its
particular charm and elegance. One such edifice is the Laleli (Tulip) Mosque
which was built by Sultan Mustafa III (reign: 1757–74) and contains his
mausoleum. It stands on a large, airy terrace, in the understorey of which
there are many shops. It appears larger from the outside than from inside, as
a special substructure supports the floor. Wide steps lead to the main entrance,
and via a ramp the terrace is connected with the Divanyolu, still one of
Istanbul's main thoroughfares. This enabled the sultan to reach the terrace on
horseback. He entered the mosque by a special entrance leading directly to
his private box. The exaggeration of the mosque's height by means of a lower
storey and elaborate quarters for the ruler and his entourage also characterized
other sultans' mosques of the period, such as the Ayazma Mosque, completed
in 1760. Frequently the architects of these mosques drew on and developed
the ideas of the architect of the Nuruosmaniye foundation complex, which
had been completed in 1755. This was the first major sultan's mosque in
which the influence of the Italian baroque is clearly apparent.[24] As a result,
specialists have tended to assess it in two very different ways. Some of them
are hostile to what they see as uncritical aping of European culture, sometimes
viewing the complex almost as a betrayal of glorious domestic architectural
traditions. On the other hand, it is often conceded that the architect responsible – he has not yet been identified with certainty – and the building's two
patrons, sultans Mahmud I (reign: 1730–54) and Osman III (reign: 1754–57),
deserve credit for their courage in experimenting with new techniques, and
for refusing to limit themselves by any tradition, however glorious.[25] The trim
little mosque of Şebsefa Kadın, built by a lady from the sultan's harem in
1787, is a particularly pleasing example of the small but charming mosques
of the late eighteenth century. Equally interesting is the Nusretiye, dating
from a later period (1822–26) and built by Mahmud II (reign: 1808–38),

which reflects its architect's interest in the rococo and the French style of the Napoleonic period.[26]

In the complexes pertaining to sultans and princesses of this time, it is often the mosques which conform most closely to the sixteenth-century tradition. They are nearly all square buildings covered by a dome. However, the ornamental stairs which were being developed in this period, as well as the design of ramps, cornices and portals, offered plenty of scope for architects to employ their imagination. In addition to this type of architecture, built by men who were familiar with motifs from the European baroque and rococo, there was another style, more heavily indebted to the classical Ottoman architecture of the sixteenth and seventeenth centuries. A good example of this style is the mosque in the Bosphorus village of Beylerbeyi, built in 1778, probably by the architect Mehmed Tahir.[27]

Small, stone kiosks with lattice windows, from which free water was dispensed, were a particularly popular form of charitable foundation in the eighteenth century. Inside them sat a servant, who was paid by the foundation to serve thirsty passers-by with a cup of water from a large jug. The day-to-day running of this sort of foundation was not very expensive, but this was probably not the only reason why they were so popular. These pavilions also offered both the patron and the architect the opportunity to experiment with curvilinear decorative forms without unduly provoking a public unused to such things. In Istanbul, projecting cornices, convex arched lattices and decorative reliefs combined to produce minor masterpieces. The effect was enhanced by the smooth, carefully constructed wall on which the decorative features were based. In Cairo these structures, known as *sebil*, were even more elaborate, generally having a second storey as well. This upper level would be occupied by a Qur'ānic school. The pavilions thus became proper buildings in their own right, and came to play a significant part in the lives of the townspeople.[28]

However, functional buildings and palaces represented a major part of architectural activity at that time. Selim III (reign: 1789–1807) ordered the construction of the vast Selimiye Barracks to the south of Üsküdar, across the Bosphorus from his capital, a building which is still in use. Around the same time, other military buildings were constructed at the estate known as Levend Çiftliği, which was then well out of town, but is now in the middle of the Istanbul district of Levent.[29] To the south of the city, at Küçükçekmece by the Sea of Marmara, powder manufacturing was set up, requiring the construction of an artificial reservoir.[30] Meanwhile, in 1839, after more than a century, work was finally completed on a 25-kilometre-long water conduit. Other achievements of this period included the Valide (Sultan's Mother) reservoir in 1796 and the coffer-dam of Mahmud II, which was completed in

1839. Both of these projects were extremely demanding in architectural terms, but henceforth they supplied Istanbul, which did not have many streams, with most of its water.[31] Water supply projects had been undertaken repeatedly ever since the time of Sultan Mehmed II (reign: 1451–81), and especially during the reign of Süleyman the Magnificent (reign: 1520–66). However, the shortage of money meant that Selim III and Mahmud II were able to continue this tradition only by giving water supply a high priority. That several of these projects also had military uses must have encouraged investments in this sector.

Hydraulic constructions are made of stone, and many of them have therefore survived. However, we have to rely largely on illustrations and literary sources with regard to the Bosphorus palaces of the sultans and princesses, which continued to be built even in this period. Most of the mainly timber buildings have since been destroyed by fire or demolished.[32] However we do have an exchange of letters which grants us an extraordinary insight into the relationship between a patroness from the sultan's family and her architect who also designed jewellery and other artefacts.[33] Although we know of a few orders from sultans to their architects and of some retrospective comments from architects regarding their patron, all dating from earlier times, there survives, so far as I have been able to determine, no direct dialogue predating this correspondence from the late eighteenth century.

Antoine Ignace Melling (1763–1831) was born in Karlsruhe and later resided in France. When he came to Istanbul in 1785, he was already fluent in French and Italian as well as German; he now had to learn the Ottoman language on the spot. For Sultana Hatice, Selim III's sister, corresponding with a foreigner seems to have been a genuine challenge; quite possibly, she had recently learned to write in Roman letters. A curious correspondence thus developed: the princess, or her secretary, wrote in a rather immature hand and struggled to represent the sounds of the Ottoman language via Roman characters. Melling's handwriting is assured, but his letters show that he had great difficulties above all with Ottoman word order and pronunciation. Both correspondents also resorted to Italian, which was still a sort of *lingua franca* in the Mediterranean area at the time. One of Melling's letters to the sultana is entirely in Italian, while Hatice Sultan dated at least one of her letters in the same language. Their somewhat unsystematic orthography was also based partly on the way that Latin letters were pronounced in Italian.[34]

Sultan Selim III and his sisters, Beyhan Sultan and Hatice Sultan, demonstrated considerable enthusiasm for the arts. Selim III was a gifted musician, and Beyhan Sultan had copies made of the poems of the Mevlevî Sheikh Galib, probably the major poet of the age.[35] One of the projects for which Hatice Sultan employed Melling was the building of her Bosphorus villa. It is thought that Selim III had encouraged his sister to contract the foreign architect; the idea was probably that if his work found favour he would go on to work for the sultan himself.[36] However, this never came about, as in 1800 Melling was dismissed from the sultana's service in disgrace. The reason for this remains a mystery.

The correspondence and other evidence makes it clear that Melling, who subsequently found fame in Europe on account of his drawings and landscape paintings, undertook a wide variety of projects for the sultana. He designed a garden and built Hatice Sultan's Bosphorus villa in the French neoclassical style; the architect's own sketches for the façade facing the water have survived. He also created splendid formal robes, the making of which he oversaw in person. One of the letters concerns some embroidery which was taking far too long for the sultana's liking, and another refers to a dressing case set with precious stones.[37] Melling seems to have worked as an all-round designer. In the correspondence, at least, he was treated by the sultana as an ordinary servant, a role which he accepted.

In terms of its size, the sultana's Bosphorus villa more or less fitted into the line of villas along the coast.[38] Like all its neighbours, it was not very high, but optical elements made it appear higher. The niche decoration that enlivened the ground floor of the pavilion was perhaps also intended to create a relationship with the neighbouring building, which seems to have been adorned by a long row of painted niches. Nevertheless, the sultana's villa must have seemed like an exotic intruder. While the neighbouring houses had two upper storeys, the sultana's villa had just a ground floor and a single upper level, allowing its ceilings to be higher. As in most Ottoman dwellings, there was a bay window on the upper floor, although in this particular case it was supported by classical columns rather than braces. However, the most conspicuous differences were at roof level, where Hatice Sultan's villa sported a pediment in the classical style, decorated with an oval shield containing three half-moons. The roof also had a balustrade, on which there were urns at regular intervals. Unfortunately, we do not know what the neighbours made of this unusual building, and nor does the correspondence offer any clues about a possible connection between Melling's work as architect and his falling from favour.

Architecture in the Provinces

In the sixteenth century most monumental buildings in the provinces were built by officials of the central government on duty in the region. Some such officials came originally from the area in question, having made a career in the central administration after forming part of the 'levy of boys'. By contrast,

12. Esenköy (Arpaz), western Anatolia. Osman Beyler Konağı, fortified house with tower dwelling (*c.* 1800). (Photograph: Prof. Ayda Arel, Istanbul)

in the second half of the eighteenth century many architectural patrons lived permanently in the area they administered, where they had roots which went back for generations.[39] Their edifices were intended to show off their local status, which is why so many of them decayed or were even torn down when the family fell from power.

Some provincial power-holders created pious foundations to consolidate their reputation among the townspeople. Two generations of the Çapanoğulları family, for example, built a remarkable double mosque in Yozgat, the town they had founded in central Anatolia.[40] The older part of the mosque was built by Mustafa Pasha in 1778, while his son Süleyman added a second chamber in 1795. The entrance hall, originally an open one, was converted to connect the two parts of the building, allowing a variety of perspectives through the complex to satisfy contemporary taste.

However, the most interesting buildings constructed by these provincial potentates and surviving today are, without doubt, their residences. The finest example is probably the palace of Ishak Pasha, not far from the small town of Doğu Beyazit and close to the Turkish–Iranian border.[41] Three generations of a local pasha family contributed to the building of the palace, which was probably finished by 1784. Oddly enough, this complex does not recall the palaces of Istanbul but instead copied Seljuk models. The golden age of this style of architecture lay about five hundred years earlier, so the choice must have been a conscious one; it was not simply a case of the style persisting in a remote province. Unfortunately, no text has emerged to shed light on the reasons behind this decision.

We enter the palace through a portal incorporating Seljuk decorative motifs reinterpreted in the manner of the eighteenth century. Within the complex one of the owners was buried, together with his wife. The mausoleum harks back to a form of tomb common at the time of the Mongolian occupation of Anatolia, in the late thirteenth and in the fourteenth centuries. As often occurred in mausolea from the Mongol period, the tombs were not actually in the mausoleum, but rather in a cellar space beneath it. However, despite this archaism Ishak Pasha's family certainly did not reject modern comforts. Winters in that region are long and cold, so most of the rooms were fairly small and each was provided with a fireplace. Since such fireplaces do not produce much warmth, there were also pipes built into the interior walls through which hot air could flow from a central boiler.

Pashas in frontier regions were often able to do more or less as they pleased. This fact was brought painfully home to Pierre Amedée Jaubert, whom Napoleon sent as an agent and envoy to the Shah of Persia in 1805. While still on Ottoman territory he was imprisoned in the citadel of Doğu Beyazit, and survived only because of the help he received from the commander of the fortress and a female member of the commander's family.[42] In the western provinces local magnates had less autonomy, but their residences were nevertheless often fortified and magnificently appointed. Recent research has revealed that the rural tower house, a form which had been popular in western Anatolia since antiquity and the Byzantine period, was frequently revived in the years around 1800.[43] This was probably due to the general sense of insecurity resulting from the disturbances created by deserters or dismissed soldiers during this time of conflict. However, the towers were probably also intended to symbolize the power of the families who built them. They probably did make a considerable impact on the peasants and nomads of the area. However, indirectly at least, these fortified houses also represented a show of strength directed at the sultan, and the message was not lost on Sultan Mahmud II. Even though most provincial potentates who came to grief were the victims of power-hungry neighbours, the latter often acted on the orders of the ruler, who could not generally rely on his own troops in the depths of the provinces.

A tower building in the area of Arpaz in the Aegean region of Anatolia, which has been thoroughly researched, possessed a separate dwelling-house as well as the tower itself. Although there was no direct connection between Ottoman and European types of fortified houses, this arrangement represents the same combination of tower and *corps de logis* which was also a common feature of medieval European castles.[44] The house had two storeys and, as was usual in Ottoman houses, the living quarters were on the first floor. A terrace afforded the inhabitants a pleasant view over the Aegean landscape. The fortress-like character of the complex was re-enforced by an exterior wall. The fortifications could not, of course, have withstood a siege by a proper army, but they did serve as an effective demonstration of power.

In the towns, the houses of powerful families were usually unfortified. A well-known example from the late eighteenth century, which can still be seen today, is the house of Çakır Fahir Ağa in the small Aegean town of Birgi. The building is not particularly large; few Ottoman dignitaries built houses which matched the dimensions of English or French country seats of the same epoch, perhaps because they seemed uncomfortable and not very intimate.[45] The upper storey, where the living quarters were located, has many windows overlooking the street and the garden. In the corners there are two distinctly belvedere-like rooms, each with an antechamber, which are particularly dis-tinguished in architectural terms. One of them seems to have been intended as a drawing-room for the summer, while the other was used in winter. These 'reception rooms' were very ornate, with carved wooden ceilings featuring a central roundel. Such ceilings were often very imaginatively conceived and in affluent homes remained popular until the late nineteenth century. This being a Mediterranean climate, the hall, which was an important part of Ottoman living quarters, opened on to the garden to become a terrace. The lower floor, where the servants lived and meals were prepared, was open towards the garden.

Decoration

Much of the paintwork, which made the house of Çakır Ağa light and colourful both inside and out, has survived. Some of the designs are abstract, such as those on the exterior walls. However, bunches of flowers, mostly garden flowers such as tulips, carnations or hyacinths arranged in a vase or tied together with a ribbon, were also popular as decorative features.[46] Such flower arrangements were often very realistic and had been characteristic of

13. Mosque of Yakub Bey, also known as Hisar Camii, in the old district of Izmir. The mosque, built in 1592, was altered in the eighteenth and nineteenth centuries. The pulpit (*minber*), which has a bas-relief townscape with mosques on its eastern side, also dates from this period. Probably the Izmir townscape is intended. (Photograph: Prof. Ayda Arel, Istanbul)

façade decorations ever since the sixteenth century. They were often to be found in the sultan's palace and in the great mosques.[47] In the eighteenth century, compositions based on fruits also became popular; one of the earliest examples, perhaps inspired by European still lifes, is to be found in a hall of the sultan's harem, which was painted in the early eighteenth century.[48] This form of decoration was also used in the bas-reliefs which often adorned the

drinking-water fountains (çeşme) of this period.[49] Fruit and flower compositions were also popular on women's tombstones, corresponding to the
head coverings, such as *ulema* turbans or dervish caps, which decorated the
funerary. There is an early example of this decoration on the tombstone of
Saliha Hatun (died 1739–40), a woman of Istanbul. On the front there are
fruits in bowls and bunches of roses in high relief, some of them in elaborately
decorated vases. On the back there is a pear tree, heavily laden with fruit; two
pears have fallen to the ground. Might these perhaps represent the children
of the deceased woman? A grave from the years 1812/13 is decorated in
flatter and more stylized relief. The deceased is commemorated by a cypress
tree around which grapevines are wound; these trees often appeared in poems,
where they were associated with tall, slim beauty, but they were also commonly
planted in cemeteries.[50] From the eighteenth century onwards, families who
wanted to proclaim a particular social and political status often erected
elaborate tombs; at any rate, more of them have survived from this period
than from previous ones. It appears as if the men's graves, with their elaborate
emblems, were designed to make such status as conspicuous as possible. The
women were seen to contribute in an indirect but not insignificant manner to
the strength of the family through their beauty and fertility.

As well as decorative fruit and flowers, the landscape picture became
fashionable in the second half of the eighteenth century. Again, interest in
this genre arose initially in Istanbul, at the sultan's court and in the princesses'
palaces.[51] However, the new subject-matter quickly spread to the provinces.
In the vestibule of the summer drawing-room of the house of Çakır Ağa,
there is a frieze, such as often separated the door and window level from the
ceiling in such houses, showing a great panorama of Istanbul.[52] This motif
was already well established in miniature painting, but here the stylized
townscape extends over an area of several metres. It is possible to recognize
the Sultan Ahmed Mosque and the Aya Sofya. In the background is Galata
and the mosque of Kılıç Ali Pasha; on the right of the picture much space
is devoted to Üsküdar with its mosques and a palace, no longer extant, on the
shore. However, the most important element in the picture is the sea, with a
small island in the foreground. Although the painter has placed the island far
too close to the Istanbul shore, it is quite clearly meant to be the Leander
Tower which, rather than the great monumental buildings, served as the
landmark of the Ottoman capital in illustrations of the city at that time. A
host of sailing ships also enliven the scene; the painter seems to have decided
to omit all the open rowing-boats which most people used for shorter trips.
This decision may have been dictated by the fact that people were always
visible in such boats; however, until the second half of the nineteenth century
both patrons and artists avoided the depiction of people and animals.[53] Other

painters, who evidently felt less constrained by the bounds of reality, illustrated open rowing-boats sallying forth over the waves without anybody visible to propel them.

Such landscape paintings do not appear to have caused any misgivings among pious people, since buildings dedicated to religious purposes exhibit the same form of decoration. Mosques adorned with illustrations of landscapes are particularly numerous in the provinces. However, the scarcity of mosque paintings of this type in Istanbul may simply be due to the fact that in the capital the landscapes have been obliterated by later restoration work.[54] Townscapes of the pilgrimage centres of Mecca and Medina often served to decorate religious edifices. The greatness of the two mosques is emphasized, and the places visited and venerated by pilgrims are prominent. This was a theme which had been popular in miniature painting for centuries and which seems to have been carried over into murals.

In formal terms, these paintings are characterized by the attempt to reproduce light effects, such as the shimmering pink and light yellow sky of sunrise and sunset. The tops of trees are often shaded in a manner intended to represent the incidence of light. These elements probably go back to European models. They may have been introduced to the Ottoman realm via paintings made in the Istanbul districts of Galata and Pera (Beyoğlu), which had substantial European populations, or via books of patterns with sketches, engravings or watercolours.[55] It is thought that the rapid spread of this form of landscape painting through Anatolia and the southern Balkans was due to itinerant artists, but no information about the lives and work of these individuals has yet come to light.

In some cases landscapes were also represented in bas-relief.[56] This was a significant innovation, since except for the decorations on some tombstones, reliefs had hitherto been restricted to abstract patterns. Reliefs were particularly popular on the structures built to dispense water, which possessed panels ideal for such ornamentation. There are beautiful examples from the trading city of Izmir, where the water dispenser of the Çakaloğlu Khan (1805) and another, known as Dönertaş (1813–14), were decorated with townscapes. A relief of the same period which adorns the pulpit in Izmir's Hisar Camii Mosque is particularly interesting. Rather than the usual representation of an imaginary town or of Istanbul motifs, this is a panorama of Izmir itself.[57] There was a school of stone-masons in Izmir between 1776 and 1839, the members of which drew on the motifs generally used in decorative painting to produce bas-reliefs. It seems that the inhabitants of this active trading town had developed a sense of their local and urban identity, which is why they commissioned artwork showing the Izmir townscape.

A Different View of Europe

We have often alluded to Ottoman architects, painters and stone-masons of
this period being interested in European artefacts. In some cases the services
of European artists were engaged by members of the Ottoman upper class,
although few of these artists were major figures. Many historians have explained the increased interest in Europe by relating it to the economic and
political crises of the time, which, they claim, shook the self-confidence of
the Ottoman élite. Interest in military, technical and later also scientific
achievements in Europe reflected a desire to achieve parity with the Ottoman
Empire's victorious enemies.[58] There is certainly a great deal of truth in this
explanation, but it is somewhat superficial. To show this, we might usefully
refer to an example from German history. The defeat of Germany in the
Second World War and the revelation of the crimes committed by the Nazis
certainly led to profound self-doubt among thoughtful Germans, and their
rejection of the past contributed to a readiness to accept aspects of American
culture. However, this acceptance did not mean that writers and film-makers,
for example, were reduced simply to copying American models. In fact, new
creative energies were released by the encounter. In the same way, it would
be wrong to underestimate the intellectual curiosity of members of the
Ottoman upper class, who had a cosmopolitan heritage of their own, with
respect to many of the artefacts arriving from Europe. The vital creativity of
Ottoman variants of the baroque and rococo, several examples of which we
have already encountered, illustrates the point.[59]

High-level members of the Ottoman élite were able to learn something of
life in contemporary Europe through ambassadors' reports. Shortly after his
return from a 1720 embassy to France, Yirmisekiz Mehmed Çelebi wrote
such an account, which became quite famous.[60] Several ambassadors' reports
were printed in their own right, and others were included, sometimes in an
abridged form, in the imperial chronicles commissioned by the Ottoman court
and subsequently printed, as well as being distributed in many manuscripts.
Ahmed Resmî, historian and political author, was ambassador to Vienna in
1757–58 and to Berlin in 1764–65. He penned a rather understated, ironic
account of the Prussian capital, a town which boasted imposing architecture
but retained a very provincial atmosphere. The curiosity of the Berliners,
who had never before encountered a Muslim, features prominently in Ahmed

14. From the festival book illustrated by Levni (Library of the Topkapı Sarayı,
Istanbul). Young people dancing on a decorated raft, with watching dignitaries in the
upper part of the picture. Ebubekir Ratıb compared such displays to the European
opera of the eighteenth century.

Resmî's report. He also alludes humorously to the Prussian king's reluctance to spend money on anything but war, diplomatic ceremony included.[61]

Ahmed Resmî was an experienced diplomat, with a much clearer understanding of the power structure of contemporary Europe than most grand viziers of his time. However, he also took a lively interest in other matters.[62] He frequently received invitations from members of the Prussian élite resident in Berlin, who were as keen to find out more about this exotic guest as they were to show off their own affluence. Ahmed Resmî's report includes observations about the passion of well-to-do Berliners for porcelain; entire rooms were filled with such objects until they resembled exotic gardens.[63] He was also struck by the popularity of conservatories, in which exotic plants were grown. Ahmed Resmî notes the king's commercial policy of banning the import of porcelain from Saxony (i.e. Dresden) and instead encouraging domestic producers. In Ahmed Resmî's view, eventually a second Saxony might develop in Berlin. But for the time being, however, the king's import bans meant that his subjects had to pay exceptionally high prices.

The Ottoman ambassador was also invited to the Berlin theatre and to fancy-dress balls; the latter must have rather shocked him.[64] Another report, that of Ebubekir Ratıb Efendi, who led a diplomatic mission to the Habsburg court in 1791–92 to announce the accession of Selim III to the throne, contains a rather fuller reaction to the theatre.[65] Ebubekir spent a considerable time in Temeşvar (Timisoara), which was in Habsburg hands at the time, and visited a performance of a tragedy. In this context, he explains that there are three types of drama: tragedy, comedy and opera. It is significant that he compares the opera to Ottoman shadow-plays (*hayal*), probably because of the scenery, which must have reminded him of the landscape pictures used for shadow-plays.[66] Ebubekir Ratıb Efendi was also struck by the similarity of comedy to the art of the Ottoman storytellers, in which mimicry was an important element. He likens the ballet interludes, which were always included in both operas and comedies, to the performances by Ottoman *cengi* dancers. Such performances are illustrated many times in the miniatures by Levnî which document the circumcision festival of 1720. Ebubekir Ratıb notes that although love stories from long ago provided the subject-matter of most works, they were often used as a vehicle for veiled satire at the expense of contemporary kings, generals and prominent figures.

Diplomats witnessed the life of the European upper classes, but we may also have a drastic description of England's 'low life', written by a former janissary named Ismail Beşe.[67] 'Beşe' was used as a title by Ottoman soldiers; in England, Ismail Beşe converted it to 'Bashaw' and eventually adopted it as his surname. Ostensibly, Ismail Beşe came originally from Edirne, where he was born into a well-to-do family in 1735. According to his own story, he resigned from his post in the Ottoman administration to turn his energies to foreign trade. He goes on to claim that he was taken prisoner by the Spaniards and had to serve for five years as a slave aboard galleys and at various construction sites. Eventually, so he writes, he managed to flee to Portugal and thence to England. In London he hoped to make contact with one of his brothers, who was also engaged in international trade and had connections with English merchants. However, before he managed to do this, all the money which he had somehow saved was stolen from him. This forced him to live the life of a vagabond, his poverty preventing him from settling anywhere in England. His marriage to an Englishwoman did nothing to help, as she too belonged to the class of those of no fixed abode. Even his baptism by the Bishop of Lincoln, following which he called himself Ismael James Bashaw, seems to have done little to improve his circumstances. In 1797 an account appeared of his adventures as an itinerant dyer, hatter, cobbler and as a worker in the iron industry. Initially this reads as a pure fiction, but in fact the family is documented in English court proceedings, the couple's children have been traced in church records, and there are also occasional references to 'Bashaw' and his wife as the recipients of charitable support. Thus, we may look forward to the publication of research dealing with the unusual fate of the former janissary, even if certain aspects of his life probably will never be elucidated. If he really came from the Ottoman Empire, Ismail Beşe evidently decided at some point in his adventures to turn his back once and for all on his former home. One would like to know more about his life story and how he, perhaps, manipulated it in the telling.

The Effects of the French Revolution

Ahmed Resmî, Ebubekir Ratıb and even Ismael J. Bashaw were confronted with more or less gradual processes such as increasing European power and the process of industrialization. They had, and took, years to consider these phenomena. Things were very different with regard to one of the most important events in European history, at least for our purposes: the French Revolution. It seems unlikely that much was known in Istanbul in 1789 of the pressure created by national debts or of the agitation against the exemption of the nobility from taxes, still less of the recent massive swing from prosperity to depression in the French economy. Yet today these circumstances are seen by historians as the main factors which sparked the revolution.[68] The event itself must therefore have come as a surprise. At first the revolution appeared to Ottoman administrators as something exotic, something conceivable only among the unbelievers and especially in France. It probably did not even occur to them that there might be direct consequences for Ottoman state and society. However, it quickly became clear that the already difficult problems facing the Ottoman ruling class at that time would before long be considerably exacerbated by the events in France.

In April 1789 Selim III, who had corresponded as a prince with the young Louis XVI, succeeded to the throne as heir to Abdülhamid I (reign: 1774–89). He planned to replace the janissaries, who were ineffective as a military force, with a troop trained in modern methods. This project was to cost him the throne in 1807, and, a few months later, his life.[69] The accession of Selim III to the throne approximately coincided with the convocation of the Estates General (5 May 1789) which marked the beginning of the French Revolution. Soon, disputes in Istanbul between European supporters and opponents of the revolution began to attract the notice of Ottoman officials. For example, after the fall of Louis XVI in 1792, the Republic sent its own ambassador to Istanbul. At first, however, the royal representative refused to turn over the embassy to the new arrival. The 'War of the Cockades', when French republicans living in Istanbul began to sport red, white and blue cockades and their royalist opponents white ones, also occasioned amazed and somewhat sarcastic reactions. In fact, the sultan's government was called in to adjudicate the ensuing dispute.

At first, the Ottoman authorities decided to remain neutral in the 'War of the Cockades' and other such conflicts, regarding them as French domestic matters. However, this changed when Napoleon attacked the Ottoman province of Egypt in 1798 and occupied it for three years. This attack was, at least in part, a consequence of the unsettled domestic situation in France itself: the Directorate which had risen to power after the fall of Robespierre had wanted to keep the dangerous general away from France for a while. From 1798 to 1802 the Ottoman Empire and France were at war with one another. This situation was something quite new in the long history of Ottoman–French relations, and must have forced those responsible for Ottoman foreign policy radically to reconsider their outlook.[70]

They were not alone in facing this problem. In the years around 1800, attitudes towards the French Revolution and Napoleonic rule decisively shaped the views of European intellectuals towards life and society in general. Goethe, Wordsworth and even Beethoven all took a stand on these issues at various turning-points in history.[71] Certain non-Muslim intellectuals of Istanbul seem to have shared this sense of the revolution's seminal importance. This is clear from the story of Mouradjea D'Ohsson, an Ottoman Armenian who was, for a time, Swedish ambassador.[72]

Mouradjea D'Ohsson was born as Ignatius Muradcan Tosunyan in 1740, the son of a Catholic family in Istanbul. His father spent many years as interpreter to the Swedish embassy, a career which his son also followed. By

1768 Muradcan Tosunyan was already chief interpreter, and when subsequently he was elevated to the Swedish nobility, he took the name of D'Ohsson, with its French overtones. Under this name and in French, he published from 1788 the multi-volume work for which he is still known among historians of the Ottoman Empire: *Tableau général de l'Empire ottoman* ('A General Survey of the Ottoman Empire').[73] Unlike other authors writing on the subject, D'Ohsson had lived in the empire for decades, and he had first-hand experience of how the Ottoman state apparatus functioned. He also spoke and wrote the Ottoman language, as he needed to in his professional capacity. His work, which was printed twice in France, therefore presents a rather special and rarely encountered perspective. On the one hand, the author was a member of an Ottoman minority, albeit one who had distanced himself from his origins, and, on the other, a foreign diplomat. Moreover, D'Ohsson showed a strong affinity for France, the centre of intellectual life in Europe. In 1799 he settled there, and he died near Paris in 1807.

Before this, however, Mouradjea D'Ohsson had created a considerable scandal in Istanbul, which led to the Sublime Porte declaring a foreign diplomat *persona non grata* for the first time in its history. As early as 1793 D'Ohsson had attracted attention to himself for his Jacobin sympathies. The monarchist ambassador Count Choiseul-Gouffier left Istanbul at that time, and his successor, the former Marquis de Ste-Croix, who had entered the service of the Republic under the bourgeois name of Descorches, took up the post in the face of strong protests from his diplomatic colleagues. At this stage D'Ohsson had acted as an intermediary, smoothing the way to the Porte for the republican envoy, who was also regarded with some scepticism by the Ottoman government. After Napoleon's attack on Egypt, the authorities in Istanbul occupied the French embassy, and documents came to light which revealed that D'Ohsson had been receiving regular payments from the French ambassador. In April 1799 D'Ohsson was recalled by the Swedish government, although it appears that he did not travel to Sweden at all, but rather moved directly to France. There he busied himself with the publication of his work. Payments to foreign sympathizers were widespread in the Europe of the *ancien régime*, and it was not always considered dishonourable to accept them. However, politics had become much more ideological in the wake of the French Revolution, and this led to a change in the way such matters were regarded. Unfortunately, no text has yet come to light in which D'Ohsson responds to the charges against him, so we do not know how he saw his own behaviour. On the other hand, perhaps there is an eloquence in this very silence ...

The 'Rehabilitation' of an Age

Research which has recently appeared or is still being undertaken has shown that, despite many economic and political crises, the period between 1770 and 1830 was one of artistic creativity and a spirit of intellectual adventure. It is not always legitimate to equate decades of political stability and the consolidation of power with periods of blossoming artistic activity, as writers on Ottoman history still tend to do rather often. Moreover, today, in an age when the national state and its associated national culture are no longer regarded as the *non plus ultra* of historical development, it is easier to appreciate the opportunities which arose, in the short term at least, from the special circumstances of the years either side of 1800. The balance between the still vibrant Ottoman literary and architectural tradition on the one hand, and the interest in European artefacts on the other, led to the creation of unique and very attractive works of art.[74] In our own times, postmodernism has modified our perspective on the phenomenon of cultural borrowing and re-established that it is artistically valid to draw on and unite heterogeneous elements. Now, perhaps, it may at last be possible to gain a better understanding of a fascinating period in which Ottoman intellectuals seem to have operated by similar principles.[75]

13

Elegance Alafranga,[†] Social Criticism and Tomatoes: Transformations in the Culture of the Ottoman Upper Class, 1840–1914

The nineteenth century – its cultural history included – is among the most thoroughly researched periods in Ottoman history. Certain arts also practised in previous centuries, such as shadow-plays and improvised theatre, now enjoyed a golden age. At the same time, members of the Ottoman élite, along with some artists and skilled craftsmen, were attempting to introduce new genres of literary and visual art, such as the novel or photography, to the Ottoman cultural domain. It is impossible to do full justice to these developments in the space of a single chapter, and so we shall restrict ourselves to brief descriptions of those areas with which we have already been concerned in the main part of this volume: architecture and the structure of urban districts, everyday figurative and literary genres, and cuisine. Even within these limitations, we shall be able to deal only with some of the many changes taking place in the course of the nineteenth century. Nevertheless, the central point should emerge clearly: although the Ottoman upper class originally saw the import of cultural innovations from Europe as a way of conserving the empire, this political motivation was only partly shared by many writers, photographers, theatre people and critics. Rather, such people had embarked on their new *métier* with the zeal of converts to a fresh cause and with a spirit of adventure. There was a real sense of *joie de vivre* in their work. However, they were repeatedly accused of showing too little respect for sacrosanct traditions, even if these traditions, like the Ottoman neo-absolutism of the time, were in fact of rather recent vintage. The conflicts and compromises which arose from this situation will form the subject-matter of the present chapter.

In the period beginning with the end of the Napoleonic Wars (1815) and lasting for about a century, the Ottoman Empire, widely known as the 'sick

---

[†] 'European style'

man of Europe', was in the process of dissolution. Just like the Habsburg Empire, the Ottoman state experienced fierce attacks from the élites of various subject populations with aspirations towards forming nation states along the lines of western European models. Again like Austria-Hungary, the Ottoman Empire is today regarded in some circles, particularly Arab ones, with a degree of nostalgia.[1] The formation of post-Ottoman states in the Balkans was complicated by the attempts of the great European powers to gain influence over the new nations. England, Russia and France all pursued this goal, and towards the end of the nineteenth century the German Empire and Austria-Hungary began to do so as well.[2] Moreover, after each lost war there were plans simply to divide up the Ottoman Empire among the great European powers. These plans always failed on account of the rivalries between those powers, but also on account of the considerable political acumen of certain members of the Ottoman government.

In economic terms, the nineteenth-century Ottoman Empire became increasingly bound up in a set of international economic relations dominated by European states. Free-trade agreements and the special rights of several among these states, known as capitulations, prevented any effective measures to protect domestic industries. European control strengthened after 1875, when the Ottoman state was no longer able to pay its debts. The increasing costs of modernizing the army and transport system contributed to this bankruptcy, but more fundamental factors included the loss of resources through unequal treaties and the independence of relatively productive provinces.[3]

The Ottoman élite attempted to counter the effects of this crisis by means of alliances with a succession of individual European states. In the early nineteenth century, Britain appeared the most reliable partner. However, British support for the Greek rebels in their battle for independence caused the Porte to look elsewhere as well. Due to tsarist policies of expansion in the Balkans and towards the Mediterranean, Russia was regarded as the most dangerous enemy. Since the founding of the German Empire (1870), military relations with Prussia, whose kings had been promoted emperors, became closer. Moreover, towards the end of the nineteenth century German firms began to offer serious competition to English and French companies, for example in the financing of the Baghdad Railway.[4] This situation at least partly explains why the Young Turk government decided in 1914 to enter the First World War against the Entente and on the German side.

The Ottoman Upper-class Experiments

Ottoman attempts to find allies in Europe also had serious consequences in domestic politics. In 1839 the sultan's decree of Gülhane was issued, named after one of the parks pertaining to the Topkapı Palace. In the decree the new sultan, Abdülmecid (reign: 1839–61), who had just succeeded his father Mahmud II (reign: 1808–39), guaranteed the security and property rights of all his subjects, regardless of religion. Translated into the reality of the Ottoman Empire at the time, this meant the abolition of the special privileges and obligations of the different religious groups which had so far coexisted more or less peacefully within the bounds of the empire.[5] The special taxes (*cizye*) levied on non-Muslims were also abolished. However, Christians and Jews could now be conscripted into the army, which Mahmud II had reconstructed along modern lines after his bloody suppression of the janissaries (1826). In theory, at least, non-Muslims could also obtain posts in the bureaucracy.[6] In fact, many of them sought to avoid military service, and indeed many of the sultan's Muslim subjects must have been equally reluctant conscripts. However, in the nineteenth century it was only the non-Muslims who were generally given the option of avoiding service in the army by paying a special tax. This concession was the result of the Ottoman government's conviction that it could not rely on the loyalty of its Christian subjects in the event of a war in the Balkans.

For the Ottoman upper class, the changes of the Tanzimat, as the period between 1839 and 1878 is generally known, meant that those of its members actively serving the sultan no longer needed to regard themselves as his virtual slaves. Even under Mahmud II things still had been very different. That monarch had restored the power of the central government by executing many provincial magnates and dignitaries, to say nothing of his slaughter of so many janissaries. In most instances, the estates of the executed men were confiscated. Yet the reforms of the Tanzimat period did not constitute a complete reversal of Mahmud II's neo-absolutism; far from it. However, Sultan Abdülhamid II, whose autocratic reign lasted for over thirty years (1876–1909), preferred to make the upper class pliant mainly by means of arrests, deportations and corruption. Although the constitutionalist appointed Grand Vizier Midhat Pasha was murdered in 1884 during his exile on the Arabian peninsula, political assassinations of members of the Ottoman élite remained exceptional.[7]

Between 1839 and 1878, when Abdülhamid abrogated the constitution established in 1876 and constructed a régime founded on the palace bureaucracy, it was in fact the grand viziers rather than the sultans who reformed the Ottoman state apparatus along the lines of the French model and governed in a rather autocratic fashion. Thus the 'Young Ottoman' writer Namık Kemal (note the analogy to the 'Young Germans' and other 'young' opposition movements of the nineteenth century) complained that the suppression of the janissaries had destroyed indigenous means of maintaining control over the state apparatus, and that no new checks and balances had been introduced.[8]

In fact, the discontent engendered by military service, lost wars, the interference of foreign states in the empire's internal affairs and the presence of foreign refugees in remote provinces only occasionally gave rise to 'grass roots' revolutionary movements in Istanbul. Probably the best-known example of such phenomena is the rebellion of 1909, which was to have restored Sultan Abdülhamid's power, just after he had been forced (in 1908) by military and bureaucratic revolts to put the constitution of 1876 back in place. This movement aimed at giving the sultan the upper hand over a bureaucracy perceived to be culturally alien. There was a desire to reaffirm the validity of an unwritten 'social contract', passed down through the oral tradition, between the ruler and his subjects.[9] Nevertheless, due to the disappearance of the janissaries, who had been the strong arm of the Istanbul lower classes, rebellions of this type were relatively rare.[10]

In these matters, the jurists and theologians, who might have provided an alternative source of leadership, did not present a united front. Since the eighteenth century at least, the most senior members of the *ulema* hierarchy formed a distinct aristocracy, whose powers had been severely curtailed by the *de facto* confiscation of pious foundations which took place in this period.[11] Moreover, high-level judges and teachers for a long time had not maintained many significant relationships with ordinary Muslims. Quite a few of them had no doubt come to the same conclusion as senior military men and bureaucrats belonging to the central administration: namely that only a radical reorganization could halt the disintegration of the empire. No doubt such opinions enjoyed rather less support at the lower levels of the *ulema* hierarchy.

After 1878 Sultan Abdülhamid used religious discourse to justify his neo-absolutist régime and this move must have done a great deal to neutralize opposition against his policies. Since the kadis' courts, particularly towards the end of the nineteenth century, were giving up ever more cases to courts which functioned on the basis of laws decreed by the ruler, the *ulema* had in any case lost considerable political influence. It must be said that the religious emphasis of his reign did not dampen Abdülhamid's enthusiasm for technical innovations, particularly those which appeared as though they might help him assert and legitimize his rule. Railways and telegraph lines came into this category, as did photography. This combination of religiosity and interest in technical progress remains characteristic of most Turkish conservatives today, which is why Abdülhamid is still a popular figure in such circles.[12]

The Assimilation of a Foreign Culture and Domestic Enlightenment

Historians have attempted to explain the decision of the Ottoman upper class to accept European cultural novelties in many aspects of life by the sense of uncertainty brought about by lost wars.[13] Well-to-do Ottomans welcomed what sultans and literary figures saw as 'European achievements' in order to participate in contemporary technical progress and save at least a part of the empire. Even the writers, journalists and politicians who campaigned on behalf of European novels, dramatic art or a more public role for women often justified their attitudes in this way. Thus, for example, in one of his best-known works, the writer Namık Kemal celebrates the heroism of a young woman who disguised herself as a man and joined in the defence of the threatened stronghold of Silistre.[14]

However, such discourse from the political élite does not tell the whole story. As popular satires at the expense of young fops and their snobbish lifestyle demonstrate, the novelty factor also contributed to the urge to experiment with European forms.[15] Moreover, borrowing from foreign cultures has often been used as a means of implementing changes in the culture of the borrower. In the European context we might cite Shakespeare's 'adoption' in Germany in the late eighteenth and early nineteenth centuries, where his work provided the model for a novel articulation of emotions on stage.[16] In the present book, we have observed the rise of 'intimate' culture from the second half of the seventeenth century onwards, which should be viewed as a major, internally generated variety of cultural change. With this in mind it is worth looking more closely at the indigenous starting points for cultural changes of the late Ottoman period as well. It would hardly be going too far to describe the changes in the culture of the élite which took place in the nineteenth century as a version of the Enlightenment, albeit one limited in its resonance.[17] I would even argue that, while in one way the many wars lost in the last century of the Ottoman Empire helped bring about major changes, they also acted as the main brake on cultural transformation. For these wars, and the open contempt for the 'Sick Man' which ensued in Europe, engendered a sense of disloyalty in those members of the élite who might otherwise have been prepared to accept European culture with open arms.[18]

The literary figures and politicians of the Tanzimat period, like their successors during the reign of Sultan Abdülhamid II, isolated themselves from the lower classes by their acceptance of a foreign culture and, *mutatis mutandis*, a comparable dichotomy persists even today. Of course this isolation was not absolute, but it did prevent the formation of alliances between elements of the upper class and political groups lower down the social scale. In a period in which the formation of nation states, and later the democratic ideal, came to be uppermost in people's minds, this isolation from the 'people' was seen as a grave moral blemish, above all by writers. Many authors addressed the sense of internal conflict which they experienced in these circumstances. Over and over again we will encounter two contradictory aims

in Ottoman nineteenth-century architecture, drama and literature. On the
one hand, architects and writers were proud of the cultural innovations they
introduced. After all, as has recently become clear, the classical and romantic
artistic tradition in Europe was not alone in placing great stock in the quality
of originality. The poet Şeyh Galib, writing at the end of the eighteenth
century and untouched by European artistic traditions, had also attempted to
find a basis for the originality and uniqueness of poetry, to which end he
invoked elements of mystic philosophy.[19] Cultural innovation, however, was
possible only if the artist was, to a degree, willing to distance him- and
sometimes herself from certain assumptions of his/her readers.

   On the other hand, unlike Şeyh Galib, the writers of the nineteenth century
were concerned above all with the social, enlightening function of literature.
They were therefore prepared to conform to existing traditions and to accept
compromises in order to satisfy current tastes and reach as large a section of
the Istanbul middle and upper classes as possible. Initially, the attraction of
new forms such as drama and the novel for Ottoman authors had little to do
with the new literary possibilities they opened up. Rather, writers aimed at
pursuing new agendas, such as the abolition of polygamy or the advantages of
marriages between consenting partners. In the long term this disproportionate
concern with didactic elements can be seen to have undermined the artistic
value of the novels and plays of the second half of the nineteenth century, and
these works are not very popular among modern readers and audiences.[20]

The Problems of Secularization

Throughout the nineteenth century the change of lifestyle championed by
the Ottoman sultans and political élites went hand-in-hand with an attempt
to separate politics from religion. This goal was pursued with varying degrees
of intensity, but in certain fields continued even during the reign of Sultan
Abdülhamid.[21] Hardly any sultans of the period were freethinkers, and
convictions of this kind, if known, probably would have endangered their
position. When a late nineteenth-century figure such as Beşir Fuad openly
admitted his atheism and ultimately affirmed his convictions by suicide, he
placed himself 'beyond the pale', and his reputation has continued to suffer
right up to the present day.[22] However, the tendency to take religion for
granted, rather than treating it as a topic for discussion, certainly existed in
the seventeenth century and probably very much earlier. It was particularly
widespread among those bureaucrats who had been educated 'on the job'
rather than in the schools of theology. Quite a few officials inclined towards
pragmatism. Thus, the influential historian, geographer and bibliographer
Kâtib Çelebi (died 1657) had strongly criticized the quarrel between the

preachers known as 'Kadızade's people' and their dervish opponents as a display of ignorance and self-conceit.[23]

A tendency towards 'creeping' secularization, which Sultan Mahmud II particularly encouraged, was therefore founded largely on practical considerations. Money had to be found to finance the new army, and bringing the existing pious foundations under state control appeared as a means to this end.[24] From 1826 onwards, pious foundations were subordinated to a special ministry and thereby to all intents and purposes nationalized. This cost the jurists and theologians, particularly the most prominent of them, considerable political influence, since they had hitherto enjoyed appreciable incomes from the administration of pious foundations. Although the schools of theology (*medreses*) were equally placed under state control, they were systematically neglected in favour of the newly-established technical colleges. Around the middle of the century, even budding jurists and theologians with intellectual promise were forced to search beyond the *medreses* for additional educational opportunities.[25] As a long-term consequence of the policies of Mahmud II and his immediate successors, intellectuals of a religious bent are comparatively scarce even in modern Turkey.[26]

At first glance we might think that this development of secular schools largely came to a standstill under Abdülhamid II, as in this period religion was used a great deal in order to legitimize the ruler's status. The Ottoman sultan was presented as the caliph of the entire Islamic world, above all in dealings with foreign Muslims, most of whom were subjects of European colonial empires.[27] In India this image of the Ottoman sultan became politically important, and the pronounced interest of Indian Muslims in the Ottoman caliphate prompted Atatürk to abolish this institution in 1924.[28] However, even under Abdülhamid secular schools were founded, designed to prepare students for technical and administrative duties in the civil service. Many members of the secularized intelligentsia had received their training in military schools. Rıfat Osman (1874–1933), for example, one of the pioneers of post-classical archaeology and the conservation of monuments, was in fact an army doctor, and Beşir Fuad (referred to above) had enjoyed a successful career as an army officer before turning to literature.[29]

However, the secularization of the intelligentsia was beset by tensions which strongly recall those we have already observed in the area of artistic endeavour. On the one hand, many intellectuals began to distance themselves more and more from religious obligations such as public Friday prayers or the fast of Ramadan. On the other hand, they nevertheless wished to be 'at one with the people', among whom religion continued to play a dominant role. This conflict was a concern of many post-Ottoman novels, particularly those written in the period between 1930 and 1970. However, it had developed very much earlier, during the process of élite secularization in the late nineteenth century, a process riven by contradictions which gained a hold only over certain limited sectors of society.[30]

Architecture and Town Planning

As a consequence of secularization and the partial adoption of European ideas, tensions emerged in art and everyday life, which also manifested themselves in the appearance of towns.[31] Practical considerations were allied to the aim of glorifying the neo-absolutist, nineteenth-century version of the Ottoman ideology of authority via the construction of public buildings, streets and squares. Sultans Abdülmecid, Abdülaziz and Abdülhamid II seem to have assumed that the capital, in particular, needed a face-lift, and this view was shared by a significant section of the Ottoman ruling class. As a result, at least the most affluent parts of Istanbul might hope to enjoy the benefits of 'civilized progress'. Clearly, the implication was that the Ottoman Empire should not be viewed as the aged, decaying imperium so often presented in the European press, but rather as a transformed, modern and dynamic state. The municipal model was basically the Paris of the Haussmann period, with which many Ottoman bureaucrats had become familiar as students or young embassy secretaries.

Constructing streets suitable for wheeled traffic through the maze of old Istanbul was both a practical necessity and a central goal in the ideology of Ottoman power. Such developments contributed to the projection of the sought-after image, as travel in carts and carriages had become a symbol of social status, particularly in the case of women. Pictures of carriages, which were often decorated, carrying women more or less invisible to the outside world on some excursion, were a popular motif among European photographers of the time. In this case however, photographers were not merely pandering to the facile exoticism of their customers. Indeed, one of the most artistically successful novels of the late nineteenth century was entitled *Carriage Love*.[32] Meanwhile, at an utterly unliterary level, the diary kept by an Istanbul bureaucrat, from a well-to-do background, between 1901 and 1909, shows how important the carriage had become in the lives of the affluent inhabitants of Istanbul. Having to sell one's carriage clearly signalled a fall in social status.[33] At a practical level, the considerable expansion of the city during the nineteenth century meant that ever more suppliers were travelling in and out of it. Although the inhabitants of Ottoman urban districts tended to be unenthusiastic about through traffic, it became evident that it was virtually impossible to distribute food, wood and other consumer goods without using wagons.

Fire-fighting was an even more urgent consideration.[34] Since Istanbul, except for the monumental buildings, consisted of wooden houses, fires had always been a dangerous fact of city life. Fires started while people were cooking, in workshops and sometimes when lighted charcoal, used to drive out the damp in winter, set fire to the cover over the brazier. As population densities increased, these fires became both more frequent and more destructive; in the so-called Hocapaşa Fire of 1865 a wide strip of the old town between the Golden Horn and the Sea of Marmara was burned to the ground.[35] In earlier times, the janissaries had been responsible for extinguishing blazes, but in the nineteenth century they were replaced by fire brigades with simple equipment mounted on wheels. Their ineffectiveness may be measured by the fact that they soon became the butt of much humour. However, in the old part of Istanbul it really was often impossible to reach the source of the fire in time.

In order to facilitate fire-fighting, the Ottoman élite of the nineteenth century therefore planned largely to get rid of cul-de-sacs and to straighten roads. For the same reason the construction of wooden houses was prohibited. Only stone and brick houses really made it harder for fires to spread. However, since poorer householders were unable to afford these materials, the Ottoman administration generally refrained from enforcing the use of stone and bricks except on those streets which were regarded as 'representative'. Elsewhere, administrators merely insisted on the erection of fireproof walls. In fact, the fires of the nineteenth century presented many opportunities to straighten roads. If more than ten houses were destroyed in a district, it would be divided into fresh lots, according to legislation introduced in 1882. Owners could be obliged to part with some of their land to enable the widening of roads. The sultan's bureaucrats were moved to introduce this regulation by the example of the similar French law of 1841, but the relevant Ottoman provisions are older than those of Italy and Prussia.[36]

Projects such as urban regeneration required a new administrative structure. In the provinces, until the nineteenth century, only the *kadi* would devote much of his time to tasks which would today be the responsibility of the municipal government. In Istanbul many officials, from the grand vizier down, were responsible for municipal affairs, but there was no administration or elected councillors specializing in these duties. Affluent townspeople were thus denied a means of exerting political influence. To remedy this situation, Ottoman bureaucrats began to experiment with town councillors after 1857.[37] At that time the sultan and his senior officials felt compelled to heed the calls of the European inhabitants of Pera for the establishment of modern municipal services such as road-building and street-lighting in that part of town, which was known as the VIth district. In order to ensure sufficient financial resources, affluent Europeans were drafted into this council, which became very active between 1857 and 1877. The private interests of its members were, of course, not neglected. In 1870 the municipal authority in the VIth district was even granted its own building, the first of its kind in Istanbul. It was very close to the banking district, and its façade still provides a backdrop to the busy square of Şişhane.[38]

In the banking district of Galata the owners of the larger banks were granted a considerable say in urban planning, as is apparent from the archive of the Camondo banking family.[39] This archive relates to several generations of a Jewish dynasty of bankers, art collectors and patrons, originally from Istanbul. Although its members moved to Paris in 1869, they hung on to their property in Galata for many years. The Camondos, probably inspired by the architecture of the financial quarter of Paris, commissioned commercial buildings which were evidently intended as an ensemble. Until recently neither the structures put up by the Camondos nor other commercial buildings in the eclectic Levantine style of the late nineteenth century were considered particularly noteworthy. Many were torn down, or destroyed by fire. When Said Naum Duhani, a Lebanese prince, in 1946 published a monograph on the old houses of Pera-Galata; it was largely ignored. However, a Turkish translation of the French original which appeared in 1982 was an instant success, and probably contributed to the cultural nostalgia which came to surround the history of Pera, now called Beyoğlu.[40]

Businesses, theatres and cafés spread along the Grand'rue de Péra (today İstiklal Caddesi), which around 1900 became a meeting place for affluent non-Muslim Ottomans, visiting Europeans and increasingly also for members of the Muslim upper class. Most of the latter were men, but some theatres also had boxes enclosed by lattice-work for women theatre-goers, or put on performances for exclusively female audiences. Many milliners also established themselves along the same street, and by the end of the nineteenth century visits to their shops had become a part of the everyday life of Ottoman ladies.[41]

At about this time, affluent Muslim families began to move into the new apartment buildings on the northern edge of the city, in the vicinity of today's Taksim Square and in Şişli. The latter, a new and developing area, would come to overshadow the shopping district of Beyoğlu in the second half of the twentieth century. Well-to-do Muslim families moved to their new homes largely because they wanted to enjoy conveniences such as street-lighting and nearby shopping opportunities. For the women in such families the move offered new spheres of activity. For in the 'modern' areas of Istanbul, just as in contemporary Europe, women – particularly the wealthier among them – were able to venture out in public at certain times without compromising themselves.[42] In the holiday resorts of the Princes Islands and certain Bosphorus villages there were similar opportunities.[43] In the twentieth century, the confectioners' shops of Beyoğlu and later those of Ankara emerged as centres for informal social contact between women.

Bursa is probably the best known of the provincial towns in which pashas who saw themselves in the vanguard of the changing times undertook major building projects. Ahmed Vefik Pasha (1823–91) was active there in 1863–64 and from 1879 to 1882. It was he who instigated the construction of the business streets which are still at the heart of Bursa's city centre.[44] In planning new buildings, Ahmed Vefik Pasha was rather more sensitive to the history of the city than was true of some of his colleagues. Around the Constantine Column (Çemberlitaş) in Istanbul, for example, the hacked-off corner of a historic public baths building and the bisected structure of the Ali Pasha *medresesi* still bear witness to the rash mid-nineteenth-century extension of the Divanyolu. By contrast, Ahmed Vefik Pasha had the mausoleum of the 'Runner' (Yürüyen Dede), a popular saint whose tomb lay right in the path of a new road, moved to another spot; he consistently attempted to preserve the historic appearance of Bursa. The pasha was also responsible for the construction of the theatre which still exists today, in which he took an enthusiastic interest. He himself translated and adapted plays by Molière and compiled a large Ottoman dictionary. However, his cultural activities ultimately led to the end of his period in office at Bursa. He had made many enemies in the town, and in Istanbul he was accused of holding back too much of his province's revenue from the treasury – always in desperate need of funds – in order to spend it on cultural and building projects.

When we compare Ottoman buildings of this period with those in European cities on the one hand, and in colonial centres such as Tunis on the other, the relatively modest size of many Ottoman enterprises is striking.[45] This was a consequence of the limited resources available to the state in this period of all but permanent crisis. Moreover, what little money there was tended to be spent on areas inhabited by the rapidly increasing European population of Istanbul or by the Ottoman upper class. As photographs from the second half of the nineteenth century show, there were pockets, even within the famed VIth district, which could not muster the necessary political influence, and which therefore remained largely untouched by the urban regeneration for a long time.

However, Istanbul was spared the stark antithesis of a modern, European-style district and a more or less neglected old town which was so common in colonies.[46] Interestingly, the contrast between the old and new parts of town continued until even very recently to be more conspicuous in Ankara than in Istanbul, where streets were improved and modern buildings constructed even in the historic peninsula. Right up to the end of the nineteenth century many upper-class families lived around the Grand Bazaar (Kapalıçarşı), as is evident from the buildings which are today used as schools, business premises and museums. In this area, the new book and newspaper district also developed, close to the grand vizier's office known as the High Gate (Babıâli). Thus, the regeneration of Istanbul took the form of a host of separate construction projects and reflected the complicated situation of the late Ottoman Empire. While the latter was no longer independent in financial and political terms, its upper class nevertheless remained largely in control of the process of architectural transformation.

New Forms of Visual Culture: Photography and Museums

Until the nineteenth century, townspeople who were not members of the inner palace circle or of certain dervish orders normally saw pictures of people and animals only on festive occasions.[47] Towards the end of the century, however, photographs and caricatures quickly turned pictures into a part of everyday culture. This development was relatively inconspicuous, but all the more effective as a factor contributing to the process of secularization. Photography, which was imported into the Ottoman Empire in the 1850s, was at first the preserve of European residents of Istanbul (James Robertson, Guillaume Berggren) and members of non-Muslim minorities such as Basile Kargopoulos or the Aliksan brothers, who signed their work as Abdullah Frères. Their customers were also generally Europeans.[48] Among the Muslims, it was army officers who first began to practise photography, which enabled them more easily to figure out the 'lie of the land'; previously the same purpose had been served by training in landscape-drawing.[49] Photography gave the inhabitants of the larger Ottoman towns access to human images in a way which was generally regarded as unproblematic in religious terms. Indeed, one of Abdülhamid's daughters recalled that her father had shown her photographs of potential candidates for her hand in marriage, and that in this way she had selected her future husband.[50]

We do not know many of the names of those first Ottomans who had studio photographs taken of themselves in 'public' attire or in the clothes they might have worn to a family celebration. It is therefore impossible to say whether they were Muslims or followers of other religions.[51] However, in the last twenty years of the nineteenth century, group photographs of people at their workplaces or, in the case of the Muslim upper class, family portraits, were already a part of everyday life.[52] Female members of that class, above all those of the younger generation, liked to be photographed without veils and in European dress; there are even photographs of princesses in this style. Sometimes the ladies are pictured at the grand piano or holding a violin.[53]

Sultan Abdülhamid was an active patron of photography. Nearly all the studio owners of his time were granted official titles. No doubt the usefulness of photography as a way of keeping a closer eye on provincial officials was a consideration. In this way the sultan could see for himself that building projects in distant locations really were progressing as rapidly as was claimed in the reports he received; at that time photomontages of Potemkinesque villages were still beyond the bounds of technical possibility. Photography also enabled Abdülhamid to project an image for the benefit of European governments. Whereas European photographs of Ottoman scenes typically showed historic buildings, picturesque landscapes, street scenes featuring artisans and pedlars, as well as studio portraits, Abdülhamid's many albums were devoted largely to photographs showing innovations of the contemporary period.[54] Apart from the inevitable parades, these pictures illustrate railway stations, hospitals and even the interior of a tobacco factory. However, these were not documentary-style snapshots, but rather carefully stylized compositions. Sometimes figures would be arranged according to their social status. Other photographs were designed to illustrate the various stages of a process of production. Thus, the Ottoman photographs of the nineteenth century constitute an important source of information about the political and social ideology of the period, even if the interest of today's Turkish intelligentsia in such photographs perhaps has more to do with their simple, documentary value.

Photography and museums go hand in hand, as both of them enable the observer to absorb a large number of images in a relatively short time. Most Turkish museums were not founded until the republican era. However, even in the second half of the nineteenth century the 'Sultan's Museum', right beside the Topkapı Palace, enabled an initially rather limited public to see major archaeological finds which had been made on Ottoman territory. This was the result of the efforts of Osman Hamdi (1842–1910), who painted historical, Oriental-style pictures which won him several prizes at Paris exhibitions. He also wrote comedies.[55]

In 1881 Osman Hamdi took over a collection of antiques which was neither valuable nor well organized. He undertook excavations which, in line with the philosophy of his time, were intended principally to turn up exhibits for his museum. He also campaigned to check the 'disappearance' abroad of valuable finds. This campaign enjoyed only limited success, but goes a long way to explaining why this much-decorated Orientalist painter has today become an inspiration for left-wing liberals.[56] In many of his paintings, moreover, he portrays the life of women from the Ottoman upper class, and he often employed his wife as a model.

The Theatre

In nineteenth-century Istanbul there were three forms of theatre. These included the shadow-play which was known for a long time as *karagöz*, and the type of drama called *orta oyunu*, which involved improvising without a stage or set text, and which depended almost entirely on the skill of the main comic.[57] Alongside these there was also theatre in the European sense of the word. French and Italian theatre troupes were particularly frequent visitors to Pera (Beyoğlu); many members of their audiences came from the resident Levantine population (whom the Ottomans dubbed 'fresh-water Franks'). As well as many second-rate troupes, it was possible to admire some of the most prestigious figures of contemporary theatre, such as the French actress Sarah Bernhardt. However, there were also home-grown theatres in which both translated European drama and Ottoman plays were staged. Between 1870 and 1880 the 'Ottoman Theatre' had a monopoly on Ottoman plays with set texts. This ended in 1884, when Sultan Abdülhamid took exception to a play produced there and ordered the theatre building to be demolished. This seems to have occurred in a single night, following which the ensemble disbanded.[58]

However, during the brief years of the Ottoman Theatre's operation, the Armenian director Güllü Agop (who became Yakub Efendi following his conversion) had created the first great repertory theatre in Istanbul. Nearly all the actors were Armenians, Ottoman Turks being very much the exception. One production of Schiller's *Robbers* was marked by the insistence of the two Turkish members of the ensemble on wearing turbans (very seldom seen in contemporary Istanbul). All the actresses were Armenians; Afife Jale Hanım, who is regarded as the first Muslim actress, did not begin her career until after 1920. This situation gave rise to a problem with diction, as the Armenian actors (some of whom also appeared in Armenian plays) spoke a very special dialect of Turkish, different from the pronunciation current in upper-class Muslim society. Moreover, many of them were unfamiliar with the elaborate written language employed by playwrights such as Namık Kemal (1840–88) and Abdülhak Hamid (1852–1937). Indeed, many of the less-educated Muslim actors also had problems with 'difficult' words. The misunderstandings which resulted were all the more unfortunate given that many Ottoman literary figures were extolling the new repertory theatre as a school of elegant expression and sophistication, unlike *karagöz* and *orta oyunu*.[59] It was Güllü Agop who arrived at a solution to this problem, when he appointed several renowned literary figures as advisers to his theatre. As well as translating, adapting and writing plays, they gave language classes to the actors and actresses. Some members of the ensemble, such as the tragic actress Hraçya, became greatly respected performers. However, the Armenian nationalist movement of the turn of the century made life difficult for these culturally 'Ottomanized' actors and actresses. Ultimately, many of them departed for the Caucasus.

Choosing appropriate plays could also be problematic. Arifi Bey, who was attached to the Ottoman embassy in Vienna and was probably the same individual who later became the Grand Vizier Ahmed Arifi Pasha, clearly articulated this problem in an interview which he gave to an Austrian journalist before 1877.[60] As he put it, the family was so hallowed an institution among Ottoman Muslims that plays which dealt with family relationships and, inevitably, exposed them to criticism, were unacceptable. Political plays were out of the question because they threatened public order; Namık Kemal's drama *The Fatherland or Silistre* had recently had been banned because it incited disorder. (Political content and family intrigues were of course un-avoidable in historical dramas, which were very popular at that time.) Only translated texts remained, but the foreign situations with which they dealt were of little interest to Ottoman audiences. It is true that very few new plays were written at the beginning of the twentieth century, when censorship controls were tightened, and the theatre relied largely on translations. After the restoration of the constitution in 1908, when indigenous plays were once again permitted, a new start had to be made on the basis of improvised texts.[61]

Ottoman writers and people involved in the theatre repeatedly attempted to push back the limitations which circumstances placed upon them. In fact, the issue of contemporary family life was one of their central concerns. Thus the comedy *The Poet's Marriage* by Şinasi (1824–71), which was one of the first successful Ottoman plays, dealt with the complications which could arise when the bride and groom had never set eyes upon one another before the wedding.[62] Playwrights were faced by the problem of how to motivate the hero's love for the heroine: how, then, had he become acquainted with her? One popular solution was to make the lovers distant relatives, who might therefore have been playmates as children. There were even attempts at political, patriotic drama, despite never-ending conflicts with the censor, and such plays became very popular in an atmosphere inflamed by lost wars and the misery of refugees. Nevertheless, it cannot be denied that the kind of theatre hoped for and demanded by Ottoman literary figures of the turn of the century, a theatre which functioned as a hothouse for new social practices, remained largely a dream.

Letters and Memoirs

Concomitant to the cultural changes of the second half of the nineteenth century, first-person narrations increased in number and popularity. Literary figures exchanged letters – we shall be looking, for example, at the correspondence between Fazlı Necib and Beşir Fuad (1852/3–1887) – which may often have been intended from the beginning for future publication. However, purely personal letters also became more common. Ahmed Cevdet (1822–95), the historian and grand vizier, encouraged his wife to learn to read and write in order that they could communicate without the intervention of a third party while the busy official was on his travels. At least a part of the correspondence has survived.[63] As well as the photographs which appeared among the possessions of prominent people, there were also resmî records of the most important events in the lives of their families. Recently, for example, notes by Osman Hamdi's father have emerged, which deal with his marriage (1841) and the births of the five children which ensued.[64]

With regard to memoirs, there are some documents from the upper political echelons, of the kind also common in contemporary Europe. Several grand viziers of the late nineteenth and early twentieth centuries have left memoirs. Among the best known publications of this kind are the texts which the son of the murdered Grand Vizier Midhat Pasha (1822–84) published in English. Addressed to a European audience, they were designed to prove that Midhat Pasha was innocent on the charges which had been levelled against him by a commission appointed by Sultan Abdülhamid and presided over by Ahmed Cevdet.[65] Ahmed Cevdet himself was also the hero of a biography written by a family member, in this case his daughter, the publicist Fatma Aliye (1864–1936). Despite the conservative environment in which she was brought up, she became one of the first influential 'new-style' women intellectuals.[66] Meanwhile, the memoirs of Aşçı Dede Ibrahim deal with a less prestigious world of middle-ranking bureaucrats and dervishes.[67] However, in addition to the texts referred to here, all of which have been thoroughly studied, there must be a great deal of unknown material, and the history of late-Ottoman memoirs remains a desideratum.

Books and Publishing[68]

In the second half of the nineteenth century the production of printed books increased considerably. Some of the various technical colleges which had been founded in Istanbul since the reign of Mahmud II printed their own course materials. Inspired by the French grandes écoles, the 'Sultan's School of Engineering' was particularly active in this regard.[69] The founders of commercial publishing houses, among whom Ebuzziya Tevfik stands out by virtue of his long and successful career, often had to take personal charge of the various stages of producing the books.[70] Ebuzziya Tevfik, for example, annotated and edited the works which he published; it was he who provided footnotes for the eighteenth-century account of Ahmed Resmî's trip to

Berlin.[71] However, Ebuzziya Tevfik's international reputation stemmed from his creativity in the field of Ottoman typography; the typographical society in Leipzig reported regularly on what he had printed.[72]

In a similar vein, the journalist and author Ahmed Mithat also had to undertake the production and publication of his books in person. This exposed him to a double risk. On the one hand, there was no guarantee that there would be a sufficient public for belletristic literature by contemporary authors, few of whose works were potential course material. Beyond this risk, one which all authors share to some extent, Ahmed Mithat had to immobilize his resources by investing in printing presses and paper. He had to ensure that both the machines and his employees worked at full capacity, which even led to his taking on the printing of a newspaper published by his 'competitor' Ebuzziya Tevfik.[73]

There were also many Armenian printing-press owners and publishers, who produced Ottoman as well as Armenian books; indeed, often Ottoman books formed the larger part of their output. Agop Boyacıyan, who had worked with the governor, lexicographer and man of the theatre Ahmed Vefik Pasha, was well known at the end of the nineteenth century for his modern technical equipment. In 1890 he printed the first edition of James Redhouse's Ottoman–English dictionary, whose later versions are still used by many readers of Ottoman texts.[74] Another reference work of continuing popularity, the encyclopaedia by the Albanian author, Şemseddin Sami, was also printed by an Armenian printer and publisher, in this case Mihran Nakkaşiyan, who came from Kayseri.[75]

One of the most difficult problems facing these publishers and printing-press owners was that of supplying their customers. Even in the 1880s packages often took so long to reach the provincial towns that subscriptions to periodicals were impracticable. According to the critic and author Beşir Fuad, who published his own literary and popular science magazine for a while, low sales were largely due to the numerous cafés in which magazines were freely available.[76] These enabled people of modest means to avoid paying for a subscription; readership may have increased, but the publisher failed to benefit. Differences with the censor were another source of trouble; censors' interventions were not merely frequent, but also difficult for authors and publishers to predict. Even simple printing errors could lead to major difficulties, if the censors suspected some ulterior motive. The problem was exacerbated by the many unofficial informers, among whom there were in fact several printers and publishers.[77] All these problems led to low output, low sales and financial losses. Publishing businesses often changed hands or disappeared altogether, particularly if the owner were banished from Istanbul, as Ebuziyya Tevfik was on several occasions.

Another problem was that many members of the Istanbul upper class seem to have regarded books as objects for collecting, and therefore preferred manuscripts, which were more attractive by virtue of their paper and script. Manuscripts were still produced, particularly in the provinces, even at the end of the nineteenth century; saints' legends continued to be copied, and indeed even tax registers from the sixteenth century might be reproduced by hand if they were needed for reference, for example in case of disputes about land.

The reading habits of male members of the Ottoman upper class are reflected in printed inventories of their libraries. These lists were produced for buyers when after their owner's death, the libraries were auctioned by an antiquarian bookseller.[78] About thirty such inventories have so far been examined, including the lists of books belonging to Ahmed Vefik Pasha, the theatre enthusiast and governor of Bursa whom we have already encountered. He owned a significant library, as did Şeyhülislam Arif Hikmet Efendi (died 1859), who donated a collection of 5,000 volumes in Medina and still retained a valuable library in his Istanbul home. Apart from such exceptions, educated Ottoman dignitaries would accumulate a few hundred, sometimes about a thousand, volumes in the course of their careers. Ottoman history and poetry were preferred, while Arabic and Persian texts were by no means uncommon. French books, however, were unusual, although the Grand Vizier Âli Pasha, a man of great and varied learning, possessed about forty works in that language. Unfortunately, we know only very little about the libraries of literary figures in more modest positions. However, the correspondence between Beşir Fuad and his friend, the publicist Fazlı Necib, shows that in such circles there was an interest in French works and, above all, in popular texts dealing with the natural sciences.[79]

In the absence of any comprehensive study of translations of this period, we shall here confine ourselves to a single example, that of the translation of works by the French Romantic poet, Victor Hugo.[80] Hugo was held in high regard in Ottoman literary circles of the late nineteenth century. Very many important authors of the period, including Namık Kemal and Samipaşazade Sezai (1860–1936), translated individual poems by the Frenchman, and there are several Ottoman translations of some of his works. Moreover, in 1885 Beşir Fuad wrote the first 'new-style' literary biography in the Ottoman domain, the subject of which was Hugo, who had died just a few months earlier. It must be said that, despite all his respect for Hugo, Beşir Fuad in fact belonged to a very different literary tradition. He regarded a knowledge of the natural sciences as an absolute prerequisite for the novelist, and insisted on the merit of Emile Zola, whose naturalistic novels were dismissed not just by many Ottoman commentators, but also by a good number of French readers, as godless and 'un-artistic'.[81]

In Ottoman literary circles of the late nineteenth century, Victor Hugo was revered mainly as a poet and, to a much lesser extent, as a dramatist. His prose works, by contrast, excited little interest. Ottoman readers were probably put off by the length of his novels, and as these works cannot be understood without a certain amount of knowledge of life in northern France or in the Channel Islands, they were especially difficult of access. Nevertheless, an Ottoman translation of Hugo's *Les Misérables*, about the life of the convict and later entrepreneur Jean Valjean and his adoptive daughter, Cosette, appeared in the same year (1862) as the original. In fact, though, the 'translation' was a brief synopsis, rather in the style of a police report.

Certain of Hugo's poems were appreciated by Ottoman writers because they deal with themes which had until then been lacking from the Ottoman poetic tradition. Children constitute a particularly striking example; Hugo evokes them many times, first from a father's and later from a grandfather's perspective. Hugo's political poetry presented even greater challenges, above all the poems directed against 'Napoleon the Small', who had seized the French throne in 1851 after a coup d'état. Writers resident in the Ottoman Empire attempted to neutralize these poems in order to get them past the censor. However, Samipaşazade Sezai, the author of an impressive translation of Hugo's poem evoking the death of a child in the fighting of 1851, refused to make such compromises and published his text in exile.[82]

The Beginnings of the Novel

Sezai was not just a translator, but also a prose author in his own right. However, his novel published in 1885, *The Adventure*, already belonged to a second stage in the development of novel writing in the Ottoman language.[83] We are constantly discovering more about the stages which had come before, namely the beginnings of the genre, so that this account should not be regarded as definitive. Until about ten years ago, a story by Şemseddin Sami, whom we have already encountered as the author of a geographical encyclo-paedia, was regarded, with certain reservations, as the first Ottoman novel (it was published in 1872). However, since then it has become clear that a number of Ottoman Christians had already turned their hands to the new form of narrative some years before. The work of Evangelinos Misailidis – who, it must be said, adapted a story originally written in Greek – and Vartan Pasha has remained unknown for so long partly because they used alphabets with which most Ottoman literary historians are not familiar. However, we should also bear in mind that the national rivalries of a later period meant that assimilated, 'Ottomanized' members of the minorities tended to be neglected.

Evangelios Misailidis, who was also a printer, translated and adapted an adventure novel, which was printed in Ottoman but using the Greek alphabet. This was because the author was a Karamanlı, thus belonging to a Turcophone Christian group which lived in Anatolia until the Greek–Turkish population exchange of 1923.[84] In 1851 Vartan Pasha, who, as his title suggests, also pursued a career in the Ottoman civil service, published a tale on the theme of Romeo and Juliet, set among the affluent Armenians of Istanbul. In such circles Ottoman was the language of everyday life, Armenian being reserved for the liturgy. The family conflict which ultimately ruins the lovers is fought out between Gregorian and Roman Catholic Armenians. In fact, in real life as well as in novels, the conversion of particular families and groups to Catholicism and later also to the Protestant churches created severe conflicts within the Armenian communities, and Vartan Pasha's work should be seen as an appeal for more tolerance and understanding.[85]

Şemseddin Sami's story of 1872 is another romantic tragedy with a subtext of social criticism. An eighteen-year-old youth named Talat falls in love with Fitnet, the stepdaughter of a tobacconist, whom he has seen at her window. His love is reciprocated. Since Fitnet is not allowed to leave her house, the young man, still beardless, disguises himself as a girl in order to visit his beloved. However, before the couple can steer matters towards their marriage, Fitnet's hand is given instead to a rich man, who, to make matters worse, turns out to be her father. The lovers commit suicide and the father loses his sanity.[86]

Among the secondary characters in the novel, the motif of a young woman unable to avoid an unwanted marriage is played out a second time. Similarly to Ottoman dramatists of the period, the author of this story emphasizes the fact that without freedom of choice a happy union becomes impossible, above all for the woman. However, the most extreme kind of unwanted marriage occurs when the principal female character is a slave. This is no doubt why Ottoman writers of the later nineteenth century, who were concerned with the issues of freedom and choice, particularly favoured such situations. Of course, the arrival of a newly-acquired slave girl also offered authors an easy and credible means of effecting the initial meeting between hero and heroine. This was a problem which was very much harder to solve if the heroine were a free-born girl, as we have seen in the cases of Talat and Fitnet.

Samipaşazade Sezai's story *Adventure* (published in 1889) revolves round the romantic figure of a beautiful slave girl who is sold by her owners when the son of the household falls in love with her and begs her freedom of his parents because he wishes to marry her. Throughout the story, the young slave girl is sold from one place to another with little opportunity to shape her own destiny. At the end of the novel she commits suicide after a *successful* escape, when she understands that she is incapable of surviving on her own, not having learned how to make a living. In fact this was a problem with which free women of that generation, as well as slave girls, were forced to come to terms.[87]

Novelists of this period were generally more interested in conveying their message than in the formal aspects of narrative. However, since this was a new genre, writers of Sezai's generation could hardly avoid reflecting on the form as well. Older Ottoman narrative traditions, as they had been practised by the *meddah*s since the seventeenth century and perhaps even earlier, demanded a narrator who intervened visibly in the action. Thus, for example, in one story a link is created from one section to the next by the narrator's explanation that 'However, whilst they [the central characters of the previous section] are on their way, let us describe the house of Anton Ağa to the dear reader.'[88] This tactic, which is also by no means uncommon in early French novels, made life very much easier for writers wishing not just to entertain but also to educate their audience. In this way they were able to address their readers in a manner already tried and trusted, and to recall for them the most important elements of their message.[89]

However, in the last quarter of the nineteenth century, working with the novel also meant coming to terms with French narrative writing of the period, and particularly with the novels of Zola, which were at once admired and despised. Here, unlike in the Ottoman tradition, an omniscient and invisible narrator made his story unfold. Visible interventions in the flow of the narrative were usually attributed to a lack of artistry on the part of the author. Moreover, this form demanded a detailed description of both the physical environment and the inner life of the main characters. These requirements were hard to reconcile with the didactic concerns which were still prevalent among Ottoman writers. Moreover, only well-read audiences can digest descriptions; those less used to reading tend to reject them as 'boring'.[90] Critics and literary scholars have always accused early Ottoman novelists of overemphasizing dialogue and action and of subordinating an artistic concern with character and environment to the didactic enterprise. This began to change only in the years around 1900.

Criticizing Western Civilization

Young, helpless girls were nearly always portrayed as positive figures in Ottoman novels. However, many authors regarded older women, particularly those making demands of an erotic nature, as a threat. The infamous 'lady with the dagger', who had already played a role in *meddah* tales, was also a wicked, conspiring presence in novels of the nineteenth century.[91] On the whole, though, social and moral criticism was directed at men. We have already described the figure of the unsympathetic, thoughtlessly conservative father, who prevents the happiness of the young lovers. Another stock figure, which was portrayed as even more reprehensible and which was also popular in drama, was that of the young fop who squanders his money in the cafés, theatres and bars of Pera without, in fact, having any understanding of European culture.

No doubt such persons did indeed exist. However, their popularity among novelists and dramatists probably had more to do with other factors.[92] At a time when the Ottoman Empire was under threat from both internal and external enemies, authors who were critical of society and who argued for a fundamental change in Ottoman culture were under considerable pressure to justify themselves. Some of them articulated their ambivalence by insisting on the moral superiority of Muslim men and women, but simultaneously suggesting that young people of both sexes needed to adapt to the educational tradition of Europe. It was for this reason that educated young women, whose knowledge by no means made them 'unfeminine', were so popular as characters in novels among authors of republican Turkey. The young fop, got up in the European style (*alafranga*), should be seen as the negative antitype to this female figure. By dwelling on the ridiculousness of the fop – and sometimes on his sorry end – the author could convey to his readers that despite all the innovations he proposed, he remained an Ottoman and had by no means become a 'turncoat'.

Changes in Social Life and Food Culture

As the Ottoman novels show, towards the end of the nineteenth century many members of the Ottoman élite changed important elements of their everyday culture. Prominent personalities, above all members of the palace, sometimes imported furniture from France, although before long it was possible to obtain chairs, tables and chests of drawers from local cabinet-makers as well. In the second half of the nineteenth century it was still rare in the Muslim upper class for the lady of the house to be present when her husband received company. Customs were different, however, among the Polish exiles who sought refuge in the Ottoman Empire after the failed revolts of the nineteenth century. Partly because of their technical expertise, many of them quickly became integrated into the Ottoman administrative structure and converted to Islam. In this milieu, women were not excluded from social occasions.[93] At the sultan's court this custom also came to prevail by the end of our period. In 1922, the last year of the Ottoman Empire, the caliph Abdülmecid Efendi, who was also a painter, invited all members of the Ottoman ruling family, men and women alike, to a social gathering.

There is still little information available about the speed at which customs changed in more 'bourgeois' circles.[94] It is rather easier to trace innovations in the menu, especially since the growth of women's magazines had turned cuisine into a theme of written culture; by the 1860s, cookery books began to appear from time to time. Many plants and whole dishes which form an integral part of modern Turkish cuisine first appeared on the menu in the second half of the nineteenth century. One particularly important example is the tomato, originally an American plant. The spread of the potato also occurred in this period; however, the potato was never used as a staple like bread and rice, it was and is still regarded by Turkish chefs as an ordinary vegetable and prepared accordingly.[95]

If the names of the new dishes can be taken to shed light on culinary relationships, Italian as well as French cuisine was particularly important. Noodles, which became a national dish only very late even in Italy, found their way into Turkish kitchens alongside the obligatory tomato sauce. It is not yet certain whether this dish had spread beyond Levantine circles in Istanbul by the time of the First World War. While the word *pasta* became an accepted part of the vocabulary of Turkish cuisine, it does not denote noodles, but rather cakes with fruit and cream fillings. Such sweets are today served at weddings, New Year celebrations and when receiving guests 'after dinner'. Chocolate in the Ottoman realm is denoted by a mixture of Italian (*çokolata*) and French (*krem şokola*) terms; its advance has not yet, so far as I am aware, been investigated in any detail. Tea became the Turkish national drink only in the 1930s, when it began to be cultivated within the region. In the last years of the Ottoman Empire it was still an exotic item.

Turkish cuisine has so far been a matter of interest mainly to ethnologists and cooks. Historical research into the topic is still in its early stages. However, even now it is clear that the cultural relationships of Istanbul's upper and middle classes are reflected in many ways in the culinary domain. Moreover, recently central European consumers have adopted innovations from what was once Ottoman food culture: *pide* or pitta bread, stuffed vine leaves, and above all *döner-gyros* and *cacık-tzatziki*.

Continuity and New Beginnings

Looking back at the late Ottoman period, from the perspective of the present day, the years between the issue of the sultan's decree of Gülhane (1839) and the official end of the Ottoman Empire (1923) appear as a time of transition. In the same perspective, this period has also been viewed as a period of preparation for the Turkish Republic proclaimed in the same year. This Republic was and to the present day remains a national state, comparable with those which had already emerged in the Balkans during the nineteenth century. Nevertheless, Turkish nationalism developed only very late, and did not acquire political relevance until after 1908. It is for this reason that the theme of 'art and nationalism' has not been touched upon in this book. It is true that in the short period between 1908 and 1914 nationalist conceptions influenced the design of certain buildings, and writers such as Ömer Seyfeddin (1884–1920) published stories which also reflected such views. But even so, texts and paintings which we would today consider 'nationalistic' were produced mainly within the republican period.[96]

Of course it is quite legitimate to regard the late Ottoman era as a period of gestation for problems which would eventually confront the citizens of the Turkish Republic, and which continue to confront them today. In terms of the class which shaped the state, there were important continuities: Atatürk himself had been an Ottoman general and had distinguished himself in the battle of 1915 in the Dardanelles. Particularly among middle-ranking officials in the early Turkish Republic there were numerous former cadres of the Young Turk organization, which had been in power for most of the time from 1908 to 1918. However, the most prominent representatives of the defunct 'Young Turk' regime went into exile (some to Germany) after the Ottoman defeat, and others were eliminated during the first years of the Republic.[97]

In view of this relative continuity of the 'personnel', it seems logical also to look for similar lines of continuity in cultural affairs. Literary figures such as Yakup Kadri Karaosmanoğlu or Mehmet Akif Ersoy had already made a name for themselves under the last sultans and continued their careers – not without obstacles – in the early Republic. Turkish historians, and public opinion even more so, regard Ottoman history as 'our' history without any equivocation. While there intervened a 'Jacobin' period of the Turkish Republic, during which the new élite forming in Ankara saw itself as revolutionary and as 'overthrowers of the throne', and distanced itself from the Ottoman past accordingly, this tendency did not last for long.[98]

Nevertheless, it would be wrong to see the role of late-Ottoman cultural life as nothing more than a 'preparation for the Republic'. After all, it is by no means certain yet that the nation state represents the summit of historical development. For our purposes it is more important that in a time of continual political and military crises there were men and women ready to explore new art-forms such as written plays, novels, oil-painting and photography. This experimentation with a secularized culture involved many late-Ottoman intellectuals in existential and spiritual conflicts. In this brief chapter we have encountered theatre people who ignored official disapproval to mock 'sacred' institutions of the state and society, and who lost their jobs as a result. We have alluded to Samipaşazade Sezai's exile and Beşir Fuad's suicide as well as to the tragedy of Armenian theatrical artists using the Ottoman language, driven into exile by the political conflicts of the turn of the century. This engagement on the part of Muslims and non-Muslims alike shows that it is a gross simplification to trace all the cultural transformations of the late nineteenth century back to the attempt to match the European powers in political and military terms.

Rather, these men and women had the courage to attempt using innovations from European culture as the starting-point for their own version of the Enlightenment. We have seen how the political context in which these attempts were made continually led to internal tensions and to restrictions which were difficult to overcome, so that artists and critics were often less than satisfied with what was produced. However, this should not blind us to the courage, the readiness to experiment, the flexibility and not least the pure enthusiasm which the artists and their public demonstrated in the process.

14

In Conclusion

We have reached the end of the story. Architects with and without formal training in the sultan's architectural staff, literary figures and painters of festive decorations, male and female diarists and letter writers, dervishes and women of the Ottoman upper class have all played a part in it. In many cases certain personalities were selected because relevant sources were accessible at first hand or because studies of them already existed. This applies to Osman Ağa from Temeşvar, who wrote about his captivity, and to Asiye Hatun from Üsküp, who corresponded with her sheikh.[1] Both were literate townspeople who cannot be assigned to the palace or *ulema* cultures, or to the oral tradition of the lower class. Since interest has recently begun to be shown in such individuals, there is little doubt that we shall soon learn of similar examples from other areas of the vast Ottoman Empire.

Giving and Taking

In other cases, figures from Ottoman palace culture have also entered our story, such as the architects Sinan and Mimar Mehmed Ağa or the historian and literary figure Mustafa Âlî – not to mention the omnipresent Evliya Çelebi.[2] However, our concern was not so much with these personalities *per se*, as with what they had to say about everyday customs or the way in which less prominent contemporaries regarded the work of these men. The culture of the Ottoman townspeople by no means excluded familiarity with artefacts from 'high culture'. People prayed in the mosques designed by Sinan and Mimar Mehmed Ağa, where there was often a section reserved for women, so that places of worship also formed part of women's day to day life. Mustafa Âlî's books (1541–1600) have influenced works by generations of historical and political writers, thereby indirectly reaching a wider audience of Ottoman bureaucrats. And if Evliya's writings were read by few before the nineteenth century, many of the stories included in his travelogue were also told by oral narrators.

Thus the culture of Ottoman townspeople developed in close contact with courtly culture, but it was also tightly bound to the traditions and aspirations of the jurists and theologians. When the artisans of Istanbul were officially invited to file past the sultan to mark a military campaign or a circumcision festival, we may assume that the living images which they created for such an occasion would not be conceived without contact with the court. Finally, it was customary to commemorate the festivities in a special book, which in two cases were even illustrated by court artists with colourful miniatures.[3] Since court artists were involved in the description of these parades, it seems certain that they were also involved in planning them. Moreover, from the seventeenth century onwards, ever greater numbers of artisans joined the janissary troops. This also facilitated an indirect link with court culture, at least in Istanbul, for the capital's janissaries had many opportunities to observe the sultan and the court at close quarters. In the religious domain, dervishes and preachers not only communicated a knowledge of officially accepted religion, but also of religious controversies. Due to the persistent disputes regarding the 'Kadızade's People', many inhabitants of the capital must have obtained a clearer insight into the substance of their religion.[4] Sometimes dervishes were also oral narrators (*meddah*) and drew on their knowledge of written culture in their stories.[5] Because of such knowledge, many of these narrators were highly esteemed even among members of the palace milieu.

Our account presupposes that the Ottoman high cultures of the court and the *ulema* were by no means just 'givers'. There were enduring interrelationships between the culture of the intellectual and political élite on the one hand and the culture of the majority of the population, which depended on oral transmission, on the other. This claim is not so trivial as it might initially appear. Among historians dealing with the European middle ages, for example, there was a movement of some influence which made the opposite assumption: the illiterate general population was thought to have received many impulses from church and aristocratic culture, but to have remained largely passive itself.[6] As a reaction to romantic conceptions of an anonymous but creative national spirit, this position even has a certain validity. However, it overlooks the fact that even the members of the medieval upper class, literate though they were, very seldom practised the arts of reading and writing. As a result, the contacts maintained by the upper classes of medieval or early modern Europe with the oral cultures around them were much more intensive than they were to be in, for example, the eighteenth and nineteenth centuries.

We must assume a similar situation in the Ottoman Empire, where the average townsperson did not speak Arabic or Persian – the two languages of religion and poetry, respectively – or the Ottoman literary language, composed of loan words from both those sources. Here, too, many members of the upper class were, in their everyday lives, immersed in a culture resting on oral transmission. The Istanbul dervish Seyyid Hasan is a good example of this.[7] He was able to read and write fluently, but oral culture provided the setting for most of the social contacts which he recorded in his diary. At a more elevated intellectual level, much the same is true of Mustafa Âlî.[8] As a courtier, and a graduate of prestigious theological schools and one of the sultan's senior officials, Âlî clearly belonged to the inner circle of Ottoman high culture. Nevertheless, exalted personality though he was, he was in no way estranged from the culture of ordinary townspeople. He associated with dervish sheikhs who were by no means among the most intellectual representatives of Islamic mysticism. This does not mean that Âlî took an uncritical attitude towards such phenomena; in fact, he reproached Sultan Murad III (reign: 1575–95) for granting too much influence to questionable sheikhs. However, we may assume that even as elevated a representative of Ottoman high culture as Mustafa Âlî was entirely familiar with the partially oral culture of the city.

For the present at least, only a few textual sources are available to those wishing to examine the interchange between oral and written culture. Most of these are legends of holy men, whose authors took it upon themselves to describe the origins and development of certain dervish convents. Sometimes it is even possible to find traces of the manipulation to which orally communicated stories of heroes and holy men were subjected before they were considered a 'usable past' for the dervish lodge in question. We can detect such manipulations because of the curiosity and broad interests of Evliya Çelebi, who was responsible for the survival of parallel versions of several such legends. Of course Evliya Çelebi, a man with a court education, was far from being the prototype of an oral narrator. We may assume that he was well acquainted with the most prominent storytellers (*meddah*) of his time – his work is often the only source in which at least the names of these artists are recorded – but his own work belongs to the realm of written culture rather than oral narration. Evliya's aim was probably both to educate and entertain the Istanbul public by descriptions of a cultural and geographical nature, in combination with stories which were often fictional.[9] By comparing these different versions of the story of one and the same holy man's life, we can probably come a little closer to the original, oral tale.

What Made Towns Special

At his death, a holy man left his followers his tomb as a source of blessings and a place of assembly. Dervishes and others who attended such a sanctified place must have identified with the man they considered as their sheikh, and in many cases, the town in which the convent lay also shared in this sense of pride. Thus, the shrine of Pirî Baba in Merzifon, described by Evliya, became the emblem of the town, a means by which it set itself apart from neighbouring and more important urban centres. In some contexts at least, Merzifon might be defined as the town of Pirî Baba, Konya as the town of Mevlana Celaleddin Rumî or Şerefli Koçhisar, in the depths of innermost Anatolia, as the town of Mahmud Hüda'î.

At a much more mundane level, local specialities also helped towns set themselves apart from others and become something out of the ordinary. These specialities might be consumer goods such as textiles or leather, or they might be food and drink. Local products which enjoyed a certain reputation might of course be copied elsewhere, but that is of only marginal significance. Similarly, it is of secondary importance that cotton yarn or woollen material was mainly produced not in the town after which it was named, but rather in the surrounding countryside. The skills of the silk weavers of Bursa, the producers of mohair cloth in Ankara or the tanners of Kayseri helped make their towns famous. This is clear from the geographical handbooks of the seventeenth century as well as from Evliya Çelebi's descriptions.[10] It would be wrong to believe that Ottoman towns of before the nineteenth century were just amorphous conglomerations, mere collections of urban districts, religious communities and guilds. Literary and pictorial evidence makes it clear that even without municipal law and self-government, the inhabitants of Ottoman towns developed a sense of having special ties to their home town.[11]

Moreover, at least as far as members of the Ottoman upper class were concerned, the mosques, covered shopping centres, theological schools and other monumental buildings made Istanbul, Bursa or Cairo into notable places. Evliya regards an Ottoman town as a configuration of citadel, mosques, theological schools, law courts and other buildings, mostly of stone. Beneath this conception lay, above all, the fact that so many Ottoman towns had grown up around foundation complexes which had been built by a ruler together with the members of his family and court. Moreover, the Ottoman administration's practice of regularly compiling lists of pious foundations probably helped consolidate the tendency of educated Ottomans to regard their towns as ensembles of monumental buildings. Admittedly, these lists were kept in the archives of the exchequer and were inaccessible to the general public, but most Ottomans who wrote books, and whose opinions we can therefore gauge, were associated in some way with the state administration or the pious foundations. They would therefore at least have been aware that such lists existed.

Among Ottoman towns Istanbul was unique. This city was a source of fascination to European painters from the sixteenth century onwards, as it was to Ottoman artists from the time of Matrakçı Nasuh (who probably died in 1564).[12] Evliya dedicated a whole book of his ten-volume travelogue to Istanbul, describing the various parts of the city: the historical centre within the Theodosian city walls, the quarter outside the fortress of the Seven Towers (Yedikule), the religious centre surrounding the grave of Eyüb Ansarî (Eyüp), Galata and its port, in addition to the Bosphorus villages. In the case of Istanbul he did not restrict himself to the buildings of the town, as he often did elsewhere. On this, his native terrain – and also when describing Cairo, his long-time residence – he used documents regarding public processions, to which he had somehow obtained access, and presented a general panorama of the male population of Istanbul.[13] The townspeople who filed past the sultan included everybody from the grand vizier to night-watchmen, from the senior jurists and theologians to innkeepers from Galata. Evliya seems to have wanted to give a complete picture, and his work complements the panorama of Istanbul by Matrakçı Nasuh.

As well as the variety of people and cultures, the sea played a not insignificant part in making Istanbul special. There is evidence that, right from the start, buildings with a view of the sea were preferred. The palace of Mehmed the Conqueror in the third courtyard of the Serail possessed a balcony with a superb view over the Bosphorus and the Sea of Marmara. In the sixteenth century the sultans built small, elegant garden pavilions (köşk) right beside the sea, and the vizier Şemsi Ahmed Pasha employed the great architect Sinan to design him a complex including a school and mosque in Üsküdar, which showed off to best advantage when viewed from the sea. However, it was the eighteenth century which really exploited the possibilities of a seaside location. Whole stretches of the Bosphorus coast filled with villas. These buildings were considered so remarkable that regular lists of them were compiled so that when on an excursion, the sultan might be informed about the properties belonging to his senior officials.[14] By building villas at the Bosphorus and celebrating lavish festivities right on the water the Ottoman upper class manifested its desire to make the most of the special situation of Istanbul, at the confluence of two seas.

Like Istanbul, the other towns of the empire, and in particular Aleppo, Damascus and Cairo, had special reputations. These might, as in the case of Cairo and Damascus, arise from the learning and piety of the local ulema, but also from the splendour of urban festivals. This was particularly true of Cairo, where the annual flooding of the Nile, the departure and return of pilgrim caravans and the days dedicated to various holy men were all celebrated amid considerable pomp. Evliya and his French contemporary, Jean

Thévenot, were both inspired to write lengthy, enthusiastic descriptions of the festive processions in Cairo.[15]

The Problems of Minorities

In this book we have concentrated on the Muslim townspeople of those parts of the empire where Ottoman-Turkish was spoken. However, even in the towns of that region there were ethnic and religious groups which followed other faiths and which evolved their own variants of urban culture. Before the second half of the nineteenth century most of them probably considered themselves to be basically Ottoman, although the process of disaffection and reorientation had been under way since the early eighteenth century. We have seen how Demetrius Cantemir, for example, in the years around 1700, attempted to create a new identity for himself as a Moldavian-Russian prince. This process seems to have been a difficult one for the author and, in his later years, he expressed a certain nostalgia for Ottoman culture.[16]

Other examples of non-Muslim Ottomans who tried to create a new identity for themselves include the Maronites of the Lebanon, the Syrian Christians and the Armenians who opted for union with Rome. In the later part of the nineteenth century a further alternative arose for Ottoman Christians in the form of Protestantism. This was brought to the empire by missionaries, many of whom were Americans. Many of the 'new' minorities were successful in trade; even as early as the second half of the eighteenth century, Syrian Catholics played an important role in Egyptian trade.[17] Their European connections, together with the social cohesion prevalent among minorities, were probably important factors in their success. Here too, however, the process of ideological reorientation from Ottoman culture towards Europe produced serious tensions. Vartan Pasha was well aware of this when he described in his novel how the relationship of a pair of lovers is destroyed by the conflict between Gregorian and Catholic Armenians.[18]

Creativity and a Cosmopolitan Outlook

This study has dealt mainly with a rather neglected period, namely the seventeenth and eighteenth centuries. As we have seen, these two hundred years were of far greater cultural significance than has hitherto been recognized. All too often has it been assumed that the 'post-classical' period in Ottoman art was a time of artistic stagnation, in which the decay of political power was mirrored in the cultural sphere, and in which only a few exceptional works of real quality were produced. However, here we have seen that in fact this was an extremely creative period. It was at this (late) stage in Ottoman cultural history that first-person narratives and writing dealing with private matters became popular. Examples include such diverse texts as Evliya Çelebi's travel writing and the work of the various diarists and autobiographers.[19] However, the seventeenth century was also the time of a cosmopolitan group of Istanbul intellectuals, whose interests ranged from geography to discussions about the subject of beauty in different cultural contexts. Of course, this was a small group, and the Kadızadeliler with their opposite ideology were very much more conspicuous. However, only by taking cognizance of the contradictions within an epoch can we begin to understand its dynamic. Furthermore, only in this way can we come closer towards explaining the cultural transformation of the nineteenth and twentieth centuries with all its associated contradictions and tensions.

It is worth inquiring why the creative aspects of seventeenth-century Ottoman culture have been ignored for so long. The key may lie in a remark by Franz Taeschner, one of the pioneers of Ottoman cultural history. He believed that Ottoman geography had fallen under the influence of Europe almost from the earliest stage of its development and had therefore been stripped of its 'originality'.[20] Taeschner was not alone in this opinion. Many people found (and continue to find) it convincing because it accommodates both the European, ultimately Romantic conception of the originality of the artist and the outlook of Turkish nationalists which, ultimately, was also of Romantic origin. Nationalists everywhere had emphasized the originality of national traditions and tended to devalue everything which came 'from outside'. However, anyone who has studied European history knows that the assimilation of classical culture in wave after wave from Carolingian times, through the Renaissance until the age of Goethe, is regarded as a great cultural achievement by today's scholars. Let us imagine, though, how someone born into a tradition linked by an unbroken chain to the culture of late antiquity might regard this process, the reactions of Byzantines with a classical education being helpful in this respect. Very probably, an observer rooted in the classicist culture even of late Roman antiquity would dismiss this western European preoccupation, at least in its medieval phase, as utterly provincial, ignorant and unoriginal. In this book, however, we have looked at cultural borrowings in a different way. Opening oneself to a foreign culture is a creative process, and those who had the courage to do it deserve more understanding than they have hitherto been shown.

Of course, many literary figures of the eighteenth and nineteenth centuries defended closer cultural contacts with Europe by arguing that it was necessary to learn from the unbelievers, in order to regain military and political initiative.[21] However, previous research has tended to look at this aspect in isolation and therefore to exaggerate it. This study has aimed to show that what might be termed, to use a rather inelegant phrase, the instrumental-ization of art and culture was in fact only a part of the story. At any rate, many Ottoman writers and scholars were very much more curious and ready to experiment than has hitherto been admitted. Evliya Çelebi's attempt to explain his appreciation of St Stephen's Cathedral and the organ music in Vienna by referring back to King David of the Old Testament is a charming and yet neglected example of such an attitude.

On the Permeability of Iron Curtains

There are also other reasons why seventeenth- and eighteenth-century Otto-man writers, who by this time had already begun to take an interest in neighbouring cultures, have received so little attention. Both European and Turkish historians often assume that there was a type of 'iron curtain' between Europe and the Ottoman world until the last years of the eighteenth century.[22] Many twentieth-century scholars believed that the Ottomans took for granted that they possessed cultural superiority along with the true religion, and that they therefore considered it unnecessary or even unhealthy to take a close interest in the 'unbelievers' and their sciences and arts. If an Ottoman Muslim encountered a skilled unbeliever and perhaps even became friendly with him, he would, according to this theory, attempt to persuade the non-Muslim to 'end his days in goodness'; that is, to convert to Islam. No doubt many people did see things thus, but this book has attempted to show that there were also many who took a wider view. They were not always members of the élite: clearly, anybody who released his slave before or after his pilgrimage to Mecca, fully aware that the former slave would return to his native land and revert to his original religion, differed from the official line in his understanding of interpersonal relationships. It seems likely that the Muslim owner released his slave because he hoped that this would be an action of religious merit at a turning-point in his own life. The liberated slave was himself responsible for what he did with his freedom.[23]

Although such views certainly were held only by a minority, it is important not to see Ottoman culture as entirely monolithic. Many merchants, fishermen, sailors and not least soldiers belonged to particular subcultures in which it was not so unusual for individuals to travel beyond the borders of the empire and remain away for long periods. Sometimes interesting perspectives resulted from such adventures. In his memoirs describing his experiences as a prisoner of the Austrians, the interpreter Osman Ağa never actually says in so many words that war is a fundamentally bad thing. However, his moving descriptions of the misery and destruction of war encourage the reader to think that such an opinion was not entirely alien to the author.[24]

In short, this book represents the view that there were minorities for whom the borders of Ottoman culture were less 'watertight' than they were for the majority of their compatriots. Perhaps the image of an 'iron curtain' is instructive in itself. Even the most recent example of such a dividing wall, together with all its associated technology, manifestly failed to prevent a host of shared developments. With the exception of a few years, there were striking parallels in literary, musical and scientific developments on each side of that curtain. Films and music, as well as books, reached audiences both west and east of the Iron Curtain, despite all the political obstacles.

Such interchanges and parallel developments, whether they occur in the middle of the sixteenth century or in the last quarter of the twentieth, do require a certain amount of common ground between the artists, writers or ordinary people who introduce and sustain these developments. It is less clear to what extent the people involved were aware of the underlying similarities between the Ottoman and European worlds. In contemporary documents, both the Ottoman and European sides constantly emphasize the divide between them, which was seen mainly in religious terms.[25] Another dividing factor arrived with the spread of humanism from the fifteenth century onwards. Educated European observers, such as the Habsburg ambassador Busbecq, were critical of their Ottoman counterparts' (relative) lack of interest in classical remains. Contemporary figures did indeed perceive themselves to be living on either side of a clearly defined border.

However, there were economic similarities which counterbalanced the cultural divide. Fernand Braudel's concept of the 'unity of the Mediterranean' in the sixteenth century is relevant in this context. In our own age, in which the pre-eminence of culture is emphasized and often overemphasized, a reference to underlying unity, based on economic similarities, may well be seen as outmoded.[26] However, we should look closely at what conceptions of space, time and interpersonal relationships were possible at all, given the technical and economic exigencies of the pre-industrial age, irrespective of the particular religious context.[27] Until the eighteenth century, many aspects of everyday life, particularly among the less affluent classes, remained very similar on both sides of the European–Ottoman frontier. Common experiences arose from the fact that the harvest was at the mercy of unpredictable events and from the frequent threat posed by infectious diseases, even if these phenomena were interpreted very differently on each side. Seyyid Hasan's diary from the time of the plague offers us insights into both such similarities and differences.[28] In this book we have been able only briefly to suggest relevant comparisons. However, it does appear as if more common ground between Ottoman and European everyday culture of the early modern period is visible from a present-day perspective than was apparent to contemporaries.

'Private Culture' in the Domestic Context

That Ottoman townspeople took an interest in certain aspects of their own 'private' lives was of course just as significant as their attitude towards the outside world. This 'private culture', which is an identifiable part of seventeenth- and eighteenth-century literature, was reflected, for instance, in the appearance of individual houses. Ottoman dwellings had been relatively small and lightly built even in the 'classical' period of the sixteenth century. Materials such as timber and sun-dried bricks were employed alone or in half-timbered constructions and were not very durable. Yet such materials were used in the construction even of houses for the empire's wealthier inhabitants, while their counterparts of early modern Europe had come to prefer stone or fired bricks. Until the nineteenth century, items which we might today describe as furniture were scarce: a few boxes and trunks, a wooden or leather mat for bowls and trays on which meals were served, built-in and sometimes ornate shelves, used for storing lamps and occasionally books. Nevertheless, it appears that affluent households, in the active trading town of Bursa, for example, had more carpets, kilims, cushions and pillows in the eighteenth century than in the early years of the Ottoman Empire. This may have to do with the early eighteenth-century revival in the fortunes of the Ottoman textile sector.[29] Since only a small proportion of these textiles were exported, a family of average wealth would now have greater amounts of material available for clothes or household use. As a working hypothesis, it seems likely that, in the eighteenth century, Bursa no longer produced the heavy brocades for which the palace was the only market. Rather, weavers and merchants probably switched to producing more modest materials to meet urban demand. If this hypothesis proves correct, it would mean that the 'private culture' to which we have referred would indeed be more than a purely literary phenomenon.

The Role of Women

It is impossible to separate this development from the role of women in urban families. It is reasonably well established that monogamy was the norm in the towns of western and central Anatolia from at least the seventeenth century, as it was in Istanbul during the late nineteenth.[30] If a man could not live with his wife he could divorce her, but it was rare for men to be married to two women at the same time. There were exceptions to this rule in and around the palace and among jurists and theologians.[31] However, as we have seen, in the early eighteenth century there were high-ranking ladies of Istanbul who attempted to impose monogamy on their husbands. This had not always been so: in the period of expansion in the fifteenth century, when slaves and slave girls were readily available at least in Bursa, many affluent men were married to former slave girls or left children born of a female slave.[32] Free-born women of Bursa of the period therefore had to compete, on their own account and for the sake of their children, with the slave girls belonging to their husbands and with their progeny.

By the early eighteenth century, though, there were few urban women with similar experiences. Slave girls were now more expensive and to be found only in a few wealthy households. However, it is also conceivable that there was a change of outlook on this issue. Romantic authors such as Namık Kemal, writing around the middle of the nineteenth century, did not, presumably, create the idea that there could be no love without free choice out of thin air. Rather, they must have been drawing on an attitude that they could assume was shared by at least a section of their readership.

'Private Culture' and the Beginning of the Novel

Emphasizing the importance of cultural activities among small groups of friends or associates inevitably means dealing with individual men and women who did not belong to the powerful Ottoman élite, and whose decisions impacted solely upon their personal lives and those of their families. We have seen how Seyyid Hasan, even while he was mourning the death of his relations, found time to describe the taste of cheese and the beauty of fruit with which he had been presented.[33] We have observed Asiye Hatun form a personal estimate of the spiritual profit she drew from corresponding with her sheikh. On the basis of this judgement, and despite a nagging conscience, she took the step, for her decisive, of changing her spiritual adviser.[34]

These and similar stories are important because, for the emerging nineteenth-century novel, they probably represent an additional source to that of the *meddah* tales. Men and women who no longer found it unusual that some of them wrote about their personal experiences probably regarded the new novels in the same light. In fact, the tradition of caricatural scenes which was familiar from the *meddah* tales sometimes complemented the first-person authors' close observation of individual characteristics and weaknesses rather well. Thus, in the first scene in Vartan Pasha's novel we encounter the hero trying to make a purchase in a shop, but so preoccupied by the desire to flirt that he forgets to tell the milliner what he actually wants. He is entirely intent on presenting himself in the correct light, and there is considerable comedy in his failure to reply appropriately to the inquiries of the frustrated milliner.[35]

Literary historians have in fact always emphasized how difficult the first generations of Ottoman novelists found the task of creating rounded personalities rather than miniature-like, stylized stereotypes.[36] Yet if certain authors of the 'second generation' who wrote around 1900 did succeed in creating convincing characters, their achievement was probably not solely due to the influence of Emile Zola, Alphonse Daudet or Guy de Maupassant. This influence was important, of course, particularly with regard to literary technique. However, it is worth asking why the early 'new-style' Ottoman writers such as Ahmed Midhat Efendi (1844–1912) considered the novel to be so effective a means of communicating their didactic messages. Without there being a 'private yet written culture' among their readers, such faith in the genre's efficacy would have been nonsensical.

Even if we acknowledge that the first Ottoman novelists overestimated the resonance of the new form in the short term, they were right at least in the sense that their novels contributed greatly to the growth of the reading public. In particular, women of the upper classes began to become readers, although they remained excluded from the political world and could therefore find little to interest them in the typical genres of established literature, such as political and ethical tracts and monumental, multi-volume chronicles. It seems clear that the gradual spread of 'private culture' from the late seventeenth century onwards prepared the way for the rapid acclimatization of the novel as a narrative form.

The Problem of Pictures

In this study we have repeatedly looked for those prerequisites for the cultural changes of the Tanzimat period which originated from within the Ottoman domain, rather than being induced from the outside world. In the same context it is worth taking a closer look at the rapid rise of the picture in the nineteenth century, a phenomenon which has not been the subject of much scrutiny. Even in previous eras there had been exceptions to the religious prohibition against likenesses of people and animals. In the Seljuk period some reliefs featuring animals and mythical beasts with human heads were produced, several well-preserved examples of which can be seen in the museum at Konya. In addition, from the thirteenth century onwards, ceramics were sometimes decorated with illustrations of people. In the fifteenth century the (sometimes sizeable) ram motif was used on gravestones.[37] Human portraits were present to a greater or lesser extent in Ottoman palace culture, depending on the taste of the reigning sultan. Ever since the reign of the Ummayads in the seventh and eighth centuries, the ruler could prove his privileged position by ostentatiously violating the prohibitions on wine and images which applied to ordinary mortals, and allowing the inner circle of the royal household to do the same.[38] Mehmed the Conqueror, for one, took advantage of this dispensation, and commissioned a portrait of himself from Gentile Bellini.[39] Even under Süleyman the Magnificent, for whom compliance with religious law was a prime objective in his later years, the court patronized the production of many miniatures showing battles and court receptions, which still survive in the Topkapı Palace. In the seventeenth century the sultans and their courtiers were less prominent patrons of the pictorial arts, even though the tradition did not die out entirely. Moreover, during the 'Tulip Age' (1718–30) and the immediately following years, important painters such as Levnî and Abdullah Buhari were once again active and receiving commissions from the court.

Many miniatures of the eighteenth century are marked by a strong interest in themes taken from domestic life. In the sixteenth century, painters of miniatures and their patrons had been more concerned with the wars and victories of the sultans and, to a lesser extent, with town panoramas and large-scale festivals. In addition, illustrations were painted for the manuscripts of literary classics and sometimes descriptions of the life of the Prophet Muhammad. In the eighteenth century, major festivals were once again documented through miniatures, with Levnî and his school also venturing to deal with 'nocturnal' aspects of the festivals, and in particular the fireworks.[40] However, of even greater relevance to our purpose are the many individual portraits of young men and women. Hammam scenes, among others, occasioned painters to attempt the portrayal of partially clothed bodies. These artists and their patrons were evidently no longer concerned exclusively with capturing the splendour of the court and the victories of the armies. In this form of art, reserved for a small public composed mostly of courtiers, individual persons now also became possible subjects for pictorial art.[41]

This court art remained invisible to the 'ordinary' townsperson. For this reason we have used such images only occasionally as historical sources, and without looking closely at the circumstances in which they were produced. However, the animals, people and mythical beasts which decorated carts in processions and were carried through the streets as confectionary sculptures or formed part of firework displays at the great festivals are a very different matter. They too were commissioned by the sultan, but these were works of art presented before a large public from beyond the world of the court. So far no contemporary texts have emerged which deal with the issue of how such objects were viewed by religious scholars, since, after all, they violated the Islamic prohibition of images. However, the materials used for these festive decorations were of course far from durable, and this probably made it easier to turn a blind eye to their dubious status. There can, after all, have been little temptation to worship as idols images made out of sugar, which were eaten at the end of the feast. Moreover, it seems likely that the presentation of such images was a part of the general, festive contravention of the rules governing everyday life. In the course of such events, the privileges usually reserved for the sultan were extended to large numbers of townspeople, albeit briefly.

Photography also entered Ottoman society initially as a symbol of authority. This, however, was not a matter of allowing the common subjects to see, in the context of a festival, the images of people and animals which were usually confined to miniatures accessible only to the court. Rather, the sovereign was concerned to make himself as tangible a presence as possible among both bureaucrats and 'ordinary' subjects. Among the earliest examples of the use of photography in Ottoman public life are the portraits of the various sultans which were to be found in more and more magistrates' offices from the middle of the nineteenth century onwards.[42] One aspect of the nineteenth-century neo-absolutist style of rule was that the sultan no longer steered the fate of the empire as an invisible power hidden behind the walls of the seraglio, but rather became a visible presence among his subjects.

As to the Ottoman élite of the Tanzimat period, a group which no longer saw itself as virtually enslaved to the sultan, it did not now feel constrained to leave the sultan a monopoly on such tokens of power. Pashas and military men also appear in photographs, surrounded by the emblems of their rank, in carefully adjusted clothes and poses.[43] Moreover, before long, photography had become a part of the 'private culture' of the Ottoman upper class. By the turn of the century the family photograph was well established in such circles as a souvenir and also as a visiting card.[44] Young couples, fathers proudly presenting their small children, and three-generation families gathered around the mother-in-law all figure in such pictures. Osman Hamdi even staged a photograph in which he poses in semi-facetious homage before his elegant daughter-in-law. Thus photography became a medium for representing domesticity and the family circle. No doubt the tradition of public art in festive contexts helped photography establish itself so quickly in both the public and private domains.

Individuals in a Non-individualistic Age

Existing historiography concerning the Ottoman Empire is based, with only a few exceptions, on the assumption that individuals were so tightly bound up in state structures, as well as in their families, town quarters and religious communities, that there was little scope for private initiatives, still less for adventure. Many factors – strict social controls, particularly on the behaviour of young people, collective liability for taxes and for unsolved crimes, diffi-culties associated with the move from village to town – did certainly contribute to the fact that new enterprises and initiatives did not always end well for those who risked embarking on them. However, research into European and North American source material from the early modern period has shown that similar risks and limitations existed in these societies as well. This did not prevent some people from making life-changing decisions and writing about their experiences. On the contrary, historians dealing with early modern European autobiographies now believe that men and women did not necessarily begin writing about themselves because family and neighbourhood ties had loosened. Rather, some people wrote because they had reflected on these ties and consciously identified themselves with certain groups.[45] The situation in the Ottoman context does not appear to have been very different. Clearly, merchants, seafarers and dervishes of both sexes, without abandoning their respective allegiances, became increasingly confident that their entirely personal experiences were worth recording. This conviction could extend even to experiences such as the taste of the cherries which made such an outstanding impression on Osman Ağa at a time of war and peril.[46]

Any study of Ottoman culture between about 1550 and 1780 must therefore take account of the way in which two basic strands are interwoven. On the one hand we are confronted by a pronounced symbolism of authority, to which modern art historians are devoting a great deal of attention.[47] On the other, we encounter a growing interest in the lives of individual people, something which found expression in the diaries and brief memoirs which they wrote. In the long term the sources might make it possible to write a history of 'private life' in the Ottoman domain. Such an undertaking would have appeared completely unrealistic just ten or fifteen years ago.

A central theme of those historians concerned with the history of 'private life' in modern Europe has been the variety of ways in which the developing absolutist principality managed to infiltrate even the domestic lives of its subjects.[48] Thus, a great deal has been written about the analogy which was made in the absolutist states of Europe between the prince and the master of even the most humble household, who, after all, 'ruled' over his wife, children and servants.[49]

Similar questions arise in the case of the Ottoman domain, particularly with regard to the eighteenth and early nineteenth centuries. It is worth reflecting on why in the eighteenth century, just when so many changes were beginning to take place in the lifestyle of the upper class and in the world of art, there were ever more official attempts to restrict even further the access of women to the world outside their homes.[50] To what extent these attempts to ban women from public life succeeded, what interests lay behind them, and why the sultans supported such policies are issues which have not yet been satisfactorily resolved. However, it seems likely that they constituted a reaction to the greater influence enjoyed by women belonging to the upper class, and by princesses in particular, during this period. The new authority of upper-class women also manifested itself in their patronage of works of art. Thus, social historians still have much work to do on the relationships between rulers and heads of families on the one hand and between heads of families and their households on the other. However, in the eighteenth century the sultan's court was no longer the only source of patronage for artists and writers. Art and literary history must therefore also take account of the development of 'private life' in the Ottoman domain.

Notes

1. Introduction

1. Turan (1990) is one of the few attempts at a synoptic presentation. Goodwin (1971) and Kuran (1987) have here been used as the basis for the architectural history.

2. Renda (1989).

3. The way in which this debate influenced the studies of a young cultural historian in the 1880s can be observed very clearly in Gombrich (1984), pp. 42ff.

4. cf. Berktay (1991) on Turkish republican historiography.

5. Gölpınarlı (1931; 1953) and others, Mardin (1962; 1983) and others.

6. Ocak (1991), Kafadar (1989).

7. See Berktay (1992) on this 'piety' towards the state and ways in which it can be overcome.

8. Muchembled (1978), Vovelle (1982), Ginzburg (1982) are good examples of this 'new-style' cultural history.

9. For more on these links see the summary of research produced by Berlioz and Le Goff relating to historically-oriented ethnology and the parallel survey by Vauchez et al. relating to the history of religious mentality, both in Duby and Balard (eds) (1991).

10. In Germany, studies dealing with everyday culture often try to discover the manner in which the population as a whole experienced industrialization, national socialism and war.

11. The works of E. P. Thompson led the way. See in particular Thompson (1971).

12. Evliya Çelebi (1896/97–1938), Vol. 10, pp. 406ff.; And (1982), Reyhanlı (1983), pp. 48ff.

13. For example: İmamoğlu (1992), And (1982), Kafadar (1989).

14. Kafadar (1989).

15. Chartier (1982), pp. 17–18.

16. Findley (1980), pp. 8ff.

17. Fleischer (1986), pp. 35ff.

18. Gölpınarlı (1953), p. 167.

19. Findley (1980), pp. 9–11.

20. Chambers (1973), p. 454.

21. Fleischer (1986), pp. 136ff.

22. Historians dealing with 'folk culture' have produced various definitions. Muchembled (1978) applies it to the culture of the illiterate, and to villagers in particular (pp. 11–19). On the other hand, Chartier (1982), pp. 88ff., defines the culture of the entire population other than members of the clergy, aristocrats and town councillors as 'popular'.

23. Chartier (1982), p. 10, writes that he wishes to avoid the term *culture populaire* 'as far as possible'.

24. See Roth (ed.) (1993) for a comprehensive treatment of popular culture in Bulgaria, Greece and the former Yugoslavia.

25. The 'grand old man' of this field, who in his many publications paid special attention to the relationship of folk poets to the written word, was, until his recent death, Pertev Naili Boratav (Paris).

26. cf. Farge (1992).

27. Sallmann (1986) makes it clear that practices which might, at first sight, appear to form part of 'folk religion' or even the realm of magic in Naples by the end of the sixteenth century, were also widespread among members of the upper class.

28. This was the practice in the Balkans for a long time: cf. Kechagioglou (1993), pp. 64ff.

29. cf. Assmann, Assmann and Hardmeier (eds) (1993), on the problem of recording in written form texts arising from the oral tradition.

30. Delumeau (1973; 1977).

31. Lewis (1982), p. 82.

32. Gölpınarlı (1963).

33. McNeill (1974).

34. Symposium (1974) (editors not named) provides an overview of the cultural activities of the Phanariots.

35. Raymond (1984), pp. 91ff.

36. cf. Popovic (1992) on authors producing Ottoman texts in the territory of the former Yugoslavia during the sixteenth century.

37. cf. Gölpınarlı (1967) for the catalogue of this collection of manuscripts.

38. See Kreiser (1979) on the definition of the Ottoman core territories.

39. Raymond (1984) and (1985) offer an introduction to Arab urban culture during the Ottoman period.

40. Vovelle (1982), pp. 25ff.

41. Bacqué-Grammont et al. (1991) and Laqueur (1993) have produced the most recent results of such work.

42. Ahmet Refik (1932).

43. İnalcık (1969).

44. For a summary of this debate cf. Le Roy Ladurie (1977), Vol. I, pp. 819ff.

45. Fleischer (1986), p. 204.

46. Ibid., p. 254.

47. Tietze (1982); Fleischer (1986), pp. 6–8.

48. Faroqhi (1979) includes some details of this event.

49. Fleischer (1986), p. 167.

50. Mardin (1962) addresses this issue.

51. A dissertation by Adnan Şişman regarding this issue has not, to my knowledge, ever been published.

52. Goubert (1966), pp. 252ff., contains moving passages about the exhaustion of France by Louis XIV's endless military campaigns.

53. Kafadar (1986).

54. Tietze (1991).

55. Bennassar and Bennassar (1989).

56. Lerner (1958).

57. Bombaci (1968), trans. Mélikoff, pp. 267ff., suggests that the 'classical' period of Ottoman literature began with a political event, that is, with the conquest of Constantinople in 1453.

58. Fleischer (1986), pp. 253ff.

59. Necipoğlu-Kafadar (1991), pp. 212ff.

60. Goodwin (1971), pp. 178 and 185.

61. Ibid., pp. 333–55.

62. Kuran (1987), p. 169.

63. Cemal Kafadar is preparing a broadly based study of this 'sense of decline'.

64. Fleischer (1990).

65. Arel (1975) is an important contribution to the re-evaluation of this period.

66. See Kuran (1987), p. 246, for a more recent and still very negative point of view.

67. See in particular Bayly (1989).

68. Ortaylı (1983).

69. Akın (1993).

70. It is most unfortunate that music had to be excluded from the present study. Ottoman music is unusual in that we have examples of scores and other information dating back to the seventeenth, and in a few cases even to the sixteenth, century. These allow us to reconstruct the manner in which the pieces in question were played. For this we are indebted to, among others, Ali Ufki Efendi, also known as Albertus Bobovius. He was an Ottoman of Polish descent who noted down the music performed in the sultan's palace. Other musical traditions included that of the Mevlevîs, whose major works are still performed today. Unfortunately, the deficiencies of my musical and musicological background do not allow me to make any useful contribution in this area. I am grateful to Andreas Tietze for his insights and in particular to Cem Behar, from whom I have learned a great deal.

2. The Emergence of an Empire

1. Vryonis (1971), pp. 69ff.

2. Ibid., pp. 285–6.

3. de Planhol (1968), pp. 220ff.

4. On the Gagauz see the article 'Dobrudja' (by Halil İnalcık) in *EI*. See Vryonis (1971), pp. 455ff., advancing the contrary point of view, that they were in fact an autochthonous group subsequently absorbed by the Turks. In his article 'Ḳarāmān' in *EI*, Howard Reed suggests that they may have been descendants of a non-Greek, autochthonous group from Asia Minor.

5. Köprülü (1929); Ocak (1989). Cf. also Ocak (1983) on the survival of Islamic motifs in Anatolian saints' legends.

6. See the article 'Barak Baba' (by Bernard Lewis) in *EI*, 2nd edn.

7. Whether Baba Ishak or Baba Ilyas was the main leader of this revolt has been hotly debated. It all depends on whether one identifies Baba Ishak or Baba Ilyas as the 'Paperraissole' (Baba Resulullāh-Baba 'God's Prophet') who appears in the chronicle of Simon de St Quentin. Simon de St Quentin, who travelled through Anatolia in the thirteenth century, almost certainly obtained his information from European mercenaries who had lived for a long time in the area: Ocak (1989), pp. 2–3. See Cahen (1969) and Ocak (1989). Most specialists seem now to support Ocak's view.

8. Ocak (1989), pp. 87–95, and Beldiceanu-Steinherr (1991). For a history of Islamic dervishes, see Trimingham (1971).

9. See Kafadar (1995) for a useful discussion of this tale.

10. cf. the article 'Karamanlılar' (by Şihabettin Tekindağ) in *İA*.

11. cf. the article 'Shāh Ismā'il' (by R. M. Savory) in *EI*, 2nd edn. 'Sunni' designates the mainstream interpretation of Islam. This recognizes the first four caliphs who ruled the Islamic world after the death of the Prophet Muhammad as 'rightly guided' and therefore legitimate. Shia supporters, on the other hand, believe that of the four only Ali (reign 656–61), nephew and son-in-law of the Prophet, ruled by right. For the period after Ali's death they believe in the spiritual rule of various religious leaders (*imam*s) descended from Ali. None of these,

however, ascended the caliphal throne, although the Fatimids (reign from 909 in North Africa and later in Egypt, 969–1171) claimed to be descended from Ali and thus to be rightful caliphs. Cf. Hodgson (1974), Vol. I, pp. 212–23, Vol. 2, pp. 23–9.

12. Sohrweide (1965), pp. 145ff.

13. Ibid., p. 159; İnalcık (1973), pp. 186ff.

14. Mélikoff (1975); Gölpınarlı (1973); Birge (1965), Ill. 6 and 7. See also the article 'Ḥurufiyya' (by A. Bausani) in EI, 2nd edn.

15. İnalcık (1953).

16. Düzdağ (1972), pp. 91ff. Moreover, in some periods converts were rewarded with money from the sultan's treasury, a piece of information for which I am indebted to Professor Machiel Kiel.

17. Vryonis (1971), pp. 288ff. For more on the Bogomils cf. Cirkovic (1986), pp. 1157–8. The Bogomils had much in common with the French, Spanish and Italian Cathars. The people of Montaillou, for instance, were Cathars: cf. Le Roy Ladurie (1975). Popovic (1992) urges caution; it is, he points out, easy to exaggerate the influence of the Bogomils.

18. Gölpınarlı (ed.) (1958), p. 56.

19. Vryonis (1971), p. 388.

20. Ibid., p. 387.

21. With regard to this matter cf. Tanyu (1967), pp. 319–21 and Hasluck (1929).

22. In the twentieth century, Mevlevî culture was impressively personified by Abdülbaki Gölpınarlı, whose writings are so frequently cited in this book, and to whose memory I would like to pay tribute.

23. 'Ibn Bībī' (by H. W. Duda) in EI, 2nd edn.

24. Cf. the article 'madrasa' (by G. Pedersen and G. Makdisi) in EI, 2nd edn.

25. Konyalı (1964), pp. 785ff.

26. See ibid., pp. 845ff. for the inscriptions in the Karatayı Medrese, today a museum.

27. Cacaoğlu Nur el-Din, ed. Temir (1959).

28. Ibn Battuta, trans. Défremery and Sanguinetti (1854), Vol. 2, pp. 334ff.

29. Uzluk (1958), pp. 11–13, reproduces a list of the books compiled in the mid-fifteenth century. In addition, cf. the article 'Ibn al-'Arabi' (by Ahmet Ateş) in EI, 2nd edn.

30. Gölpınarlı (1953), pp. 60ff.

31. Elvan Çelebi (1984).

32. cf. the article 'Othmānlı-Literature' (by Gönül Alpay Tekin) in EI, 2nd edn.

33. Many mainly historical or biographical works even in the fifteenth and sixteenth centuries included an initial chapter influenced by legend: cf. Tašköprüzäde, trans. Rescher (1927), p. 5, and Aşık-Paşa's son (Aşık-paşazade), trans. Kreutel (1959), p. 25. There are similar instances to be found in European Renaissance and baroque historical literature.

34. Cf. Neumann (1994). This codification, known as the Mecelle, corresponds to the Hanifi conception of law. The Hanifite school of law is one of the four schools (mezhep) of Sunni Islam, which are all regarded as equally orthodox, despite their many variations. The Hanifites were predominant in the Ottoman Empire, just as they are in modern Turkey. The Muslim schools of law are not the religious denominations for which they are so often mistaken.

35. Cahen (1988), pp. 148ff.

36. Ibid., pp. 211–24.

37. The following articles in EI, 2nd edn: 'Nīshāpur' (by E. Honigmann and C. E. Bosworth); 'Marw' (by A. Yakubowskii and C. E. Bosworth).

38. Gölpınarlı (1959), p. 40.

39. cf. the article 'Masdjid' (by R. Hillenbrand) in EI, 2nd edn.

40. Goodwin (1971), pp. 59ff.

41. Özergin (1965); Erdmann (1961).

42. Cacaoğlu Nur el-Din, ed. Temir (1959), p. 165.

43. Çulpan (1975).

44. cf. the article 'Kubād-abād' (by M. Meinecke) in *EI*, 2nd edn.

45. cf. the article 'Ankara' (by F. Taeschner) in *EI*, 2nd edn. In a number of sizeable articles, Tuncer Baykara has attempted to reconstruct the appearance of Anatolian towns of this period.

46. cf. Arel (1968) for an initial overview.

47. Foss (1979).

48. Taeschner (1968).

49. Particularly Ankara Tapu ve Kadastro Genel Müdürlüğü 139 (992/1584).

50. Inalcık (1973), p. 95.

51. cf. ibid., pp. 78, 87 for the argument that those who entered the sultan's service via the levy of boys (*devşirme*) were not slaves. Behrens-Abouseif (1994), pp. 52–3 shows how problematic certain Egyptian contemporaries found the status of these state servitors.

52. Kunt (1974).

53. Ṭašköprüzāde, trans. Rescher (1927), pp. 75–6.

54. Dilger (1967) has suggested that the *Kanunname* (collection of sultan's orders) of Mehmed II does not really stem from that ruler, but in fact was collected mainly as late as the sixteenth century. Objections to this argument include those of Fleischer (1986), p. 199 (and the authors cited there) and Necipoğlu-Kafadar (1991), p. 20.

55. Babinger (1962b), p. 367.

56. Cvetkova (1963).

57. cf. Goodwin (1971), ill. 293, 313, 351 for mosques of the 'classical' period in Sıvas, Kayseri and Elmalı. There are many other examples.

58. Necipoğlu-Kafadar (1991), pp. 212ff., 250.

59. Ibid., p. 51.

60. Necipoğlu (1992).

61. Aşık-Paşa Zade, trans. Kreutel (1959), pp. 41, 55 and many other examples.

62. Yérasimos (1990), pp. 62ff., 183ff.

63. On the ideal of power and political reality in the seventh century, cf. Hodgson (1974), Vol. I, pp. 197ff.

64. Inalcık (1970); cf. also the same author's article 'Istanbul' in *EI*.

65. Ayverdi (1958).

66. Regarding architectural form cf. Goodwin (1971), pp. 121–31; regarding their function cf. Barkan (1963).

67. On the Karamanoğulları foundations in Konya see Konyalı (1964), p. 967.

68. Inalcık (1973), pp. 9–10.

69. Alexandrescu-Dersca (1977); Inalcık (1973), pp. 16–17.

70. Inalcık (1973), pp. 35–40.

71. Inalcık (1954a) and (1954b).

72. Recent contributions to this debate include those of Lindner (1983) and Kafadar (1995).

73. Beldiceanu-Steinherr (1971); Lindner (1983), pp. 9ff.

74. Fleischer (1986), pp. 296–7. From this point of view the wars of Murad III seem to the historian Mustafa Âlî to have been self-destructive and motivated by the personal ambitions of certain viziers. See also Abou-El-Haj (1984), p. 22.

75. Fleischer (1986), pp. 59ff., provides a striking description of the historian Mustafa Âlî's experiences at the wartime frontier during the second half of the sixteenth century.

76. Inalcık (1973), pp. 35–7.

77. Bayburtluoğlu (1973).

78. Labib (1965), pp. 381–5.

79. Brummet (1991).

80. Article 'Mamluk' (by D. Ayalon) in *EI*, 2nd edn.

81. Abou-El-Haj (1982).

82. Barbir (1979/80).

83. Behrens-Abouseif (1994), pp. 1–14.

84. Uzunçarşılı (1972), p. 23.

85. Reid (1969).

86. Başbakanlık Arşivi-Osmanlı Arşivi, section Mühimme Defterleri (MD) 28, p. 139, No. 331 (984/1576–77).

87. Inalcık (1973), pp. 57–8.

88. Fleischer (1986), pp. 157ff., 253ff. On the ethnic stereotypes of the Ottoman upper class in the seventeenth and early eighteenth centuries, see Cantemir, ed. Dutu and Cernovodeanu (1973), pp. 52–3.

89. A good example is the Sokollu vizier family; cf. Fleischer (1986), pp. 305ff.

90. Kiel (1990).

91. Cf. Šamic (1986), for example.

92. For a discussion of this issue in the Bulgarian context, cf. Kiel (1985).

93. From the names of taxpayers listed in the tax registers it is sometimes possible to deduce the ethnic group of the persons in question. Sometimes we also encounter a part of the town which, at least originally, was inhabited by one particular ethnic group.

94. Inalcık (1973), pp. 65–9.

95. For this very reason, nationalist Turkish historians were sometimes inclined to demonize the ruling class of the Ottoman Empire – with the exception of those who were demonstrably Turks; cf. Danişmend (1971), *passim*.

3. The Economic and Social Structure of the Ottoman Empire in Early Modern Times

1. Barkan and Meriçli (1988), p. 9; Barkan (1951), p. 12. Erder (1975) suggests another method, based on the number of adult men relative to the whole population in a wide variety of societies. In many cases the two methods give very similar results, tending to support the contention that five is a realistic estimate of the size of households in many parts of the Ottoman Empire. In the case of Bursa, 6,190 married and 1,813 unmarried taxpayers, added to an 'extra' 10 per cent of non-taxpayers, would suggest a population of about 36,000 in 1530–31.

2. With regard to migrants from the lower orders, cf. the still-unpublished study by Seng (1991). I am grateful to the author for allowing me to read her work.

3. I am indebted to Machiel Kiel for the information about Athens.

4. Barkan (1951), p. 22.

5. For a description of Buda from the year 1554, just after the completion of the conquest of Hungary, cf. Busbeck, trans. von den Steinen (1926), pp. 20–1.

6. Raymond (1979).

7. Regarding the educated world of Cairo in the late middle ages, cf. Petry (1981).

8. Behrens-Abouseif (1989).

9. Raymond (1973/74), Vol. I, p. 204. If all these people were heads of households the total would be 750,000 souls. However, in view of the large number of apprentices and other non-masters, who were generally single, that is certainly an overestimate. On the other hand, there were also many Mamluks and others who did not work. At the end of the eighteenth century, Cairo probably had between about 263,000 and 300,000 inhabitants. A probable decline in the population during the previous hundred years should be taken into account.

10. Dalsar (1960), pp. 125ff.

11. Raymond (1979).

12. Busbeck, trans. von den Steinen (1926), pp. 25–6 describes smaller caravanserais on the Balkan peninsula.

13. Barkan (1942a).

14. Orhonlu (1967), p. 62.

15. Steensgaard (1974), pp. 60ff.

16. Tilly (1985).

17. Faroqhi (1984a), p. 52.

18. Ülgener (1981), p. 22.

19. Gloves were, however, worn more seldom than in early modern Europe.

20. Lane (1968).

21. Braudel (1966), Vol. I, pp. 510ff. The first edition dates from 1949. On the collapse of the seventeenth century cf. Sella (1968).

22. Raymond (1973/74), Vol. 2, pp. 400ff.

23. İnalcık (1979/80).

24. Hattox (1988), pp. 72ff.

25. Aymard (1989), p. 475; Sella (1968).

26. Raymond (1973/74), Vol. 1, pp. 100, 174–9.

27. Wirth (1986).

28. Stoianovich (1960); Panzac (1992), p. 193.

29. Reference is to oral communications presented at a symposium in Aix-en-Provence organized by Professor Daniel Panzac (autumn 1991).

30. Redhouse (1921), p. 1625. I am grateful to Heidi Stein for drawing my attention to this passage.

31. The stereotype of the 'static' Orient may have played a part in this; cf. Said (1978).

32. Immanuel Wallerstein has put forward this point of view in several books and articles. See in particular Wallerstein et al. (1987).

33. As well as Wallerstein (1974), cf. also Braudel (1979), Vol. 3, in particular pp. 12–70, upon which the following section is based.

34. Wallerstein (1974), pp. 301ff.

35. Barkan (1975a).

36. Çızakça (1987). Gerber (1988), pp. 13, 88, suggests, however, that the crisis in silk manufacturing was much less severe than has hitherto been assumed.

37. Çızakça (1985).

38. Abdel Nour (1982), pp. 276ff.

39. For a discussion of this problem with regard to Aleppo cf. Masters (1988), pp. 75ff.

40. Genç (1984).

41. Regarding the attempts of the Ottoman financial administration to deal with the crisis by purely fiscal means cf. Y. Cezar (1986).

42. Güçer (1964) analyses this problem with regard to the late sixteenth century. For an examination of the logistics of an Ottoman campaign cf. Finkel (1988). Murphey (1999), p. 189 disagrees with this evaluation.

43. See Y. Cezar (1986) on the financing of war in the eighteenth century.

44. Lowry (1986), pp. 23, 34.

45. Fekete (1960) provides a good example of the material goods which were accumulated by a military man based in Hungary.

46. Aktepe (1958b), pp. 38–9.

47. Çizakça (1985), pp. 370ff.

48. With regard to this issue cf. also İslamoğlu-İnan (1987), pp. 19ff., although this author concentrates on the political resources of the Ottoman state while I am dealing with its economic resources in the widest sense.

49. Braudel (1979), Vol. 3, pp. 268ff.

50. Todorov (1967/68).

51. Issawi (1980), pp. 74–8.

52. Quataert (1983), pp. 71ff.

53. For an example cf. Issawi (1980), p. 120.

54. Sırman (1988) deals with the division of labour and women's networks in modern western Anatolia, but unfortunately remains unpublished. I am grateful to the author for the opportunity to consult her study.

55. Faroqhi (1984a), p. 244; Reindl-Kiel (1997).

56. Faroqhi (1986b).

57. İnalcık (1973), pp. 104–18.

58. İnalcık (1965), pp. 135–6.

59. Barkan (1975b), p. 23.

60. Güçer (1964), p. 57.

61. Faroqhi (1984a), p. 57.

62. Veinstein (1983) sheds light on the problem from the *timar*-holders' point of view.

63. Akdağ (1963), pp. 44–7.

64. Faroqhi (1984a), p. 270.

65. On the rapid settlement of nomadic immigrants to Anatolia cf. de Planhol (1968), pp. 226–8.

66. İnalcık (1980), p. 288.

67. Kunt (1981), pp. 54ff.

68. İnalcık (1974).

69. Akdağ (1963), pp. 214–15.

70. İnalcık (1980), pp. 300ff.

71. Akdağ (1963), pp. 198, 221; Griswold (1983), pp. 24–59.

72. Adanır (1982).

73. Faroqhi (1984a), p. 271.

74. İnalcık (1985); McGowan (1981), pp. 155ff.

75. McGowan (1981), pp. 56ff.

76. Ibid., p. 73.

77. Stoianovich (1960); McGowan (1981), pp. 62–7.

78. Sanır (1949), p. 168; Braudel (1979), Vol. I, pp. 423–8.

79. İnalcık (1973), pp. 68–9.

80. Akdağ (1963), pp. 150ff.; Faroqhi (1992a), p. 30.

81. İnalcık (1980).

82. Necipoğlu-Kafadar (1986b); Ca'fer Efendi, ed. Crane (1987), p. 67.

83. Such permission was also necessary for the renovation of at least the larger mosques. I am grateful to Machiel Kiel for this information. On the larger issue cf. Kiel (1985).

4. Images of the World and the Times

1. Because of such actions, occasionally sultans' decrees were issued dealing with particular grievances; cf. İnalcık (1965) and Faroqhi (1992a).

2. de Planhol (1968), pp. 220ff.

3. Faroqhi (1984a), p. 49.

4. Planhol (1968), pp. 235–8.

5. İnalcık (1980), pp. 304ff.

6. Kunt (1981), pp. 22ff.

7. Faroqhi (1994); cf. also Ch. 2.

8. Düzdağ (1972), p. 9, where the Kızılbaş are described as *kâfir*. Elsewhere, however, it is stated that it was forbidden to enslave them (p. 111).

9. Faroqhi (1984a), pp. 100–1.

10. Bennassar and Bennassar (1989), pp. 251ff.

11. Eickhoff (1992), p. 193.

12. Bennassar and Bennassar (1989), pp. 238ff., 366ff.

13. Uzunçarşılı (1965), pp. 19–32 provides an overview of the curriculum.

14. İnalcık (1973), pp. 70–5.

15. Zilfi (1988), pp. 57ff.

16. Ibid., pp. 216ff, describes the life of Fethullah (died 1703), who was murdered as a young man together with his father, the former *şeyhülislam* Feyzullah.

17. Regarding the relationship between the historian Mustafa Âlî and Baki cf. Fleischer (1986), pp. 57–8.

18. Zilfi (1988), pp. 129ff.

19. Gölpınarlı (1953), pp. 166–7, discusses this affair from the point of view of the Mevlevî dervishes, who were particularly affected.

20. Zilfi (1988), pp. 145–6.

21. Ibid., p. 157.

22. Ibid., p. 211.

23. Regarding the manipulations of ecclesiastical income sources in eighteenth-century France see Soboul (1970), pp. 298–302.

24. İslamoğlu-İnan (1987), pp. 20ff.

25. Kißling (1953).

26. Gölpınarlı (1953), pp. 156–8, describes the administrative duties of the leaders of orders in the seventeenth century; Faroqhi (1981a), pp. 93ff.

27. cf. the article 'Nakshbandiyya' (by Hamid Algar and K. A. Nizam) in *EI*, 2nd edn.

28. In the seventeenth century it was usual to appoint dervish sheikhs as mosque preachers, but a knowledge of theology or religious law was required for the position; cf. Kafadar (1989).

29. Karamustafa (1994) contains interesting observations regarding this topic.

30. Başbakanlık Arşivi – Osmanlı Arşivi, section Mühimme Defterleri (MD) 79, p. 323, No. 815 (1019/ 1610–11).

31. MD 82, pp. 74 and 76 (1027–1617).

32. Clogg (1982).

33. Braude (1982); Clogg (1982), on the other hand, adheres to the more traditional opinion that the *millet* system goes back to the fifteenth century.

34. Runciman (1968), p. 204.

35. Ibid., p. 219.

36. Ibid., pp. 214–19. On Venice as a link between the eastern church and the artistic and scholastic world of Europe cf. also McNeill (1974).

37. Fra Paolo Sarpi was a Venetian theorist of the secular state at the beginning of the seventeenth century. He was employed as legal counsel to the Venetian government.

38. Runciman (1968), pp. 259–88; Hering (1968).

39. K. Schwarz (1970), pp. 51ff., 93.

40. Taeschner (1923) is still a good overview of the Ottoman geographers. See also Adnan-Adıvar (1943), pp. 55–104.

41. Pirî Re'is, ed. H. Alpagut and F. Kurtoğlu (1935).

42. Mughul (1965).

43. Adnan-Adıvar (1943), pp. 68–9.

44. Naṣūḥü's-silāḥī (Matrakçı), ed. Hüseyin G. Yurdaydın (1976), pp. 58ff.

45. Ibid. contains facsimiles of the miniatures.

46. Ibid., facsimiles 8b and 9a.

47. Fleischer (1986), p. 110.

48. Kâtib Çelebi (1732), p. 629.

49. Taeschner (1923), pp. 48ff., 68.

50. Evliya Çelebi, ed. Van Bruinessen et al. (1988), p. 6.

51. Gdoura (1985).

52. Sahillioğlu (1975).

53. Raymond (1973/74), Vol. 2, pp. 482–96.

54. Khachikian (1967); Kévonian (1975); Erim (1991).

55. Kafadar (1986).

56. Faroqhi (1990), p. 220.

57. Mantran (1962), pp. 187–93.

58. Faroqhi (1992a).

59. Aktepe (1958a), p. 11. Mahmud I went so far in 1731 as to prohibit completely individual complainants. Only the delegates of whole towns and districts were to be allowed to come to Istanbul.

60. In the eighteenth century European consulates often had many real and ostensible interpreters, as many non-Muslim subjects attempted to gain the protection of a foreign power in this way; cf. Bağış (1983).

61. For an example cf. Delumeau (1967), pp. 219–20.

62. cf. Mustafā 'Ālî, trans. Tietze (1978 and 1982).

63. Abou-El-Haj (1991), pp. 24ff., has expressed doubts that the 'Counsel Books' (*nasihat-name*), according to İnalcık (1969) part of the 'mirror for princes' tradition of Iranian literature, really constitute 'objective' commentaries on political reality. He is no doubt right to assert that the statements made in these tracts were in fact weapons in political disputes and can be evaluated accurately only in this light. There were also European parallels to Ottoman 'mirror

for princes' literature: the texts dealing with imperial reforms in late medieval Germany on the one hand, and, on the other, the writings of the Spanish Arbitristas during the sixteenth and seventeenth centuries.

64. Fleischer (1990).

65. Evliya Çelebi, trans. Kreutel (1957), pp. 77, 228–30.

66. Ibid., p. 259; cf. also the article 'Dadjdjāl' (by S. H. Longrigg) in *EI*, 2nd edn.

67. MD 29, p. 96, No. 231 (984/1576–77).

68. Faroqhi (1971).

69. Fleischer (1986), pp. 134–8.

70. Ibid., p. 134.

71. Flemming (1987).

72. Fleischer (1992).

73. Sholem (1973).

74. Fleischer (1992).

75. MD 5, p. 196, No. 487 (973/1565–66).

76. Sholem (1973), pp. 667ff. provides a detailed description of Sabbatai's conversion.

77. Stoianovich (1960).

5. Borders and Those Who Crossed Them

1. cf., for example, Raymond (1984); Behrens-Abouseif (1992).

2. Arık (1976); Renda (1989).

3. For example, the historian Mustafa Naima (1655–1716), cf. Thomas (1972); cf. also Barbir (1979/80).

4. Tietze in the introduction to Vartan Pasha, ed. Andreas Tietze (1991), p. ix.

5. de Planhol (1958), p. 111 also cites Evilya Çelebi, according to whom the Greeks of Antalya already spoke only Turkish in the seventeenth century.

6. The main source for details about the figure of Cantemir is the biography included in the English translation of Cantemir's Ottoman history which appeared in 1734: Cantemir, trans. Tindal (1734), pp. 455–60; reprinted in the selection by Dutu and Cernovodeanu (1973), pp. 286–98.

7. Cantemir, who also composed himself, wrote two books on this subject.

8. Cantemir, ed. Dutu and Cernovodeanu (1973), p. 12.

9. Cantemir, trans. Tindal (1734) and the German version of 1745, based on the English one. The French edition dates from 1743.

10. Cantemir, ed. Dutu and Cernovodeanu (1973), p. 13; cf. also Fleischer (1986), pp. 267ff.

11. Many of the notes are reprinted in the anthology of 1973, in which the actual historical presentation is omitted.

12. Cantemir, trans. Tindal (1734), opposite p. 1.

13. Cantemir, ed. Dutu and Cernovodeanu (1973), p. 130. In fact, the four minarets are very similar in appearance.

14. The illustration is on the same page as the map. For a description of his town palace cf. ibid., p. 122.

15. Cantemir, trans. Tindal (1734), p. 360. On pp. 423–5 there is an extremely vivid account of the clumsy 'diplomacy' of the French ambassador, Ferréol.

16. He rarely omits to attach a disrespectful adjective to each reference to the Islamic religion.

17. Cantemir, trans. Tindal (1734), pp. 172–3 and 217.

18. Ibid., p. 351.

19. Ibid., p. 354.

20. Reference is to Halil Inalcık: Cantemir, ed. Dutu and Cernovodeanu (1973), p. 9.

21. cf. the bibliography in ibid.

22. cf. Orhonlu (1974) on Ethiopia, H. Yavuz (1984) on Yemen and İnalcık (1948) on the northern steppes.

23. Faroqhi (1986b).

24. Aktepe (1958b).

25. cf. Ch. 9.

26. Osman Ağa, trans. Kreutel and Spies (1954) and (1962). The 1962 edition has been used here.

27. cf., for example, Osman Ağa, trans. Kreutel and Spies (1962), p. 107.

28. Ibid., pp. 35ff.

29. Ibid., p. 13.

30. Kafadar (1989), p. 132.

31. Used by Montesquieu (1986) and Defoe (1975), for example.

32. Evliya Çelebi (1896/97–1938), Vol. 9, p. 123 and Evliya Çelebi, trans. Kreutel (1957), p. 109.

33. cf. Evliya Çelebi, trans. Kreutel (1957) with Schweigger (1986), Busbeck, trans. von den Steinen (1926) or even Dernschwam (1923).

34. Evliya Çelebi, trans. Kreutel (1957), pp. 144–5.

35. Ibid., p. 78; cf. also the new edition revised by Erich Prokosch and Karl Teply (1987).

36. Ibid., pp. 160ff; and Hüttl (1976), p. 135.

37. Ibid., pp. 126ff.

38. Humanists also often frowned upon the (relative) lack of interest exhibited by many Ottomans in Greek and Roman antiquity, cf. Busbeck, trans. von den Steinen (1926).

39. Evliya Çelebi, trans. Kreutel (1957), p. 114.

40. Faroqhi (1994), pp. 152–3.

41. Kunt (1974).

42. Fleischer (1986), pp. 154–9.

43. Dernschwam (1923), p. 121.

44. Başbakanlık Arşivi - Osmanlı Arşivi, section Mühimme Defterleri 48, p. 121, No. 322, August 1587. The nuns' convent may have been that of St Philothei which was famous – or, in Ottoman eyes, notorious – for being a refuge for released or fleeing slave women: Mackenzie (1992), pp. 46–7. In the Ottoman text, however, Rusula is named as the founder.

45. Wild (1964) *passim*, gives a full account of such problems.

46. Ibid., pp. 228–30; Wild describes how his release came about.

47. Sahillioğlu (1985).

48. For a survey of Ottoman slavery cf. Sahillioğlu (1985).

49. Tietze (1942).

50. Ibid., pp. 176–8.

51. Ibid., p. 190.

52. Bennassar and Bennassar (1989), p. 309.

53. Ibid., *passim*.

54. Ibid., pp. 202–26. See also Kahane et al. (1958).

55. A new biography by Cem Behar appeared as an introduction to Behar (1990).

56. Ibid., p. 11.

57. Ibid., pp. 55ff.

58. Ibid., p. 21.

59. Ibid., p. 9.

60. Ibid., pp. 25ff., 33.

61. cf. the article 'Ibrāhīm Müteferriḳa' (by Niyazi Berkes) in *EI*, 2nd edn, and also Berkes (1962).

62. This served as the basis for Berkes's comments.

63. Berkes (1962), p. 718; cf. also Mikes (1978).

64. See the article 'Maṭbaʿa' (section written by Günay Alpay Kut) in *EI*, 2nd edn, which gives a good overview of the problem as a whole.

65. Gdoura (1985), pp. 89ff.

66. Ibid., p. 97.

67. Ibid., pp. 99ff.

68. See Atıl (1987), pp. 64–73, for reproductions of a few particularly beautiful examples.

69. Gdoura (1985), pp. 104–6, discusses the religious opposition to printing.

70. Evliya Çelebi, trans. Kreutel (1957), p. 114.

71. Gdoura (1985), p. 97.

72. Montagu (1993), pp. 62–3.

73. Runciman (1968), pp. 272–4.

74. Gdoura (1985), pp. 90–1.

75. Ibid., pp. 115, 230ff.; cf. also his discussion of Ibrahim Müteferrika's printing propaganda: pp. 113ff.

76. Karamustafa (1994).

77. Köprülü (1935).

78. Gölpınarlı and Boratav (1991), pp. 50–1.

79. Ibid., pp. 42–5. For a dating into the seventeenth century cf. Jansky (1964).

80. Evliya Çelebi, trans. Dankoff (1990).

81. Faroqhi (1990), pp. 89–95.

82. Cantemir, trans. Tindal (1734), pp. 457–8.

83. Montagu (1993), p. 136; see also Bennassar and Bennassar (1989), pp. 289–307.

84. Bennassar and Bennassar (1989), p. 133.

85. Uluçay (1980), p. 34.

86. Montagu (1993), p. 119.

87. Osman Ağa, trans. Kreutel and Spies (1962), pp. 147–8.

88. cf. also Bennassar and Bennassar (1989), pp. 288–307.

6. Women's Culture

1. Jennings (1973); Gerber (1980).

2. According to Islamic religious law, a woman's evidence is worth only half of a man's. In many cases, two male witnesses are required, or one man and two women; Schacht (1982), p. 193.

3. The work resulting from this new wave of interest includes, in Germany, the studies by Wunder (1992) and Ennen (1991).

4. With regard to the household accounts of Ottoman princesses of the eighteenth century, cf. the study being prepared by Tülay Artan. I am grateful to the author for allowing me to read her work.

5. Schacht (1982), p. 132.

6. However, non-Muslim wives could not inherit from Muslim husbands, and nor could such husbands inherit from their wives.

7. Alexander (1985).

8. Başbakanlık Arşivi – Osmanlı Arşivi, section Ahkâm Defterleri (AD) Vol. 1, pp. 182, 185 (1156/1743–44).

9. AD Vol. 2, p. 213 (1159/1746).

10. On this and related issues, although with regard to the twentieth century, cf. the unpublished dissertation by Sırman (1988).

11. My own knowledge relates to Ankara and Kayseri (sixteenth–seventeenth centuries) and Bursa (early eighteenth century).

12. Jennings (1973).

13. Montagu (1993), p. 72.

14. Artan, oral information.

15. Artan (1988), pp. 366ff. and Artan (1992).

16. Duben and Behar (1991), p. 156.

17. Evliya Çelebi, trans. Dankoff (1991), pp. 230–5.

18. Ibid., p. 234.

19. Ibid., pp. 259ff.

20. Artan (in publication). I am grateful to the author for having made her manuscript available to me.

21. Montagu (1993), pp. 120–1. The 'us' is probably the 'modest plural' which is still used in modern Turkish.

22. Uluçay (1950), p. 11; the letters, in modern Turkish characters, are on pp. 29–47.

23. Ibid., p. 27.

24. The sultan had inquired why Hurrem was angry with this pasha. Hurrem postponed her reply: Uluçay (1950), p. 31.

25. Ibid., p. 31.

26. Ibid., p. 43.

27. Ibid., pp. 8–9.

28. Montagu (1993), pp. 76–9.

29. Ibid., pp. 58–60; cf. also Melman (1992), pp. 77–98.

30. cf. a European engraving, reproduced in Theunissen et al. (1989), Ill. no. 38.

31. Renda et al. (1993), Ill. no. 58.

32. This was also where Sultan Ahmed III (reign 1703–30) built the palace known as the Sa'adabad. The numerous kiosks surrounding it were demolished after the sultan's deposition. For a contemporary illustration cf. And (1982), Ill. no. 20.

33. cf., for example, the miniature reproduced in Renda et al. (1993), Ill. no. 59.

34. Montagu (1993), pp. 106–7.

35. Özdeğer (1988) calculates that in the inheritance records which he investigated, relating to the period 1489 to 1640, there are 3,121 deceased persons, leaving 1,659 sons and 1,402 daughters. Unfortunately, we do not know how many children altogether were born in these families. The register refers only to those who were still alive at the death of the father or mother (the table does not make it clear which). Moreover, we should probably assume that

estates were entered in official registers above all when the number of heirs was small. It was in such cases that there was a danger of the estate passing to the state by default. This danger could be reduced by official registration which demonstrated the existance of heirs, even if the latter might live in other towns and villages. I am grateful to Christoph Neumann for discussing this issue with me.

36. Montagu (1993), pp. 90, 117.

37. Bursa Kadı Sicilleri B160 and 162, *passim.*

38. Ibid.

39. Although these were worn by well-to-do ladies of Istanbul: cf. Montagu (1993), p. 115, and see also the catalogue of the Museum für Kunsthandwerk, Frankfurt am Main (1985), Vol. 2, Ill. no. 87.

40. Bursa Kadı Sicilleri B160 and 162, *passim.*

41. cf., for example, Illustration no. 17 in Patlagean (1977) showing early Byzantine earrings the likes of which, dating from the twentieth century, can still be found today in Turkish antique shops. See also the catalogue of the Museum für Kunsthandwerk, Frankfurt am Main (1985), Vol. 2, Ill. no. 7/11 a–c.

42. Sırman (1988), p. 117.

43. Faroqhi (1980), p. 77.

44. Evliya Çelebi (1896/97–1938), Vol. 9, p. 781.

45. Helmecke (1993), p. 27.

46. At least, this is the impression given by Lady Mary Wortley Montagu's descriptions; cf., for example, Montagu (1993), pp. 89 and 115.

47. There are several miniatures, mainly from the eighteenth century, which illustrate the dress of well-to-do ladies; cf. Renda et al. (1989), Ill. nos. 57 and 62.

48. İnalcık (1973), Ill. nos. 28 and 30.

49. Mackenzie (1992), p. 64.

50. P[itton] de Tournefort (1982), Vol. 1, between pp. 178 and 179.

51. Renda et al. (1993), Ill. no. 7.

52. On the opportunities for women to hold a *timar* cf. Reindl-Kiel (1997).

53. Jennings (1973), p. 75.

54. Ibid., pp. 106–7.

55. Ibid., pp. 195–6.

56. Çızakça (1996).

57. Bursa Kadı Sicilleri B160 and 162, *passim.*

58. Faroqhi (1984a), pp. 279–80.

59. Gerber (1980), p. 237.

60. Faroqhi (1984b), particularly p. 217.

61. Uluçay (1985), p. 18.

62. [Seyyid Hasan], 'Sohbetname', Topkapı Sarayı Kitaplığı, Hazine 1426, folio 29b.

63. Ibid., folio 30a.

64. Berkey (1991), particularly p. 151.

65. Schacht (1982), p. 127.

66. Abou-El-Haj (1984), pp. 57–8.

67. Derin (1959), cf. also Feyzullah, trans. Türek and Derin (1969/70). In his autobiography the writer also provides some information about his married life.

68. Derin (1959), p. 102.

69. Kafadar (1992). The title 'Hatun' ('Woman') was still a term of respect in the seventeenth century.

70. Kafadar (1992), pp. 172–3.

71. Ibid., p. 174.

72. Ibid., p. 190.

73. Karamustafa (1994).

74. Kafadar (1992), pp. 170–1, 175. I am grateful to Christoph Neumann for his ideas.

75. Ibid., p. 190.

76. Gölpınarlı and Boratav (1991), pp. 50–1.

77. This is the problem which seems to have undermined the career of Zeyneb, a poetess and friend of Mihri Hatun; cf. Gibb (1900–1905), Vol. 2, p. 135ff.

78. cf. the article 'Mihri' (by Theodor Menzel and Edith Ambros) in *EI*, 2nd edn.

79. Ibid.; İz and Kut (1985), Vol. 2, p. 227.

80. İz and Kut (1985), Vol. 2, pp. 229–30.

81. Erünsal (1977–79); cf. also Kappert (1976), p. 88.

82. Such as those of Aşık Çelebi and Latifi; cf. also the passage in Gibb (1900–1905), Vol. 2, pp. 123ff.

83. Ibid., Vol. 3, p. 170.

84. Ibid., Vol. 4, pp. 150–9.

85. Ibid., pp. 152–3.

86. See the article 'Fitnat' (by Ali Canib Yöntem) in *İA*.

87. Baer (1983).

88. Goodwin (1971), pp. 396, 414; Arel (1975), p. 71; Uluçay (1980), p. 109.

89. Artan (1988).

90. Ibid.

91. Quataert (1986).

92. Helmecke (1993), p. 27.

93. Montagu (1993), p. 118.

94. Helmecke (1993), p. 27.

95. Ibid., p. 28.

96. Tezcan et al. (1980), p. 173.

97. Gerber (1982), pp. 237–8.

98. Helmecke (1993), p. 32.

99. Ibid., pp. 25 and 32.

100. Ibid., p. 20.

101. Quoted by Kafadar (1992), p. 171.

102. Montagu (1993), p. 88.

103. Friedrich Schleiermacher, 1798, 10th commandment in 'Katechismus der Vernunft für edle Frauen', in Schleiermacher (1984), Part 1, Vol. 2, pp. 154ff. I am grateful to Hadumod Bußmann and Wolfgang Birus for the quotation.

104. İz and Kut (1985), Vol. 2, pp. 229–30.

7. Architects, Foundations and Architectural Aesthetics

1. Hugo (1972), pp. 238–40.

2. For a new summary see Erlande-Brandenbourg (1989).

3. Yérasimos (1990).

4. Evliya Çelebi (1896/97–1938), Vol. 1.

5. Gdoura (1985), pp. 79ff.

6. Barkan (1972, 1979), Vol. 1, pp. 332ff.

7. Maury et al. (1983); Gaube and Wirth (1984), p. 113; İmamoğlu (1992).

8. See the article 'Malatya' (by Suraiya Faroqhi) in *EI*, 2nd edn.

9. Thus, the summer palaces of Ottoman princesses and dignitaries on the shores of the Bosphorus were always built of wood.

10. Öney (1971).

11. Konyalı (1964), pp. 629–91, Faroqhi (1976).

12. Yérasimos (1990), pp. 143ff.

13. Kuran (1987), pp. 298–300.

14. Ahmet Refik (1977), pp. 139–52ff.

15. Ca'fer Efendi (1987).

16. Faroqhi (1999).

17. Ahmet Refik (1977), p. 116.

18. Faroqhi (1990), p. 154.

19. Kuran (1987), p. 298.

20. Turan (1963).

21. The Ottoman buildings in Cairo constitute an exception; cf. Behrens-Abouseif (1989).

22. Kuran (1987), p. 286.

23. Ahmet Refik (1988), pp. 58–61.

24. Orhonlu (1984b).

25. See the article 'Istanbul' (by Halil Inalcık) in *EI*, 2nd edn.

26. See the article 'Waḳf' *EI*, 2nd edn. Many Muslim jurists believe that *wakf* (Turk. *vakıf*) already existed in the age of the Prophet Muhammad.

27. Barkan and Ayverdi (1970), pp. xxff.

28. Barkan (1980a); for a further discussion see Barnes (1980).

29. Barkan (1963), p. 252.

30. Çağatay (1971), pp. 50–1.

31. Mandaville (1979).

32. Barkan and Ayverdi (1970), pp. x–xxxvii.

33. Faroqhi (1984a), p. 31.

34. Barkan (1966), pp. 56–7; Kreiser (1986).

35. Akarlı (1985/86).

36. Gaube and Wirth (1984), pp. 146–7.

37. See Barkan and Ayverdi (1970), p. 117 on turning a private house into a foundation.

38. Faroqhi (1984a), pp. 23–48.

39. On Sinan there is a great deal of literature, cf. particularly Kuran (1987), pp. 39ff.; on Mehmed Ağa cf. Ca'fer Efendi, trans. Crane (1987), pp. 32f.

40. Sai Çelebi (1988), pp. 29–30, 72–3; Saatçı (1990), pp. 69, 83–5.

41. Konyalı (1964), pp. 461–82.

42. cf. the articles 'Manisa' (by Çagatay Uluçay), 'Tokat' (by Tayyıp Gökbilgin), 'Trabzon' (by Shihabettin Tekindağ) in *İA*.

43. Kuran (1987), pp. 46ff.; cf. also the article 'Ḵhurrem Sultan' (by Susan Skilliter) in *EI*, 2nd edn.

44. Bates (1978), pp. 254–5.

45. There are various opinions concerning the reasons why female members of the dynasty tended to build their mosques in Üsküdar. Bates (1978), p. 254, suggests that the women members of the sultan's family had to be content with sites in less visible areas which the ruler was inclined to concede to them. Peirce (1988), however, argues that female members of the dynasty preferred to have their foundations at the ends of caravan routes. This is also the view taken by Machiel Kiel, to whom I am indebted for a discussion of this matter.

46. Behrens-Abouseif (1989).

47. Kuran (1987), pp. 114ff. The full list of viziers who undertook building projects in their home towns would be a very long one.

48. Ibid., pp. 150–3, regarding the bridge.

49. cf. the article 'Mamluk' (by David Ayalon and P. Holt) in *EI*, 2nd edn.

50. There is a survey of this literature in Maury et al. (1983), Vol. 2.

51. Behrens-Abouseif (1989).

52. Başbakanlık Arşivi – Osmanlı Arşivi, section Mühimme Defterleri 33, p. 39, No. 82 (985/1577–78).

53. Kiel (1985), pp. 148ff.

54. Veselá-Premosilová (1978/79); see also Kiel (1985), p. 149.

55. Regarding painting, cf. Kiel (1985), pp. 273ff.

56. Anonymous (1974).

57. Faroqhi (1990), pp. 16off.

58. Mustafā 'Ālī (1978–1982), Vol. 1, p. 54.

59. Necipoğlu-Kafadar (1986a).

60. Barkan (1972, 1979), Vol. 2, p. 211.

61. Faroqhi (1990), pp. 140–1; Burton (1964), Vol. 2, p. 294.

62. Barkan (1972, 1979), Vol. 1, pp. 51, 348.

63. Bates (1978), pp. 258–9.

64. Necipoğlu-Kafadar (1986b), p. 107.

65. Barkan (1972, 1979), Vol. 1, pp. 351ff.

66. Ibid., Vol. 1, pp. 359–60, 381ff.

67. Faroqhi (1990), pp. 135, 140–1.

68. Barkan (1972, 1979), Vol. 1, pp. 336–43; Rogers (1982).

69. Delumeau (1975), p. 76.

70. Maury et al. (1983).

71. Faroqhi (1984a), p. 79.

72. Barkan (1972, 1979), Vol. 1, pp. 361–80.

73. Ibid., Vol. 1, pp. 364–5.

74. Faroqhi (1990), p. 130.

75. Ca'fer Efendi, trans. Crane (1987), pp. 64–76.

76. Evliya Çelebi, trans. Kreutel (1957), pp. 105–22.

77. Ca'fer Efendi, trans. Crane (1987), p. 20.

78. Ibid., p. 67; Necipoğlu-Kafadar (1986).

79. Ca'fer Efendi, trans. Crane (1987), pp. 73ff.

80. One of the most recent contributions to the literature on this inexhaustible theme is Allen (1993). Unfortunately I have been unable to see this work, which has been published only in electronic form.

81. Ca'fer Efendi, trans. Crane (1987), pp. 68–9.

82. Evliya Çelebi, trans. Kreutel (1957), p. 105.

83. Ibid., pp. 112–14.

84. cf. for example the Cecilia music by Henry Purcell and Georg Friedrich Handel, in which the organ has a special role to play among the instruments of the orchestra. The texts for Handel's music are by John Dryden.

85. Faroqhi (1992b).

86. Moreover, Evliya is not content to suggest that only Muslims and Christians possess, in their religious traditions, the basis for a common aesthetic sense. He also includes the Jews, pointing out that Psalter and Thorah are the holy books of the Jews; cf. Evliya Çelebi, trans. Kreutel (1957), p. 113.

8. Town Life: Urban Identity and Lifestyle

1. For an attempt to represent towns as being of minor importance in the economic and social life of Syria and Egypt, cf. Lapidus (1969).

2. Thieck (1985).

3. Denny (1970) and Arık (1976) discuss many townscapes of the late eighteenth century, as well as of later periods.

4. On the other hand, in certain periods, such as the seventeenth century, the sheikhs of the Mevlana convent came into severe conflict with the local taxpayers; cf. Gölpınarlı (1953), pp. 154–64.

5. This theme is a popular one in the Ottoman erotic literature of the eighteenth century, but also occurs in the writing of Evliya Çelebi: e.g. Evliya Çelebi (1896/97–1938), Vol. 9, p. 781, in a discussion of the women and young people of Mecca.

6. Marcus (1989), p. 316.

7. On the districts of Istanbul in the fifteenth century, see Barkan and Ayverdi (1970), pp. x–xiv.

8. It must be said that the complexity and mystery of the Ottoman town's layout has often been exaggerated, cf. Raymond (1985), pp. 214ff.

9. Faroqhi (1984a), pp. 23–48.

10. Orhonlu (1984a).

11. Marcus (1989), pp. 293–5.

12. Ibid., p. 294.

13. Ahmet Refik (1988), p. 40.

14. Oral information from the Institute for Restoration in the Faculty of Architecture, Middle East Technical University, Ankara, Turkey, for which I am grateful to Professors Ömür Bakırer and Emine Caner-Saltık.

15. Faroqhi (1987), p. 113.

16. Tülay Artan is working on a study of the princesses' palaces on the Bosphorus.

17. İmamoğlu (1992) includes several interesting examples.

18. On Cairo cf. Maury et al. (1983).

19. Faroqhi (1987), p. 113.

20. Arık (1976) provides a host of examples relating to this type of decoration.

21. Eldem (no date).

22. Faroqhi (1987), pp. 65–115.

23. cf. Marcus (1989) and Hanna (1991).

24. In Kayseri there was a heatable living room known as a *togana* which, in addition, served as a kitchen and larder. İmamoğlu (1992), pp. 49ff.

25. In many affluent homes the *selamlık* was appointed with particular splendour.

26. Faroqhi (1985/86).

27. This is clear from the estate inventories which exist for several Ottoman towns, cf. Barkan (1966).

28. Batári (1980).

29. Ibid.

30. Ibid.

31. Barkan (1949/50, 1951/52, 1953/54), part 1, p. 557.

32. I was able to see parts of these collections myself in 1972.

33. Ydema (1990), p. 123.

34. Ibid., p. 7.

35. Ibid., pp. 27ff., discusses the designs of the Anatolian carpets which appear in Dutch paintings. See also King (1983), p. 25.

36. On carpets featured in paintings by the Italian masters cf. Erdmann (1962).

37. Ydema (1990), pp. 31, 44.

38. Rageth (1999).

39. Mills (1983), p. 14.

40. Ibid., p. 16.

41. Ydema (1990,), pp. 48–51.

42. Faroqhi (1984a), p. 138.

43. King (1983), p. 26.

44. Oral information from a museum official of the 1970s (Museum of Antalya).

45. Koçu (1969), p. 152.

46. Faroqhi (1984a), p. 181.

47. Faroqhi (1976).

48. Raby (1986), p. 285.

49. Ibid., pp. 72, 98.

50. Ibid., pp. 28off.

51. For an example cf. İmamoğlu (1992), p. 110.

52. Braudel (1979), Vol. 1, pp. 259–62.

53. İmamoğlu (1992), pp. 83–4, says much the same of the houses in Kayseri, although that town is located in an area with a distinctly continental climate.

54. This comparison is based on Abdel Nour (1982), Faroqhi (1987), Marcus (1989) and Hanna (1991).

55. Marcus (1989), p. 282.

56. cf. the illustrations in Faroqhi (1987) and Hanna (1991).

57. Abdel Nour (1982), pp. 125–36; Marcus (1989), p. 294.

58. Hanna (1991), p. 57.

59. Marcus (1989), pp. 314–28, discusses this topic in detail.

60. Hanna (1991), p. 57.

61. Ibid., pp. 42–3.

62. Splendid houses belonging to Christians were by no means uncommon either in Kayseri at the end of the seventeenth, or in Aleppo during the eighteenth century; cf. Marcus (1989), p. 318.

63. Hanna (1991), p. 42.

64. cf. Arel (1982).

65. Ibid.

66. Faroqhi (1984a), pp. 275ff.

67. Ibid., p. 276.

68. Aktepe (1958a).

69. Dernschwam (1923).

70. Raby (1982), p. 81.

71. On the observations made by Evliya, cf. Faroqhi (1992b).

72. Evliya Çelebi (1897–1938), Vol. 9, p. 200.

9. Ceremonies, Festivals and the Decorative Arts

1. Eyice (1962/63). In the present volume, 'dervish convent' and 'dervish lodge' are used interchangeably.

2. Tanyu (1967) gives an overview of holy tombs in the Ankara area.

3. On the revival of the Bektashi shrine of Merdivenköy cf. Bacqué-Grammont et al. (1991).

4. Hasluck (1929).

5. Yérasimos (1990), p. 202.

6. There is a good example of a *meydanevi* at the Divan Edebiyatı Müzesi in Istanbul, the former Mevlevîhane of Galata.

7. Birge (1965), p. 176.

8. Barkan (1942a).

9. cf., for example, Evliya Çelebi (1896/97–1938), Vol. 9, p. 274.

10. Gölpınarlı (1953), pp. 391–3.

11. On this subject see Thévenot (1980), pp. 237ff., as well as the description by Dr Covel of the circumcision celebration of 1675; cf. Nutku (1972). With regard to the sixteenth century, cf. Reyhanlı (1983), pp. 55–8.

12. cf. Gökyay (1986).

13. And (1959) and (1982).

14. Babinger (1962a).

15. Nutku (1972), p. 42.

16. Ibid., pp. 72–3; And (1982), pp. 207–26.

17. Başbakanlık Arşivi-Osmanlı Arşivi, section Maliyeden Müdevver (MM) 4729.

18. On the construction of the *nahil*s cf. And (1982), p. 213.

19. MM 4729, pp. 5ff.

20. Ibid., pp. 14ff.

21. And (1982), p. 92, summarizes accounts which document the preparation of confectionary for the circumcision festival of 1582.

22. Ibid., p. 94.

23. Ibid., p. 92.

24. The *keyl* is a dry measure which varies from one place to another. A *keyl/kile* of 12.8kg was probably meant in this case; cf. Hinz (1955), p. 41.

25. On the regular expenditure of the palace kitchen cf. Barkan (1979); see ch. 11 for a discussion of eating and drinking outside court festivals.

26. Cf. Atasoy (1998); see also And (1982), p. v for a list of the pages reproduced in his book.

27. Mantran (1962), pp. 349–57.

28. Many excerpts from the text in And (1959) and (1982). See the unpublished dissertation by Atıl (1969) and her essay on the same topic: Atıl (1993) and most recently Atıl (1999).

29. Mantran (1962), p. 356.

30. cf. And (1982), Ill. no. 132.

31. Ibid., Ill. no. 26.

32. Ibid., pp. 227ff.

33. Haus-, Hof- und Staatsarchiv, Vienna, Turcica I, f. 89ff. (9.10.1720).

34. And (1982), pp. 214ff.

35. Nutku (1972), Ill. no. 39.

36. And (1982), Ill. no. 46.

37. Nutku (1972), pp. 46ff.

38. Ibid., p. 52.

39. Reyhanlı (1983), Ill. no. 100.

40. Necipoğlu-Kafadar (1986a).

41. And (1982), Ill. no. 60, cf. also his remarks on p. 68.

42. On this problem cf. Kreiser (1978), cf. pp. 200, where a similar, but not identical, miniature is reproduced.

43. And (1982), pp. 123ff.

44. Ibid., pp. 130–1.

45. Ibid., pp. 104ff.

46. Ibid., pp. 104–5.

47. Faroqhi (1990), pp. 53, 73.

48. And (1982), p. 115. On European fireworks, cf. also Kohler and Villon- Lechner (1988).

49. Hafız Hüseyin Ayvansarayî (1864/65), p. 140, claims that the air-filled 'clubs' of the festival stewards were invented by a certain Hüsameddin, and that this opened the way to a *ulema* career for the inventor. However, the details he provides are contradictory.

50. And (1982), p. 38, draws on the report by the Englishman, Dr Covel, who witnessed the circumcision festival of 1675.

51. Ibid., p. 198; however, the account he draws on here is not from a first-hand witness.

52. For French and English examples from the Renaissance period, cf. Yates (1985), pp. 127ff.

53. Busbeck, trans. von den Steinen (1926), pp. 64–9, praises Süleyman's regime as an absolutist one; his observations relate to a court garden party which he witnessed.

54. Goubert (1966), p. 108.

55. cf. the miniatures reproduced in And (1982) and Atıl (1993).

56. And (1982), pp. 227ff.

57. With regard to Sa'adabad, cf. the attempts at a reconstruction in Eldem (1977).

58. Castan (1989), pp. 434–5.

59. İnalcık (1973), Ill. no. 27.

60. Evliya Çelebi (1896/97–1938), Vol. 9, p. 54 mentions *mesire*s even for a small place such as Alaşehir.

61. And (1982), p. 38.

62. Başbakanlık Arşivi – Osmanlı Arşivi, section Mühimme Defterleri (MD) 6, p. 562, No. 1222.

63. Bennassar and Bennassar (1989), pp. 314–17.

64. Faroqhi (1981a).

65. MD 19, p. 260, No. 521.

66. Faroqhi (1991).

67. Reyhanlı (1983), p. 66.

68. And (1982), p. 98, although this information only dates from the nineteenth century.

69. Ahmet Refik (reprinted 1988), pp. 40–1.

10. Readers, Writers and Storytellers

1. The most famous such case is probably that of Pir Sultan Abdal, see Gölpınarlı (1953), pp. 99–103.

2. cf. Kafadar (1989).

3. Köprülü (1966), pp. 392ff.

4. This 'middle' zone, the meeting point of court and scholarly culture on the one hand and oral culture on the other, has been examined by, among others, Pertev Naili Boratav; cf. Boratav (1973).

5. Such colleges are to be found, for example, in an unpublished register of the religious foundations of Istanbul dating from 1546; see Barkan and Ayverdi (1970).

6. Başbakanlık Arşivi – Osmanlı Arşivi, section Maliyeden Müdevver (MM) 9771.

7. This was taught in several dervish convents, such as those of the Mevlevîs and the Nakşbendîs; cf. Chambers (1973). Gölpınarlı (1953), pp. 90ff., shows how the poetry of Mevlana Celaleddin was reworked by later Mevlevî poets.

8. Chartier (1982), p. 87ff.

9. This became clear from an inspection of the Bursa *kadi* registers B 160 and B 162, which relate to the 1730s. They are kept in the National Library in Ankara.

10. On the huge number of dervish convents in sixteenth-century Istanbul cf. Barkan and Ayverdi (1970).

11. Birge (1965), pp. 57–8.

12. Ibid., pp. 171–2, with details of Albanian Bektashis entering the order and marrying.

13. Barkan (1942a).

14. Thus, for example, the historian and writer Mustafa Âlî visited the main convent of the Bektashis and described his stay: Fleischer (1986), p. 167.

15. cf. Gölpınarlı (1967). El-Buharî (810–70) was active in the Hejaz and in and around Buhara. His work known as *Sahih* is one of the most treasured texts of this kind. Muslim b. el-Haccac (817–75) wrote a work with the same title, which is held in almost equally high esteem by the experts.

16. El-Gazalî (1058–1111) was a theologian, jurist, mystic and religious reformer who tried to achieve a creative synthesis of mysticism and theology, which had generally been seen as antitheses until his time.

Farid al-Din 'Attar (died at the end of the twelfth or beginning of the thirteenth century) was a poet and mystic writer.

Ibn 'Arabî (1165–1240), an Andalusian mystic, lived in Anatolia for a while. Some of his books have survived to the present day in Konya, via his son-in-law, Sadreddin Kunevî. Although Ibn 'Arabî was heavily criticized by some theologians, he was held in high regard in the Ottoman domain. After the conquest of Syria and Egypt (1516–18), Sultan Selim I ordered the construction of an important foundation at the tomb of Ibn 'Arabî.

17. Celaleddin Rumî (1207–73) moved from Balkh, today in Afghanistan, to settle in Konya in about 1217. There he became involved in mysticism, after meeting the dervish Şemseddin Tebrizî. Among the most influential of his works are the Mesnevî, a didactic text in verse, and his poetry.

Camî (1414–92) lived in Herat, where he composed both poetry and prose, many of the poems being mystic in character. Sultan Mehmed II attempted to persuade him to settle in Istanbul, and he was held in high esteem in Ottoman literary circles.

Hafız (c. 1325–c. 1390) lived in Shiraz and was the Persian master of the lyric form, with special emphasis on the gazel.

Sa'dî, who produced both verse and rhyming prose (between 1213–19–c. 1292), lived in Shiraz. His Gülistan ('Rose Garden') and Bostan ('Garden') are particularly renowned. A degree of scepticism, religious tolerance and 'everyday' morality figure among the elements of his work. Many of his coinages became part of Persian conversational language.

Kaygusuz Abdal (died 1415), perhaps a follower of Abdal Musa, whose tomb is venerated near Elmalı, was one of the founders of Turkish mystic poetry. His works are characterized by their zest for life, satire and irony.

Süleyman the Magnificent (Turkish Kanunî, 1494–1566) wrote poetry under the literary pseudonym of Muhibbî.

Nearly all the information in notes 15, 16 and 17 was taken from the corresponding articles in EI, 2nd edn. On Sa'dî see Rypka (1959), pp. 241ff., on Süleyman the Magnificent see the relevant İA article.

18. There is a survey of the major Mevlevî writers in Gölpınarlı (1953), pp. 128–50.

19. Ibid., pp. 109–10.

20. Ibid., pp. 132ff.

21. See the articles 'Niyazi-i Mısrî' and 'Ismail Hakkı' (by Franz Babinger and Günay Kut) in EI, 2nd edn. Niyazî-i Mısrî (1617/18–1694) was held in high regard as an inspired mystic, but exiled to Lemnos several times by the Ottoman government. Isma'il Hakkı (1652–1725) was a mystic, scholar and poet. His commentaries on older mystic writings take both linguistic and religious issues into account.

22. Elvan Çelebi (1984).

23. Ibid., pp. xxxivff.

24. Faroqhi (1981b), pp. 99ff.

25. Mehmed Birgevî (c. 1520–73), himself a Bayramî dervish and şeriat scholar, fiercely opposed all innovations and deviations from şeriat law. See the article 'Birgevî' (by Kasım Kufrevî) in EI, 2nd edn.

26. Bakî (1526–1600), army judge of Rumelia and one of the most important Ottoman poets. His elegy on the death of Sultan Süleyman (1566) became particularly renowned.

Famed for his poems in honour of many contemporary dignitaries, Fuzulî (c. 1480–1556) came from Iraq. He was a Sufi who avoided becoming involved in disputes between schools, and was particularly highly regarded by the Bektashis; cf. the relevant article in EI, 2nd edn.

27. The poet Nizamî Gencevî (c. 1141–the beginning of the thirteenth century), one of the greatest figures in Persian literature, wrote a romantic epic about Hüsrev and Şirin, which is regarded as one of the great works of world literature. There is an epic about Yusuf and Züleyha by Camî; cf. the biographies of these two poets in EI, 2nd edn.

28. For an example of an unpublished collection of legal pronouncements (fetva) see Düzdağ (1972).

29. Faroqhi (1981b), p. 100.

30. When I used this manuscript it was located in the Cebeci Semt Kütüphanesi, Ankara.

31. On this biography cf. Beldiceanu-Steinherr (1971).

32. Faroqhi (1979).

33. On Amasya as a residence of princes and the sultan, see Kappert (1976).

34. Only a small part of the legend is included in the printed edition of Vol. 2 (see Evliya Çelebi 1896/97–1938), but it is to be found in the manuscript Bağdat Köşkü 304 in the library of the Topkapı Sarayı, folios 346–9. This has recently been published in a full transcription: Evliya Çelebi (1999).

35. Gölpınarlı (ed.) (1958).

36. In the copy located in the Cebeci Semt Kütüphanesi the founding legend is on pp. 40ff.

37. Boratav (1973), pp. 37ff.

38. Gölpınarlı (ed.) (1958), pp. xxii–xxiii.

39. Kißling (1945–49).

40. Yérasimos (1990), p. 244.

41. Ibid., pp. 76, 128ff.

42. Ibid., pp. 77ff., 182ff.; cf. also ch. 1.

43. Gölpınarlı (ed.) (1958), p. xxiii.

44. Ibid., p. xxiii; Mélikoff (1975).

45. Kafadar (1989), p. 124; cf. also Zilfi (1977).

46. Cemal Kafadar has played a major part in this re-evaluation, and the following paragraphs are indebted to his work on the subject. See Kafadar (1989).

47. Ibid.

48. Osman Ağa, trans. Kreutel and Spies (1954).

49. Gökyay (1985); Kafadar (1989). The following remarks are also based on the first volume of the diary itself: Topkapı Sarayı Kütüphanesi (Istanbul), section Hazine 1426.

50. Kafadar (1989), p. 143.

51. On 'soul helva' cf. also Evliya Çelebi (1896/97–1938), Vol. 9, p. 590. From this text we understand that there was a certain moral obligation to accept the helva offered in the name of a deceased individual.

52. Topkapı Sarayı Kütüphanesi (Istanbul), section Hazine 1426, folio 24aff.; Kafadar (1989), pp. 143ff. On behaviour during times of plague, see Panzac (1985), pp. 280ff.

53. Topkapı Sarayı Kütüphanesi (Istanbul), section Hazine 1426, folio 27b ff.

54. Ibid., folio 28a.

55. Ibid., folio 28a, 29b. See also Kafadar (1989).

56. For biographical details see Gökyay (1985) and Kafadar (1989).

57. Topkapı Sarayı Kütüphanesi (Istanbul), section Hazine 1426, folio 29b.

58. cf., for example, ibid., folio 24a.

59. Beldiceanu-Steinherr (1961).

60. Ibid., pp. 13ff.

61. de Groot (1978), p. 61.

62. Beldiceanu-Steinherr (1961), p. 15.

63. Ibid., p. 12.

64. Ibid., p. 98.

65. Gölpınarlı (1953), pp. 108ff., 136ff. The autobiography is to be found in Süleymaniye Kütüphanesi (Istanbul), section Halet Ef.-Ilave No. 74, but the present remarks are based on Gölpınarlı's work only. Şahidî and Divane Mehmed Çelebi were evidently among those mystics who claimed that people who had attained a certain level of perfection needed take no account of religious laws, relevant only to the external, visible world. There were many supporters of this view among the Bektashi dervishes in particular.

66. Augustinus (1985).

67. Gölpınarlı (1953), pp. 77ff.

68. Zilfi (1986).

69. Kreutel (1971), pp. 273ff.

70. See the article 'Evliya Çelebi' (by Cavit Baysun) in İA.

71. Dankoff has published the report of this sojourn in an English translation with a commentary. See Evliya Çelebi, trans. Dankoff (1990).

72. Reference is to Volume 1 of his work on travel: Evliya (1896/97–1938).

73. Evliya Çelebi, trans. Kreutel (1957), p. 199.

74. Taeschner (1923).

75. Hodgson (1974), Vol. 1, pp. 324ff.

76. Köprülü (1966), pp. 380ff.

77. Ibid., p. 380.

78. Evliya Çelebi (1896/97–1938), Vol. 9, p. 273.

79. Ibid., Vol. 9, p. 275.

80. Ibid., Vol. 2, manuscript Topkapı Sarayı, Bağdat Köşkü 304, folio 279b–280a.

81. See the article 'hadjdj' (by A. J. Wensinck and J. Jomier) in EI, 2nd edn.

82. Evliya Çelebi (1896/97–1938), Vol. 9, pp. 3–4.

83. Köprülü (1966), pp. 319–20.

84. Kafadar (1989) describes these first-person narrators individually.

11. Food, Drink and Sociability

1. This chapter is based upon the excellent and informative article 'Matbakh' (by Halil İnalcık) in EI, 2nd edn. See also Faroqhi (1988), p. 55.

2. Faroqhi (1984a), p. 222.

3. Montagu (1993).

4. Nan-ı aziz is a term often used to denote bread in the source literature. The word aziz can mean both 'holy' and 'precious, esteemed'. On the part played by Ottoman cereals in the food supply of the Mediterranean region during the sixteenth century, cf. Braudel (1966), Vol. 1, pp. 517–47.

5. İslamoğlu and Faroqhi (1979), p. 416.

6. Evliya Çelebi, trans. Dankoff (1990), pp. 144–5.

7. cf. e.g. Evliya Çelebi (1896/97–1938), Vol. 9, pp. 97, 169, 359.

8. Gonzalez de Clavijo, trans. Markham (1970), p. 68.

9. Gökyay (1985), p. 60.

10. There is a somewhat different list of bread and pastries in Kütükoğlu (1978). For the early sixteenth century cf. Barkan (1942b), p. 331, where there are accounts for meals and baking.

11. Such ovens were also to be found in larger private homes.

12. Kütükoğlu (1983), p. 91.

13. Algar (1992).

14. Busbeck, trans. von den Steinen (1926), pp. 58, 110.

15. Ergenç (1975), pp. 160–1.

16. Kütükoğlu (1983), p. 92.

17. See, for example, Faroqhi (1988), pp. 53ff.

18. Evliya Çelebi, trans. Dankoff (1990), pp. 144–5.

19. Evliya Çelebi (1896/97–1938), Vol. 9, p. 777.

20. Evliya Çelebi, trans. Van Bruinessen et al. (1988), p. 170–1; Evliya Çelebi, trans. Dankoff (1990), pp. 144–5.

21. Faroqhi (1988), pp. 53–4; Evliya Çelebi, ed. Van Bruinessen et al. (1988), pp. 178–9.

22. Wild (1964), p. 246; Kütükoğlu (1983), p. 93.

23. Evliya Çelebi (1896/97–1938), Vol. 9, p. 126; Kütükoğlu (1983), pp. 93–4.

24. McGowan (1969).

25. Kütükoğlu (1983), pp. 91, 93.

26. On the *dirhem* equivalent, cf. Hinz (1955), p. 5. On Ottoman weights, see also İnalcık (1983).

27. Evliya Çelebi (1896/97–1938), Vol. 9, p. 25.

28. e.g. ibid.

29. Evliya Çelebi, trans. Dankoff (1988), pp. 144–5.

30. Kreiser (1975), pp. 236ff.

31. Kütükoğlu (1983), p. 94.

32. Evliya Çelebi (1896/97–1938), Vol. 2, p. 92.

33. Ibid., p. 93.

34. Faroqhi (1988), p. 67.

35. Doughty (1979), Vol. 2, p. 551.

36. Evliya Çelebi, trans. Dankoff (1988), pp. 144–5.

37. Caoursin, trans. Vatin (1997), p. 301. Nicolas Vatin was kind enough to draw this point to my attention. Kâtib Çelebi (1154/1732), p. 600.

38. Evliya Çelebi (1896/97–1938), Vol. 9, p. 25.

39. Ibid., p. 97.

40. Ibid., p. 338; Evliya Çelebi, trans. Van Bruinessen et al. (1988), pp. 178–9.

41. Evliya Çelebi, trans. Dankoff (1990), pp. 144–5.

42. Kreiser (1975), pp. 236ff.; Wild (1964), pp. 246–7 reports how partaking of the fruits of Antalya helped him recover quickly after severe illness.

43. [Hasan], 'Sohbetname', Topkapı Sarayı Kitaplığı, Hazine 1426, Vol. 1, folio 25a.

44. Osman Ağa, trans. Kreutel and Spies (1962), p. 21.

45. Faroqhi (1978), p. 60.

46. R. Jennings (1993), *passim*, includes a great deal of evidence relating to sugar production on Cyprus from the Ottoman conquest until 1640.

47. Kütükoğlu (1983), p. 98.

48. Reindl-Kiel and Kiel (1991).

49. Evliya Çelebi (1896/97–1938), Vol. 9, p. 114.

50. Kütükoğlu (1983), p. 99. In fact, Evliya maintains that there is another, more widespread sort of *sakız*; ibid., p. 126.

51. Evliya Çelebi, trans. Dankoff (1990), pp. 118–19. A jam is still made of carrots today in Iran, a piece of information for which I am grateful to Dr Eberhard Krüger of Munich.

52. Evliya Çelebi, trans. Dankoff (1990), pp. 144–5.

53. Evliya Çelebi (1896/97–1938), Vol. 9, p. 169; Busbeck, trans. von den Steinen (1926), p. 58.

54. Başbakanlık Arşivi – Osmanlı Arşivi, section Maliyeden Müdevver (MM) 4729.

55. Evliya Çelebi, trans. Dankoff (1990), pp. 144–5.

56. Kütükoğlu (1983), pp. 200, 316.

57. Evliya Çelebi, trans. Van Bruinessen et al. (1988), pp. 170–1.

58. Kreiser (1975), p. 237; Kütükoğlu (1983), p. 101.

59. Kütükoğlu (1983), p. 310.

60. Evliya Çelebi (1896/97–1938), Vol. 9, p. 590.

61. Mélikoff (1964). The following account is based on her article. On the consumption of sweets in dervish circles cf. Algar (1992).

62. On the history of this pudding cf. Algar (1992).

63. Faroqhi (1976); Algar (1992).

64. cf. the article 'Istanbul' (by Halil İnalcık) in *EI*, 2nd edn.

65. Evliya Çelebi, trans. Van Bruinessen et al. (1988), p. 170.

66. Raby and Yücel (1986); also Raby (1986).

67. Braudel (1979), Vol. 1, p. 179, emphasizes this aspect in relation to butter; Ahmed Refik (1988), p. 40.

68. Kafadar (1989), p. 143.

69. Referred to by Rombauer and Rombauer-Becker (1973), p. 18.

70. Montagu (1993), pp. 88, 116.

71. Evliya Çelebi, trans. Dankoff (1990), pp. 118–19.

72. [Seyyid Hasan], 'Sohbetname', Vol. 2, folio 67b.

73. Ibid., folio 62b.

74. Caoursin, trans. Vatin (1997), p. 301.

75. Evliya Çelebi (1896/97–1938), Vol. 9, p. 123; Evliya Çelebi, trans. Dankoff (1990), pp. 144–5.

76. Busbeck, trans. von den Steinen (1926), pp. 20, 27; Dernschwam (1923), pp. 101–3.

77. On these mercenaries cf. Akdağ (1963), Cezar (1965), İnalcık (1980).

78. Tietze (1942), pp. 187–90.

79. Yıldırım (1976).

80. Faroqhi (1981b), p. 56.

81. Kißling (1957); Anonymous (1980); Hattox (1988); Desmet-Grégoire (1991).

82. Faroqhi (1986a), p. 91.

83. Ibid., p. 89.

84. Faroqhi (1986b), p. 72; on Istanbul see Mantran (1962), pp. 209–10.

85. Raymond (1973/74), Vol. 1, pp. 131ff.

86. Kißling (1957), pp. 353–4.

87. Hammer (1834), Vol. 2, p. 503.

88. Tapu ve Kadastro Genel Müdürlüğü, Ankara, Kuyudu Kadime 171, folio 22bff. The *berş* mentioned here may have been laudanum, hemp or opium syrup.

89. Evliya Çelebi (1896/97–1938), Vol. 9, pp. 33–4.

90. MM 88, p. 81.

91. Kißling (1957) gives a sumary of Katib Çelebi's arguments.

92. Montagu (1993), p. 87.

93. Ibid., p. 88.

94. Abou-El-Haj (1991), pp. 44ff.

95. Lady Mary describes such a visit in a passage which has become famous: Montagu (1993), pp. 58–60; cf. also the commentaries by Melman (1992), pp. 77–98.

96. Evliya Çelebi (1896/97–1938), Vol. 2, p. 26.

97. Busbeck, trans. von den Steinen (1926), pp. 180–1.

98. Cantemir, trans. Tindal (1734), pp. 249–50; Jacob (1904).

99. Kafadar (1989), p. 143, quotes the maxim that, in respectable circles, one should avoid food prepared 'in the market' so far as possible.

100. Beldiceanu-Steinherr (1960), pp. 55–8.

101. With regard to salons and the etiquette attached to them in the second half of the sixteenth century, cf. Fleischer (1986), p. 23.

102. Montagu (1993), *passim*, e.g. pp. 53–4, 137–8.

12. Crises and New Beginnings, 1770–1839

1. This applies to Urfa, for example; cf. the article 'al-Ruha' (Ottoman and modern age) (by Suraiya Faroqhi) in *EI*, 2nd edn.

2. Genç (1984); Stoianovich (1960).

3. Aksan (1995).

4. Raymond (1973/74), Vol. 1, pp. 155ff.

5. Stoianovich (1960), p. 257.

6. Genç (1984); cf. also pp. 64–72.

7. Ibid.

8. Daniel Roche (1989), pp. 126–7, has shown that it was only rarely possible to enforce the import ban relating to Indian cotton materials ordered by both the English and French kings.

9. Fukasawa (1987), p. 133ff.

10. Stoianovich (1960), pp. 265–6; Sandgruber (1993), pp. 675–6.

11. Dermigny (1964), Vol. 3, pp. 249–50.

12. Paskaleva (1993), p. 1,050.

13. Tsirpanlis (1993).

14. Shaw (1977), p. 17.

15. Panzac (1992); Tsirpanlis (1993).

16. Todorov (1980), pp. 149ff., 163–5.

17. Roth (1993), p. 20.

18. Todorov (1980), pp. 217ff.

19. Skowronski (1993), pp. 137–9.

20. cf. İnalcık (1980), McGowan (1981); on the events of 1808 see Lewis (1968), p. 75.

21. Y. Cezar (1986), pp. 100–4.

22. Akarlı (1985/86).

23. As early as the seventeenth century, Koçi Bey criticized the expansion of religious foundations and their exploitation for private purposes: Barnes (1980), pp. 134ff.

24. Arel (1975), pp. 59ff., 69ff.

25. This ambivalence is also evident in Arel (1975), although this book has made a major contribution to the re-evaluation of eighteenth-century Ottoman architecture.

26. Goodwin (1971), p. 417.

27. Ibid., pp. 398–9.

28. Arel (1975), pp. 70ff.; Behrens-Abouseif (1992).

29. Shaw (1971), pp. 128ff.

30. Çeçen (1991), p. 117.

31. Müller-Wiener (1977), pp. 514–19.

32. Artan (1993–96) makes perceptive observations about the history of land use on the shores of the Bosphorus.

33. Anhegger (1991).

34. Ibid., pp. 29–30.

35. cf. the article 'Şeyh Galib' (by Abdülbaki Gölpınarlı) in *İA*.

36. Perot (1991), p. 20.

37. Anhegger (1991), p. 28.

38. Reproduction in Boschma and Perot (1991), pp. 26–7.

39. Veinstein (1976) gives a good insight into the exercise of power by the Karaosmanoğlu dynasty in the Aegean coastlands of Anatolia, based on French sources.

40. Goodwin (1971), pp. 400–1.

41. Ibid., pp. 404–7.

42. Jaubert (1821), pp. 44–74. Jaubert was confined to the citadel and therefore did not see the nearby Ibrahim Paşa Sarayı. However, he recounts that the palace had a bad reputation in the area because it occasioned extra charges on the hard-pressed local population. As early as 1805, the current head of the family returned to the citadel of Doğu Beyazit.

43. Arel (1993).

44. Ibid.

45. Eldem (no date), p. 71; Goodwin (1971), pp. 435–7.

46. cf. the photographs reproduced in Goodwin (1971), pp. 435–7.

47. For an example see Goodwin (1971), p. 267.

48. Renda (1989), pp. 70–1.

49. In drinking water fountains (*çeşme*) the water flows from a large tank which is filled through a water pipe. The *sebil* does not require piping since the water is presented in cups.

50. Laqueur (1993), Ill. Plate 14.

51. Renda (1989), pp. 73–4.

52. Illustrations: Goodwin (1971), p. 433 and Arık (1976), p. 87.

53. Renda (1989), pp. 78–86, where there is a general description of Ottoman mural painting.

54. Examples of mosque decorations in Arık (1976), pp. 27–85; these, however, date largely from the nineteenth century.

55. Renda (1989), p. 79.

56. Arık (1976), pp. 103–18; Arel (1986).

57. Arel (1986).

58. Lewis (1968), pp. 41ff.

59. cf. Cerasi (1986), who elaborates on this aspect from an architect's point of view.

60. Göcek (1987) offers a discussion of this text; see Mehmed Efendi, ed. Veinstein (1981) for a translation into French.

61. Ahmed Resmî (1303/1886), pp. 45–7. The following sections are very much indebted to Virginia Aksan's study of this historian and diplomat.

62. On Ahmed Resmî's assessment of the political situation, see Ahmed Resmî (1303/1886), pp. 39–40, 55ff.

63. Ibid., pp. 35–6.

64. Ibid., pp. 49–50.

65. On Ebubekir Ratıb cf. Uçman (1989). This essay includes an account of Ebubekir's visit to a theatre in modern Turkish characters (p. 158).

66. For examples of such so-called *göstermelik* landscapes cf. And (1975), p. 45.

67. I am grateful to Aykut Kansu, who is preparing a book about Ismail Beşe/Ismael James Bashaw, for information about that individual.

68. The historiographical debate about the French Revolution is both vast and continuing. An interesting contribution is Hobsbawm (1990).

69. Shaw (1971) describes the intricacies of these events in detail.

70. Ibid., pp. 249–89.

71. In *Hermann und Dorothea* Goethe expressed his disappointment with the way the French Revolution had developed. In 1792, he had regarded the revolution in a much more neutral way, appreciative of its global historical significance. Schiller was made an honorary citizen of the French Republic when Gironde was in power; he too was disappointed by subsequent developments. Beethoven initially dedicated his Third Symphony (Eroica) to Napoleon, but withdrew the dedication when Napoleon had himself crowned emperor.

72. This section is based on Beydilli (1984), which also contains an excellent discussion of the political background. See also Lewis (1968), pp. 53ff.; Shaw (1971), pp. 247ff.

73. D'Ohsson (1788–1824).

74. Cerasi (1986), pp. 9–10.

75. Holbrook (1992) gives food for thought along these lines.

13. Elegance Alafranga, Social Criticism and Tomatoes

1. On the political events of this period cf. Shaw (1977) and Castellan (1991).

2. Trumpener (1968); Ortaylı (1981).

3. Blaisdell, trans. Kuyucak and Dalgıç (1979); Shaw (1977), p. 223.

4. Trumpener (1968), pp. 5–7.

5. Davison (1973), pp. 38ff.

6. Findley (1989), pp. 142–3.

7. Shaw (1977), p. 172, regards the reign of Abdülhamid as the peak of the Tanzimat, but most historians assume that this period ends with the dissolution of the first Ottoman parliament in 1878. On the deposition and death of Midhat Pasha cf. ibid., p. 216.

8. Mardin (1962), p. 310.

9. Mardin (1988).

10. Shaw (1977), pp. 279ff.

11. Barnes (1986), p. 127.

12. Shaw (1977), pp. 221ff.

13. Lewis (1968), p. 45.

14. And (1972), pp. 102–3, 367. Ortaylı (1983) gives a clear picture of the problems confronting the Ottoman upper class of this period; cf. also Neumann (1994).

15. Evin (1983), pp. 85–7; Mardin (1974).

16. Reinterpretations of Greek and Roman art and literature were used as a vehicle for cultural change in the European 'renaissances' of the twelfth to thirteenth, fifteenth to sixteenth as well as the late eighteenth and early nineteenth centuries.

17. Evin (1983), pp. 9–21; Maştakova (1994).

18. I am grateful to Huri İslamoğlu-İnan for a discussion of this issue; cf. also Timur (1986).

19. Mardin (1974); Holbrook (1992).

20. Evin (1983), pp. 9–21, 127.

21. On this matter cf. Berkes (no date).

22. Selâhattin Hilâv in his introduction to Beşir Fuad (no date), p. 8.

23. İnalcık (1973), p. 185. Although Kâtib Çelebi had himself received an *ulema* education, he was out of sympathy with the extremists.

24. Barnes (1986), pp. 84, 118ff.

25. Chambers (1973).

26. İhsanoğlu (1987).

27. Deringil (1991).

28. cf. Özcan (1997).

29. Rıfat Osman (1989); Okay (no date), pp. 41ff.

30. The life-work of the poet Nazım Hikmet (1902–63) could be seen in this light.

31. Çelik (1986) is the basis for this section.

32. *Araba sevdası*; cf. Evin (1983), pp. 158–72, Moran (1991), pp. 57–67.

33. Dumont (1986).

34. Denel (1982), pp. 58ff.

35. Atasoy and Raby (1989), pp. 15–18 gives a good overview of fires in Istanbul; Çelik (1986), p. 55.

36. Çelik (1986), pp. 51, 167–8.

37. Ortaylı (1985), p. 45.

38. Çelik (1986), p. 46. Between 1865 and 1869 overall planning for the Istanbul region was also the responsibility of a commission composed of Ottoman bureaucrats; ibid., p. 63.

39. Seni (1994).

40. Duhani (1982).

41. And (1972), p. 100. With regard to the 'excursions' of an Ottoman lady of around 1900, cf. Dumont (1986).

42. With regard to women 'stepping out' in European cities of the late nineteenth century, see Walkowitz (1992), pp. 46–50.

43. Belge (1994), pp. 255–60, elegantly portrays these islands.

44. Erder (1976), pp. 239ff. and And (1972), p. 89, describe the autocratic methods by which Ahmed Vefik attempted to oblige the inhabitants of Bursa to attend performances at 'his' theatre.

45. Çelik (1986), pp. 153–63.

46. Ibid., pp. 49–81. Janet Abu-Lughod has invented the term 'urban apartheid' to denote this phenomenon: Abu-Lughod (1980).

47. Creatures composed of letters of the alphabet were popular in such circles; cf. Birge (1965), Ill. 5, 6, 8, 9. However, most of the surviving compositions of this sort probably date from the nineteenth century.

48. Öztuncay (1992); Beaugé and Çizgen (no date).

49. Beaugé and Çizgen (1993), pp. 222ff.

50. Ibid., p. 179.

51. Ibid., pp. 137ff.

52. There are beautiful examples in Duben and Behar (1991).

53. Renda et al. (1993), p. 249.

54. Beaugé and Çizgen (no date), pp. 200–11.

55. cf. the article 'Othmān Hamdī' (by P. and S. Soucek) in *EI*, 2nd edn.

56. Rona (ed.) (1993).

57. And (1983), pp. 118ff.

58. And (1972), pp. 217–18, 238–44.

59. Ibid., pp. 116–35.

60. Ibid., pp. 104–5.

61. Ibid., p. 253.

62. Ibid., p. 322.

63. Kütükoğlu (1986), p. 202, as well as the lecture given by the author on this theme. On p. 210 she quotes a letter in which the pasha assures his wife that he cannot conceive of anything other than monogamous marriage: 'So far nothing else has occurred to me, and may God forbid [the contrary].'

64. Koç (1993).

65. See the article 'Midhat Pasha' (by Roderic H. Davison) in *EI*, 2nd edn.

66. Chambers (1973) draws largely from this source.

67. Findley (1989) makes heavy use of this text.

68. The history of the press is not included here; on that topic see the article 'Matbuât' (by Vedat Günyol) in *İA*.

69. Strauss (1993).

70. See Eidam (1993) on the beginnings of publishing and bookselling in Bulgaria, about which much more is known.

71. Ahmed Resmî (1303/1886).

72. Strauss (1992), p. 327.

73. Ibid., pp. 314–15.

74. Redhouse (1921); Strauss (1992), p. 324.

75. Strauss (1992), p. 322.

76. Beşir Fuad (no date), pp. 59–60.

77. Strauss (1992), p. 323.

78. Kut (1994).

79. Beşir Fuad (no date), *passim*.

80. The study on this topic by Kerman (1978) includes a great deal of source material and, from this particular viewpoint, is most enlightening.

81. The writer Sezai is distinguished from other individuals bearing the same first name by the patronymic 'Son of Sami Pasha'. Surnames did not become obligatory until the 1930s. However, many writers of that period continued to sign their work with their first names only (Yaşar Kemal, Nazım Hikmet etc.). Among the newer generation which has entered literary life since about 1960, however, it has become more usual for authors to sign their work with both their first names and surnames. See also Beşir Fuad (no date), *passim*.

82. Kerman (1978), pp. 351–2; Özön (1985), p. 122; Kerman (1978), pp. 325–33.

83. Evin (1983), pp. 146ff.

84. Misailidis (1986).

85. Vartan Pasha (1991); Maştakova (1994).

86. Evin (1983), pp. 55–64.

87. Mardin (1974); Evin (1983), p. 157; Parlatır (1987).

88. Vartan Pasha (1991), p. 6.

89. Evin (1983), pp. 18–20, 32.

90. Emile Zola's novels also contained a message which could easily have led to a didactic style of narration; the author was, after all, concerned with the effects of inherited pre-dispositions on human destiny. However, he took care to imply his message, so far as was possible, in his story, without presenting it explicitly and in didactic terms; cf. also Evin (1983), pp. 173ff.

91. Ibid. pp. 33–5. However, Timur (1991), pp. 33–7, points out that, even before 1900, Hüseyin Rahmi Gürpınar defended women who attempted to realize their own ideas in erotic relationships.

92. On this issue see Mardin (1974) and Timur (1991), p. 38.

93. Ortaylı (1983), p. 179.

94. However, see Dumont (1986).

95. On the cultural problems which sometimes accompanied the arrival of French cuisine, cf. Mardin (1974), p. 430.

96. On the nationalist message which could be implicit in neo-Ottoman buildings of the early twentieth century, cf. Y. Yavuz (1981), pp. 110ff. On Ömer Seyfeddin's nationalism cf. Mardin (1974), p. 438.

97. The novel *Kurt Kanunu* ('The Law of the Wolf') by Kemal Tahir reflects the atmosphere of these years: Kemal Tahir (1969).

98. Berktay (1991), pp. 106ff.

14. In Conclusion

1. Osman Ağa, trans. Kreutel and Spies (1954 and 1962); Kafadar (1992).

2. Kuran (1987); Ca'fer Efendi (1987), Fleischer (1986); Evliya Çelebi (1896/97–1938).

3. Atıl (1993); And (1982).

4. Zilfi (1986).

5. Köprülü (1966), pp. 361–412.

6. Duby (1973), pp. 299–308.

7. Kafadar (1989).

8. Fleischer (1986), pp. 111–296.

9. Haarmann (1976).

10. Evliya Çelebi (1896/97–1938), *passim*.

11. Marcus (1989) draws heavily on the Aleppo Chronicle of Yusuf al-Halabî from the eighteenth century, which beautifully documents such local patriotism.

12. Naşūḥü's-Silāḥī, ed. Yurdaydın (1976), Ill. 8B and 9A; Evliya Çelebi (1896/97–1938), Vol. 1.

13. Evliya Çelebi (1896/97–1938), Vol. 1, pp. 484ff.

14. At the end of the eighteenth and beginning of the nineteenth centuries, when the Ottoman treasury was acutely short of money, entering a property in this register was probably sometimes also the first step towards confiscation.

15. Gran (1979), pp. 35–91; Thévenot (1980), pp. 237–48; Evliya Çelebi (1896/97–1938), Vol. 10, pp. 315ff., 393ff. and elsewhere.

16. İnalcık in his foreword to Cantemir (1973), p. 9. I am grateful to Christoph Neumann for a discussion of this issue.

17. Marcus (1989), p. 47, Raymond (1973/74), Vol. 2, pp. 483ff.

18. Vartan Pasha (1991).

19. Kafadar (1989).

20. Taeschner (1923), p. 32.

21. Lewis (1968), pp. 60, 83–9.

22. Lewis (1982), p. 39.

23. Bennassar and Bennassar (1989), p. 455.

24. Osman Ağa, trans. Kreutel and Spies (1962), pp. 34, 37 and elsewhere.

25. Bennassar and Bennassar (1989) show very clearly how religious differences manifested themselves in the everyday lives of people outside the political élites.

26. Hess (1978).

27. This question was first formulated in historical research by Lucien Febvre; see Febvre (1977).

28. Panzac (1985), pp. 279–311; Kafadar (1989).

29. This is the impression given by a cursory examination of the Bursa inheritance registers of the fifteenth and eighteenth centuries (National Library, Ankara).

30. Among the Ankara inheritance records of the seventeenth century there are, for example, few cases in which a man left more than one widow. However, no systematic study has yet been made of this topic.

31. Duben and Behar (1991), pp. 148ff.

32. This emerges from reading a Bursa inheritance register from the years 892–94/1487–89.

33. Topkapı Sarayı, Kütüphanesi (Istanbul), secton Hazine 1426, folio 25a.

34. Kafadar (1992), pp. 174ff.

35. Vartan Pasha (1991), p. 2.

36. Evin (1983), pp. 129ff.

37. cf. the article 'Akhlat' (by Franz Taeschner) in *EI*, 2nd edn. I am grateful to Hans-Peter Laqueur for kindly drawing my attention to this fact.

38. Grabar (1973).

39. Necipoğlu-Kafadar (1991), p. 14.

40. And (1982), Ill. 48–52.

41. Renda et al. (1989), pp. 63–8.

42. Beaugé and Çizgen (no date), p. 176.

43. Ibid., p. 181.

44. Ibid., p. 180.

45. Kafadar (1989), p. 135.

46. Osman Ağa, trans. Kreutel and Spies (1962), p. 21.

47. cf. in particular the work of Gülru Necipoğlu-Kafadar.

48. Chartier (1989).

49. Wunder (1992), pp. 261ff.

50. On this issue cf. the works by Artan.

Chronology

1240–42(?)	Revolt of the Babaîs. After the defeat, the fleeing *baba*s probably disperse all over Anatolia, founding dervish settlements in the process.
1248	Battle of Kösedağ establishes Mongolian control over the principalities of Anatolia.
1207–73	Mevlânâ Celâleddîn Rûmî.
1274	Death of Sadreddîn-i Konevî, the son-in-law of Ibn 'Arabî. He leaves an important library in Konya.
1312	Death of Sultan Veled, son of Celâleddîn Rûmî. He was one of the first to use Anatolian Turkish for literary purposes.
1362	Conquest of Edirne, which then becomes the main residence of the sultans until the second half of the fifteenth century.
1358–1416	Bedreddin, son of the Judge of Sımavna, Sufi, law scholar and, in the last part of his life, rebel against Sultan Mehmed I.
1391–95	Construction of the Mosque of Sultan Bayezid Yıldırım in Bursa.
1402	Battle of Ankara, Timur captures Bayezid I.
1419–21	Construction of the Green Mosque and its annexes in Bursa.
1453	Conquest of Constantinople (Istanbul) by Sultan Mehmed II, the Conqueror. The Hagia Sophia is turned into the Aya Sofya Mosque.
from 1459	Construction of the Topkapı Sarayı.
1463–70	Construction of the Mosque of Mehmed the Conqueror, together with theological schools, guest-house and other pious foundations.
1480	Gentile Bellini at the court of Mehmed II.
c. 1481	Surviving version of the Hacı Bektaş legend book (*Vilâyet-nâme*). An anonymous chronicler strongly criticizes the choice of Istanbul as the new imperial capital.
1489/90–1588	Sinan the Architect.
c. 1500	Mihri Hatun writing in Amasya.
1514	Selim I occupies Tabriz for a short period and imports many skilled craftsmen to the Ottoman Empire.

1516–17	Conquest of Syria and Egypt by Sultan Selim I. Mosques in the Ottoman style are henceforth constructed in these provinces. Many skilled craftsmen, particularly from Egypt, present in Istanbul.
1520/2–73	Mehmed Birgevî, renowned theologian and opponent of any innovation in religious practices.
1520–66	Reign of Sultan Süleyman ('the Magnificent', 'the Lawgiver').
1539	Sinan's appointment as chief architect to the sultan.
1539	Construction of the mosque complex of Haseki Hurrem.
1541–1600	Mustafa Âlî, historian and literary figure.
1543/44–1628/29	Mahmud Hüda'î, influential dervish sheikh.
c. 1544	Divane Mehmed Çelebi represents the 'enthusiastic' movement within the Mevlevî order.
1545	Mosque of Prince (Şehzade) Mehmed begun.
1550	Death of the dervish Şahidî, disciple of Divane Mehmed Çelebi and author of an autobiography.
1550–59	Construction of Sultan Süleyman's foundation complex in Istanbul (mosque, theological schools, hospital).
1562 (?)	Completion of the Rüstem Pasha Mosque, famous for its tilework.
1564 (?)	Construction of a series of aqueducts to supply Istanbul.
1565 (?)	Construction of the mosque of Princess Mihrimah, the daughter of Sultan Süleyman and Hurrem Sultan (Roxelane), sited in Istanbul at the Edirne Gate.
1565–72	Construction of the foundation complex of Sokollu Mehmed Pasha in Istanbul; the mosque is famous for its tilework.
1572–1638	Cyrillos Lucaris, Greek Orthodox patriarch of Istanbul, promoter of printing; as a theologian, he is sympathetic towards the Calvinists.
1574–75	Completion of the Selimiye Mosque in Edirne, zenith of Sinan's architectural career.
1582	Circumcision of the future Sultan Mehmed III celebrated amid great festivities which are documented in a book lavishly illustrated with miniatures.
1596	Return of Sultan Mehmed III after the victory at Mezökeresztes marked by great celebrations.
1597–1664	The sultan's mother, Safiye Sultan, starts the construction of the Yeni Valide Mosque (Bahçekapı), which is eventually completed by another sultan's mother, Turhan Sultan, in 1664.
1609–20	Construction of the Sultan Ahmed Mosque by Mimar Mehmed Ağa.

1609–57   Kâtib Çelebi, historian, bibliographer and geographer.

1610–after 1683   Evliya Çelebi travels through the Ottoman Empire.

1620–88   Seyyid Hasan, dervish sheikh and diarist.

1626–76   Sabhatai Sevi, from 1666 Aziz Mehmed Efendi.

after 1631   Demolition and reconstruction of the Kaaba after its destruction
                 in a flood.

c. 1642–43   Asiye Hatun, female Halvetiye dervish in Üsküb/Skopje.

mid-17th c.   Ali Ufkî Efendi records the pieces of music sung by the palace
                 pages.

1655–1716   Mustafa Naima, historian.

c. 1670–1745   Ibrahim Müteferrika, founder of the first printing press using the
                 Arabic alphabet to produce books in Ottoman.

1673–1713   Demetrius Cantemir.

1675   Great circumcision festival for the sons of Mehmed IV at Edirne.

1688   Osman Ağa, prisoner of war, begins an odyssey through Austria.

1702   Autobiographical writings of Şeyhülislam Feyzullah Efendi, the
                 former tutor to Mustafa II.

1708   Famous tulip festival at the palace.

1717–18   Visit of Lady Mary Wortley Montagu to Istanbul.

1718–30   Grand Vizier Damad Ibrahim Pasha from Nevşehir, the major
                 building patron of the Tulip Age.

1718–30   'Tulip Age'.

1720–21   Visit of the Ottoman ambassador, Yirmisekiz Mehmed Çelebi to
                 Paris.

1720   Splendid circumcision festival for the sons of Ahmed III. The
                 official record of the festivities is lavishly decorated with mini-
                 atures.

c. 1720   The painter Levnî is active.

1720   Theological school of Damad Ibrahim Pasha in Istanbul.

1726   Mosque of Damad Ibrahim Pasha in Nevşehir.

1734   Mosque, library and other foundations by Grand Vizier Hekimoğlu
                 Ali Pasha.

1755   Completion of the Nuruosmaniye Mosque, with baroque elements.

1757–60   Construction of the Ayazma Camii in honour of Mihrişah Emine
                 Sultan, mother of Sultan Mustafa III.

1757–99   Seyh Galib, Mevlevî sheikh and poet.

1759–63   Construction of the Laleli Mosque together with its foundation
                 complex.

1762	Library of Rağıb Pasha.
after 1767	Reconstruction of the Mosque of Mehmed the Conqueror and his mausoleum, destroyed by an earthquake.
1778	Construction of the mosque at the Bosphorus village of Beylerbeyi for Sultan Abdülhamid I.
1778–95	Mosque of the Çapanoğulları in Yozgat.
1780	Death of the poetess Fitnat.
before 1784	Construction of the Ishak Paşa Sarayı in Doğu Beyazit, near the Iranian border.
1787	Mosque of Şebsefa Kadın in Unkapanı/Istanbul.
1804	Mosque of Selim III outside Üsküdar.
1822–95	Ahmed Cevdet, historian, jurist and senior bureaucrat.
1828	Watchtower for fires: 'Beyazit Tower' (in the Istanbul district of the same name) over 50 metres in height.
1839	The Tanzimat ('[re]organization') period begins with the Decree of Gülhane.
1840–88	Namık Kemal, poet and bureaucrat, constitutionalist, journalist, historian and playwright. Leader of the Young Ottoman opposition against Abdülhamid II, uniting Islamic convictions with liberal doctrines.
1842–1910	Osman Hamdi, orientalist painter and museum founder.
1845	The first bridge over the Golden Horn, built by the Sultana Mother, Bezm-i Alem.
1850–1904	Şemseddin Samî, narrative writer, lexicographer and journalist.
1850–1912	Career of Basile Kargopoulos in Istanbul and Edirne, court photographer to Sultans Murad V (1876) and Abdülhamid II (1876–1909).
1851	A novel by the Armenian Vartan Pasha, *The Story of Akabi*, published in the Ottoman language.
1852–67	James Robertson (1813–88) and his brother-in-law, Felice Beato, operate a photographic studio in Istanbul.
from 1855	Renovation of the Istanbul port installations.
1855–1914	Ahmed Midhat, journalist, publisher and narrative writer.
from 1857	Founding of a local authority in Istanbul's 'Sixth District' (denoting Pera/Beyoğlu). Many improvements are made here, particularly after the fire of 1870: sewage disposal, street-lighting, land-register.
1858–98	Photographic careers of the Aliksan brothers, known professionally as Abdullah Frères.
1859	Şinasi's comedy *The Poet's Wedding*.

1864–1935   Fatma Aliye, literary figure and publicist, daughter of Ahmed Cevdet Pasha.

1865–69   The 'Commission for Street Reconstruction' straightens and widens many Istanbul streets.

1867–1914   Tevfik Fikret, poet, publisher of the important literary periodical *Servet-i Fünun* ('Wealth of Knowledge') and teacher at the French language state school of Galatasarayı Lisesi.

1870–1905   Career of the Swedish photographer Guillaume Berggren in Istanbul.

1870   Güllü Agop is granted a fifteen-year privilege for staging plays in the Ottoman language.

1872   Namık Kemal's romantic drama *The Fatherland or Silistre*.

1872   *The Love-Story of Talat and Fitnet* by Şemseddin Samî, one of the earliest Ottoman novels.

1874   First railway connecting Istanbul and Sofia, construction of the Sirkeci railway station.

1875   Opening of the 'Tünel', the underground railway between Galata and Pera (Beyoğlu).

1875   *Felâtun Bey and Rakım Efendi* by Ahmed Midhat, a satirical narrative featuring the young, superficially 'Europeanized' fop.

1879–82   Consolidation of Ottoman national debts. European creditors, organized into the 'Dette Ottomane', are accorded a significant say in the management of Ottoman financial affairs.

1884   Closure and destruction of the Gedikpaşa Theatre, run by Güllü Agop.

1889   Halit Ziya [Uşaklıgil]'s story *Forbidden Love*, first as a *feuilleton*, then as a book. This is considered the first novel to be a success in literary terms.

1908   The 'Young Turk' opposition forces Sultan Abdülhamid II to reintroduce the annulled constitution of 1876.

1909   Sultan Abdülhamid II is deposed.

Bibliography

Abdel Nour, Antoine (1982) *Introduction à l'histoire urbaine de la Syrie ottomane (XVIe–XVIIIe siècle)* (Beirut: Université Libanaise and Librairie Orientale).

Abou-El-Haj, Rifa'at (1982) 'The Social Uses of the Past: Recent Arab Historiography of Ottoman Rule' in, *International Journal of Middle East Studies*, 14, pp. 185–201.

— (1984) *The 1703 Rebellion and the Structure of Ottoman Politics* (Istanbul and Leiden: Nederlands Historisch-Archeologisch Instituut).

— (1991) *Formation of the Ottoman State. The Ottoman Empire Sixteenth to Eighteenth Centuries* (Albany, NY: SUNY Press).

Abu-Lughod, Janet (1980) *Rabat, Urban Apartheid in Morocco* (Princeton, NJ: Princeton University Press).

Adanır, Fikret (1982) 'Haiduckentum und osmanische Herrschaft. Sozialgeschichtliche Aspekte der Diskussion um das frühneuzeitliche Räuberunwesen in Südosteuropa', in *Südost-Forschungen*, 41, pp. 43–116.

Adnan-Adıvar, Abdülhak (1943) *Osmanlı Türklerinde İlim* (Istanbul: Maarif Vekilliği).

Ahmed Resmî (1303/1886) *Sefaretname* (Istanbul: Kitabhane-yi Ebuzziya).

Ahmet Refik (1932) *Onaltıncı asırda Rafızîlik ve Bektaşîlik, Onaltıncı asırda Türkiye'de Rafızîlik ve Bektaşîliğe dair Hazinei evrak vesikalarını havidir* (Istanbul: Muallim Ahmet Halit).

— (1977) *Türk Mimarları (Hazine-i evrak Vesikalarına göre)* (Istanbul: Sander).

— (1988) *Onuncu Asr-ı hicrîde Istanbul Hayatı (1495–1591)* (Istanbul: Enderun Kitapevi).

Akarlı, Engin (1985/86) 'Gedik: Implements, Mastership, Shop Usufruct and Monopoly among Istanbul Artisans, 1750–1850', in *Wissenschaftskolleg-Jahrbuch*, pp. 223–32.

Akdağ, Mustafa (1963) *Celalî Isyanları (1550–1603)* (Ankara: AÜ Dil ve Tarih Coğrafya Fakültesi).

Akın, Günkut (1993) 'Tanzimat ve bir Aydınlanma Simgesi', in *Osman Hamdi Bey ve Dönemi, 17–18 Aralık 1992* (Ankara: Tarih Vakfi Yurt Yayınları), pp. 123–33.

Aksan, Virginia (1995) *An Ottoman Statesman in War and Peace:* Ahmed Resmi Efendi 1700–1783 (Leiden: E. J. Brill).

Aktepe, Münir (1958a) 'Istanbul nüfus meselesine dair bazı vesikalar', in *Tarih Dergisi*, IX, 13, pp. 1–30.

— (1958b) *Patrona İsyanı (1730)* (Istanbul: İstanbul Üniversitesi Edebiyat Fakültesi).

Aktüre, Sevgi (1978) *19. Yüzyıl Sonunda Anadolu Kenti, Mekânsal Yapı Çözümlemesi* (Ankara: O. D. T. Ü. Mimarlık Fakültesi).

Alexander, John (1985) 'Law of the Conqueror (the Ottoman State) and Law of the Conquered (the Orthodox Church): The Case of Marriage and Divorce', in *XVIe Congrès International des Sciences Historiques, Rapports* (2 vols) (Stuttgart: Comité International des Sciences Historiques), Vol. I, pp. 369–71.

Alexandrescu-Dersca, Marie-Mathilde (1977) *La campagne de Timur en Anatolie* (London: Variorum).

Algar, Ayla (1992) 'Food in the Life of the Tekke', in *The Dervish Lodge, Architecture, Art and*

Sufism in Ottoman Turkey, ed. Raymond Lifchez (Berkeley: University of California Press), pp. 296–306.

Allen, Terry (1993) *Imagining Paradise in Islamic Art*, electronic publication (Sebastopol, CA: Solipsist Press).

And, Metin (1959) *Kırk Gün Kırk Gece. Eski Donanma ve Şenliklerde Seyirlik Oyunları* (Istanbul: Taç Yayınları).

— (1972) *Tanzimat ve Istibdat Döneminde Türk Tiyatrosu 1839–1908* (Ankara: Türkiye İş Bankası).

— (1975) *Karagöz, Türkish Shadow Theatre* (Ankara: Dost Yayınları).

— (1982) *Osmanlı Şenliklerinde Türk Sanatları* (Ankara: Kültür ve Turizm Bakanlığı).

— (1983) *Türk Tiyatrosunun Evreleri* (Ankara: Turhan Kitabevi).

Anhegger, Robert (1991) 'Melling et la Sultane Hadigé', in Cornelis Boschma, Jacques Perot et al. (eds), *Antoine-Ignace Melling (1763–1831), artiste-voyageur* (Paris: Editions Paris Musées), pp. 28–32.

Anonymous (ed.) (1974) *Symposium 'L'époque phanariote', 21–25 octobre 1970, à la mémoire de Cléobule Tsourkas* (Salonica: Institute for Balkan Studies).

Anonymous (ed.) (1980) *Le café en Méditerranée, histoire, anthropologie, économie, XVIIIe–XXe siècle* (Aix-en-Provence: Institut de Recherches Méditerranéennes).

Arel, Ayda (1968) 'Menteşe Beyliği Devrinde Peçin Şehri', in *Anadolu Sanatı Araştırmaları*, I, pp. 69–98.

— (1975) *18 Yüzyılda Istanbul Mimarisinde Batılılaşma Süreci* (Istanbul: ITÜ Mimarlık Fakültesi).

— (1982) *Osmanlı Konut Geleneğinde Tarihsel Sorunlar* (Izmir: Ege Üniversitesi Güzel Sanatlar Fakültesi).

— (1986) 'Image architecturale et image urbaine dans une série de basreliefs ottomans de la region égéenne', in *Turcica*, XVIII, pp. 83–117.

— (1993) 'Gothic Towers and Baroque Mihrabs: The Post-classical Architecture of Aegean Anatolia in the Eighteenth and Nineteenth Centuries', in *Muqarnas, X, Essays in Honor of Oleg Grabar*, pp. 212–18.

Arık, Rüçhan (1976) *Batılılaşma Dönemi Anadolu Tasvir Sanatı* (Ankara: Türkiye İş Bankası).

Artan, Tülay (1988) 'Architecture as a Theatre of Life: Profile of the Eighteenth-Century Bosphorus', unpubl. PhD Dissertation, Massachusetts Institute of Technology, Cambridge MA.

— (1992) 'Topkapı Sarayı Arşivindeki Bir Grup Mimari Çizimin Düşündürdükleri', in *Topkapı Sarayı Müzesi, Yıllık*, 5, pp. 7–55.

— (1993) 'From Charismatic Leadership to Collective Rule, Introducing Materials on the Wealth and Power of Ottoman Princesses in the Eighteenth Century', in *Toplum ve Ekonomi*, 4, pp. 53–94.

— (1993–96) 'Early 20th Century Maps and 18th–19th Century Court Records: Sources for a Combined Reconstruction of Urban Continuity on the Bosphorus', in *Environmental Design*, 13, 14.

'Aşık-Paşa (zade) (1959) *Vom Hirtenzelt zur Hohen Pforte, Frühzeit und Aufstieg des Omanenreiches nach der Chronik 'Denkwürdigkeiten und Zeitläufe des Hauses Osman vom Derwisch Ahmed ...'* trans. Richard Kreutel (Vienna, Graz and Cologne: Styria).

Assmann, Aleida, Jan Assmann and Christof Hardmeier (eds) (1993) *Schrift und Gedächtnis, Archäologie der literarischen Kommunikation* I (Munich: Wilhelm Fink Verlag).

Atasoy, Nurhan (1998) *Surname-i humayun* (Istanbul: Koçbank).

Atasoy, Nurhan and Raby, Julian (1989) *Iznik, the Pottery of Ottoman Turkey* (London: Alexandria Press).

Atıl, Esin (1969) 'Surname-i Vehbi: An Eighteenth-Century Ottoman Book of Festivals', unpubl. PhD Dissertation, distrib. by University Microfilms.

— (1987) *The Age of Sultan Süleyman the Magnificent* (Washington DC, New York: National Gallery of Art and Harry N. Abrams)

— (1993) 'The Story of an Eighteenth-Century Ottoman Festival', in *Muqarnas*, 10, *Essays in Honor of Oleg Grabar*, pp. 181–200.

— (1999) *Levni and the Surname: The Story of an Eighteenth-Century Festival* (Istanbul: Koçbank).

Augustinus, Aurelius (1985) *Die Bekenntnisse* (Munich: dtv).

Aymard, Maurice (1989) 'Friends and Neighbours', in *The History of Private Life*, Vol. III, *Passions of the Renaissance*, trans. Arthur Goldhammer (Cambridge, MA: Belknap Press and Harvard University Press), pp. 447–92.

Ayverdi, Ekrem Hakkı (1958) *Fatih Devri Sonlarında Istanbul Mahalleleri, Şehrin Iskânı ve Nüfusu* (Ankara: Vakıflar Umum Müdürlüğü).

Babinger, Franz (1962a) 'Mehmeds II. Heirat mit Sitt-Chatun (1449)', in *Aufsätze und Abhandlungen zur Geschichte Südosteuropas und der Levante* (Munich: Südosteuropa Verlagsgesellschaft), Vol. I, pp. 225–39.

— (1962b) 'Beiträge zur Geschichte der Malqoč-Oghlus', in *Aufsätze und Abhandlungen zur Geschichte Südosteuropas und der Levante* (Munich: Südosteuropa Verlagsgesellschaft), Vol. I, pp. 355–69.

Bacqué-Grammont, Jean-Louis et al. (1991) *Anatolia Moderna, Yeni Andadolu* (Istanbul, Paris: Institut Français d'Études Anatoliennes and Librairie d'Amérique et d'Orient).

Baer, Gabriel (1983) 'Women and Waqf: An Analysis of the Istanbul Tahrîr of 1546', in *Asian and African Studies*, 17, pp. 9–27.

Bağış, Ali Ihsan (1983) *Osmanlı Ticaretinde Gayrimüslimler, Kapitülasyonlar, Beratlı Tüccarlar ve Hayriye Tüccarları (1750–1839)* (Ankara: Turhan Kitapevi).

Barbir, Karl (1979/80) 'From Pasha to Efendi: The Assimilation of Ottomans into Damascene Society 1516–1783', in *International Journal of Turkish Studies*, I, 1, pp. 68–83.

Barkan, Ömer Lütfı (1942a) 'Osmanlı İmparatorluğunda bir İskân ve Kolonizasyon Metodu Olarak Vakıflar ve Temlikler', in *Vakıflar Dergisi*, II, pp. 279–386.

— (1942b) 'Bazı Büyük Şehirlerde Eşya ve Yiyecek Fiyatlarının Tesbit ve Teftişi Hususlarını Tanzim Eden Kanunlar', in *Tarih Vesikaları*, I, 5, pp. 326–40; II, 7, pp. 15–40; II, 9, pp. 168–77.

— (1949/50, 1951/52, 1953/54) 'Osmanlı İmparatorluğunda bir İskân ve Kolonizasyon Metodu Olarak Sürgünler', in *İstanbul Üniversitesi İktisat Fakültesi Mecmuası*, XI, 1–4, pp. 524–69; XIII, 1–4, pp. 56–78; XV, 1–4, pp. 209–37.

— (1951) 'Tarihî Demografi Araştırmaları ve Osmanlı Tarihi', in *Türkiyat Mecmuası*, X, pp. 1–26.

— (1963) 'Şehirlerin Teşekkül ve İnkişafi Tarihi Bakımından: Osmanlı İmparatorluğunda İmaret Sitelerinin Kuruluş ve İsleyiş Tarzına ait Araştırmalar', in *İstanbul Üniversitesi İktisat Fakültesi Mecmuası*, 23, 1–2, pp. 239–96.

— (1966) 'Edirne Askeri Kassam'ına ait Tereke Defterleri (1545–1659)', in *Belgeler*, III, 5–6, pp. 1–479.

Barkan, Ömer Lütfı and Ekrem Ayverdi (1970) *Istanbul Vakıfları Tahrîr Defteri, 953 (1546) Tarîhli* (Istanbul: İstanbul Fetih Cemiyeti).

— (1972, 1979) *Süleymaniye Cami ve İmareti İnşaatı* (2 vols) (Ankara: Türk Tarih Kurumu).

— (1975a) 'Feodal' Düzen ve Osmanlı Tımarı', in *Türkiye İktisat Tarihi Semineri, Metinler/Tartışmalar ...*, ed. Osman Okyar and Ünal Nalbantoğlu (Ankara: Hacettepe Üniversitesi), pp. 1–32.

— (1975b) 'The Price Revolution of the Sixteenth Century: A Turning Point in the Economic History of the Near East', in *International Journal of Middle East Studies*, 6, pp. 3–28.

— (1979) 'İstanbul Saraylarına ait Muhasebe Defterleri', in *Belgeler*, IX, 13, pp. 1–380.

— (1980) 'Türk Toprak Hukuku Tatbikatının Osmanlı İmparatorluğunda aldığı Şekiller: Imparatorluk Devrinde Toprak Mülk ve Vakıflarının Hususiyeti (I)', in *Türkiye'de Toprak Meselesi, Toplu Eserler*, Vol. I, ed. Abidin Nesimi, Mustafa Şahin and Abdullah Özkan (Istanbul: Gözlem Yayınları), pp. 249–80.

Barkan, Ömer Lütfi and Enver Meriçli (1988) *Hüdavendigâr Livası Tahrir Defterleri I* (Ankara: Atatürk Kültür, Dil ve Tarih Yüksek Kurumu).

Barnes, John Robert (1980) 'Evkaf-ı humayun; Vakıf Administration under the Ottoman Ministry for Imperial Religious Foundations 1839 to 1875', unpubl. PhD Dissertation, University of California, Los Angeles.

— (1986) *An Introduction to Religious Foundations in the Ottoman Empire* (Leiden: E. J. Brill).

Batári, Ferenc (1980) 'Turkish Rugs in Hungary', in *Halı*, 3, 2, pp. 82–90.

Bates, Ülkü (1978) 'Women as Patrons of Architecture in Turkey', in *Women in the Muslim World*, ed. Lois Beck and Nikki Keddie (Harvard: Harvard University Press), pp. 245–60.

Bayburtluoğlu, M. Zafer (1973) 'Kahraman Maraş'ta bir Grup Dulkadiroğlu Yapısı', in *Vakıflar Dergisi*, X, pp. 234–50.

Bayly, Christopher A. (1989) *Imperial Meridian: the British Empire and the World 1780–1830* (London and New York: Longman).

Beaugé, Gilbert and Engin Çizgen (no date, probably 1993) *Images d'empire, Aux origines de la photographie en Turquie, Türkiye'de Fotoğrafın Öncüleri* (Istanbul: Institut d'Etudes Françaises d'Istanbul).

Behar, Cem (1990) *Ali Ufkî ve Mezmurlar* (Istanbul: Pan Yayıncılık).

Behrens-Abouseif, Doris (1989) *Islamic Architecture in Cairo – an Introduction* (Leiden: E. J. Brill).

— (1992) 'The 'Abd al-Rahmān Katkhudā Style in 18th Century Cairo', in *Annales Islamologiques*, 26, pp. 117–26.

— (1994) *Egypt's Adjustment to Ottoman Rule, Institutions, waqf and Architecture in Cairo* (Leiden: E. J. Brill).

Beldiceanu-Steinherr, Irène (1960) *Scheich Üftāde, der Begründer des Gelvetijje Ordens* (Munich: self-publ.).

— (1971) 'La Vita de Seyyid 'Ali Sultan et la conquête de la Thrace par les Turcs', in *Proceedings of the Twenty-Seventh International Congress of Orientalists*, Ann Arbor, Michigan, 13–19 August 1967 (Wiesbaden), pp. 275–6.

— (1991) 'Les Bektaši à la lumière des recensements ottomans (XVᶜ–XVIᶜ siècles)', in *Wiener Zeitschrift für die Kunde des Morgenlandes*, 81, pp. 21–73.

Belge, Murat (1994) *Istanbul Gezi Rehberi* (2nd edn) (Istanbul: Tarih Vakfı Yurt Yayınları).

Bellan, Lucien-Louis (1932) *Chah 'Abbas I, Sa vie, son histoire* (Paris: Paul Geuthner).

Bennassar, Bartholomé and Lucile Bennassar (1989) *Les chrétiens d'Allah* (Paris: Perrin).

Berkes, Niyazi (1962) 'İlk Türk Matbaası Kurucusunun Dinî ve Fikrî Kimliği', in *Belleten*, XXVI, 104, pp. 715–37.

— (no date [probably 1978]) *Türkiye'de Çağdaşlaşma* (Istanbul: Doğu-Batı Yayınları).

Berkey, Jonathan (1991) 'Women and Islamic Education in the Mamluk Period', in *Women in Middle East History*, ed. Nikki Keddie and Beth Baron (New Haven: Yale University Press), pp. 143–60.

Berktay, Halil (1991) 'Der Aufstieg und die gegenwärtige Krise der nationalistischen Geschichtsschreibung in der Türkei', in *Periplus*, I, pp. 102–25.

— (1992) 'The Search for the Peasant in Western and Turkish History/Historiography', in *New Approaches to State and Peasant in Ottoman History*, ed. Halil Berktay and Suraiya Faroqhi (London: Frank Cass), pp. 109–84.

Beşir, Fuad (no date) *Ilk Türk Materyalisti Beşir Fuad'ın Mektuplar*, intro. Selâhattin Hilâv, ed. C. Parkan Özturan (Istanbul: ARBA Yayınları).

Beydilli, Kemal (1984) 'Ignatius Mouradgea D'Ohsson (Muradcan Tosunyan)', in *Istanbul Üniversitesi Edebiyat Fakültesi Tarih Dergisi*, 34, pp. 247–314.

Birge, John Kingsley (1965) *The Bektashi Order of Derwishes* (London: Luzac).

Blaisdell, Donald (1979) *Osmanlı İmparatorluğunda Avrupa Malî Denetimi 'Düyunuumumiye'*, trans. H. A. Kuyucak and Ali İhsan Dalgıç (Istanbul: Doğu-Batı Yayınları).

Bode, Wilhelm von and Ernst Kühnel (1984) *Antique Rugs from the Near East*, trans. and ed. Charles Grant Ellis (London: Bell and Hyman).

Bombaci, Alessio (1968) *Histoire de la littérature turque*, trans. Irène Mélikoff (Paris: C. Klincksieck).

Boratav, Pertev Naili (1973) *100 Soruda Türk Halk Edebiyatı* (2nd edn) (Istanbul: Gerçek Yayınevi).

Boratav, Pertev Naili and Gölpınarlı Abdülbakî (1943) *Pir Sultan Abdal* (Ankara: Ankara Üniversitesi Dil ve Tarih-Coğrafya Fakültesi).

Boschma, Cornelis, Jacques Perot et al. (eds) (1991) *Antoine-Ignace Melling (1763–1831), artiste-voyageur* (Paris: Editions Paris Musées).

Braude, Benjamin (1982) 'Foundation Myths of the Millet System', in *Christians and Jews in the Ottoman Empire*, ed. Benjamin Braude and Bernard Lewis (2 vols) (New York and London: Holmes and Meier), Vol. I, pp. 69–88.

Braudel, Fernand (1966) *La Méditerranée et le monde méditerranéen à l'époque de Philippe II* (2 vols; 2nd edn) (Paris: Armand Colin).

— (1979) *Civilization matérielle, économie et capitalisme* (3 vols) (Paris: Armand Colin).

Brummett, Palmira (1991) 'Competition and Coincidence: Venetian Trading Interests and Ottoman Expansion in the Early Sixteenth Century Levant', in *New Perspectives on Turkey*, 5–6, pp. 29–52.

Burton, Richard (1964) *Personal Narrative of a Pilgrimage to al-Madinah & Meccah* (2 vols) (New York: Dover Publications).

Busbeck, Ogier Ghiselin von (1926) *Vier Briefe aus der Türkei*, trans. and annotated Wolfram von den Steinen (Erlangen: Verlag der Philosophischen Akademie).

Cacaoğlu Nur el-Din (1959) *Kırşehir Emiri Caca oğlu Nur el-Din'in 1272 Tarihli Arapça-Moğolca Vakfiyesi*, ed. Ahmet Temir (Ankara: Türk Tarih Kurumu).

[Ca'fer Efendi], Howard Crane (ed.) (1987) *Risāle-i mi'māriyye, an Early-Seventeenth-century Ottoman Treatise on Architecture* (Leiden: E. J. Brill).

Çağatay, Neşet (1971) 'Osmanlı İmparatorluğunda Rıba-Faiz Konusu Para Vakıfları ve Bankacılık', in *Vakıflar Dergisi*, IX, pp. 39–57.

Cahen, Claude (1969) 'Baba Ishaq, Baba Ilyas, Hadjdji Bektash et quelques autres', in *Turcica*, I, pp. 53–64.

— (1988) *La Turquie pré-ottomane* (Istanbul and Paris: Institut Français d'Etudes Anatoliennes).

Cantemir, Demetrius (1734) *The History of the Growth and Decay of the Ottoman Empire*, trans. N. Tindal (London: John James and Paul Knapton).

— (1743) *Histoire de l'Empire Othoman où se voyent les causes de son aggrandissement et de sa décadence*, trans. M. de Joncquières (4 vols) (Paris: Huart).

— (1973) *Dimitrie Cantemir, Historian of South East European and Oriental Civilizations, Extracts from 'The History of the Ottoman Empire'*, ed. Alexandru Dutu and Paul Cernovodeanu, foreword by Halil Inalcık (Bucharest: Association Internationale d'Études du Sud-Est Européen).

Caoursin, Guillaume (1997) 'De casu regis Zizimi', in *Sultan Djem, Un prince ottoman d'après deux sources contemporaines: Vakî'ât-ı Sultân Cem, Œuvres de Guillaume Caoursin*, trans. Nicolas Vatin (Ankara: Tarih Kurumu).

Castan, Nicole (1989) 'The Public and the Private', in *History of Private Life*, Vol. III, ed. Philippe Ariès and Roger Chartier, trans. Arthur Goldhammer (Cambridge MA: Belknap), pp. 403–46.

Castellan, Georges (1991) *Histoire des Balkans, XIVᵉ–XXᵉ siècle* (Paris: Fayard).

Çeçen, Kâzım (1991) *Istanbul'un Vakıf Sularından Halkalı Suları* (Istanbul Büyükşehir Belediyesi and İSKİ).

Çelik, Zeynep (1986) *The Remaking of Istanbul, Portrait of an Ottoman City in the Nineteenth Century* (Seattle and London: University of Washington Press).

Cerasi, Maurice (1986) *La città del Levante, Civiltà urbana e architettura sotto gli Ottomani nei secoli XVIII–XIX* (Milan: Jaca Book).

Cezar, Mustafa (1965) *Osmanlı Tarihinde Levendler* (Istanbul: İstanbul Güzel Sanatlar Akademisi).

Cezar, Yavuz (1986) *Osmanlı Maliyesinde Bunalım ve Değişim Dönemi (XVIII. yydan Tanzimat'a Mali Tarih)* (Istanbul: Alan Yayıncılık).

Chambers, Richard (1973) 'The Education of a Nineteenth-century Ottoman *alim*, Ahmed Cevdet Paşa', in *International Journal of Middle East Studies*, 4, pp. 440–64.

Chartier, Roger (1982) *Lectures et lecteurs dans la France d'Ancien Régime* (Paris: Editions du Seuil).

Chartier, Roger (ed.) (1989) *A History of Private Life*, Vol. 3, *Passions of the Renaissance*, trans. by Arthur Goldhammer (Cambridge, MA and London: Belknap Press of Harvard University Press).

Cirkovic, Sima (1986) 'Die östlichen Teile Jugoslawiens 1350–1650', in *Handbuch der europäischen Wirtschafts- und Sozialgeschichte*, ed. Wolfram Fischer and Hermann Kellenbenz (Stuttgart: Klett Cotta), Vol. I, pp. 1149–87.

Çizakça, Murat (1985) 'Incorporation of the Middle East into the European World Economy', in *Review*, VIII, 3, pp. 353–78.

— (1987) 'Price History and the Bursa Silk Industry: A Study in Ottoman Industrial Decline, 1550–1650', in *The Ottoman Empire and the World Economy*, ed. Huri İslamoğlu-İnan (Cambridge and Paris: Cambridge University Press and Maison des Sciences de l'Homme), pp. 247–61.

— (1996) *A Comparative History of Business and Finance: Islamic World and the West, from the Seventh Century to the Present* (Leiden: E. J. Brill).

Clogg, Richard (1982) 'The Greek Millet in the Ottoman Empire', in *Christians and Jews in the Ottoman Empire*, ed. Benjamin Braude and Bernard Lewis (2 vols) (New York and London: Homes and Meier), Vol. I, pp. 185–208.

Çulpan, Cevdet (1975) *Türk Taş Köprüleri, Ortaçağdan Osmanlı Devri Sonuna kadar* (Ankara: Türk Tarih Kurumu).

Cvetkova, Bistra (1963) 'Sur certaines réformes du régime foncier au temps de Mehmet II', in *Journal of the Economic and Social History of the Orient*, VI, pp. 104–20.

Dall'Oglio, Marino (1978) 'Transylvanian Rugs – Some Considerations and Opinions', in *Halı*, I, 3, pp. 274–7.

Dalsar, Fahri (1960) *Türk Sanayi ve Ticaret Tarihinde Bursa'da İpekçilik* (Istabul: İstanbul Üniversitesi İktisat Fakültesi).

Danişmend, Ismal'il Hami (1971) *Izahlı Osmanlı Tarihi Kronolojisi* (5 vols) (Istanbul: Türkiye Yayınevi).

Davison, Roderic H. (1973) *Reform in the Ottoman Empire 1856–1876* (2nd edn) (New York: Gordian Press).

Defoe, Daniel (1975) *Robinson Crusoe* (Munich and Zurich: Winkler Verlag).

Delumeau, Jean (1967, 1973) *La civilisation de la Renaissance* (Paris: Arthaud).

— (1973) *Naissance et affirmation de la Réforme* (Paris: PUF).

— (1975) *Rome au XVIe siècle* (Paris: Hachette).

— (1977) *Catholicism between Luther and Voltaire: a New View of the Counter-Reformation*, intro. John Bossy (London and Philadelphia: Burns & Oates and Westminster Press).

Denel, Serim (1982) *Batılılaşma Sürecinde Istanbul'da Tasarım ve Dış Mekanlarda Değişim ve Nedenleri* (Ankara: ODTÜ Mimarlık Fakültesi).

Denny, Walter B. (1970) 'A Sixteenth-Century Architectural Plan of Istanbul', in *Ars Orientalis*, 8, pp. 49–63.

Derin, Fahri (1959), 'Şeyhülislam Feyzullah Efendi'nin Nesebi Hakkında bir Risale', in *Tarih Dergisi*, X, 14, pp. 97–103.

Deringil, Selim (1991) 'Legitimacy Structures in the Ottoman State: The Reign of Abdülhamid II (1876–1909)', in *International Journal of Middle East Studies*, 23, 3, pp. 345–59.

Dermigny, Louis (1964) *La Chine et l'Occident, Le commerce à Canton au XVIIIe siècle 1719–1833* (3 vols) (Paris: SEVPEN).

Dernschwam, Hans (1923) *Tagebuch einer Reise nach Konstantinopel und Kleinasien (1553–55)*, ed. and annotated Franz Babinger, from original text in the Fugger archive (Munich and Leipzig: Duncker und Humblot).

Desmet-Grégoire, Helène (1991) *Contribution au thème du et des cafés dans les sociétés du Proche-Orient*, Cahiers de l'IREMAM (Aix and Marseilles: Centre National de la Recherche Scientifique).

Dilger, Konrad (1967) *Untersuchungen zur Geschichte des osmanischen Hofzeremoniells im 15. und 16. Jahrhundert* (Munich: Dr Rudolf Trofenik).

D'Ohsson, Mouradjea (1788–1824) *Tableau général de l'Empire Ottoman* (2nd edn; 7 vols) (Paris: L'Imprimerie de Monsieur and Firmin Didot).

Doughty, Charles M. (1979) *Travels in Arabia Deserta*, intro. T. E. Lawrence (New York: Dover Publications).

Duben, Alan and Cem Behar (1991) *Istanbul Households, Marriage, Family and Fertility 1880–1940* (Cambridge: Cambridge University Press).

Duby, Georges (1973) *Hommes et structures du Moyen âge* (Paris and The Hague: Mouton).

Duby, Georges and Michel Balard (eds) (1991) *L'histoire médiévale en France, bilan et perspectives* (Paris: Société des Historiens Médiévistes de l'Enseignement Supérieur and Editions du Seuil).

Duhani, Said Naum (1982) *Eski Insanlar, Eski Evler, XIX Yüzyılda Beyoğlu'nun Sosyal Topografisi*, trans. Cemal Süreyya (Istanbul: Türkiye Turing ve Otomobil Kurumu).

Dumont, Paul (1986) 'Said Bey. The Everyday Life of an Istanbul Townsman at the Beginning of the XXth Century', in *Osmanistische Studien zur Wirtschafts- und Sozialgeschichte in memoriam Vančo Boškov*, ed. Hans Georg Majer (Wiesbaden: Otto Harrassowitz), pp. 1–16.

Düzdağ, M. Ertuğrul (1972) *Şeyhülislam Ebusuud Efendi Fetvaları Işığında 16. Asır Türk Hayatı* (Istanbul: Enderun).

Eflakî, Ahmet (1973) *Ariflerin Menkıbeleri*, trans. Tahsin Yazıcı (Istanbul: Hürriyet Yayınları).

EI (1960–) *The Encyclopedia of Islam* (New York edn) (Leiden: E. J. Brill).

Eickhoff, Ekkehard (1992) *Venedig, Wien und die Osmanen, Umbruch in Südosteuropa 1645–1700* (2nd edn) (Stuttgart: Klett-Cotta).

Eidam, Liliana (1993) 'Der Weg zur Professionalismus: Bulgarische Popularautoren 1878–1944', in *Südosteuropäische Popularliteratur im 19. und 20. Jahrhundert*, ed. Klaus Roth (Münchner Vereinigung für Volkskunde und Südosteuropa-Gesellschaft), pp. 97–110.

Eldem, Sedad Hakkı (1977) *Sa'dabad* (Istanbul: Kültür Bakanlığı).

— (no date) *Türk evi plan tipleri* (Istanbul: Istanbul Üniversitesi Mimarlık Fakültesi).

Elvan Çelebi (1984) *Menakıbu'l-kudsiyye fi Menasıbi'l-ünsiyye, Baba İlyas-ı Horasânî ve Sülâlesinin Menkabevî Tarihi*, ed. Ismail Erünsal and Ahmet Yaşar Ocak (Istanbul: İstanbul Üniversitesi Edebiyat Fakültesi).

Ennen, Edith (1991) *Frauen im Mittelalter* (4th edn) (Munich: C. H. Beck).

Erder, Leila (1975) 'The Measurement of Preindustrial Population Changes: The Ottoman Empire from the 15th to the 16th Century', in *Middle Eastern Studies*, XI, 3, pp. 284–301.

— (1976) 'The Making of Industrial Bursa: Economic Activity and Population in a Turkish City 1835–1975', unpubl. PhD Dissertation, Princeton University.

Erdmann, Kurt (1961) *Das anatolische Karavansaray des 13. Jahrhunderts* (Berlin: Gebrüder Mann).

— (1962) *Europa und der Orientteppich* (Berlin and Mainz: Florian Kupferberg).

Ergenç, Özer (1975) '1600–1615 Yılları Arasında Ankara İktisadi Tarihine Ait Araştırmalar', in *Türkiye İktisat Tarihi Semineri, Metinler-Tartışmalar ...*, ed. Osman Okyar and Ünal Nalbantoğlu (Ankara: Hacettepe Üniversitesi).

Erim, Neşe (1991) 'Trade, Traders and the State in Eighteenth Century Erzurum', in *New Perspectives on Turkey*, 5–6, pp. 123–50.

Erlande-Brandenburg, Alain (1989) *La Cathédrale* (Paris: Fayard).

Erünsal, Ismail E. (1977–79) 'Türk Edebiyatı Tarihine Kaynak Olarak Arşivlerin Değeri', in *Türkiyat Mecmuası*, XIX, pp. 213–22.

Evin, Ahmet Ö. (1983) *Origins and Development of the Turkish Novel* (Minneapolis: Bibliotheca Islamica).

Evliya Çelebi (1896/97–1938) *Seyahatnamesi* (Istanbul: İkdam and elsewhere).

— (1957) *Im Reiche des Goldenen Apfels, Des türkischen Weltenbummlers Evliya Çelebi denkwürdige Reise in das Giaurenland und in die Stadt und Festung Wien anno 1665*, trans. and commentary Richard F. Kreutel (Graz: Verlag Styria).

— (1999) *Evliya Çelebi Seyahatnamesi, Topkapı Sarayı Bağdat 304 Yazmasının Transkripsyonu, Dizini*, 2. Kitap, ed. Zekerya Kurşun, Seyit Ali Kahraman, Yücel Dağlı (Istanbul: Yapı ve Kredi Yayinlari).

[Evliya Çelebi] (1987) *Im Reiche des Goldenen Apfels ...* , trans. with commentary Richard F. Kreutel, greatly extended edition produced by Erich Prokosch and Karl Teply (Graz, Vienna and Cologne: Styria).

— (1988) *Evliya Çelebi in Diyarbekir*, ed. and trans. Van Bruinessen et al. (Leiden: E. J. Brill).

— (1990) *Evliya Çelebi in Bitlis, the Relevant Sections of the Seyahatname*, trans. and ed. with commentary and introduction Robert Dankoff (Leiden: E. J. Brill).

— (1991) *The Intimate Life of an Ottoman Statesman, Melek Ahmed Paşa (1588–1662) as Portrayed in Evliya Çelebi's Book of Travels*, trans. and intro. Robert Dankoff and Rhoads Murphey (Albany, NY: SUNY Press).

Eyice, Semavi (1962/63) 'İlk Osmanlı Devrinin Dini-İçtimai bir Müessesesi, Zaviyeler ve Zaviyeli Camiler', *İstanbul Üniversitesi İktisat Fakültesi Mecmuası*, 23, 1–2, pp. 3–80.

Farge, Arlette (1992) *Dire et mal dire. L'opinion publique au XVIIIe siècle* (Paris: Editions du Seuil).

Faroqhi, Suraiya (1971) 'Der Aufstand des Yaḥya ibn Yaḥya al-Suwaydī', in *Der Islam*, 47, pp. 67–92.

— (1976) 'The *tekke* of Hacı Bektaş: Social Position and Economic Activities', in *International Journal of Middle East Studies*, 7, pp. 28–69.

— (1978) 'The Early History of the Balkan Fairs', in *Südost-Forschungen*, XXXVII, pp. 50–68.

— (1979) 'The Life Story of an Urban Saint in the Ottoman Empire', in *Tarih Dergisi*, XXXII, pp. 655–78, 1,009–18.

— (1980) 'Textile Production in Rumeli and the Arab Provinces: Geographical Distribution and Internal Trade (1560–1650)', in *Osmanlı Araştırmaları*, I, pp. 61–83.

— (1981a) 'Seyyid Gazi Revisited: The Foundation as Seen Through Sixteenth and Seventeenth-century Documents', in *Turcica*, XIII, pp. 90–122.

— (1981b) *Der Bektaschi-Orden in Anatolien (vom späten fünfzehnten Jarhhundert bis 1826)* (Vienna: Verlag des Instituts für Orientalistik).

— (1984a) *Towns and Townsmen of Ottoman Anatolia, Trade, Crafts and Food Production in an Urban Setting* (Cambridge: Cambridge University Press).

— (1984b) 'Mohair Manufacture and Mohair Workshops in Seventeenth Century Ankara', in *İstanbul Üniversitesi İktisat Fakültesi Mecmuası*, 41, 1–4, Ord. *Prof. Ömer Lütfi Barkan'a Armağan*, pp. 211–36.

— (1985/86) 'Stadt-Landbeziehungen und die regionale Organisation im osmanischen Anatolien des 16.-17. Jahrhunderts', in *Jahrbuch zur Geschichte und Gesellschaft des Vorderen und Mittleren Orients* (Berlin: Edition Parabolis), pp. 137–63.

— (1986a) 'Coffee and Spices: Official Ottoman Reactions to Venetian-Egyptian Trade in the Later Sixteenth Century', in *Wiener Zeitschrift für die Kunde des Morgenlandes*, 76, pp. 87–93.

— (1986b) 'Town Officials, *tımar*-holders and Taxation: The Late Sixteenth Century Crisis as Seen from Çorum', in *Turcica*, XVIII, pp. 53–82.

— (1987) *Men of Modest Substance, House Owners and House Property in Seventeenth-century Ankara and Kayseri* (Cambridge: Cambridge University Press).

— (1988) 'Agricultural Crisis and the Art of Flute-playing: The Worldly Affairs of the Mevlevî Dervishes (1595–1652)', in *Turcica*, XX, pp. 43–70.

— (1990) *Herrscher über Mekka, die Geschichte der Pilgerfahrt* (Munich and Zurich: Artemis).

— (1991) 'Black Slaves and Freedmen Celebrating (Aydın, 1576)', in *Turcica*, XXI–XXIII, pp. 205–15.

— (1992a) 'Political Activity among Ottoman Taxpayers and the Problem of Sultanic Legitimation (1570–1650)', in *Journal of the Economic and Social History of the Orient*, XXXV, pp. 1–39.

— (1992b) 'Red Sea Trade and Communications as Observed by Evliya Çelebi (1671/72)', in *New Perspectives on Turkey*, 5–6, pp. 87–106.

— (1994) 'The Life and Death of Outlaws in Çorum', in *Armağan Festschrift Andreas Tietze*, ed. Ingeborg Baldauf, Suraiya Faroqhi and Rudolf Vesely (Prague: Oriental Institute, Charles University).

— (1999) 'A Builder as Slave Owner and Rural Moneylender: Hacı Abdullah of Bursa, Campaign Mimar', in *Arab Historic Review for Ottoman Studies*, 19–20, Mélanges Prof. Machiel Kiel, pp. 601–15.

Febvre, Lucien (1977) *Life in Renaissance France*, trans. Marian Rothstein (Cambridge, MA: Harvard University Press).

Fekete, Lajos (1960) 'Das Heim eines türkischen Herrn in der Provinz im XVI. Jahrhundert', in *Studia Historica Academiae Scientiarum Hungaricae*, 29, 5, pp. 3–30.

[Feyzullah Efendi] trans. Ahmed Türek and Çetin Derin (1969/70) 'Feyzullah Efendi'nin kendi Kaleminden Hal Tercümesi', in *Tarih Dergisi*, 23, pp. 205–18; 24, pp. 69–93.

Findley, Carter V. (1980) *Bureaucratic Reform in the Ottoman Empire, the Sublime Porte 1789–1922* (Princeton, NJ: Princeton University Press).

— (1989) *Ottoman Civil Officialdom, A Social History* (Princeton, NJ: Princeton University Press).

Finkel, Caroline (1988) *The Administration of Warfare: the Ottoman Military Campaigns in Hungary, 1593–1606* (2 vols) (Vienna: VWGÖ).

Fleischer, Cornell H. (1986) *Bureaucrat and Intellectual in the Ottoman Empire, the Historian Mustafā Âlî (1541–1600)* (Princeton, NJ: Princeton University Press).

— (1990) 'From Şehzade Korkud to Mustafa Âli: Cultural Origins of the Ottoman Nasîhatname', in *Congress on the Economic and Social History of Turkey* ... , ed. Heath Lowry and Ralph Hattox (Istanbul: İSİS Press), pp. 67–78.

— (1992) 'The Lawgiver as Messiah: The Making of the Imperial Image in the Reign of Süleyman', in *Soliman le Magnifique et son temps, Actes du Colloque de Paris, Galéries Nationales du Grand Palais, 7–10 mars 1990* (Paris: La Documentation Française), pp. 159–78.

Flemming, Barbara (1987) 'Sahib-kıran und Mahdi: Türkische Endzeiterwartungen im ersten Jahrzehnt der Regierung Süleymans', in *Between the Danube and the Caucasus*, ed. Györgi Kara (Budapest: Verlag der Akademie der Wissenschaften), pp. 43–62.

Foss, Clive (1979) *Ephesus After Antiquity: A Late Antique, Byzantine and Turkish City* (Cambridge: Cambridge University Press).

Fukasawa, Katsumi (1987) *Toilerie et commerce du Levant, d'Alep à Marseille* (Paris: Editions du CNRS).

Gaube, Heinz and Eugen Wirth (1984) *Aleppo. Historische und geographische Beiträge zur baulichen Gestaltung, zur sozialen Organisation und zur wirtschaftlichen Dynamik einer vorderasiatischen Fernhandelsmetropole* (2 vols) (Wiesbaden: Dr Ludwig Reichert).

Gdoura, Wahid (1985) *Le début de l'imprimerie arabe à Istanbul et en Syrie: Evolution d l'environnement culturel (1706–1787)* (Tunis: Institut Supérieur de Documentation).

Genç, Mehmet (1984) 'Osmanlı Ekonomisi ve Savaş', in *Yapıt*, 49, 4, pp. 52–61; 50, 5, pp. 86–93.

Gerber, Haim (1980) 'Social and Economic Position of Women in an Ottoman City, Bursa 1600–1700', in *International Journal of Middle East Studies*, 12, pp. 231–44.

— (1988) *Economy and Society in an Ottoman City: Bursa, 1600–1700* (Jerusalem: The Hebrew University).

Gibb, E. J. W., (1900–1905) *A History of Ottoman Poetry*, ed. Edward G. Browne (4 vols) (London: Luzac and Co.).

Ginzburg, Carlo (1982) *The Cheese and the Worms, the Cosmos of a Sixteenth-century Miller*, trans. John and Anne Tedeschi (Harmondsworth: Penguin Books).

Göçek, Fatma Müge (1987) *East Encounters West: France and the Ottoman Empire in the Eighteenth Century* (Oxford and New York: Oxford University Press).

Gökyay, Orhan Şaik (1985) 'Sohbetname', in *Tarih ve Toplum*, 3, pp. 128–36.

— (1986) 'Bir Saltanat Düğünü', in *Topkapı Sarayı Yıllığı*, 1, pp. 21–56.

Gölpınarlı, Abdülbaki (1931) *Melamîlik ve Melamîler* (Istanbul: Devlet Matbaası).

— (1953) *Mevlânâ'dan sonra Mevlevîlik* (Istanbul: İnkilap Kitabevi).

— (ed.) (1958) *Manakıb-ı Hacı Bektaş-ı Veli, Vilâyet- Nâme* (Istanbul: İnkilap Kitabevi).

— (1959) *Mevlânâ Celâleddin, Hayatı, Felsefesi, Eserleri, Eserlerinden Seçmeler* (Istanbul: İnkilap Kitabevi).

— (1963) *Alevî-Bektasî Nefesleri* (Istanbul: Remzi Kitabevi).

— (1967) *Mevlana Müzesi Yazmalar Kataloğu* (3 vols) (Ankara: Milli Eğitim Bakanlığı).

— (1973) *Hurufîlik Metinleri Kataloğu* (Ankara: Türk Tarih Kurumu).

Gölpınarlı, Abdülbaki and Pertev Naili Boratav (1991) *Pir Sultan Abdal* (Istanbul: Der Yayınları).

Gombrich, Ernst H. (1984) *Aby Warburg, eine intellektuelle Biographie* (Frankfurt a. M.: Suhrkamp).

Gonzalez de Clavijo, Ruy (1970) *Narrative of the Embassy of Ruy Gonzalez de Clavijo to the Court of Timur in Samarcand, AD 1403–1406* ... , trans. and annotated Clements R. Markham (New York: Franklin).

Goodwin, Godfrey (1971) *A History of Ottoman Architecture* (London: Thames and Hudson).

Goubert, Pierre (1966) *Louis XIV et vingt millions de Français* (Paris: Fayard).

Grabar, Oleg (1973) *The Formation of Islamic Art* (New Haven and London: Yale University Press).

Gran, Peter (1979) *Islamic Roots of Capitalism, Egypt, 1760–1840* (Austin and London: University of Texas Press).

Griswold, William (1983) *The Great Anatolian Rebellion 1000–1020/1591–1611* (Berlin: Klaus Schwarz Verlag).

Groot, Alexander H. de (1978) *The Ottoman Empire and the Dutch Republic, A History of the Earliest Diplomatic Relations 1610–1630* (Leiden and Istanbul: Nederlands Instituut voor het Nabije Oosten).

Groß, Erich (1927) *Das Vilayet-name des Haǧǧî Bektasch, Ein türkisches Derwisch-Evangelium* (Leipzig: Mayer und Müller).

Güçer, Lütfi (1964) *XVI–XVII Asırlarda Osmanlı İmparatorluğunda Hububat Meselesi ve Hububattan Alınan Vergiler* (Istanbul: İstanbul Üniversitesi İktisat Fakültesi).

Haarmann, Ulrich (1976) 'Evliyā Čelebis Bericht über die Altertümer von Gize', in *Turcica*, VIII, 1, pp. 157–230.

Hafiz Hüseyin Ayvansarayî (1864/65) *Hadikatü 'l-cevami* (Istanbul: Matbaa-yı amire).

Hanna, Nelly (1991) *Habiter au Caire. La maison moyenne et ses habitants aux XVIIe et aux XVIIIe siècles* (Cairo: Institut français d'Archéologie Orientale du Caire).

[Hasan, Seyyid] 'Sohbetname', Topkapı Sarayı, Bibliothek, Hazine 1426, Vol. I. (Hazine 1418 = Vol. 2.)

Hasluck, F. W. (1929) *Christianity and Islam under the Sultans*, ed. Margaret Hasluck (Oxford).

Hammer, Joseph von (1834) *Geschichte des Osmanischen Reiches, größtenteils aus bisher unbenützten Handschriften und Archiven* (4 vols) (Pesth: C. A. Hartleben).

Hattox, Ralph (1988) *Coffee and Coffeehouses: The Origins of a Social Beverage in the Medieval Near East* (Seattle and London: Washington University Press).

Helmecke, Gisela (1993) 'Die Stickereien', in *Reich an Samt und Seide, Osmanische Gewebe und Stickereien*, ed. Christian Erber (Bremen: Edition Temmen), pp. 25–33.

Hering, Gunnar (1968) *Ökumenisches Patriarchat und europäische Politik 1620–1638* (Mainz and Wiesbaden: Institut für Europäische Geschichte).

Hess, Andrew (1978) *The Forgotten Frontier. A History of the Sixteenth Century Ibero-African Frontier* (Chicago and London: University of Chicago Press).

Hinz, Walther (1955), 'Islamische Maße und Gewichte umgerechnet ins metrische System', in Handbuch der Orientalistik, ed. Berthold Spuler (Supplementary Vol. 1, H 1) (Leiden: E. J. Brill).

Hobsbawm, E. J. (1990) *Echoes of the Marseillaise, Two Centuries Look Back on the French Revolution* (London and New York: Verso).

Hodgson, Marshall G. S. (1974) *The Venture of Islam, Conscience and History in a World Civilization* (Chicago and London: University of Chicago Press).

Holbrook, Victoria Rowe (1992) 'Originality and Ottoman Poetics: In the Wilderness of the New', in *Journal of the American Oriental Society*, 112, 3, pp. 440–54.

Hugo, Victor (1972) *Nôtre Dame de Paris*, intro. Jean Maurel (Paris: Librairie Générale).

Hüttl, Ludwig (1976) *Max Emanuel, Der Blaue Kurfürst 1679–1726, Eine politische Biographie* (Munich: Süddeutscher Verlag).

İA (1950–86) *İslam Ansiklopedisi, Tarih, Coğrafya, Etnografya ve Biyografya Lugatı* (Istanbul: Millî Eğitim Bakanlığı).

Ibn Battuta (1854) *Voyages d'Ibn Batoutah* (4 vols) ed. and trans. C. Défrémery and B. R. Sanguinetti (Paris: Librairie Impériale).

İhsanoğlu, Ekmeleddin (1987) 'Some Critical Notes on the Introduction of Modern Sciences to the Ottoman State and the Relation between Science and Religion up to the End of the Nineteenth Century', in *Comité International d'Etudes Pré-ottomanes et Ottomanes, VI Symposium, Cambridge 1–4 July 1984*, ed. Jean Louis Bacqué-Grammont and Emeri van Donzel (Istanbul, Paris and Leiden: The Divit Press), pp. 235–52.

İmamoğlu, Vacit (1992) *Geleneksel Kayseri Evleri, Traditional Dwellings in Kayseri* (Ankara: Halkbank).

İnalcık, Halil (1948) 'Osmanlı-Rus Rekabetinin Menşei ve Don-Volga Kanalı Teşebbüsü (1569)', in *Belleten*, XII, pp. 349–402.

— (1953) 'Stefan Duşan'dan Osmanlı İmparatorluğuna: XV Asırda Hıristiyan Sipahiler ve Menşeleri', in *Fuad Köprülü Armağanı/Mélanges Fuad Köprülü* (Istanbul: AÜ Dil ve Tarih-Coğrafya Fakültesi), pp. 207–48.

— (1954a) *Hicri 835 Tarihli Sûret-i Defter-i Sancak-i Arvanid* (Ankara: Türk Tarih Kurumu).

— (1954b) 'Ottoman Methods of Conquest', in *Studia Islamica*, III, pp. 103–29.

— (1965) 'Adâletnâmeler', in *Belgeler*, II, 3–4, pp. 42–149.

— (1969) 'Capital Formation in the Ottoman Empire', in *The Journal of Economic History*, XIX, pp. 97–140.

— (1970) 'The Policy of Mehmed II toward the Greek Population of Istanbul and the Byzantine Buildings of the City', in *Dumbarton Oaks Papers*, 23, pp. 213–49.

— (1973) *The Ottoman Empire, the Classical Age 1300–1600* (London: Weidenfeld and Nicolson).

— (1974) 'The Socio-Political Effects of the Diffusion of Fire-Arms in the Middle East', in *War, Technology and Society in the Middle East*, ed. Bela Király (London: Oxford University Press), pp. 195–217.

— (1979/80) 'Osmanlı Pamuklu Pazarı, Hindistan ve İngiltere: Pazar Rekabetinde Emek Maliyetinin Rolü', in *ODTÜ Gelişme Dergisi*, special issue *Türkiye İktisat Tarihi Üzerine Araştırmalar*, II, pp. 1–66.

— (1980) 'Military and Fiscal Transformation in the Ottoman Empire, 1600–1700', in *Archivum Ottomanicum*, VI, 283–337.

— (1983) 'Introduction to Ottoman Metrology', in *Turcica*, XV, pp. 311–48.

— (1985) 'The Emergence of Big Farms, *çiftliks*: State, Landlords and Tenants', in *Studies in Ottoman Social and Economic History*, VIII (London: Variorum).

— (1993) 'Dervish and Sultan: an Analysis of the Otman Baba Vilayet-namesi', in *Manifestations of Sainthood in Islam*, ed. Grace Martin Smith and Carl W. Ernst (Istanbul: İSİS), pp. 209–24.

— (1994) 'How to Read 'Ashık Pasha-Zâde's history', in *Studies in Ottoman History in Honour of Professor V. L. Ménage*, ed. Colin Heywood and Colin Imber (Istanbul: İSİS Press), pp. 139–56.

Islamoğlu, Huri and Suraiya Faroqhi (1979) 'Crop Patterns and Agricultural Production Trends in Sixteenth-Century Anatolia', in *Review*, II, 3, pp. 401–36.

İslamoğlu-İnan, Huri (1987) 'Introduction: "Oriental Despotism" in World System Perspective', in *The Ottoman State and the World Economy*, ed. Huri İslamoğlu-İnan (Cambridge and Paris: Cambridge University Press and Maison des Sciences de l'Homme), pp. 1–26.

Issawi, Charles (1980) *The Economic History of Turkey 1800–1914* (Chicago: University of Chicago Press).

İz, Fahir and Günay Kut (1985) 'XV. Yüzyılda Nazım', in *Başlangıcından Günümüze Kadar*

Büyük Türk Klâsikleri, Tarih-Antoloji-Ansiklopedi, (Istanbul: Ötüken and Söğüt), Vol. 2, pp. 109–260.

Jacob, Georg (1904) 'Traditionen über Bekri Mustafa Aga', in *Revue orientale,* pp. 1–7.

Jansky, Herbert (1964) 'Zeitgeschichtliches in den Liedern des Bektaşî-Dichters Pir Sultan Abdal', in *Der Islam,* 39, pp. 130–42.

Jaubert, Pierre Amedée (1821) *Voyage en Arménie et en Perse dans les années 1805 et 1806* (Paris: Pélicier and Nepveu).

Jennings, Ronald C. (1973) 'Loan and Credit in Early 17th Century Ottoman Judicial Records: The Sharia Court of Anatolian Kayseri', in *Journal of the Economic and Social History of the Orient,* XVI, II–III, pp. 168–216.

— (1975) 'Women in Early 17th Century Ottoman Judicial Records – The Sharia Court of Anatolian Kayseri', in *Journal of the Economic and Social History of the Orient,* XVIII, I, pp. 53–114.

— (1993) *Christians and Muslims in Ottoman Cyprus and the Mediterranean World, 1571–1640* (New York: New York University Press).

Kafadar, Cemal (1986) 'A Death in Venice (1575): Anatolian Muslim Merchants Trading in the Serenissima', in *Journal of Turkish Studies,* 10, *Raiyyet Rüsumu, Essays presented to Halil Inalcık on his Seventieth Birthday by his Colleagues and Students,* pp. 191–218.

— (1989) 'Self and Others: The Diary of a Dervish in Seventeenth-century Istanbul and First-person Narratives in Ottoman Literature', in *Studia Islamica,* LXIX, pp. 121–50.

— (1992) 'Mütereddit bir Mutasavvıf: Üsküplü Asiye Hatun'un Rüya Defteri 1641–43', in *Topkapı Sarayı Yıllığı,* 5, pp. 168–222.

— (1995) *Between Two Worlds: The Construction of the Ottoman State* (Berkeley and Los Angeles: University of California Press).

Kahane, Henry, Renée Kahane and Andreas Tietze (1958) *The Lingua Franca in the Levant, Turkish Nautical Terms of Italian and Greek Origin* (Urbana: University of Illinois Press).

Kappert, Petra (1976) *Die osmanischen Prinzen und ihre Residenz Amasya im 15. und 16. Jahrhundert* (Istanbul: Nederlands Historisch-Archeologisch Instituut).

Karamustafa, Ahmet T. (1994) *God's Unruly Friends, Dervish Groups in the Islamic Later Middle Period, 1200–1550* (Salt Lake City: University of Utah Press).

Kâtib Çelebi (1145/1732) *Cihân-numâ* (Istanbul: İbrahim Müteferrika).

Kechagioglou, Giorgos (1993) 'Neugriechische belletristische Volksbücher, Vorüberlegungen zu bibliographischen sowie literatur- und gattungsgeschichtlichen Fragen', in *Südosteuropäische Popularliteratur im 19. und 20. Jahrhundert,* ed. Klaus Roth (Munich: Münchener Vereinigung für Volkskunde und Südosteuropa-Gesellschaft), pp. 55–66.

Kemal, Tahir (1969) *Kurt Kanunu* (Ankara: Bilgi Yayınevi).

Kerman, Zeynep (1978) *1862–1910 Yılları Arasında Victor Hugo'dan Türkçeye Yapılan Tercümeler üzerinde bir Araştırma* (Istanbul: İ.Ü. Edebiyat Fakültesi).

Kévonian, Kéram (1975) 'Marchands arméniens au XVIIᵉ siècle. A propos d'un livre arménien publié à Amsterdam en 1699', in *Cahiers du Monde Russe et Soviétique,* XVI, pp. 199–244.

Khachikian, Levon (1967) 'Le registre d'un marchand arménien en Perse, en Inde et au Tibet', in *Annales, Economies Sociétés Civilisations,* 22, pp. 231–78.

Kiel, Machiel (1985) *Art and Society of Bulgaria in the Turkish Period, A Sketch of the Economic, Juridical and Artistic Preconditions of Bulgarian Post-Byzantine Art and its Place in the Development of the Art of the Christian Balkans, 1360/70–1700* (Assen and Maastricht: Van Gorcum).

— (1990) *Studies on the Ottoman Architecture of the Balkans* (London: Variorum).

King, Donald (1983) 'The Carpets in the Exhibition', in *The Eastern Carpet in the Western*

World, from the 15th to the 17th Century, ed. Donald King and David Sylvester (London: Arts Council of Great Britain), pp. 24–32.

Kißling, Hans-Joachim (1945–49) 'Eine bektašitische Version der Legende von den zwei Erzsündern', in *Zeitschrift der Deutschen Morgenländischen Gesellschaft*, 99, pp. 181–201.

— (1953) 'Aus der Geschichte des Chalvetijje-Ordens', in *Zeitschrift der Deutschen Morgenländischen Gesellschaft*, 103, pp. 233–89.

Kißling, Hans-Joachim (1957) 'Zur Geschichte der Rausch- und Genußgifte im Osmanischen Reiche', in *Südost-Forschungen*, XVI, pp. 342–56.

Koç, Havva (1993) 'Bir Belge Işığında İbrahim Edhem Paşa ve Ailesi Hakkında Hatırlamalar', in *Osman Hamdi Bey ve Dönemi, 17–18 Aralık 1992*, ed. Zeynep Rona (Istanbul: Tarih Vakfı Yurt Yayınları), pp. 27–40.

Koçu, Reşat Ekrem (1969) *Türk Giyim Kuşam ve Süslenme Sözlüğü* (Ankara: Sümerbank).

Kohler, Georg and Alice Villon-Lechner (1988) *Die schöne Kunst der Verschwendung, Fest und Feuerwerk in der europäischen Geschichte* (Zurich and Munich: Artemis).

Konyalı, Ibrahim Hakkı (1964) *Abideleri ve Kitabeleri ile Konya Tarihi* (Konya: Yeni Kitap Basımevi).

Köprülü, Mehmed Fuad (1929) *Influence du chamanisme turco-mongol sur les ordres mystiques musulmans* (Istanbul: İstanbul Darülfünunu Türkiyat Enstitüsü).

— (1935) *Türk Halkedebiyatı Ansiklopedisi, Ortaçağ ve Yeniçağ Türklerinin Halk Kültürü Üzerine Coğrafya, Etnoğrafya, Etnoloji, Tarih ve Edebiyat Lugatı*, No. I Aba-Abdal Musa (no more appeared) (Istanbul).

— (1966) *Edebiyat Araştırmaları* (Ankara: Türk Tarih Kurumu).

Kreiser, Klaus (1975) *Edirne im 17. Jahrhundert nach Evliyā Çelebi, Ein Beitrag zur Kenntnis der osmanischen Stadt* (Freiburg i. Br.: Klaus Schwarz Verlag).

— (1978) '" … dan die Türckhen leiden khain Menschen Pildnuss": über die Praxis des "Bildverbots" bei den Osmanen', in *Fifth International Congress of Turkish Art*, ed. G. Fehér (Budapest: Verlag der Ungarischen Akademie der Wissenschaften), pp. 549–56.

— (1979) 'Über den Kernraum des Osmanischen Reichs', in *Die Türkei in Europa* … , ed. Klaus-Detlev Grothusen (Göttingen: Vandenhoeck und Ruprecht), pp. 53–63.

— (1986) 'Icareteyn: Zur "Doppelten Miete" im Osmanischen Stiftungswesen', in *Journal of Turkish Studies*, 10, *Raiyyet Rüsûmu, Essays presented to Halil Inalcık on his Seventieth Birthday by his Colleagues and Students*, pp. 219–26.

Kreutel, Richard (1971) 'Neues zur Evliyā-Čelebi-Forschung', in *Der Islam*, 48, pp. 269–79.

Küçükömer, Idris (1969) *Düzenin Yabancılaşması Batılaşma* (Istanbul: Ant).

Kunt, Metin (1974) 'Ethnic-regional Solidarity in the Seventeenth-century Ottoman Establishment', in *International Journal for Middle East Studies*, V, pp. 233–9.

— (1981) *Bir Osmanlı Valisinin Gelir-Gideri Diyarbekir, 1670–71* (Istanbul: Boğaziçi Üniversitesi Yayınları).

Kuran, Aptullah (1987) *Sinan, the Grand Old Master of Ottoman Architecture* (Washington and Istanbul: Institute of Turkish Studies and Ada Press).

Kut, Turgut (1994) 'Terekelerde Çıkan Kitapların Matbu Satış Defterleri', in *Müteferrika* 2, pp. 3–24.

Kütükoğlu, Mübahat (1978) '1009 (1600) Tarihli Narh Defterine göre İstanbul'da çeşidli Eşya ve Hizmet Fiatları', in *Tarih Enstitüsü Dergisi*, 9, pp 1–86.

— (1983) *Osmanlılarda Narh Müessesesi ve 1640 Tarihli Narh Defteri* (Istanbul: Enderun Kitapevi).

— (1986) 'Cevdet Paşa ve Aile İçi Münasebetleri', in *Ahmed Cevdet Paşa Semineri*, ed. Mübahat Kütükoğlu (Istanbul: I.Ü. Edebiyat Fakültesi) pp. 199–222.

Labib, Subhi Y. (1965) *Handelsgeschichte Ägyptens im Spätmittelalter (1171–1517)*, Vierteljahresschrift für Sozial- und Wirtschaftsgeschichte, suppl. issue 46 (Wiesbaden: Franz Steiner).

Lane, Frederick (1968) 'The Mediterranean Spice Trade: Further Evidence of its Revival in the Sixteenth Century' (1940), in *Crisis and Change in the Venetian Economy in the Sixteenth and Seventeenth Centuries*, ed. Brian Pullan (London: Methuen), pp. 47–58.

Lapidus, Ira (1969) 'Muslim Cities and Islamic Societies', in *Middle Eastern Cities*, ed. Ira Lapidus (Berkeley and Los Angeles: University of California Press).

Laqueur, Hans-Peter (1993) *Osmanische Friedhöfe und Grabsteine in Istanbul* (Tübingen: Ernst Wasmuth Verlag).

Lerner, Daniel (1958) *The Passing of Traditional Society* (Glencoe IL: Free Press).

Le Roy Ladurie, Emmanuel (1975) *Montaillou, village occitan de 1294 à 1324* (Paris: Gallimard).

— (1977) 'Les masses profondes: la paysannerie', in *Histoire économique et sociale de la France*, Vol. 1, 2, pp. 483–865.

Lewis, Bernard (1968) *The Emergence of Modern Turkey* (2nd edn) (London: Oxford University Press).

— (1982) *The Muslim Discovery of Europe* (New York and London: W. W. Norton).

Lindner, Rudi (1983) *Nomads and Ottomans in Medieval Anatolia* (Bloomington: Indiana University Press).

Lowry, Heath (1986) 'Changes in Fifteenth-century Ottoman Peasant Taxation: The Case Study of Radilofo (Radolibos)', in *Continuity and Change in Late Byzantine and Early Ottoman Society*, ed. Anthony Bryer and Heath Lowry (Birmingham and Washington: University of Birmingham Press and Dumbarton Oaks), pp. 23–38.

Mackenzie, Mollie (1992) *Turkish Athens, The Forgotten Centuries 1456–1832* (Reading: Ithaca Press).

Majer, Hans Georg (1990) 'Zur Ikonographie der osmanischen Sultane', in *Das Bildnis in der Kunst der Orients*, ed. Martin Kraatz et al. (Stuttgart: Franz Steiner).

— (1992) 'The Harem of Mustafa II (1695–1703)', in *Osmanlı Araştırmaları*, XII, pp. 431–44.

Mandaville, Jon E. (1979) 'Usurious Piety: The Cash waqf Controversy in the Ottoman Empire', in *International Journal of Middle East Studies*, X, 3, pp. 289–308.

Mantran, Robert (1962) *Istanbul dans la seconde moitié du dix-septième siècle, Essai d'histoire institutionelle, économique et sociale* (Istanbul and Paris: Institut Français d'Archéologie d'Istanbul and Adrien Maisonneuve).

Marcus, Abraham (1989) *The Middle East on the Eve of Modernity, Aleppo in the Eighteenth Century* (New York: Columbia University Press).

Mardin, Şerif (1962) *The Genesis of Young Ottoman Thought, a Study in the Modernization of Turkish Political Ideas* (Princeton, NJ: Princeton University Press).

— (1974) 'Super Westernization in Urban Life in the Ottoman Empire in the last Quarter of the Nineteenth Century', in *Turkey, Geographic and Social Perspectives*, ed. Peter Benedict, Erol Tümertekin and Fatma Mansur (Leiden: E. J. Brill), pp. 403–46.

— (1983) *Jön Türklerin Siyasi Fikirleri 1895–1908* (Istanbul: Iletişim).

— (1988) 'Freedom in an Ottoman Perspective', in *State, Democracy and the Military, Turkey in the 1980s*, ed. Metin Heper and Ahmet Evin (Berlin and New York: Walter de Gruyter), pp. 23–36.

Maštakova, Elena I. (1994) 'Eine neue Bereicherung für die Turkologie (Bemerkungen zum ersten türkischen Roman)', in Ingeborg Baldauf, Suraiya Faroqhi and Rudolf Vesely (eds), *Armağan, Festschrift für Andreas Tietze* (Prague: Enigma Corporation), pp. 143–50.

Masters, Bruce (1988) *The Origins of Western Economic Dominance in the Middle East, Mercanilism and the Islamic Economy in Aleppo, 1600–1750* (New York: New York University Press).

Maury, Bernard, André Raymond, Jacques Revault and Mona Zakarya (1983) *Palais et maisons du Caire*, Vol. 2, *Époque ottomane (XVIᵉ–XVIIIᵉ siècles)* (Paris: Éditions du CRNS).

McGowan, Bruce (1969) 'Food Supply and Taxation on the Middle Danube (1568–1579)', in *Archivum Ottomanicum*, I, pp. 139–96.

— (1981) *Economic Life in Ottoman Europe, Taxation, Trade and the Struggle for Land 1600–1800* (Cambridge and Paris: Cambridge University Press and Maison des Sciences de l'Homme).

McNeill, William H. (1974) *Venice, the Hinge of Europe 1081–1797* (Chicago and London: Chicago University Press).

Mehmed Efendi (1981) *Le Paradis des infidèles, Un ambassadeur ottoman en France sous la Régence*, ed. Gilles Veinstein (Paris: François Maspéro/La Découverte).

Mélikoff, Irène (1975) 'Le problème kızılbaş', in *Turcica*, VI, pp. 49–67.

Melman, Billie (1992) *Women's Orients, English Women and the Middle East, 1718–1918, Sexuality, Religion and Work* (London: Macmillan).

Mikes, Kelemen (1978) *Briefe aus der Türkei*, trans. and ed. Gyula Zathureczky, Sybille Baronin Manteuffel-Szöege, Thomas von Boyay and Antal Szerb (Graz, Vienna and Cologne: Styria).

Miller, Barnette (1970) *Beyond the Sublime Porte: The Grand Seraglio of Stambul*, intro. by Halide Edib (New York: AMS).

Mills, John (1978) 'Two Aspects of the Small Pattern Holbein Carpets', in *Halı*, I, 4, pp. 324–329.

— (1983) 'The Coming of the Carpet to the West', in *The Eastern Carpet in the Western World, from the 15th to the 17th Century*, ed. Donald King and David Sylvester (London: Arts Council of Great Britain), pp. 11–23.

Misailidis, Evangelinos (1986) *Seyreyle Dünyayı Temaşa-i Dünya ve Cefakâr- u Cefakeş*, ed. Robert Anhegger and Vedat Günyol (Istanbul: Cem Yayınevi).

Montagu, Lady Mary Wortley (1993) *Turkish Embassy Letters*, ed. M. Jack and A. Desai (London: William Pickering and Chatto).

Montesqieu, Charles-Louis de (1986) *Perserbriefe* (Frankfurt a. M.: Insel).

Moran, Berna (1991) *Türk Romanına Eleştirel bir Bakış*, Vol. 1, *Ahmet Mithat'tan A. H. Tanpınar'a* (4th edn) (Istanbul: İletişim Yayınları).

Muchembled, Robert (1978) *Culture populaire et culture des élites dans la France moderne (XVᵉ–XVIIIᵉ siècles)* (Paris: Flammarion).

Mughul, Yakub (1965) 'Portekizlilerle Kızıldeniz'de Mücadele ve Hicaz'da Osmanlı Hakimiyetinin Yerleşmesi Hakkında bir Vesika …', in *Belgeler*, II, 3–4, pp. 37–47.

Müller-Wiener, Wolfgang (1977) *Bildlexikon zur Topographie Istanbuls, Byzantion Konstantinupolis-Istanbul bis zum Beginn des 17. Jahrhunderts* (Tübingen: Ernst Wasmuth).

Murphey, Rhoads (1988) 'Provisioning Istanbul: The State and Subsistence in the Early Modern Middle East', in *Food and Foodways*, 2, pp. 217–63.

— (1999) *Ottoman Warfare 1500–1700* (London: UCL Press).

Museum für Kunsthandwerk, Frankfurt am Main (1985) *Türkische Kunst und Kultur aus osmanischer Zeit* (2 vols) (Recklinghausen: Aurel Bongers).

Mustafā 'Ālī (1978–1982) *Mustafā 'Ālī's Counsel for Sultans of 1581*, ed. and trans. Andreas Tietze (2 vols) (Vienna: Verlag der Österreichischen Akademie der Wissenschaften).

Naṣūḥū's-Silāḥī (Maṭrakçı) (1976) *Beyān-i Menāzil-i Sefer-i 'Irāḳeyn-i Sulṭān Suleymān Ḫān*, ed. Hüseyin G. Yurdaydın (Ankara: Türk Tarih Kurumu).

Nayır, Zeynep (1975) *Osmanlı Mimarlığında Sultan Ahmet Külliyesi ve Sonrası (1609–1690)* (Istanbul: İTÜ Mimarlık Fakültesi).

Necipoğlu, Gülru (1992) 'The Life of an Imperial Monument: Hagia Sophia after Byzantium', in *Hagia Sophia from the Age of Justinian to the Present*, ed. Robert Mark and Ahmet S. Çakmak (Cambridge: Cambridge University Press), pp. 195–225.

Necipoğlu-Kafadar, Gülru (1986a) 'Plans and Models in 15th and 16th Century Ottoman Architectural Practice', in *Journal of the Society of Architectural Historians*, XLX, 3, pp. 224–43.

— (1986b) 'The Süleymaniye Complex in Istanbul: An Interpretation', in *Mukarnas*, 3, pp. 92–117.

— (1991) *Architecture, Ceremonial and Power. The Topkapı Palace in the Fifteenth and Sixteenth Centuries* (Cambridge, MA: Architectural History Foundation and MIT Press).

Neumann, Christoph (1994) *Das indirekte Argument. Ein Plädoyer für die Tanzimāt vermittels der Historie, Die geschichtliche Bedeutung von Ahmed Cevdet Paşas Ta'rih* (Münster and Hamburg: Lit Verlag).

Nutku, Özdemir (1972) *IV. Mehmet'in Edirne Şenliği (1675)* (Ankara: Türk Tarih Kurmu).

Ocak, Ahmer Yaşar (1983) *Bektasî Menâkibnâmelerinde İslam Öncesi İnanç Motifleri* (Istanbul: Enderun Kitabevi).

— (1989) *La révolte de Baba Resul ou la formation de l'hétérodoxie musulmane en Anatolie au XIIIᵉ siècle* (Ankara: Conseil Suprême d'Atatürk pour Culture, Langue et Histoire).

— (1991) 'Les réactions socio-religieuses contre l'ideologie officielle ottomane et la question de *zendeqa ve ilhād* (hérésie et athéisme) au XVIᵉ siècle', in *Turcica*, XXI–XXIII, pp. 71–82.

Okay, M. Orhan (no date) *Ilk Türk Pozitivist ve Natüralisti Beşir Fuad* (Istanbul: Dergâh Yayınları).

Öney, Gönül (1971) *Ankara'da Türk Devri Yapıları, Turkish Period Buildings in Ankara* (Ankara: Dil ve Tarih-Coğrafya Fakültesi Yayınları).

Orhonlu, Cengiz (1967) *Osmanlı İmparatorluğunda Derbend Teşkilatı* (Istanbul: İstanbul Üniversitesi Edebiyat Fakültesi).

— (1974) *Osmanlı İmparatorluğunun Güney Siyaseti, Habeş Eyaleti* (Istanbul: İstanbul Üniversitesi Edebiyat Fakültesi).

— (1984a) 'İstanbul'da Kayıkçılık ve Kayık İşletmeciliği', in *Osmanlı İmparatorluğunda Şehircilik ve Ulaşım*, ed. Salih Özbaran (Izmir: Ege Üniversitesi Edebiyat Fakültesi), pp. 83–103.

— (1984b) 'Şehir Mimarları', in ibid., pp. 1–26.

Ortaylı, İlber (1981) *Ikinci Abdülhamit Döneminde Osmanlı İmparatorluğunda Alman Nüfuzu* (Ankara: AÜ Siyasal Bilgiler Fakültesi).

— (1983) *İmparatorluğun en Uzun Yüzyılı* (Istanbul: Hil Yayını).

—. (1985) *Tanzimattan Cumhuriyete Yerel Yönetim Geleneği* (Istanbul: Hil Yayını).

Osman, Ağa (1954) *Leben und Abenteuer des Dolmetschers Osman Aga, Eine türkische Autobiographie aus der Zeit der großen Kriege gegen Österreich*, trans. and commentary Richard F. Kreutel and Otto Spies (Bonn: Orientalisches Seminar der Universität Bonn).

— (1962) *Der Gefangene der Giauren, Die abenteuerlichen Schicksale des 'Osman Ağa aus Temeschwar, von ihm selbst erzählt*, trans. and intro. Richard F. Kreutel and Otto Spies (Graz, Vienna and Cologne: Verlag Styria).

Özcan, Azmi (1997) *Pan-Islamism, Indian Muslims, the Ottomans and Britain (1877–1924)* (Leiden: E. J. Brill).

Özdeğer, Hüseyin (1988) *1463–1640 Yılları Bursa Şehri Tereke Defterleri* (Istanbul: İstanbul Üniversitesi İktisat Fakültesi).

Özergin, M. Kemal (1965) 'Anadolu'da Selçuklu Kervansarayları', in *Tarih Dergisi*, XV, 20, pp. 141–70.

Özön, Mustafa Nihat (1985) *Türkçede Roman* (2nd edn) (Istanbul: İletişim Yayınları).

Öztuncay, Bahattin (1992) *James Robertson, Pioneer of Photography in the Ottoman Empire* (Istanbul: Eren).

Panzac, Daniel (1985) *La peste dans l'Empire Ottoman, 1700–1850* (Louvain: Editions Peeters).

— (1992) 'International and Domestic Maritime Trade in the Ottoman Empire during the 18th Century', in *International Journal of Middle East Studies*, 24, pp. 189–206.

Parlatır, Ismail (1987) *Tanzimat Edebiyatında Kölelik* (Ankara: Türk Tarih Kurumu).

Paskaleva, Virginia (1993) 'Die bulgarischen Gebiete 1700–1850', in *Handbuch der europäischen Wirtschafts- und Sozialgeschichte*, Vol. 4, ed. Wolfram Fischer et al. (Stuttgart: Klett-Cotta), pp. 1,948–59.

Patlagean, Evelyne (1977) *Pauvreté économique et pauvreté sociale à Byzance, 4ᵉ–7ᵉ siècles* (Paris and The Hague: Mouton).

Peirce, Leslie (1988) 'Shifting Boundaries: Images of Ottoman Royal Women in the 16th and 17th Centuries', in *Critical Matrix*, 4, I, pp. 43–81.

— (1993) *The Imperial Harem, Women and Sovereignity in the Ottoman Empire* (New York and Oxford: Oxford University Press).

Perot, Jacques (1991) 'Melling à Constantinople', in Cornelius Boschma, Jacques Perot et al. (eds) *Antoine-Ignace Melling (1763–1831), artiste-voyageur* (Paris: Editions Paris Musées), pp. 15–27.

Petry, Carl (1981) *The Civilian Elite of Cairo in the Later Middle Ages* (Princeton, NJ: Princeton University Press).

Pirî, Re'is (1935) *Kitabı Bahriye*, ed. Haydar Alpagut and Fevzi Kurtoğlu (Istanbul: Türk Tarih Kurumu).

Planhol, Xavier de (1958) *De la plaine pamphylienne aux lacs pisidiens, nomadisme et vie paysanne* (Paris: Institut Français d'Archeologie d'Istanbul and Adrien Maisonneuve).

— (1968) *Les fondements géographiques de l'histoire de l'Islam* (Paris: Flammarion).

Popovic, Alexandré (1992) 'Représentation du passé et transmission de l'identité chez les musulmans du Balkans', in *Les Balkans à l'époque ottomane, Revue du monde musulman et de la Méditerranée*, 66, ed. Daniel Panzac (Aix-en-Provence: Editions Edisud), pp. 139–144.

Quataert, Donald (1983) *Social Disintegration and Popular Resistance in the Ottoman Empire, 1881–1908* (New York: New York University Press).

— (1986) 'Machine Breaking and the Changing Carpet Industry of Western Anatolia, 1860–1908', in *Journal of Social History*, 19, 3, pp. 473–89.

Raby, Julian (1982) *Venice, Dürer and the Oriental Mode* (London: Islamic Art Publications, Sotheby).

— (1983) 'Mehmed the Conqueror's Greek Scriptorium', in *Dumbarton Oaks Papers*, 37, pp. 15–34.

— (1986) 'The Porcelain Trade Routes', in *Chinese Ceramics in the Topkapı Saray Museum, Istanbul, Complete Catalogue, I Yuan and Ming Dynasty Celadon Wares*, ed. Regina Krahl and John Ayers (London: Sotheby's), pp. 55–64.

Raby, Julian and Ünsal Yücel (1986) 'Chinese Porcelain at the Ottoman Court', in ibid., pp. 27–54.

Rageth, Jürg (ed.) (1999) *Anatolian Kilims and Radiocarbon Dating* (Basel: Edition Jürg Rageth und Freunde des Orientteppichs).

Raymond, André (1973/74) *Artisans et commerçants au Caire au XVIIIᵉ siècle* (2 vols) (Damascus: Institut Français de Damas).

— (1979) 'La conquête ottomane et le développement des grandes villes arabes. Le cas du Caire, de Damas et d'Alep', in *Revue de l'Occident musulman et de la Méditerranée*, I, pp. 115–34.

— (1984) *The Great Arab Cities in the 16th–18th Centuries, an Introduction* (New York and London: New York University Press).

— (1985) *Grandes villes arabes à l'époque ottomane* (Paris: Sindbad).

Redhouse, James W. (1921) *A Turkish and English Lexicon* (Istanbul: American Board Mission and H. Matteosian).

Reid, Anthony (1969) 'Sixteenth-century Turkish Influence in Western Indonesia', in *Journal of Southeast Asian History*, X, 3, pp. 395–414.

Reindl-Kiel, Hedda (1997) 'A Woman *Tımar*-Holder in Ankara Province during the Second Half of the 16th Century', in *Journal of the Economic and Social History of the Orient*, 40, 2, pp. 207–38.

Reindl-Kiel, Hedda and Machiel Kiel (1991) 'Kaugummi für den Sultan, Ein Beitrag zur Wirtschaftsgeschichte der Insel Chios im 17. Jahrhundert', in *Osmanlı Araştırmaları*, XI, pp. 181–205.

Renda, Günsel (1989) 'Die traditionelle türkische Malerei und das Einsetzen der westlichen Einflüsse', in *Geschichte der türkischen Malerei* (Istanbul: Palasar SA), pp. 15–86.

Renda, Günsel et al. (1993) *Çağlarboyu Anadolu'da Kadın, Anadolu Kadınının 9000 Yılı* (Ankara: TC Kültür Bakanlığı).

Reyhanlı, Tülay (1983) *İngiliz Gezginlerine göre XVI. Yüzyılda İstanbul'da Hayat (1582–1599)* (Ankara: Kültür ve Turizm Bakanlığı).

Rifat Osman (1989) *Edirne Sarayı*, ed. Süheyl Ünver (Ankara: Türk Tarih Kurumu).

Roche, Daniel (1989) *La culture des apparences, l'histoire du vêtement (XVIIᵉ et XVIIIᵉ siècles)* (Paris: Fayard).

Rodinson, Maxime (1987) *Europe and the Mystique of Islam*, trans. Roger Veinus (Seattle and London: University of Washington Press).

Rogers, Michael (1982) 'The State and the Arts in Ottoman Turkey', in *International Journal of Middle East Studies*, 14, pp. 71–86, 283–313.

Rombauer, Irma S. and Marion Rombauer-Becker (1973) *The Joy of Cooking* (New York: New American Library).

Rona, Zeynep (ed.) (1993) *Osman Hamdi Bey ve Dönemi, Sempozyum 17–18 Aralık 1992* (Istanbul: Tarih Vakfı Yurt Yayınları).

Roth, Klaus (1993) 'Populare Lesestoffe in Südosteuropa', in *Südosteuropäische Popularliteratur im 19. und 20. Jahrhundert*, ed. Klaus Roth (Munich: Münchener Vereinigung für Volkskunde, Südosteuropa-Gesellschaft), pp. 11–32.

Runciman, Steven (1968) *The Great Church in Captivity: A Study of the Patriarchate of Constantinople from the Eve of the Turkish Conquest to the Greek War of Independence* (Cambridge: Cambridge University Press).

Saatçı, Suphi (1990) 'Tezkiret-ül Bünyan'in Topkapı Sarayı Revan Kitaplığındaki Yazma Nüshası', in *Topkapı Sarayı Yıllığı*, 4, pp. 55–102.

Sack, Dorothée (1989) *Damaskus, Entwicklung und Struktur einer orientalisch-islamischen Stadt* (Mainz/Rhein: Verlag Philipp von Zabern).

Sahillioğlu, Halil (1975) 'Bursa Kadı Sicillerinde İç ve Dış Ödemeler Aracı Olarak "Kitabü'l-Kadı" ve "Süfteceler", in *Türkiye İktisat Tarihi Semineri Metinler-Tartışmalar ...* , ed. Osman Okyar and Ünal Nalbantoğlu (Ankara: Hacettepe Üniversitesi), pp. 103–44.

— (1985) 'Slaves in the Social and Economic Life of Bursa in the late 15th and early 16th Centuries', in *Turcica*, XVII, pp. 43–112.

Sai Çelebi (1988) *Tezkiretü'l bünyan*, ed. Sadık Erdem (Istanbul: Binbirdirek Yayını).

Said, Edward (1978) *Orientalism* (New York: Random House).

Sallmann, Jean-Michel (1986) *Chercheurs de trésors et jeteuses de sorts, La quête du surnaturel à Naples au XVIᵉ siècle* (Paris: Aubier).

Šamic, Jasna (1986) *Divan de Ka'imî, Vie et œuvre d'un poète bosniaque du XVIIᵉ siècle* (Paris: Institut Français d'Études Anatoliennes and Editions Recherche sur les Civilisations).

Sandgruber, Roman (1993) 'Österreich 1650–1850', in *Handbuch der europäischen Wirtschafts- und Sozialgeschichte, Vol. 4, Europäische Wirtschafts- und Sozialgeschichte von der Mitte des 17.*

Jahrhunderts bis zur Mitte des 19. Jahrhunderts, ed. Wolfram Fischer and Ilja Mieck (Stuttgart: Klett Cotta), pp. 619–87.

Sanır, Ferruh (1949) *Sultan Dağlarından Sakarya'ya, Akşehir, Eşme ve Turgut ovalariyle Yukarı Sakarya'dan iki Vadi boyu ve Akşehir* (Ankara: Ulus Basımevi).

Schacht, Joseph (1982) *An Introduction to Islamic Law* (Oxford: Oxford University and Clarendon Press).

Schleiermacher, Friedrich Daniel Ernst (1984) *Kritische Gesamtausgabe*, 1st part, Vol. 2 *Schriften aus der Berliner Zeit 1796–1799*, ed. Günter Meckenstock (Berlin and New York: De Gruyter).

Schwarz, Hans-Günther (1990) *Der orientalische Teppich in der westlichen Literatur, Ästhetik und Kunst* (Munich: Iudicium Verlag).

Schwarz, Klaus (1970) *Osmanische Sultansurkunden des Sinai Klosters in türkischer Sprache* (Freiburg i. Br.: Klaus Schwarz Verlag).

Schweigger, Salomon (1986) *Zum Hofe des türkischen Sultans*, ed. and commentary Heidi Stein (Leipzig: FA Brockhaus).

Sella, Domenico (1968) 'Crisis and Transformation in Venetian Trade', in *Crisis and Change in the Venetian Economy in the Sixteenth and Seventeenth Centuries*, ed. Brian Pullan (London: Methuen), pp. 88–105.

Seng, Yvonne (1991) 'The Üsküdar Estates (*tereke*) as Records of Daily Life in an Ottoman Town 1521–24', unpublished dissertation, University of Chicago.

Şeni, Nora (1994) 'The Camondos and their Imprint on 19th-century Istanbul', in *International Journal of Middle East Studies*, 26, pp. 663–75.

Shaw, Stanford J. (1971) *Between Old and New. The Ottoman Empire under Sultan Selim III, 1789–1807* (Cambridge MA: Harvard University Press).

—— (1977) *History of the Ottoman Empire and Modern Turkey* Vol. 2 (with Ezel Kural Shaw), *Reform, Revolution and Republic: The Rise of Modern Turkey, 1808–1975* (Cambridge: Cambridge University Press).

Sholem, Gershom (1973) *Sabbatai Sevi, the Mystical Messiah, 1626–1676*, trans. R. J. Zwi Werblowsky (Princeton: Princeton University Press).

Sievernich, Gereon (ed.) (1989) *Europa und der Orient: 800–1900* (Berlin, Gütersloh and Munich: Berliner Festspiele and Bertelsmann).

Sırman, Ayşe Nüket (1988) 'Peasants and Family Farms: the Position of Households in Cotton Production in a Village of Western Turkey', unpublished dissertation, University College, London.

Skowronski, Monika (1993) 'Die Distribution bulgarischer Volksbücher im 19. und 20. Jahrhundert (bis 1944)', in *Südosteuropäische Popularliteratur im 19. und 20. Jahrhundert*, ed. Klaus Roth (Munich: Münchener Vereinigung für Volkskunde, Südosteuropa-Gesellschaft), pp. 137–58.

Smith, Grace M. (1983) 'Food Practices at the "Kadirihane" Dergah in Istanbul', in *Journal of Turkish Studies*, 7, pp. 403–6.

Soboul, Albert (1970) *La civilisation et la révolution française*, I, *La crise de l'Ancien Régime* (Paris: Arthaud).

Sohrweide, Hanna (1965) 'Der Sieg der Safawiden in Persien und seine Rückwirkungen auf die Schiiten Anatoliens im 16. Jahrhundert', in *Der Islam*, 41, pp. 95–223.

Soysal, Ismail (1964) *Fransız İhtilâlı ve Türk-Fransız Diplomasi Münasebetleri* (1789–1802) (Ankara: Türk Tarih Kurumu).

Steensgaard, Niels (1974) *The Asian Trade Revolution of the Seventeenth Century. The East India Companies and the Decline of the Caravan Trade* (Chicago: University of Chicago Press).

Stoianovich, Traian (1960) 'The Conquering Balkan Orthodox Merchant', in *Journal of Economic History*, XX, pp. 234–313.

Strauss, Johann (1992) 'Zum Istanbuler Buchwesen in der zweiten Hälfte des 19. Jahrhunderts', in *Osmanlı Araştırmaları*, XII, pp. 307–38.

— (1993) 'İstanbul'da Kitap Yayını ve Basımevleri', in *Müteferrika*, I, pp. 5–18.

Symposium (eds not named) (1974) *L'époque phanariote, 21–25 Octobre 1970. A la mémoire de Cléobule Tsourkas* (Saloniki: Institute for Balkan Studies).

Taeschner, Franz (1923) 'Die geographische Literatur der Osmanen', in *Zeitschrift der Deutschen Morgenländischen Gesellschaft*, 2, I, pp. 31–56.

— (1968) 'Kırşehir, ein altes Kulturzentrum aus spät- und nachseldschukischer Zeit', in *Necati Lugal Armağanı* (Ankara: Türk Tarih Kurumu), pp. 577–92.

Tanyu, Hikmet (1967) *Ankara ve Çevresinde Adak ve Adak Yerleri* (Ankara: Ankara Üniversitesi Basımevi).

Taşköprüzāde (1927) *Eš-šaqāʾiq en-nomānijje von Taşköprüzāde, enthaltend die Biographien der türkischen und im osmanischen Reiche wirkenden Gelehrten, Derwisch-Scheiḫ's und Ärzte von der Regierung Sultan 'Otmān's bis zu der Sülaimāns des Großen*, trans. O. Rescher (Istanbul: Phoenix).

Terzioğlu, Derin (1995) 'The Imperial Circumcision Festival of 1582: An Interpretation', in *Muqarnas*, 12, pp. 84–100.

Tezcan, Hülya, Selma Delibaş and John Michael Rogers (1980) *Topkapı Sarayı Museum, Textilien*, trans. Karin Hein (Herrsching/Ammersee: Schuler Verlagsgesellschaft).

Theunissen, Hans, Annelies Abelman and Wim Meulenkamp (1989) *Topkapı en Turkomanie, Turks-Nederlandse ontmoetingen sinds 1600 in samenwerking met Museum voor Volkenkunde, Rotterdam, Museum Het Princessehof, Leeuwarden* (Amsterdam: De Bataafsche Leeuw).

Thévenot, Jean (1980) *Voyage du Levant* (abridged) ed. and intro. Stéphane Yérasimos (Paris: Maspéro).

Thieck, Jean-Pierre (1985) 'Décentralization ottomane et affirmation urbaine à Alep à la fin du XVIIIème siècle', in *Mouvements communautaires et espaces urbains au Machreq* (Beirut: Centre d'Études et de Recherches sur le Moyen Orient Contemporain), pp. 117–68.

Thomas, Lewis (1972) *A Study of Naima*, ed. Norman Itzkowitz (New York: New York University Press).

Thompson, E. P. (1971) 'The Moral Economy of the English Crowd in the Eighteenth Century', in *Past and Present*, 50, pp. 76–136.

Tietze, Andreas (1942) 'Die Geschichte vom Kerkermeister-Kapitän, Ein türkischer Seeräuberroman aus dem 17. Jahrhundert', in *Acta Orientalia*, 19, pp. 152–210.

— (1992) 'Mustafā ʿĀlī on Luxury and the Status Symbols of Ottoman Gentleman', in *Studia Turcologica Memoriae Alexii Bombaci Dicata* (Naples: Istituto Universitario Orientale), pp. 577–90.

Tilly, Charles (1985) 'War Making and State Making as Organized Crime', in *Bringing the State back in*, ed. Peter B. Evans, Dietrich Rueschemeyer and Theda Skocpol (Cambridge: Cambridge University Press), pp. 169–91.

Timur, Taner (1986) *Osmanlı Kimliği* (Istanbul: Hil Yayın).

— (1991) *Osmanlı-Türk Romanında Tarih, Toplum ve Kimlik* (Istanbul: AFA Yayınları).

Todorov, Nikolay (1967/68) '19. cu Yüzyılın İlk Yarısında Bulgaristan Esnaf Teşkilatında Bazı Karakter Değişmeleri', in *İstanbul Üniversitesi İktisat Fakültesi Mecmuası*, 27, 1–2, pp. 1–36.

— (1980) *La ville balkanique aux XVe–XIXe siècles, Développement socio-économique et démographique* (Bucharest: AIESEE).

Tournefort, Joseph P[itton] de (1982) *Voyage d'un botaniste* ed. Stéphane Yérasimos (2 vols) (Paris: François Maspéro and La Découverte).

Trimingham, Spencer (1971) *The Sufi Orders in Islam* (Oxford and London: Oxford University Press).

Trumpener, Ulrich (1968) *Germany and the Ottoman Empire 1914–1918* (Princeton NJ: Princeton University Press).

Tsirpanlis, Zacharias (1993) 'Der griechische Raum 1650–1850', in *Handbuch der europäischen Wirtschafts- und Sozialgeschichte*, Vol. 4, ed. Wolfram Fischer et al. (Stuttgart: Klett-Colta), pp. 1,060–70.

Turan, Şerafettin (1963) 'Osmanlı Teşkilatında Hassa Mimarları', in *Tarih Araştırmaları Dergisi*, I, 1, pp. 157–202.

— (1990) *Türk Kültür Tarihi, Türk Kültüründen Türkiye Kültürüne ve Evrenselliğe* (Ankara: Bilgi Yayınevi).

Uçman, Abdullah (1989) 'Ebubekir Ratıp Efendi'nin Nemçe Seyahatnamesi', in *Tarih ve Toplum*, 69, pp. 155–60.

Ülgener, Sabri (1981) *İktisadi Çözülmenin Ahlak ve Zihniyet Dünyası* (Istanbul: DER Yayınları).

Uluçay, Çağatay (1950) *Osmanlı Sultanlarına Aşk Mektupları* (Istanbul: Tarih Dünyası Mecmuası Yayınları).

— (1956) *Harem'den Mektuplar* (Istanbul: Vakıt Matbaası).

— (1980) *Padişahların Kadınları ve Kızları* (Ankara: Türk Tarih Kurumu).

— (reprinted 1985) *Harem II* (Ankara: Türk Tarih Kurumu Basımevi).

Ursinus, Michael (1989) 'Klassisches Altertum und europäisches Mittelalter im Urteil spätosmanischer Geschichtsschreiber', in *Zeitschrift für Türkeistudien*, 2, 2, pp. 69–78.

Uzluk, Feridun Nafız (1958) *Fatih Devrinde Karaman Eyaleti Vakıfları Fihristi, Tapu ve Kadastro Umum Müdürlüğü Arşivindeki Deftere Göre* (Ankara: Vakıflar Umum Müdürlüğü).

Uzunçarşılı, Ismail Hakkı (1945) *Osmanlı Devletinin Saray Teşkilatı* (Ankara: Türk Tarih Kurumu).

— (1965) *Osmanlı Devletinin İlmiye Teşkilatı* (Ankara: Türk Tarih Kurumu).

— (1972) *Mekke-i mükerreme Emirleri* (Ankara: Türk Tarih Kurumu).

Vartan Paşa (1991) *Akabi Hikâyesi, İlk Türkçe Roman* (1851), ed. Andreas Tietze (Istanbul: Eren).

Vatin, Nicolas (1997) *Sultan Djem, Un prince ottoman dans l'Europe du XVe siècle d'après deux sources contemporaines: Vāḳiʿāt-i Sulṭān Cem, Oeuvres de Guillaume Caoursin* (Ankara: Türk Tarih Kurumu and IFEA).

Veinstein, Gilles (1976) '"Ayân" de la région d'Izmir et commerce du Levant (Deuxième moitié du XVIIIe siècle)', in *Etudes balkaniques*, XII, 3, pp. 71–83.

— (1983) 'L'hivernage en campagne, talon d'Achille du système militaire ottoman classique, à propos des sipāhī de Roumélie en 1559–1560', in *Studia Islamica*, LVIII, pp. 109–43.

Veselá-Premosilová, Zdenka (1978/79) 'Sur l'activité du monastère de Ste-Cathérine de Sinai en Bosnie', in *Prilozi za Orientalnu Filologiju*, XXVIII–XXIX, pp. 257–67.

Vovelle, Michel (1982) *Idéologies et mentalités* (Paris: François Maspéro).

Vryonis, Ir Speros (1971) *The Decline of Medieval Hellenism in Asia Minor and the Process of Islamization from the Eleventh through the Fifteenth Century* (Berkeley and Los Angeles: University of California Press).

Walkowitz, Judith R. (1992) *City of Dreadful Delight: Narratives of Sexual Danger in Late Victorian London* (Chicago and London: Chicago University Press).

Wallerstein, Immanuel (1974) *The Modern World System, Capitalist Agriculture and the Origins of the European World Economy in the Sixteenth Century* (New York and San Francisco, London: Academic Press).

Wallerstein, Immanuel, Hale Decdeli and Reşat Kasaba (1987) 'The Incorporation of the Ottoman Empire into the World Economy', in *The Ottoman Empire and the World Economy*, ed. Huri İslamoğlu-İnan (Cambridge and Paris: Cambridge University Press and Maison des Sciences de l'Homme), pp. 88–100.

Wild, Johann (1964) *Reysbeschreibung eines Gefangenen Christen Anno 1604*, ed. Georg A. Narciß and Karl Teply (Stuttgart: Steingrüben Verlag).

Wirth, Eugen (1974/75) 'Der Orientteppich und Europa. Ein Beitrag zu den vielfältigen Aspekten west-östlicher Kulturkontakte und Wirtschaftsbeziehungen', in *Mitteilungen der Fränkischen Geographischen Gesellschaft*, 21–2, pp. 291–400.

— (1986) 'Aleppo im 19. Jahrhundert – ein Beispiel für die Stabilität und Dynamik spätosmanischer Wirtschaft', in *Osmanische Studien zur Wirtschafts- und Sozialgeschichte, in memoriam Vančo Boškov* (Wiesbaden: Otto Harrassowitz), pp. 186–205.

Wunder, Heide (1992) *Er ist die Sonn, sie ist der Mond. Frauen in der frühen Neuzeit* (Munich: C. H. Beck).

Yates, Frances A. (1985) *Astraea: The Imperial Theme in the Sixteenth Century* (London: Routledge and Kegan Paul).

Yavuz, Hulusi (1984) *Kabe ve Haremeyn için Yemen'de Osmanlı Hakimiyeti (1517–1571)* (Istanbul: publisher not given).

Yavuz, Yıldırım (1981) *Mimar Kemalettin ve Birinci Ulusal Mimarlık Dönemi* (Ankara: ODTÜ Mimarlık Fakültesi).

Ydema, Onno (1990) *Carpets and their Datings in Netherlandisch Paintings 1540–1700* (Wappingers Falls NY: Antique Collectors Club).

Yérasimos, Stephane (1990) *La Fondation de Constantinople et de Sainte-Sophie dans les traditions turques* (Istanbul and Paris: Institut Français d'Études Anatoliennes and Librairie d'Amérique et d'Orient).

Yıldırım, Dursun (1976) *Türk Edebiyatında Bektaşi Tipine Bağlı Fıkralar (İnceleme-Metin)* (Ankara: Kültür Bakanlığı).

Zilfi, Madeline (1977) 'The Diary of a Müderris: A New Source for Ottoman Biography', in *Journal of Turkish Studies*, I, pp. 157–73.

— (1986) 'Discordant Revivalism in Seventeenth-century Istanbul', in *Journal of Near Eastern Studies*, 45, 4, pp. 251–69.

— (1988) *The Politics of Piety: The Ottoman Ulema in the Postclassical Age (1600–1800)* (Minneapolis: Bibliotheca Islamica).

Index

Words which occur on almost every page, such as 'Ottoman' or 'Istanbul', have not been included in the index.